ORTHODOX RUSSIA

edited by Valerie A. Kivelson and Robert H. Greene

ORTHODOX RUSSIA

BELIEF AND PRACTICE UNDER THE TSARS

The Pennsylvania State University Press

UNIVERSITY PARK, PENNSYLVANIA

Library of Congress Cataloging-in-Publication Data

Orthodox Russia : belief and practice under the tsars /
edited by Valerie A. Kivelson and Robert H. Greene.
p.   cm.
Includes bibliographical references and index.
ISBN 0-271-02349-X (cloth : alk. paper)
1. Russkaia pravoslavnaia tserkov'—History.
2. Orthodox Eastern Church—Russia—History.
3. Russia—Church history.
4. Russkaia pravoslavnaia tserkov'—Soviet Union—History.
5. Orthodox Eastern Church—Soviet Union—History.
6. Soviet Union—Church history.
I. Kivelson, Valerie A. (Valerie Ann). II. Greene, Robert H., 1975– .

BX485 .O77 2003
281.9′47—dc21   2002153319

CONTENTS

Part IV: Living Orthodoxy

ACKNOWLEDGMENTS

This collection developed from a pair of workshops held at the University of Michigan, Ann Arbor, titled "Russian Orthodoxy in Lived Historical Experience." Inspired by the insights and spirited debate at those workshops, we looked for a way to capture the experience in print. Although that proved impossible, some of the provocative ideas raised may be seen in the articles appearing in this volume.

We would like to thank everyone who participated in the workshops and shared their ideas and insights about approaches to the history of Orthodoxy and of religion more generally. In particular, John Fine, who knows everything there is to know about Orthodoxy, has been extremely helpful in clarifying points of theology and doctrine. Gregory Bruess, Jane Burbank, Laura Downs, David Frick, Jennifer Hedda, Susan Juster, Michael Makin, David Prestel, Anatole Senkevich, Tanya Senkevich, Tom Wolfe, and Christine Worobec added enormously with their various perspectives as commentators and participants. We would like to single out for our gratitude those who bravely took on the task of commenting from fields outside Russia and religion. In particular, Sue Juster's insights on millenarian thought and gendered spiritualities in early modern Western traditions were enormously thought-provoking, and Tanya Senkevitch's explanations of Florenskii's visual theories clarified the structures and meanings of Orthodox iconography. Roberta Nerison-Low, Marysia Ostafin, Donna Parmelee, and the staff at the Center for Russian and East European Studies (CREES) took care of all organizational aspects of the workshops and buoyed us with their enthusiasm. We also thank CREES, the Department of History, the International Institute, and the Rackham Graduate School at the University of Michigan for their generous financial support.

We also thank Michael Khodarkovsky and Tim Hofer for logistical and intellectual help, Peter Potter for his support of this project, and our contributors for their extraordinary patience through all of the vagaries of the editorial and publication process.

ILLUSTRATIONS

CHRONOLOGY

860–1240 Period of Kievan Rus'

980–1015 Reign of Grand Prince Vladimir

988 Conversion of Kievan Rus' to Eastern Orthodox Christianity

1054 Eastern Orthodox and Latin Catholic Churches fall into schism

1223–1326 Period of the Mongol Invasions and Domination, Appanage Period

1223 First appearance of the Mongols on the River Kalka

1237–1240 Mongol invasions; Kiev is destroyed; Rus' is compelled to pay heavy taxes to the Mongol khan, and Rus' princes must be confirmed in office by Mongol patent of rule

1299 Metropolitan Maksim moves from Kiev to Vladimir

1326–1700 Rise of Muscovy and the Muscovite Period

1326 Metropolitan Peter moves from Vladimir to Moscow

1327 Mongols support the princes of Moscow against their rivals, the princes of Tver

1327–41 Ivan I Kalita of Moscow appointed grand prince of Vladimir by Mongol Khan

1337 Founding of Trinity–St. Sergei Monastery

1359–89 Reign of Dmitrii Donskoi as grand prince of Moscow

1425–62 Reign of Vasilii II, grand prince of Moscow

1437–39 Council of Florence—effort to reunite Eastern and Western churches; Russia rejects the effort and discredits Metropolitan Isador, who participated at the council

1448 Bishop Iona of Riazan selected metropolitan without the consent of the patriarch of Constantinople

1453 Fall of Constantinople

1462–1505 Reign of Grand Prince Ivan III, the Great, of Moscow

1470–1505 Judaizers Heresy

1492 Anticipated End of Time, calculated to be seven thousand years from Creation; Metropolitan Gennadii creates new Easter tables

1505–33 Reign of Vasilii III, grand prince of Moscow

1533–84 Reign of Ivan IV, the Terrible

1547 Ivan IV crowned first tsar of Russia

1551 Stoglav (Hundred Chapters) Church Council

1552 Conquest of Kazan

1556 Conquest of Astrakhan

1564 Publication of first book in Moscow

1581–82 First conquests in western Siberia

1584–98 Reign of Tsar Fedor Ivanovich, regency of Boris Godunov

1589 Creation of an autocephalous Moscow patriarchate

1598–1605 Reign of Tsar Boris Godunov

1605–13 The Time of Troubles (succession of tsars and pretenders to the throne, the False Dmitriis; time of invasions and social unrest)

1613 Mikhail Alekseevich, first Romanov tsar, crowned (reigns 1613–45)

1645–76 Reign of Tsar Aleksei Mikhailovich

1652 Nikon consecrated as patriarch

1653–54 Church reforms, standardization of texts and practices

1666–67 Church council condemns Nikon and the Old Believers, leading to the schism

1676–82 Reign of Tsar Fedor Alekseevich

1682 Old Believer leader, Archpriest Avvakum, burned at the stake

1682 Peter the Great crowned co-tsar with half-brother Ivan V, under regency of Sofiia

1689–1725 Reign of Peter the Great

1700–1917 Imperial Russia

1700 Adoption of Julian calendar
      Death of Patriarch Adrian; seat left vacant; church headed by Stefan Iavorskii as locum tenens

1703 Foundation of St. Petersburg, which becomes the new capital city

1721 Peter the Great abolishes patriarchate, creates the Holy Synod; promulgation of the Spiritual Regulation

1725–27 Reign of Catherine I

1727–30 Reign of Peter II

1730–40 Reign of Anna

1740–41 Reign of Ivan VI with Anna Leopol'dovna as regent

1741–62 Reign of Elizabeth Petrovna

1740s–50s State-sponsored missionary work among the peoples of the East

1762–96	Reign of Catherine the Great
1770s	Origins of the *startsy*, holy elders; founding of numerous women's monastic orders; origins of the sect of self-castrastors
1764	Secularization of church lands and peasants
1767	Prohibition of forcible conversion of non-Orthodox
1773	Decree of Religious Toleration
1796–1801	Reign of Paul I
1801–25	Reign of Alexander I
1812	Napoleon invades Russia and is defeated
1825–55	Reign of Nicholas I, policy of "Orthodoxy, Autocracy, Nationality"
1828	Missions founded in Viatka, Kazan, and Simbirsk provinces
1832	Creation of the Department of Spiritual Affairs of Foreign Confessions under the Ministry of Internal Affairs
1855–81	Reign of Alexander II
1861	Emancipation of the serfs
1865–85	Conquest and incorporation of Central Asia
1867–69	Church reforms
1881–94	Reign of Alexander III
1885–1900	Policies of "Russification" in the borderlands
1894–1917	Reign of Nicholas II
1904–5	Russo-Japanese War
1905	Revolution of 1905
	Declaration of Freedom of Conscience
	October Manifesto of political reforms and civil rights
1914–17	World War I
1917	February Revolution deposes the tsar and installs the Provisional Government; patriarchate reestablished

1917–1991 Soviet Period

1917	October Revolution: the Bolsheviks take power; policy of militant atheism adopted; church property nationalized
1918–21	Civil War
1921–28	New Economic Policy (NEP)
1924	Death of Lenin; rise of Stalin
1925	Death of Patriarch Tikhon; Metropolitan Sergei serves as locum tenens
1927	Metropolitan Sergei as locum tenens swears loyalty to the Soviet regime

INTRODUCTION

Orthodox Russia

VALERIE A. KIVELSON AND ROBERT H. GREENE

After seventy years of neglect, the study of Russian religious life has entered an exciting period of growth in the decade since the fall of the Soviet Union. Long proscribed as a topic of study in the antireligious Soviet Union, religion, when it did appear in scholarly works, was treated primarily as primitive superstition or as a manifestation of an oppressive, ruling-class ideology. Russian religious history was overlooked nearly as completely by Western scholars, who concentrated on more popular and pressing subjects of political and social history. By fortuitous coincidence, the transformation of the political climate of Russia since 1991 coincided with shifts in the intellectual currents of Western scholarship, where renewed interest in cultural anthropology has driven a rush of work on religious life and culture. Thus, serious study of Russian Orthodoxy in a cultural context is relatively new, a product of the last ten to fifteen years. Recent scholarship, by Gregory Freeze and others, has fundamentally altered the ways in which we can understand Orthodoxy in its historical context.[1] This is still an emerging field, and the authors represented in this collection are among the major players in making the study of Russian Orthodoxy as dynamic as it is today.

Until recently, most American students came into contact with Russian Orthodoxy through terse stereotypes in textbooks, which dispensed with the

---

1. A more complete treatment of the literature may be found in the annotated bibliography. Of Gregory L. Freeze's many contributions, see in particular, "Handmaiden of the State? The Church in Imperial Russia Reconsidered," *Journal of Ecclesiastical History* 36 (1985): 82–102; "The Orthodox Church and Serfdom in Pre-Reform Russia," *Slavic Review* 48 (1989): 361–87; "The Rechristianization of Russia: The Church and Popular Religion, 1750–1850," *Studia Slavica Finlandensia* 7 (1990): 101–36; "Subversive Piety: Religion and the Political Crisis in Late Imperial Russia," *Journal of Modern History* 68 (1996): 308–50; and "Institutionalizing Piety: The Church and Popular Religion, 1750–1850," in *Imperial Russia: New Histories for the Empire*, ed. Jane Burbank and David L. Ransel (Bloomington: Indiana University Press, 1998), 210–49. Robert O. Crummey's early contribution is *The Old Believers and the World of Antichrist: The Vyg Community and the Russian State, 1694–1855* (Madison: University of Wisconsin Press, 1970).

Map of Imperial Russia c. 1900

OCEAN

Bering
Sea

Kamchatka

Turukhansk

S I B E R I A

Iakutsk

Lena

Enisei

Sea
of
Okhotsk

Eniseisk

Krasnoiarsk

Lake
Baikal

Irkutsk

Nerchinsk

Amur

Sakhalin

MANCHURIA

Vladivostok

MONGOLIA

C H I N A

KOREA

| 0 | 500 | 1000 Miles |

topic in a dutiful paragraph or two, or sequestered religion in a decidedly skippable chapter titled "Religion and Culture," or something similar. For instance, one textbook explains that "Byzantine Christianity, while raising Kievan Rus to a new cultural level, introduced into its cultural tradition a degree of rigidity and formalism, which would inhibit future Russian cultural development."[2] Another widely used textbook emphasizes that "the Russian Church had developed especially in the direction of religious ceremony, ritualism, and formalism." "Religion occupied a central position in Muscovite Russia and reflected the principal aspects and problems of Muscovite development: the growth and consolidation of the state; ritualism and conservatism; parochialism and the belonging to a larger world; ignorant, self-satisfied pride, and the recognition of the need for reform." But even the reformers of the seventeenth century "confus[ed] the letter with the spirit," mistaking superficial ritual practices for theological doctrine. "Religious content lagged behind form." The religious ritualism of Orthodoxy offered the believers "a great unifying bond and tangible basis for their daily life," but gave them little room for enlightenment or spiritual development.[3]

Such characterizations perpetuate a fixed image of what Orthodox religion meant for Russia: rigid, hierarchical structure; superficial conception of doctrine; and static, repetitive ritualism. Paired with fast and free use of religion as a key to a purportedly mournful, deep, or fatalistic Russian soul, sweeping statements about Russian Orthodoxy surface frequently in discussions of Russian exceptionalism. Formulaic stereotypes are still frequently invoked in efforts to resolve the haunting question of Russia's relation to and difference from the West. If Orthodoxy, or the variants that it assumed in Russia, explains any significant aspects of Russian history, then it is a task of some urgency to identify the specific ways in which Russian experience was inflected by Orthodoxy. With the opening of archives and the unprecedented access to primary source materials on the history of religion in Russia, it is now possible to pursue this project in depth, perhaps for the first time since the Revolution.

Studies of Russian Orthodoxy as a topic in itself, rather than as an expression of other political or social forces, traditionally have focused on church controversies or structural developments detached from everyday life. That

2. David MacKenzie and Michael Curran, *A History of Russia, the Soviet Union and Beyond,* 5th ed. (Belmont, Calif.: West/Wadsworth, 1999), 46.

3. Nicholas V. Riasanovsky, *A History of Russia,* 4th ed. (Oxford: Oxford University Press, 1984), 197, 201. The seventeenth-century church schism is said to demonstrate the powerful hold that Orthodox ritual had on the Muscovite population, but "it also marked the dead end of that culture" (201).

is, Orthodoxy has been seen alternatively as a practice of class oppression or of folk custom, devoid of theological, spiritual, or genuine religious content, or as a rarefied realm of doctrine and ecclesiastical institutions, populated by a handful of educated churchmen and unconnected to the world of the laity. In keeping with more recent developments in the field, the essays collected here interrogate the place of religion and religious belief in the lives of Russian subjects and collectively try to resituate the history of Orthodoxy more squarely into history itself. The chapters of this book examine lived religious experience between the fifteenth century and the immediate aftermath of the Bolshevik Revolution of 1917.

In twelve essays, the authors address questions of how Orthodoxy touched the lives of a wide variety of subjects of the Russian state, from clerics awaiting the Apocalypse in the fifteenth century to nuns adapting to the attacks on organized religion under the Soviets, and from unlettered military servitors at the court of Ivan the Terrible to peasants and urban dwellers in the last years of the imperial regime. Examining the role of religion in the lives of Russians and non-Russians, Orthodox believers and sectarians, clerics and laity, elites and commoners, men and women, the authors bring together the fields of religious and sociocultural history. By melding traditionally distinct approaches, the authors allow us to see Orthodoxy as a lived, adaptive, and flexible cultural system, rather than as a static set of rigidly applied rules and dictates.

Orthodox Christianity came to Russia from Byzantium by official fiat in 988 and remained the official religion until the Bolshevik Revolution of 1917. Vladimir, the tenth-century grand prince of Kiev credited with converting the "Rus' people" from paganism, chose Greek Orthodoxy from the array of monotheisms—Islam, Judaism, Catholicism, Orthodoxy—presented to him. In spite of the solemn princely mandate for conversion and the willingness of the Greek missionaries to translate liturgical texts into a more or less comprehensible Slavonic language, the spread of Christianity was a long, slow, faltering process. Christianity remained concentrated in cities and monastic outposts, only slowly filtering out to the sparsely populated, heavily forested lands beyond the walls. Some scholars have argued that Orthodox Christianity never made deep inroads into the peasant mentality, but rather coexisted with traditional pre-Christian pagan practices and superstitions in a dual belief system called *dvoeverie*.[4]

4. On "dvoeverie," see, for example, M. M. Gromyko, *Mir russkoi derevni* (Moscow: Molodaia gvardiia, 1991). A criticism of this position is advanced in E. B. Smilianskaia, *Volshebniki, bogokhul'niki, eretiki. Narodnaia religioznost' i dukhovnye prestupleniia v Rossii XVIII veka* (Moscow: Indrik, 2002), and

As the new religion gradually took root in Russia, a series of religious schisms and institutional restructurings affected Christendom at large and, by extension, Russia. Relations between the Byzantine Greeks and the Latin West, already tense in the ninth and tenth centuries when the Slavic peoples converted to Christianity, were strained over questions of theology and ecclesiastical authority. At issue were questions such as the nature of the Trinity, the use of leavened or unleavened bread for communion, and the legitimacy of clerical marriage. Another point of contention was the Latin claim to the primacy of the pope, which clashed with the Greek commitment to conciliar decision-making within the church. Matters reached a breaking point in 1054, when the Eastern and Western churches severed their ties. Russia remained under the institutional jurisdiction of the Greek patriarch even after Constantinople fell to the Ottoman Turks in 1453 and the center of Eastern Christianity itself came under the rule of the Muslim sultan. An independent or autocephalous Moscow Patriarchate was founded in 1589, but proved short-lived.

Leaving the post unfilled after the death of the last patriarch, in 1721 Peter the Great entrusted control of the church to a newly created administrative institution, the Holy Synod, which remained in charge of church affairs until the end of the imperial era. The abolition of the patriarchate signified a radical change in the relationship between church and state in Russia. The Holy Synod operated as a branch of the bureaucratic, secular government and was headed by a layperson appointed by the tsar. The eighteenth century witnessed further decline of the institutional church, when Catherine II secularized the extensive church land holdings and left an impoverished and weakened institution behind. Some scholars have extrapolated from the dependent status of the church a theory that the clergy subscribed to and propagated an ethos of submissiveness. Gregory Freeze has questioned this

---

idem, "Sudebno-sledstvennye dokumenty kak istochnik po istorii obshchestvennogo soznaniia (Iz opyta izucheniia 'dukhovnykh del' pervoi poloviny XVIII v.)," in *Issledovaniia po istorii knizhnoi i traditsionnoi narodnoi kul'tury Severa. Mezhvuzovskii sbornik nauchnykh trudov,* ed. T. F. Volkov et al. (Syktyvkar: Syktyvkarskii universitet, 1997), 168–75. The argument that Orthodoxy barely touched the Russian laity is made in Edward L. Keenan, "Muscovite Political Folkways," *Russian Review* 45 (1986): esp. 138–48, and idem, "Semen Shakhovskoi and the Condition of Orthodoxy," *Harvard Ukrainian Studies* 12/13 (1988/1989): 795–815. Countering the position that Orthodoxy made only slight inroads, P. P. Tolochko claims that close to ten thousand churches had been constructed in Rus' by the 1240s. See Tolochko, *Drevniaia Rus': Ocherki sotsial'no-politicheskoi istorii* (Kiev: Naukova Dumka, 1987), 195. On the debate over elite and popular religious cultures in Western Christianity, see Natalie Zemon Davis, "From 'Popular Religion' to Religious Cultures," in *Reformation Europe: A Guide to Research,* ed. Steven Ozment (St. Louis: Center for Reformation Research, 1982), 321–42, and Thomas Tentler, "Seventeen Authors in Search of Two Religious Cultures," *Catholic Historical Review* 71 (1985): 248–57.

harsh judgment against the church as "handmaiden of the state" and pointed out that government regulation produced a more educated clergy in the eighteenth century.[5] He and others have shown that, freed from the worldly burdens of managing land and people, the Russian church experienced a burgeoning of new forms of spirituality, religious devotion, and moral engagement. The most powerful example of this new kind of rigorous spiritual expression is the eighteenth- and nineteenth-century movement of the holy elders, *startsy,* who combined traditions of Orthodox monasticism with elements of Catholicism and Pietism that were filtering in from the West. The mode of religious life they created, *starchestvo,* melded the hermit's contemplative retreat with a theology of engaged action in the world.[6]

With the Bolshevik Revolution of 1917, Orthodoxy not only lost its status as the official state religion but also found itself banned and anathematized by a militantly atheistic state. Marxism and historical materialism replaced Orthodoxy as the official state doctrine. The patriarchate enjoyed a brief restoration after the fall of the tsar in 1917, but was abandoned in the early Soviet period, only to be reestablished as an appeal to Russian patriotism by Joseph Stalin during the Second World War.[7] After the war the church survived in various forms: as an officially sanctioned institution, more or less aligned with the Soviet regime; as an émigré church abroad; and as an underground movement periodically persecuted by state and party. Because the Revolution ushered in such a profoundly different era for the church, and because the context and issues confronting religion were so completely altered after 1917, we have chosen to concentrate in this volume on the years in which Orthodoxy enjoyed imperial support.[8]

Even during the long era of official Orthodoxy, however, religious life was not unchanging. Historical events affected many of the fundamental terms of the church as an institution, and the cultural milieu altered as well. Although firmly ensconced as the official Russian religion, Orthodoxy faced continual challenges. It had to struggle to establish secure roots among the

5. See Freeze, "Handmaiden of the State."

6. Robert L. Nichols, "The Orthodox Elders (*Startsy*) of Imperial Russia," *Modern Greek Studies Yearbook* 1 (1985): 1–30. For more on new forms of spiritual expression in the eighteenth century, see the discussion in the bibliography to this volume.

7. On the restoration of the patriarchate, see Catherine Evtuhov, "The Church in the Russian Revolution: Arguments For and Against Restoring the Patriarchate at the Church Council of 1917–1918," *Slavic Review* 50 (1991): 497–511.

8. The same surge of scholarly interest in religion that has enriched the study of the prerevolutionary era has also produced some excellent work on religion during the Soviet period. For further reading, see the bibliography.

sparse, dispersed pagan population, then to create and enforce unity of belief and practice within the Orthodox flock, and ultimately, to maintain its primacy in a diverse, multiethnic empire, in which a wide variety of religions coexisted and interacted. Within its own ranks of Russian Christians, Orthodoxy confronted more heterogeneity than outright heresy in its early centuries, partly because of its inability to police the beliefs and practices of its scattered flock. For instance, the Russian church did not institute the convenient surveillance mechanism of mandatory annual confession until the early eighteenth century, five hundred years later than its Western counterpart. Parish registers and confessional books, convenient for tracking and controlling Christian births, deaths, marriages, and taking the sacraments, did not come into active use until well into the eighteenth century.[9] Moreover, Russian church services did not routinely include sermons until the late seventeenth century, which meant that the ecclesiastical establishment had one less mode of communicating its rules and expectations to the faithful. Unable to check up on its parishioners, for most of its history the church could neither establish rigid conventions nor identify and punish violators. This late development of mechanisms of control or standardization lent Orthodoxy a rather attractively expansive, inclusive character, whereby local variation and idiosyncrasy were generally tolerated by default, unless they happened to catch the eye or rouse the ire of the authorities.

Not coincidentally, as the church developed control mechanisms and attempted to standardize religious practice, it confronted increasing challenges from believers who found themselves newly numbered among the schismatics or heretics. A very small circle in the late fifteenth century earned the dubious distinction of being labeled Judaizers and heretics, and some died for their beliefs. These few operated at the heart of the Moscow court and could hardly have escaped detection. A broader-based movement would not emerge until the church itself had the ambition and manpower to attempt to enforce standard practice throughout the land. The first major internal schism occurred in the late seventeenth and eighteenth centuries, with the rise of the so-called Old Belief, a movement that purported to defend traditional Russian devotional practices from the reformist innovations introduced by the patriarch and the clerical establishment. The eighteenth and nineteenth centuries produced a richer array of sectarian movements, prompting the church to step up its efforts to enforce a unitary set of practices. Religious toleration was codified into law only after the revolution of 1905, and

9. A. S. Lavrov, *Koldovstvo i religiia v Rossii, 1700–1740 gg.* (Moscow: Drevlekhranilishche, 2000).

until then deviance or apostasy could be considered criminal as well as sinful. Even after 1905, religious affiliation and practice remained matters of concern to the state as well as the church.

This brief institutional history gives some idea of the sharply changing circumstances of the church itself during the many centuries of Russia's relationship with Orthodoxy. If one shifts one's gaze from the formal configuration of the church to the circumstances in which the religion was taught, internalized, or practiced at a local level, the particularities and peculiarities of any historical moment multiply infinitely. This is the level of analysis that forms the core of the following essays and constitutes their major contribution to the study of Russian religion.

Grand claims have been made about the effect of Prince Vladimir's choice on the development of Russian history from the tenth century to the post-Soviet present. But all of these claims tend to be either static or rather mystical, generalizing about a putative common Russian soul or national character, and they fail to consider variation over time or even the tremendous variety within a single era. At each historical moment, Orthodoxy incorporated elements of the changing world and adapted to new conditions. Michael Flier's study of late-fifteenth-century apocalyptic fear traces significant transformations in the millenarian outlook over the course of a few decades, and thus refutes any "timeless" ideas about Russian apocalypticism. Further along the chronological spectrum, Laura Engelstein and Gary Marker highlight the remarkable religious creativity of the late eighteenth century, when a wide variety of spiritual movements developed, covering the gamut from stringent Orthodoxy, to fringe sectarianism, to individualized religious devotion. Nadieszda Kizenko and William Wagner explore Orthodox accommodations with the various hurdles and complications raised by secularization, urbanization, commercialization, and ultimately, communism. The juxtaposition of these studies from a broad chronological span, covering the late fifteenth century to the early Soviet period, exposes the dynamism and variety in religious understanding across time, place, population, and circumstance. By organizing this collection thematically rather than chronologically, we hope to highlight particular aspects of Orthodoxy as a lived religion.

In spite of its demonstrable historical variation, Orthodox Christianity should not be understood as completely amorphous and adaptable. Certain traits or tendencies characterize Russian Orthodoxy throughout its many manifestations, and this collection of particularized studies helps to define the outlines of a strong and lasting Orthodox culture. In line with a long tradition of descriptions (and even caricatures) of the Russian church, the authors here confirm that Orthodoxy has been grounded primarily in practice and experience. Religion structured daily practices in ways that bypassed the cognitive. Daniel Kaiser's examination of rites of passage reveals how religion saturated daily life. The Orthodox calendar regulated marriage practices, burial rituals, the naming of babies, and even sexual congress. Vera Shevzov's piece on *tserkovnost'*, or "churchness," similarly demonstrates how religion was embedded in community practices and structures. Unlike Protestantism and Judaism, based so centrally on Scripture and textual exegesis, Russian Orthodoxy valued altars, relics, and icons over complex theological argument. The material realm quite literally embodied the incandescent presence of the divine. The sensory and experiential dominated over the textual. Of the senses, vision held pride of place. Icons and frescoes played a crucial function in conveying theological ideas and biblical tales to the worshipers, while inner vision allowed for direct interaction with the saints.

What is different or new, then, in the picture of Russian Orthodoxy presented in this book? The authors here go beyond the overly easy binaries of ritual practice versus intellectual inquiry, image versus text, to explore the interplay between them. The chapters by Daniel Rowland and Michael Flier describe how Orthodox painters carefully structured icons and fresco cycles to communicate biblical lessons and to open the believer's soul to grace. Orthodoxy employs beauty—the beauty of God's Creation, the beauty of "the Uncreated Light," the beauty of the choir, the liturgy, the incense and icons during services—as effectively as any more textually based religion might deploy the sermon or the Word, to inculcate religious lessons. Beauty, after all, is presented in the medieval Russian Primary Chronicle as the single most compelling reason for St. Vladimir's choice of Orthodox Christianity over other world religions. Vladimir reportedly chose Orthodoxy at least in part in response to reports of the dazzling beauty of the Orthodox liturgy in the Hagia Sofia in Constantinople, which left his emissaries not knowing whether they "were in Heaven or on earth."[10]

Embodying both visual and spiritual beauty, icons play a crucial role in Orthodox practice. Western commentators and critics from early modern times on have carped that Russians "worshiped" their painted icons. Assuming that the Russian faithful did not distinguish between the representation and the immaterial sanctity it represented, travelers, particularly Protestants,

---

10. This insight into the relationship between beauty and Orthodoxy comes from George P. Fedotov, *The Russian Religious Mind*, vol. 1, *Kievan Christianity: The Tenth to the Thirteenth Centuries* (Cambridge: Harvard University Press, 1946; reprint, New York: Harper, 1960), 371–74.

derided Russian ritual as empty of significance and the worshipers as ignorant of the meanings of their obeisances. Shocked at the absence of sermons
or formal religious education among the Russian laity, Western observers
sneered that Orthodox worshipers continued in blind idolatry because nothing is told of what it all means."[11] However, to the Orthodox faithful, visual
messages were evidently quite clear, if not always accurate, as the chapters that
follow demonstrate.[12] In his chapter on the Kremlin frescoes, for instance,
Daniel Rowland does something very original, examining not just the intended meaning but also the reception and creative misinterpretation of
political-theological frescoes by their unschooled, largely illiterate viewers.
He bases his reconstruction on evidence from the cultural world in which
Muscovite soldiers and court servitors lived and fought. He is then strongly
positioned to assess how and to what extent Orthodoxy actually touched the
lives of Russian military men in the sixteenth century. Kaiser's chapter confirms these findings by looking at other areas in which religious messages
shaped lived experience through routine behaviors and conventions. Orthodoxy left its imprint on the patterns of daily life, demonstrating the prosaic
ways in which religion provided an organizing structure for lived experience
on the most intimate as well as the most public level. Once the problem of
the mode of transmission between a learned clerical elite and an illiterate, or
barely literate, populace resolves itself, doubts about the extent and impact
of Orthodoxy on the masses seem far less pressing, and it is easier to believe
that an unlettered people actually considered itself Christian. Michael Flier's,
Eve Levin's, and Isolde Thyrêt's studies of manifestations of popular religion
establish that Orthodoxy had indeed reached deeply into Russian culture by
the early modern, Muscovite era.

Radically recasting older ideas about Orthodoxy's ritualism and superficial-
ity, these studies reveal the active, creative deployment of religious concepts
by ordinary people in their daily lives and dispel the notion that a ritual-based
religion is necessarily an unthinking, superficial, or unproductive one. This
volume brings into focus the empowering qualities of a religion that integrated theology into practice and imbued ritual with sanctity. Ordinary
Orthodox Russians interpreted religious texts and doctrines all the time in

---

11. Samuel Baron, trans. and ed., *The Travels of Olearius in Seventeenth-Century Russia* (Stanford:
Stanford University Press, 1967), 256.

12. Inspiration for this effort to reconstruct Orthodoxy's cultural logic derives from various sources.
For some the invitation to try to reconstruct the internal logic of a very alien culture is taken from Clifford
Geertz, "Religion as a Cultural System," in his *Interpretation of Cultures: Selected Essays* (New York: Basic
Books, 1973), 87–125.

their daily lives and practices. In his reflections on the resonances and contradictions between Christian linear time, stretching from Creation to the Last Judgment, and traditional East Slavic cyclical time, marking the seasons year after year, Flier suggests a productive interplay of ideas about resurrection and salvation. The idea of resurrection fit nicely with ancient Slavic ancestor cults, but the idea of a general resurrection at the end of time did not. The peasants and townspeople of Eve Levin's and Kizenko's chapters improvised adeptly on the core themes of Orthodox Christianity by constructing cults of saints, and imagining lives for those saints, that fit the classical hagiographic models. These studies, as well as Thyrêt's, show how commonly believers appealed to saints for intercession and practical aid in their daily lives. The local peasant communities negotiated, sometimes successfully, sometimes unsuccessfully, with the church establishment for the right to venerate their saints, just as Vera Shevzov's peasants negotiated for official acknowledgment of their miracle-working icons. Examining rural communities in the nineteenth century, Shevzov shows that laypeople found ways to interpret church teachings that favored their own local practices and to win clerical support for their local interpretations. Pushing this reasoning further, she casts into doubt the assumption that a sharp divide separated clerics, as representatives of an official church, from the laity. She argues instead that the community of believers was defined as integral to the essence of the church itself.

Viewed through the lens of gender, the empowering qualities of Orthodoxy as a religion that enabled the illiterate and uneducated believer to encounter the divine on his or her own terms become all the more intriguing. Not only men, but women as well could interact with the material embodiments of the sacred and assume religious agency on their own, without the learned mediation of priests or texts. A consideration of gender suggests that the sacrality of the material and the immediacy of the sacred may have functioned to level some of the gendered hierarchies at work in the Catholic and Protestant West. Astonishingly little work has applied gender as a category of analysis in the field of Russian religious history, aside from Brenda Meehan's pioneering book on women's religious experience in imperial Russia and Levin's and Thyrêt's on the Muscovite period.[13] Here, Marker, Wagner,

---

13. Brenda Meehan, *Holy Women of Russia: The Lives of Five Orthodox Women Offer Spiritual Guidance for Today* (San Francisco: Harper, 1993; reprint, Crestwood, N.Y.: St. Vladimir's Seminary Press, 1996); Eve Levin, *Sex and Society in the World of the Orthodox Slavs, 900–1700* (Ithaca: Cornell University Press, 1989); Isolde Thyrêt, *Between God and Tsar: Religious Symbolism and the Royal Women of Muscovite Russia* (DeKalb: Northern Illinois University Press, 2001). See also Adele Lindenmeyr, *Poverty Is Not a Vice: Charity, Society, and the State in Imperial Russia* (Princeton: Princeton University Press, 1996).

Kizenko, and Thyrêt all touch on gender, and all show how women could put Orthodox models to use flexibly and creatively. Perhaps most striking in their chapters is the way in which the women they examine turned to religion and prayer to provide practical, tangible improvements in their daily lives or to ameliorate the conditions of others in the here and now. Gary Marker shows that with her thoughtful and effective acts of intercession and charity the eighteenth-century Anna Labzina enacted a form of Marian virtue in her daily life, thereby melding theology and practice. Labzina found in religion a moral justification for her involvement in charitable works, and public intercession for prisoners and the poor. Her social activism in turn allowed her to develop a peculiarly female public world. Wagner too shows ways in which women could expand their traditional roles as intercessors and nurturers to allow for broader social, religious, and political participation. The nuns of the Convent of the Exaltation of the Cross found ways to address the particular problems facing women in late imperial society, while acting within the roles and structures allowed to female religious. Wagner also shows that the growth of female religiosity paralleled that found across Europe in the late nineteenth century, but he reveals an active, publicly engaged, entrepreneurial, urban convent, which somewhat muddies expectations of cloistered female piety.

Kizenko further challenges expectations of pious female behavior as she traces in the development of the cult of the cross-dressing St. Kseniia a fascinating amalgam of traditional female preoccupations with a strikingly "unfeminine" vindictiveness and vulgarity. Comparing St. Kseniia with St. Ioann of Kronstadt, both of whom appealed particularly to female supplicants and to the poor, she finds some gender-specific aspects of Orthodox practice, along with a shared focus on miracles that produced tangible improvement in the believers' daily lives. These saints, like those discussed by Eve Levin, gained followers when they could offer practical results. Thyrêt argues for a more strongly gender-divided religious system, in which women and men approached the sacred differently. She presents a picture of a gender system more similar to a Western model than those provided by Kizenko or Marker. She provides convincing structural and institutional reasons for her arguments that women's experiences with the divine were more emotional, more isolated, and less institutionalized than men's. The pious women she studies relied on direct spiritual access and inner vision because they were denied entry into the exclusively male monasteries where most saints' relics resided. These contributions in no way add up to a new consensus regarding gender and faith in Russia, but they open the doors to further research on a topic that deserves serious study, and that may prove exceptionally fruitful as a way to understanding Russian cultural development.

Coming to terms with the diversity and mutability of Orthodox practice, Shevzov argues that we should not conclude that there were multiple orthodoxies or "heterodoxies." Rather, such a discovery allows us to recognize that Orthodoxy was an enterprise capacious enough to accommodate a community of conversation, with room for disagreement, negotiation, and even contradiction. Engelstein too encourages us to consider an "Orthodox spectrum ... broad enough to embrace a range of styles" or to accommodate "different registers of the creed." Werth's study of Orthodox conversion efforts among the non-Russian peoples of the middle Volga region shows that capaciousness at its greatest, and also demonstrates its limits. Conversion by definition blurred and reconfigured boundaries between Orthodox and non-Orthodox, and within the context of Russian imperial expansion and incorporation, complicated seemingly obvious and eternal divisions between Russians and non-Russians. Werth exposes some of the anxieties and ambiguities that accompanied that process of redefining people from one category to another. Both Russian missionaries and members of the target populations used categories of difference to assert identity. At the same time, conversion and the associated process of Russification forced participants to confront the sometimes convenient and sometimes disturbing porousness of categorical labels, as they encountered such baffling hybrid categories as Orthodox Tatars or, later, Christian Communists.[14] The wide embrace of the church, however, could not expand to include the sectarian movements of the seventeenth, eighteenth, and early nineteenth centuries. Where new Eastern converts, hazy on the basic tenets of Christianity, were militantly shepherded into the flock, sectarians were labeled heretics and definitively excluded from the Orthodox fold.

In a volume commemorating the first millennium of the Russian Orthodox Church, Boris Gasparov writes of the "special—implicit and amalgamative—character of the Christian tradition" among the Eastern Slavs, that is, a tendency to leave rules unstated and institutions and procedures informal. "It may be that the most characteristic feature of the Christian tradition among the Eastern Slavs, apparent from its very origin and evident in the

---

14. See Paul W. Werth, "The Limits of Religious Ascription: Baptized Tatars and the Revision of 'Apostasy,' 1840s–1905," *Russian Review* 59 (2000): 493–511, and Agnès Kefeli, "The Role of Tatar and Kriashen Women in the Transmission of Islamic Knowledge, 1800–1870," in *Of Religion and Empire: Missions, Conversion, and Tolerance in Tsarist Russia*, ed. Robert P. Geraci and Michael Khodaskovsky (Ithaca: Cornell University Press, 2001), 250–73.

whole span of its thousand-year history, is its 'implicitness.' . . . [B]oth the Church itself and the religious sphere of social life generally relied more on the continuity of tradition and the collective mind of its members than on objectified and abstracted regulations and institutions."[15] If this is one of the defining traits of Russian Orthodoxy, as the studies in this collection confirm, then Orthodoxy would be best understood not as dogmatic and rigid, as it has been so commonly cast, but rather as the opposite: malleable and flexible. This lack of formal codification (in spite of occasional clerical efforts to do so) may well explain the generativeness of local practice and the sometimes astounding tolerance for spontaneous interpretive religious practice.

Overall, this volume testifies to the limited utility of the kinds of dualistic models that have so commonly shaped perceptions of Russian history and culture.[16] None of the papers in this volume fits neatly within a dualistic framework. Rather, they all blur binary divisions. Engelstein does so most dramatically. Under her rigorous analysis, the sharp, clear divides between heresy and Orthodoxy, elite religion and popular, theology and practice, become far more complex and mutually implicated. The sectarian self-castrators unambiguously and even defiantly crossed the line from Orthodoxy into heresy, and yet even here, Engelstein challenges the sharply dichotomous categories so often invoked in the literature, arguing that these heretics' "practices can also be understood as an extreme variation on a common theme." She proposes that a model of a continuum running between popular and elite, sectarian and official, styles of worship reflects the religious spectrum more accurately than a bipolar framework. Shevzov's study of *tserkovnost'* subjects the artificial division of high and low, prescribed and applied, to explicit critique and finds that these divides simply cannot be maintained. In the same vein, Marker shows how Labzina's world observed no preordained boundaries. Public and private, male and female, traditional and progressive, religious and secular, Orthodox and Enlightened, oral and written, meld into a far richer concoction than a binary model would allow. Kaiser explores a

15. Boris Gasparov, "Introduction," in *Christianity and the Eastern Slavs*, vol. 1, *Slavic Cultures in the Middle Ages*, ed. Boris Gasparov and Olga Raevsky-Hughes, California Slavic Studies 16 (Berkeley and Los Angeles: University of California Press, 1993), 2–3.

16. The importance of binaries in Russian culture is most clearly articulated in the influential article by Iurii M. Lotman and Boris A. Uspenskii, "Binary Models in the Dynamics of Russian Culture (to the End of the Eighteenth Century)," in *The Semiotics of Russian Cultural History*, ed. Alexander D. Nakhimovsky and Alice Stone Nakhimovsky (Ithaca: Cornell University Press, 1985), 30–66. The other particularly relevant binary formulation is Edward L. Keenan's two-culture theory, discussed more thoroughly in Daniel Rowland's chapter in this volume.

sphere of behavior profoundly structured by Orthodoxy and yet with no discernible ties to doctrine, allowing for the possibility of a prosaic religiosity as yet unexamined by historians. Wagner shows that religious commitment does not rule out commercial pragmatism. The resourceful nuns of the Exaltation of the Cross Convent in Nizhnii Novgorod demonstrate how seemingly separate spheres intermingled with no perceptible disturbance of either sphere of activity. All of these chapters work to replace binaries with spectrums. Yet binaries arise in these essays and in the material at hand all the time, and the polarized pairs are never entirely vanquished. David Frick points out elsewhere that binaries are fundamentally attractive to the human mind, that people like to think in binary categories. Hence the paired opposites— theology and practice, understanding and ritual, Orthodox and heretic, Christian and pagan, male and female, elite and popular—assume cultural weight and explanatory power. Fortunately, Frick reminds us, people also like to escape binaries that are imposed upon them, and often do so in remarkably creative ways.[17] The contributors to this volume, like the people they study, have done so to extraordinary effect.

Finally, the findings about Russian Orthodoxy in this volume allow for a more productive comparison of Orthodoxy with Western Christianity, a comparison which demonstrates the problems inherent in relying on binary oppositions. As Thomas Tentler observes in his concluding remarks, since early modern times, conventional comparisons have counterposed flattened, ideal-types of Russia and the West. Most comparative treatments have been reflexively Eurocentric, describing Russians as ignorant, idolatrous, and obscurantist. The reaction to that stereotype substitutes another in its place that is just as unsatisfactory, as it extols Russian piety, devotion, and faith. In either case, however, the units of comparison have generally been cartoon images. On one side stands an abstract and idealized West, most perfectly represented by Protestantism in its demythologized, Calvinist forms, whose believers are imagined as educated, highly literate, probing, informed about their religious precepts, fully conversant with biblical texts, and aware of the meanings and implications of their convictions. In this East-West comparison, Catholicism too is viewed as seeking a more intellectual comprehension of revealed truth through reasoned, dialectical argumentation. On the other side of the East-West divide looms a dark and ignorant Russia, steeped in

---

17. David Frick, "Misrepresentations, Misunderstandings, and Silences: Problems of Seventeenth-Century Ruthenian and Muscovite Cultural History," in *Religion and Culture in Early Modern Russia and Ukraine,* ed. Samuel H. Baron and Nancy Shields Kollmann (DeKalb: Northern Illinois University Press, 1997), 149–68.

superstition, incense, and blind faith. Such invidious comparisons between a stereotypically obscurantist Orthodoxy and an idealized literate Protestantism or a codified seminarian Catholicism are of little value for the understanding of lived religion in either East or West.

Recent work in Western European religious history has radically revised older assumptions about religious developments in Catholic and Protestant Europe. Western Christianity, even Reformation churches, made slow progress in teaching even basic doctrine.[18] Furthermore, it is clear that religious practices in much of the West were far closer to those encountered in Russia than these idealized generalizations allow. Russian Orthodoxy was not alone in venerating holy images and relics, in seeking inner vision, or in preferring direct contact to intellectual comprehension of the divine. Music, incense, and iconography continued to communicate the faith to Catholic laypeople, even as literacy gradually increased throughout Western Europe. Notwithstanding the continued popularity of models that contrast "transcendent" Protestantism with "immanent" Catholicism, it is just as clear that mystery and the inscrutability of the divine remained enshrined at the core of both Catholic scholasticism and Protestant textuality, in spite of all efforts by the various Western churches to generate abstract formulations and to represent religious thought as reasoned logic.[19] Moreover, as Western scholars have turned their attention to the kind of lived religion that form the focus of this volume, they have found a similar diversity of local practice and emphasis on the material, the ritual and the routine, over the theological and rational. Even among Protestants, there was plenty of room for local custom and aberrant practice, and literacy made for a less uniform set of religious beliefs and attitudes than previously assumed. Throughout history, Western Europe variously nurtured or condemned a wide array of strains of religious

18. The Reformers' efforts to instruct the faithful in the new theology and the difficulties inherent in this project are treated in Gerald Strauss, *Luther's House of Learning: Indoctrination of the Young in the German Reformation* (Baltimore: Johns Hopkins University Press, 1978), and Robert W. Scribner, *For the Sake of Simple Folk: Popular Propaganda for the German Reformation* (New York: Oxford University Press, 1994). For the Catholic case, see Jean Delumeau, *Catholicism Between Luther and Voltaire: A New View of the Counter-Reformation* (London: Burns and Oates, 1977); and John Bossy, *Christianity in the West, 1400–1700* (Oxford: Oxford University Press, 1985). See also David Warren Sabean, *Power in the Blood: Popular Culture and Village Discourse in Early Modern Germany* (Cambridge: Cambridge University Press, 1987).

19. The typology of "transcendence" versus "immanence" is treated in Carlos M. N. Eire, *War Against the Idols: The Reformation of Worship from Erasmus to Calvin* (Cambridge: Cambridge University Press, 1986). It should be noted, however, that the tensions between mystery and the supernatural, on the one hand, and religious rationality, on the other, were not necessarily irreconcilable. See Trevor Johnson, "Blood, Tears, and Xavier-Water: Jesuit Missionaries and Popular Religion in the Eighteenth Century Upper Palatinate," in *Popular Religion in Germany and Central Europe, 1400–1800,* ed. Bob Scribner and Trevor Johnson (London: Macmillan, 1996), 183–202.

mysticism, spiritualism, ritualism, and every other attribute connected with Russian Orthodoxy.

Comparing Russian Orthodoxy with Christianity in its Western guises, Tentler's concluding piece suggests directions for meaningful exploration of these neighboring and organically related religious traditions that took on such different forms in different historical circumstances. To make clear and easy distinctions between Russia's religious path and that of a normative and unitary "West" requires substituting stereotypes for research. We do not need to ignore the contrasts. Protestantism cut the ties between the living and the dead, and both Catholic and Protestant churches worked effectively to bring the miraculous under some kind of official surveillance. The Russian church began its first serious forays into regulating the miraculous only in the seventeenth century, and the effort continued in an erratic and sometimes desultory way through the eighteenth century, but even then with very limited effect. Protestantism and then Roman Catholicism actively promoted a literate and catechized laity, whereas similar projects were not broached in Russia until the nineteenth century and even then were greeted with skepticism. Through creeds, seminaries, church ordinances, visitations, and bureaucracy in general, the Western churches tried to bring the laity to practice a more orderly religion, in ways that entered Orthodox organization and practice only slowly and inefficiently.[20] Orthodoxy as a flexible and loosely codified belief system may have allowed more room for diversity of expression, more tolerance, or perhaps simply less effective surveillance and regulation, than the more controlling, and narrowly defined systems developed over centuries in the West.

Orthodox Christianity was perhaps most distinctive in its overall success in maintaining loosely defined religious unity (in spite of the Old Belief, the Uniate challenge, and the multitude of sectarian groups) and in purveying its particular theology through visual, ceremonial, and practical means. Orthodoxy influenced the Russian historical experience more through the contingencies of the moment than by shaping an essentially Russian soul. Leaving the abstract realm of the soul to others, the chapters that follow present religion as applied in belief and practice. In this regard, Christine Worobec's observation holds as true for the West as for Russia: unless we take *practice* into account, "the label 'Christian' becomes meaningless, referring only to a

---

20. On the Orthodox Church's early (and ineffective) efforts to regulate popular practice, see Levin's chapter in this volume, and also Paul Bushkovitch, *Religion and Society in Russia: The Sixteenth and Seventeenth Centuries* (New York: Oxford University Press, 1992). On the eighteenth-century reforms and their failure, see Lavrov, *Koldovstvo i religiia*.

tiny spiritual and educated elite that knew how to interpret evangelical texts and church dogma correctly."[21] Historical religion cannot be usefully defined by high theology alone; only in examining its lived articulation can one learn about its substance and historical meaning. That is precisely what the contributors to this volume have succeeded in doing.

---

21. Christine D. Worobec, "Death Ritual Among Russian and Ukrainian Peasants: Linkages Between the Living and the Dead," in *Cultures in Flux: Lower-Class Values, Practices, and Resistance in Late Imperial Russia,* ed. Stephen P. Frank and Mark D. Steinberg (Princeton: Princeton University Press, 1994), 14–15.

PART I

DESTABILIZING DICHOTOMIES

I

OLD AND NEW, HIGH AND LOW

Straw Horsemen of Russian Orthodoxy

LAURA ENGELSTEIN

There are many dimensions to the study of Eastern Orthodoxy in the centuries of imperial rule. At the highest level, the Orthodox Church played a central role in the legitimation of secular authority. Bishops presided at official ceremonies and delivered sermons on state occasions; priests served as chaplains with the armed forces. Nicholas I in the nineteenth century cemented this alliance by designating the Orthodox religion one of the three pillars of empire, along with autocracy and some unspecified ethnic principle. At a local level, in the empire's many parish churches, the clergy ministered to the needs of the flock, teaching the catechism, performing the sacraments, thwarting the influence of competing faiths, and marking the limits of acceptable devotion. As a social world in its own right, the church included both monks and priests, some highly trained, some equipped with only rudimentary skills. As a community of believers, it included a broad range of laypeople, from cosmopolitan aristocrats to illiterate peasants and workers. In defending a coherent, identifiable creed, the church authenticated certain elements of doctrine and ritual and condemned others as deviant or heretical.

Nicholas I's slogan, supplied by his minister of education, Sergei Uvarov, affirmed a connection between the empire's core cultural identity (*narodnost'*), the form of political authority (*samoderzhavie*), and the character of the historically dominant faith (*pravoslavie*). Even in accepting this equation, however, nineteenth-century church leaders and lay intellectuals debated how exactly to define the faith that was so central to the empire's history and mission. Although the Orthodox Church was historically tied to the Russian lands and the Russian princes, what it stood for in spiritual and cultural terms was, by the nineteenth century, no longer taken for granted. Three key distinctions organized the thinking of laymen and clergy on this subject: the difference between Eastern and Western Christian traditions; the difference between the meaning of Orthodoxy in the lives of the Westernized elite and in the existence of ordinary Russian-speaking people; and the line between true belief (authorized doctrine, prescribed rituals) and deviation (ranging from the Old Believers to the numerous splinter sects).[1]

In seeking to understand the historical operation of Orthodoxy, both as an institution and a cultural system, scholars must make their way through the debates and representations inherited from the self-conscious exponents of tradition. In relation to the character of popular observance, opinions varied. The degree to which formal standards of belief affected ordinary parishioners had been a subject of concern since the eighteenth century. Some clergymen complained of the peasantry's ignorance of doctrine and blind adherence to ritual; others deplored their neglect of pious obligations under the stress of daily life. As part of their critique of European civilization, with its increasingly secular and rationalist ethos, the Slavophiles had a different view. These religiously oriented thinkers from cultivated gentry families interpreted what they imagined to be the routine quality of village devotion as a sign of its closeness to the source of inspiration, an internalized piety untroubled by the torments of reflection. They celebrated the folk style as an organic and nationally distinctive understanding of the faith, from which, they believed, the Europeanized elite had grown distant. The impact of their ideas can be felt in the persistent identification of Orthodoxy in general and the Russian tradition in particular with the innate spirituality they admired. "Orthodoxy," wrote one theologian, "steadfastly and fundamentally preaches that Christianity is life and not simply doctrine. Therefore, any theoretical teaching is only secondary, reflecting and rationalizing the real manifestations of life."[2]

The nineteenth-century picture of a faith divided between elite and folk versions testifies to a real cultural split, but the Slavophile vision has often been interpreted as an accurate reflection of what Orthodoxy meant for ordinary believers. Writing in the 1930s and 1940s, George Fedotov and Pierre Pascal praise the immanence of the sacred in peasant culture.[3] "In the person

1. I have developed some of the ideas in this essay at greater length elsewhere: see Laura Engelstein, "Holy Russia in Modern Times: An Essay on Orthodoxy and Cultural Change," *Past and Present* 173 (2001): 129–56.

2. N. N. Glubokovskii, *Russkaia bogoslovskaia nauka v ee istoricheskom razvitii i noveishem sostoianii* (Warsaw: Sinodal'naia tipografiia, 1928; reprint, [Russia]: Izdatel'stvo Sviato-Vladimirskogo Bratstva, 1992), 111. Cf. Tomas Spidlik, *The Spirituality of the Christian East: A Systematic Handbook*, trans. Anthony P. Gythiel (Kalamazoo, Mich.: Cistercian Publications, 1986), 7: "Dogma and devotion . . . are inseparable in the consciousness of the church."

3. G. P. Fedotov, *Stikhi dukhovnye: Russkaia narodnaia vera po dukhovnym stikham*, ed. A. L. Toporkov (Paris: YMCA, 1935; reprint, Moscow: Gnozis, 1991); Pierre Pascal, *Religion of the Russian People*, trans. Rowan Williams (Crestwood, N.Y.: St. Vladimir Seminary Press, 1976).

of Christ," comments Pascal, "God is . . . a dweller and wanderer on the soil of Russia."[4] In this same line, Andrei Siniavskii emphasizes the palpable character of folk belief, in which saints preside over daily life and the sacred figures as an element in earthly existence.[5] Gregory Freeze describes the religious landscape of the late eighteenth century as divided between the "virtuoso" or "cognitive enlightened Orthodoxy" of the church, on the one hand, and the "particularist, localized, perceptualist and immanent sacrality of the village," on the other. The church, he explains, "failed to discern the interpenetration of the secular and profane, the spiritual and sensual, that imparted immediacy and meaning to popular religious life. Symbols and ritual, especially for an illiterate flock, [were] concrete manifestations—not mere representations—of the sacred. . . . [T]he abstract teaching of virtuoso religion—the moral teachings of sermons, the spiritual histories, the catechization—bore scant meaning for the religious experience and expectations of the village."[6] Some post-Soviet Russian scholars, freed from the obligation to disparage the piety of intellectuals and praise the anticlericalism of the common folk, have returned to a vision of peasant culture as a repository of enduring patterns, including a pervasive religious sense.[7]

There is no doubt that Orthodoxy was absorbed and practiced in different ways by different social groups. The common folk may have favored a more ritualized style of worship than educated believers, but the Slavophiles had a political and philosophical interest in making such distinctions. By celebrating tradition, they were attempting to repair the consequences of what they felt as its loss. As Georges Florovsky (and with him, Viktor Zhivov) remark about the seventeenth century, its concern for tradition was already a symptom not of tradition's strength but of its perceived weakness.[8] In postulating the coherence of the national spirit, the Slavophiles were themselves being modern. They were engaging in the same "invention of tradition" that

---

4. Pascal, *Religion*, 26.

5. Andrei Siniavskii, *Ivan-durak: Ocherk russkoi narodnoi very* (Paris: Syntaxis, 1991).

6. Gregory L. Freeze, "The Rechristianization of Russia: The Church and Popular Religion, 1750–1850," *Studia Slavica Finlandensia* 7 (1990): 114–15.

7. M. M. Gromyko, "O narodnom blagochestii u russkikh XIX veka," in *Pravoslavie i russkaia narodnaia kul'tura*, bk. 1, ed. Iu. B. Simchenko and V. A. Tishkov (Moscow: Institut antropologii i etnologii Rossiiskoi Akademii nauk, 1993), 5–30. Also idem, *Mir russkoi derevni* (Moscow: Molodaia gvardiia, 1991), esp. 111–25. Also S. V. Kuznetsov, "Religiozno-nravstvennye osnovaniia russkogo zemledel'cheskogo khoziaistva," in *Pravoslavie i russkaia narodnaia kul'tura*, 33, and A. A. Panchenko, *Issledovaniia v oblasti narodnogo pravoslaviia: Derevenskie sviatyni Severo-Zapada Rossii* (St. Petersburg: Aleteiia, 1998), introduction.

8. Georges Florovsky, *Ways of Russian Theology*, 2 vols., ed. Richard S. Haugh, trans. Robert L. Nichols (Belmont, Mass.: Nordland Publishing, 1979), 1:86–87; Victor M. Zhivov, "Religious Reform and the Emergence of the Individual in Russian Seventeenth-Century Literature," in *Religion and Culture in Early Modern Russia and Ukraine*, ed. Samuel H. Baron and Nancy Shields Kollmann (DeKalb: Northern Illinois University Press, 1997), 184–98.

flourished in Europe at the time.[9] Not even the monarchy could escape this conundrum. Richard Wortman, for example, has characterized Nicholas I, that most traditional of nineteenth-century tsars, as a man in search of old-fashioned styles with which to legitimize up-to-date strategies of rule.[10] Andrei Zorin's reflection on the instrumentality of the "Orthodoxy" in Uvarov's famous triad underscores the perception that the autocrats operated with the tools of their day, while invoking an idiom that recalled the past.[11]

In short, what kind of "tradition" are we dealing with? Is Russia, as out-siders—often persuaded by the Russians' own self-presentation—tended to perceive it, the repository of outmoded cultural styles? Or was Russia en-gaged in the same business as other countries: producing a past as counter-weight to the increasingly mobile present? Should Russian culture be thought of as struggling between the heavy weight of "custom," "tradition," or "reli-gion," on the one side, and the active striving of "modernity" or seculariza-tion, on the other?

The Slavophiles wished to believe that access to the past was least obstructed at the level of the common believer. They cherished the conviction that the folk practiced Orthodoxy in a manner after its own heart, distinct from the religious culture of the church and Westernized elite. The question remains, however, as to which of these poles (if poles they were) was further removed from the essence of the faith. Were the teachings of the church the best guide to "true Orthodoxy," or was folk Orthodoxy a repository of authentic tradi-tion from which the hierarchy itself had fallen away or willingly departed?

The study of the church, no less than of folk religion, demands a critical attitude toward received ideas. Gregory Freeze depicts a church that was not insulated from the surrounding secular culture. Caught between the pres-sure of a state that professed its attachment to tradition while enlisting the church in its modernizing schemes (confiscating its lands, imposing bureau-cratic oversight, demanding political cooperation) and the apparent archa-ism of the flock, the clergy forged a middle road of cautious adaptation. Like Freeze, Robert Nichols sees the ecclesiastical establishment as forward-, not

9. *The Invention of Tradition,* ed. Eric Hobsbawm and Terence Ranger (Cambridge: Cambridge University Press, 1983). See also, the involvement of elites in resurrecting (sometimes creating) folk art tradi-tions: Wendy R. Salmond, *Arts and Crafts in Late Imperial Russia: Reviving the Kustar Art Industries, 1870–1917* (Cambridge: Cambridge University Press, 1996).

10. Richard S. Wortman, *Scenarios of Power: Myth and Ceremony in Russian Monarchy,* vol. 1 (Prince-ton: Princeton University Press, 1995), part 4.

11. Andrei Zorin, "Ideologiia 'Pravoslaviia-Samoderzhaviia-Narodnosti': Opyt rekonstruktsii," *Novoe literaturnoe obozrenie* 26 (1997): 71–104.

backward-, looking. Eighteenth-century churchmen, he reminds us, participated actively in the intellectual renewal associated with the Russian Enlightenment. Schooled in contemporary philosophy, they were also exposed to
Protestant and Pietist styles of Christianity current in Europe at the time,
which emphasized the personal dimension of religious experience. The problem facing the church at the beginning of the nineteenth century was thus
not simply the gap between the informed piety of the clergy (at least at its
upper reaches) and the ignorance of their followers. Some churchmen feared
they themselves had lost touch with the Eastern tradition. Metropolitan Filaret
(Drozdov), himself no stranger to Western learning, attempted to recover the
"true face of Orthodoxy"[12] by reviving biblical scholarship and encouraging
the development of theology. Thus, at the beginning of the nineteenth century, leading clerics felt in need not of catching up with the secular world but
of reestablishing the church's own distinctive voice.

Wishing to transmit knowledge of the corrected tradition to the populace at large, Filaret sponsored the translation of Holy Scripture from Old
Slavonic into the Russian of everyday life. The enterprise of shoring up the
faith thus entailed a simultaneous step forward, to meet the needs of a "back-
ward" populace whose lack of education cut them off from the past. Indeed,
the translation was temporarily suppressed by conservative statesmen who
feared the effects of innovation—and possibly also of making the faith transparent to the ordinary soul. Revitalizing and disseminating the Orthodox
creed, Western-trained clergymen thus attempted to repair the neglect into
which they believed popular consciousness had fallen. It bears observing,
however, that Filaret did not merely dust off a neglected tradition ready at
hand or carefully preserved in monastic archives. The refurbishing of the
canon, creating Russian-language versions of the holy texts and a catechism
for instruction, was a nineteenth-century achievement.[13]

Russia was not the only place, moreover, in which religion emerged from
the shadows of cultural neglect to achieve a new centrality in projects of
national self-definition. Catholicism, for example, languished among the poor
and ill-educated rural population of early-nineteenth-century Ireland. Only
after the famine had decimated the ranks of the destitute and driven others
into emigration, did the clergy devote itself to discipline and instruction.

---

12. Quoted in Robert L. Nichols, "Orthodoxy and Russia's Enlightenment, 1762–1825," in *Russian
Orthodoxy Under the Old Regime,* ed. Robert L. Nichols and Theofanis George Stavrou (Minneapolis:
University of Minnesota Press, 1978), 84.

13. See Robert Lewis Nichols, "Metropolitan Filaret of Moscow and the Awakening of Orthodoxy"
(Ph.D. diss., University of Washington, 1972).

Along with these church-directed efforts, popular religiosity also acquired a new lease on life, and it was then that Catholicism became a dominant feature in the Irish self-conception.[14] What became their proverbial piety is in fact of rather recent date.

The stereotypes of popular devotion in imperial Russia reflect the contrasting impressions left by contemporary observers: the admiring Slavophile vision of a grounded peasant faith, on the one hand, and on the other, the disgruntled clergy's complaint about the peasants' ignorance of church teachings, their blind observance of local customs, or worse, pagan holdovers, and their tendency to wander beyond the limits of approved belief into the heretical wilds. On the critical side of the ledger, it has also been remarked, with reference to the peasants' frequent passivity in the face of Bolshevik attacks on religion, that anticlericalism was widespread in the countryside.[15] Yet Vera Shevzov has convincingly shown that village piety was deeply connected to parish institutions, and there is evidence that many peasants actively resisted the Bolsheviks' atheist assault.[16] Villages clearly accommodated a religious culture nurtured by the church, but which also took forms marginal to institutional belief. Its expressions ranged from communal support of parish priests and chapels, to the extravagant piety of pilgrims and lay contemplatives, the unsanctioned veneration of local icons, and the "self-willed" initiatives of preachers and prophets that attracted clerical censure. Both Shevzov and Freeze document the church's attempts to come to terms with some of these practices, which it was in any case fruitless to oppose.[17] Increased literacy may have raised the level of conformity to church rules, but, Shevzov argues, it also encouraged independent activity among devout villagers, without, however, moving them to leave or even challenge the church. Most understood where the line was drawn between the irregular and the transgressive.[18]

14. See Emmet Larkin, *The Historical Dimensions of Irish Catholicism* (Washington, D.C.: The Catholic University of America Press, 1976, 1984), chap. 2, "The Devotional Revolution in Ireland, 1850–75," and S. J. Connolly, *Priests and People in Pre-Famine Ireland, 1780–1845* (New York: St. Martin's Press, 1982).

15. Stefan Plaggenborg, "Volksreligiosität und antireligiöse Propaganda in der frühen Sowetunion," *Archiv für Sozialgeschichte* 32 (1992): 102.

16. Vera Shevzov, "Popular Orthodoxy in Late Imperial Rural Russia" (Ph.D. diss., Yale University, 1994); William B. Husband, "Soviet Atheism and Russian Orthodox Strategies of Resistance, 1917–1932," *Journal of Modern History* 70 (1998): 74–107.

17. Gregory L. Freeze, "Institutionalizing Piety: The Church and Popular Religion, 1750–1850," in *Imperial Russia: New Histories for the Empire*, ed. Jane Burbank and David L. Ransel (Bloomington: Indiana University Press, 1998), 231–34.

18. For recent work on folk Orthodoxy, see Simon Dixon, "How Holy Was Holy Russia? Rediscovering Russian Religion," in *Reinterpreting Russia,* ed. Geoffrey Hosking and Robert Service (London:

In celebrating the intensity of village religion, Marina Gromyko points to intermediate forms such as extramonastic seclusion (*keleinichestvo*), pilgrimages (*palomnichestvo*), processions, and the spiritual guidance provided by holy elders (*starchestvo*).[19] Pilgrims and elders were not exclusively lower class, however, and though these practices straddle the boundary between the church and the world, they are not incidental to mainstream Orthodoxy but relate in one degree or other to the ascetic monasticism integral to the Eastern legacy.[20] Precisely this element of Orthodox culture appealed to intellectuals of the early-twentieth-century Silver Age, so fascinated by nonrational forms of experience. The ascetic tradition had deep roots, but its appeal to the common folk was not necessarily a sign of their closeness to primordial forms of belief. In the wake of the state's assault on institutional monasticism in the eighteenth century, and in connection with the influence of Pietism in court and clerical circles, Orthodox spirituality acquired new meanings. The nineteenth-century *startsy* were not direct holdovers from ancient times but the product of a revival that began in the 1760s and 1770s. *Starchestvo* did not first take hold among indigent holy men but among well-educated clerics devoted to the retrieval and editing of the teachings of the Church Fathers. Reactivated monasticism of this type thrived at the intersection of institutional and free-floating spirituality. The contemplative style, writes Robert Nichols with reference to Serafim of Sarov, "promoted the religious life at the outer edge of what ecclesiastical and civil authorities would allow."[21] "At once so traditional and so surprising in its novelty," as Vladimir Lossky remarks,[22] *starchestvo* was associated with the upsurge in monasticism as both calling and institution. Perhaps a third of monasteries in operation in the late 1800s were less than a hundred years old. Fyodor Dostoevsky composed the figure of Father Zosima, in the novel *Brothers Karamazov* (1879–80), from contemporary models. The portrait's accuracy was challenged in the literary press,

Arnold; New York: Oxford University Press, 1999), 21–39; also Vera Shevzov, "Miracle-Working Icons, Laity, and Authority in the Russian Orthodox Church, 1861–1917," *Russian Review* 58 (1999): 26–48; idem, "Chapels and the Ecclesial World of Prerevolutionary Russian Peasants," *Slavic Review* 55 (1996): 585–613; and Chris J. Chulos, "Myths of the Pious or Pagan Peasant in Post-Emancipation Central Russia (Voronezh Province)," *Russian History* 22 (1995): 181–216.

19. Gromyko, "O narodnom blagochestii."

20. Sergei Hackel, "The Eastern Tradition from the Tenth to the Twentieth Century: Russian," in *The Study of Spirituality*, ed. Cheslyn Jones, Geoffrey Wainwright, and Edward Yarnold, S.J. (Oxford: Oxford University Press, 1986), 259–82.

21. Robert L. Nichols, "The Orthodox Elders (*Startsy*) of Imperial Russia," *Modern Greek Studies Yearbook* 1 (1985): 12. See also Vladimir Lossky and Nicolas Arseniev, *La paternité spirituelle en Russie aux XVIIIème et XIXème siècles* (Bégrolles-en-Mauge: Abbaye de Bellefontaine, 1977), 36–39, 91–93.

22. Vladimir Lossky, "Les starets d'Optino," in Lossky and Arseniev, *La paternité spirituelle*, 93.

but it nevertheless became a prototype of its kind for much of the reading public.[23] This same public was likely to visit a monastery as a form of spiritual tourism.[24]

The monasticism of the charismatic *startsy,* who were respected by the church and revered by Slavophile thinkers, drew on the hesychast legacy for inspiration. Renewing the contemplative tradition of the Church Fathers, the Optina hermitage reached out to ordinary believers, while offering room for the idiosyncratic piety of individual men. Brenda Meehan has shown that spontaneous monastic devotion attracted women as well.[25] Unmarried peasant girls sometimes announced spiritual vocations and withdrew from communal life without leaving the village behind. Upper-class matrons founded charitable communities, some later formalized by the church. The *startsy,* like the female religious, defined their mission to include work in the world as well as seclusion. The Orthodox spectrum was broad enough to embrace a range of styles, from the intellectual articulations of the ecclesiastical academies, to the spiritual rigor of the contemplative life, to the social outreach of the monasteries, to the improvisational piety of peasants. These examples suggest that distinctions in the performance of Orthodox religiosity may conform not so much to divisions in the social landscape, as to different registers of the creed.[26] The vitality of certain styles associated with traditional forms of worship (*starchestvo,* for example) may, furthermore, have less to do with their resilience in the face of time than with the force of their revival.

The way in which old and new, high and low come together in Orthodox practice in the modern era is dramatically illustrated in the case of the Skoptsy, or self-castrators.[27] This community of outcasts from Orthodoxy derived their ascetic principles (refusal of meat, alcohol, profanity, and sex) and form of worship (group chants and dancing) from an existing mystical

23. William Mills Todd III, "Dostoevsky's Russian Monk in Extra-Literary Dialogue: Implicit Polemics in *Russkii vestnik, 1879–1881*," in *Christianity and the Eastern Slavs,* vol. 2, *Russian Culture in Modern Times,* ed. Robert P. Hughes and Irina Paperno, California Slavic Studies 17 (Berkeley and Los Angeles: University of California Press, 1994), 124–33.

24. For travel advice, they might consult A. A. Pavlovskii, ed., *Vseobshchii illiustrirovannyi putevoditel' po monastyriam i sviatym mestam Rossiiskoi Imperii i sv. g. Afonu,* 2d ed. (Nizhnii Novgorod: Mashistov, 1907; reprint, New York: Possev, 1988).

25. Brenda Meehan, *Holy Women of Russia: The Lives of Five Orthodox Women Offer Spiritual Guidance for Today* (San Francisco: Harper, 1993); also Nichols, "Orthodox Elders," 11, 21–23.

26. For a vivid example of belief patterns and practices that crossed the social spectrum, see Nadieszda Kizenko, "Ioann of Kronstadt and the Reception of Sanctity, 1850–1988," *Russian Review* 57 (1998): 325–44, and idem, *A Prodigal Saint: Father John of Kronstadt and the Russian People* (University Park: Pennsylvania State University Press, 2000).

27. For a general treatment, see Laura Engelstein, *Castration and the Heavenly Kingdom: A Russian Folktale* (Ithaca: Cornell University Press, 1999).

sect, the Khristovshchina or Khlysty, which emerged in the first half of the eighteenth century. Following a prophetic leader, the Skoptsy adopted the practice of ritual castration, which they considered an extension of their basic ascetic vows and a kind of baptism guaranteeing personal salvation. First discovered in 1772, they were subject before 1917 to periodic arrest and exile as dangerous heretics, but succumbed to repression by the Soviet regime only at the end of the 1920s. Unlike the Old Believers, who initially withdrew into their own communities, the Skoptsy lived among the Orthodox peasantry and townsfolk. Though sometimes denounced by neighbors, they were often tolerated on the margins of village life. They may even have been valued as exemplars of godliness. However shocking (though also impressive) the rite of self-castration may have appeared, their practices can be understood as an extreme variation on a common theme. The renunciation of bodily pleasure and the repression of sexual desire, taken as means to spiritual transcendence, develop motifs central to mystical asceticism. The charismatic role of the Skoptsy prophets, men and women of humble stature who detached themselves from worldly life, parallels that of the educated *startsy*. Sectarian leaders who made defiance of the church central to their appeal have something in common with the inspired eccentrics accused of "self-will" who insisted on their good faith and sought clerical approval.

Yet the Skoptsy were indeed different. It was easy to think of them as vestiges of a primitive age. Silver Age intellectuals imagined that mystical sects preserved an enduring spiritual legacy, and some recent commentators have evoked the Skoptsy as a symbol of persistently archaic features in the Russian cultural tradition.[28] The church, however, condemned castration as a heretical distortion of the faith. Castration itself was a skill derived from animal husbandry; and it had folkloric as well as Christian sources. Its adepts were almost all to be found among peasants, small-scale merchants, and lowly townspeople. The sect emerged, however, in the same general period in which the Optina hermitage became the center of the revived *starchestvo* and when Pietism was flooding in from Protestant Europe.[29] Having attracted the interest of mystical enthusiasts at Alexander I's court, the Skoptsy benefited for a

---

28. See comments on recent work by Aleksandr Etkind and Sergio Ingerflom, in Laura Engelstein, "Paradigms, Pathologies, and Other Clues to Russian Spiritual Culture: Some Post-Soviet Thoughts," *Slavic Review* 57 (1998): 864–77.

29. Viktor Zhivov, "Skoptsy v russkoi kul'ture," *Novoe literaturnoe obozrenie* 18 (1996): 396–400. See also A. A. Panchenko, "'On de i mnogikh delal skoptsami . . . dlia togo, chtob skopit' Tsarstvie Bozhie': Antiseksual'nost' v russkoi narodnoi kul'ture," in *Mifologiia i povsednevnost': Gendernyi podkhod v antropologicheskikh distsiplinakh,* ed. K. A. Bogdanov and A. A. Panchenko (St. Petersburg: Aleteiia, 2001), 48. Thanks to Olga Tsapina for this reference.

time from elite protection. Descriptions of the Skoptsy faith purporting to come from them may have been edited or elaborated by educated sympathizers or even by educated opponents. The famed folklorist and lexicographer Vladimir Dal' compiled the material used by Nikolai Nadezhdin in drafting the report of the commission appointed by Nicholas I to investigate the Skoptsy. It is not impossible that Dal' may have shaped some of the documents for publication. The Skoptsy, for their part, had no trouble accepting the published texts as authentic. Early in the next century, they appealed to the Bolshevik agitator, Vladimir Bonch-Bruevich, who had reasons of his own for wanting to gain their trust, to publish "improved" versions of their stories. Indeed, throughout the community's history, the Skoptsy came to understand themselves partly through their interaction with the world. When brought before the courts of law, they were obliged to account for their lives and their beliefs. Those who could read were familiar with what was written about them. Without renouncing their allegiance to the faith, some aspired to inclusion in the wider world of Russian letters.

It is thus, by studying believers who thought of themselves as loyal members of the church, as well as those who deliberately set themselves outside it, that we can test the relevance of some of the distinctions imbedded in the historical record: between doctrinal and enacted piety (precept and praxis), high and low (elite and folk), old and new (tradition and innovation). How to achieve a perspective that takes into account the stories Russians told (and tell) about themselves, without being bound by them, is—as always—the historian's task.

2

TWO CULTURES, ONE THRONE ROOM

Secular Courtiers and

Orthodox Culture in the Golden Hall

of the Moscow Kremlin

DANIEL ROWLAND

Many of the most distinguished American historians of Muscovite Russia have come to believe that the health, prosperity, even the survival of the Muscovite state throughout all of its life depended on the maintenance of a consensus among members of the ruling elite and the monarch. Robert Crummey, Edward Keenan, Nancy Shields Kollmann, and Valerie Kivelson[1] have all helped to explain how this consensus was developed and maintained. Since, like many premodern states, the Muscovite state lacked the wealth, the bureaucratic reach, and the military power to compel obedience from all its subjects, it had to rely on symbolic action to maintain this consensus. From the moment of the conversion of Kievan Rus', ecclesiastics had been working to piece together an ideology of state power, expressing their ideas in images and architecture as well as in texts. In the second half of the fifteenth century, and especially in the sixteenth century, the Muscovite church expended a considerable amount of intellectual energy on this task. In the middle of the sixteenth century in particular, the church sponsored a number of works in various media on subjects that we would call political. These works

I would like to thank the conference participants and, particularly, the editor of this volume for many helpful suggestions. I am also grateful to Dr. Sandy Isenstadt of the University of Kentucky College of Architecture and other members of the College's Seminar on Critical Issues for clarifying several points connected with reception theory.

    1. Robert O. Crummey, *Aristocrats and Servitors: The Boyar Elite in Russia, 1613–1689* (Princeton: Princeton University Press, 1983); Edward L. Keenan, "Muscovite Political Folkways," *Russian Review* 45 (1986): 138–48; Nancy Shields Kollmann, *Kinship and Politics: The Making of the Muscovite Political System, 1345–1547* (Stanford: Stanford University Press, 1987); Valerie A Kivelson, *Autocracy in the Provinces: The Muscovite Gentry and Political Culture in the Seventeenth Century* (Stanford: Stanford University Press, 1996).

took many forms, including literary texts, orations, buildings, icons, mural cycles, thrones, battle standards, and a coronation service. But for these ideas to work in the political sphere to produce a consensus, they needed to be understood outside the narrow group of elite churchmen who conceived and executed them. Were lay members of the court able to understand these impressive products of Orthodox culture, or did they remain chiefly the preoccupation of the narrow circles that produced them?

In this essay, I would like to examine the Golden Hall, one of the two main throne rooms of Muscovite Russia, and in particular the murals there,[2] as one site where ideas may have passed between the educated church elite and the far less educated secular elite that frequented these important spaces. As we shall see at the end of this essay, the murals were most probably painted after the great Moscow fire of 1547. We know from the accounts of numerous foreign ambassadors that courtiers spent a good deal of time there. And, as we shall see, the murals illustrated most if not all of the major themes current in ecclesiastical thinking about politics. Although these ecclesiastical "literary" ideas were separated from the elite by the barrier of literacy, were they accessible nonetheless through the medium of painting? To state the problem in a more general way, were the secular elite of early modern Russia Orthodox to any meaningful extent? Could visual means, including not only painting but architecture, have educated illiterate courtiers to the fundamental tenets of Orthodox political culture worked out within the literate and relatively well educated circles of the church hierarchy? The murals of the Golden Hall can serve as one example that might suggest an answer to this important question.

Our task is an unusual one, then. We need to divine not the overall meaning of the murals in the Golden Hall (a task already well carried out by Michael Flier)[3] but the meaning(s) that may have been seen in these murals

---

2. The most important published accounts of the Golden Hall murals are O. I. Podobedova, *Moskovskaia shkola zhivopisi pri Ivane IV* (Moscow: Izdatel'stvo Nauka, 1972), 59–68, and the most useful appendix, with reconstructions of the murals, by K. K. Lopialo, ibid., 193–98; Frank Kampfer, "'Russland an der Schwelle zur Neuzeit': Kunst, Ideologie und Bewusstsein unter Ivan Groznyj," *Jahrbücher für Geschichte Osteuropas* 23 (1975): 504–24. The most thorough and most convincing interpretation of the overall meaning of the murals is Michael Flier, "Putting the Tsar in His Place: The Apocalyptic Dimension of the Golden Hall Throne Room" (paper delivered at the annual convention of the American Association for the Advancement of Slavic Studies [AAASS], 1991). I have also given two papers at the AAASS relating to the murals: "The Artist's View of Politics: The Golden Palace" (1990), and "Political Messages in the Golden Palace Murals" (1995). The second of these papers forms the basis for this article. I would like to take this opportunity to thank Professor Flier for help and advice over the many years we have both been thinking about these murals.

3. Flier, "Putting the Tsar in His Place."

by a particular audience, the boyars (the highest members of the court elite) and other secular members of the court.

I raise this question in part as a response to a powerful and eloquent argument stated some time ago by Edward Keenan: his theory of two separate cultures in Muscovy, one clerical and one lay, with few connections between them. In 1971, he wrote in *The Kurbskii-Groznyi Apocrypha*, his book about a correspondence conventionally attributed to Ivan the Terrible (reigned 1547–84) and Prince Andrei Kurbskii, one of Ivan's courtiers who deserted to Lithuania:

> One of the distinctive features of Muscovite cultural life in the mid-sixteenth century is a rather sharp contrast between secular and religious cultures. Muscovite monastic culture, having inherited traditions and techniques familiar to students of medieval Western literature and philosophy, remained relatively free, during the sixteenth century, of outside influence, while the traditions and techniques of the court and counting house continued, by and large, the practices evolved by the great states that had preceded Muscovy as lords of the East European plain. There are very limited interchange and interaction between these [secular and lay] cultures: no strong traditions of formal education in the essentially religious formal culture were developed by the ruling dynasty or the warrior class; few if any princes of the Church succumbed to the lure of secular culture which so compromised Western clerics.[4]

Keenan then goes on to note the linguistic differences found in texts produced by clerical writers on one hand and lay writers on the other.

To understand Keenan's argument accurately, a couple of comments may be in order here. First, the two-culture hypothesis was invoked primarily in a linguistic context, to argue how unlikely it was that either Prince Kurbskii or Tsar Ivan the Terrible could have been the authors of the letters or other texts traditionally ascribed to them. In a recent restatement of his case, Keenan again emphasized the linguistic issue.[5] Second, Keenan sharply limits the duration of this cultural separation between the two cultures to the sixteenth

---

4. Edward L. Keenan, *The Kurbskii-Groznyi Apocrypha: The Seventeenth-Century Genesis of the "Correspondence" Attributed to Prince A. M. Kurbskii and Tsar Ivan IV,* with an appendix by Daniel C. Waugh (Cambridge: Harvard University Press, 1971), 53–54.

5. Edward L. Keenan, "Response to Halperin, 'Edward Keenan and the Kurbskii-Groznyi Correspondence in Hindsight,'" *Jahrbücher für Geschichte Osteuropas* 46 (1998): 404–18, especially 413–14.

and earlier centuries. These differences, in his opinion, became "less rigid" in the seventeenth century.[6]

This hypothesis and the rhetorical skill of its author have dampened enthusiasm for investigating Orthodox culture and have made it difficult to propose schemes of historical causation in which this culture plays a major part. I would like to argue against the two-culture hypothesis as a general proposition, and to argue in favor of the robust historical role played by culture in general, and Orthodox culture in particular, in the way the secular elite and the court behaved.

I also believe that Keenan's thesis has played a most useful role, since it has made impossible the innocent, Neoslavophile assumption, often cloaked in references to "the Russian soul," that all Russians were knowledgeable and committed Orthodox Christians and that interpretative methods from Orthodox culture from any time or place could be applied to the understanding of evidence from Muscovite Rus'. We cannot now posit the existence, to say nothing of the importance, of a religious idea in Muscovy without demonstrating the presence of texts or other sources through which Muscovites could have learned that idea and providing either direct evidence or a reasonable hypothesis that a certain person or group of people knew about the idea. In other words, Keenan has reminded us of our duties as careful historians or responsible literary critics. Yet the two-culture hypothesis has blocked important avenues of investigation and has made us perhaps too skeptical of the importance of Orthodoxy within the culture and history of Muscovy.

To start, it may be useful to talk about the assumptions that we bring to the question. These assumptions play an especially large role because the amount of direct evidence we have about the worldviews of laymen before 1600 is so small. First, and most obvious, it is as much an assumption that *no one* outside the church hierarchy knew anything about Orthodoxy as it is that *everyone* did. For the period before 1600, we know little about the frequency or quality of church services or other religious rituals, but we do know that members of the court spent a lot of time in the Kremlin churches and in the throne rooms. The state spent a great deal of scarce resources to make these spaces, and the ceremonies in them, as impressive as possible. Can we assume that the elaborate rituals, the singing, images, the liturgical or other texts left all laymen cold and unmoved? Given the evidence brought forward in this volume, it seems likely that major events in the lives of lay

---

6. Keenan, *Kurbskii-Groznyi Apocrypha,* 54.

courtiers—baptism, marriage, death—were all accompanied by Orthodox rituals. If we know so little about the opinions of lay sixteenth-century Muscovites, is it not just as arbitrary to assume that Russians were all self-serving cynics as to argue that they were all Father Zosimas[7] in training? Certainly Church Slavonic was not immediately intelligible to everyone, but neither is the sixteenth-century English of the Book of Common Prayer, which has so many fans among contemporary Episcopalians. The popularity of Latin within the Catholic Church in the era of Vatican II is an even better example. Another conception that bears examination is the notion that certain ways of thinking that were basic to Orthodox culture were too sophisticated to have been understood by most ordinary people. Who might have understood, for example, the idea that the army depicted in the icon *Blessed Is the Host of the Heavenly Tsar* (better known as "The Church Militant") represented at once the contemporary army of Muscovy, the army of Israel in Old Testament times, and the army of God at Armageddon?[8] To the twentieth-century historian, this idea seems complex and far-fetched, yet the pattern of biblical typology and historical recurrence that underlie it were absolutely basic to Orthodox culture, embedded as they were in virtually all liturgical texts. Our modern progressive linear concept of time, by contrast, was largely absent. We need to examine the notion of what is, and what is not, a complex theological idea in the context of the culture of the period we are discussing.

Not being a linguist, I cannot dispute Keenan's point about the linguistic separation of the two cultures. And I am more convinced than ever that he is right about the origins of the famous correspondence ascribed to Kurbskii and Ivan the Terrible. Further, he is surely right to concentrate on education and the transfer of ideas as a key point in discovering what Muscovite laymen actually knew. The introduction of *visual evidence*, however, changes the equation somewhat, since acquaintance with high-style Slavonic texts, or even the ability to read, were not prerequisites for understanding ideas presented in visual form. Let us then turn to our example, the murals in the Golden Hall, one of the most important political spaces in early modern Russia.

7. Father Zosima is a charismatic monk and elder (*starets*) in Dostoevsky's *Brothers Karamazov* and one of the most memorable religious figures in all of literature.

8. On this icon and its meaning for mid-sixteenth-century Russians, see Daniel Rowland, "Biblical Military Imagery in the Political Culture of Early Modern Russia: The Blessed Host of the Heavenly Tsar," in *Medieval Russian Culture*, vol. 2, ed. Michael S. Flier and Daniel Rowland, California Slavic Studies 19 (Berkeley and Los Angeles: University of California Press, 1994), 163–81.

As the places where the Boyar Duma met and the tsar and his court received foreign ambassadors, Muscovy's two throne rooms, the Golden Hall and the Faceted Hall, were places of extraordinary importance. Both are surely examples of what Clifford Geertz called a glowing center. Such centers are, according to Geertz, "essentially concentrated loci of serious acts; they consist in the point or points in a society where its leading ideas come together with its leading institutions to create an arena in which the events that most vitally affect its members' lives take place."[9] The entire Kremlin was such a center, but the throne rooms occupied a special place even within the rarefied and sacred space of the Kremlin as a whole.

One reason, then, for using this mural cycle as a location where ideas could flow from the ecclesiastical, literary culture to the secular culture is that the Golden Hall was at the center of a nested set of hierarchical spaces.[10] As Geertz put it, the Golden Hall was of central importance as a place where society's important ideas (as represented in the murals, as well as by the architecture of the Hall and rituals that took place there) and its important people (the tsar and his courtiers, lay and clerical) came together to do important things. This importance was underlined both architecturally and ritually. The Golden Hall was at the end of a sequence of hierarchically arranged spaces that began in Red Square outside the Kremlin and ended in the throne rooms. The courtier or visitor would typically pass through the massive masonry walls of the Kremlin via the Spasskii Gates, then proceed down a narrow street next to the Voznesenskii Monastery to Cathedral Square. From the square one climbed one of three staircases to the so-called Boyars' Porch; only from there could one enter either of the throne rooms (fig. 1). Access to these spaces was progressively restricted, from the general populace in Red Square, to the highly select courtiers who were allowed into the vestibules of the throne rooms, to the even smaller number of courtiers admitted to the throne rooms themselves. This spatial hierarchy was reinforced by the rituals used in the reception of foreign diplomats. Here the spatial sequence began at the border of the state and continued by carefully detailed stages to Moscow, then to the Kremlin, to Cathedral Square, and finally to the throne rooms.[11] Thus architecture and ritual made the throne

9. See Clifford Geertz, "Centers, Kings, and Charisma: Reflections on the Symbolics of Power," in *Rites of Power: Symbolism, Ritual, and Politics Since the Middle Ages*, ed. Sean Wilentz (Philadelphia: University of Pennsylvania Press, 1985), 13–38.

10. For a perceptive discussion of a similar nesting of architectural and social hierarchies, see Dell Upton, *Holy Things and Profane: Anglican Parish Churches in Colonial Virginia* (New Haven: Yale University Press, 1997), esp. 199–218. I am indebted to Julie Riesenweber for this reference.

11. I have discussed both architecture and ritual in greater detail in "Architecture, Image and Ritual

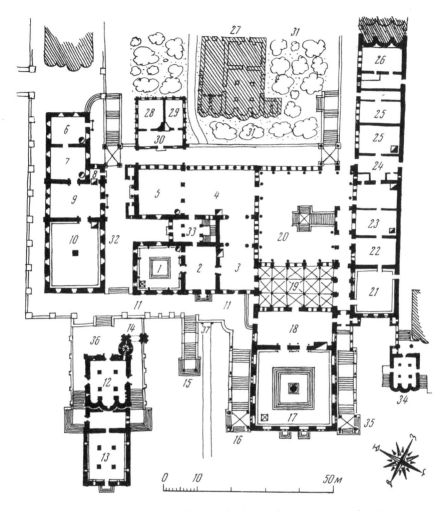

FIG. I Map of the central portion of the royal palace in the Moscow Kremlin. Reconstruc-
tion by K. K. Lopialo, from an appendix in O. I. Podobedova's *Moskovskaia shkola zhivopisi*
(Moscow: Izdatel'stvo Nauka, 1972). The space below the diagram represents Cathedral
Square. From there, diplomats and courtiers would climb to the Splendid Upper Porch or
Boyars' Porch (11) via the stairs next to the Annunciation Cathedral (12), the Central Golden
Stair (15), or the Great Splendid Golden Stair (16). From the Boyars' Porch, one entered the
vestibule (2) and throne room (1) of the Golden Hall. Further along the balcony was the
entrance to the vestibule (18) and throne room (17) of the Faceted Hall, the other main
throne room in the Kremlin.

rooms the political center of the Kremlin, which was in turn the center of the Muscovite state. The space of the Golden Hall, therefore, was especially potent as a locus for the communication of ideas.

I have also been inspired by reading the work of Valerie Kivelson[12] to ask an important question to which the Golden Palace murals seem to provide at least a partial answer. This question leads me to approach the murals from an angle that is a bit different from that used in earlier scholarship. By examining a large number of gentry petitions and other documents from the seventeenth century, Kivelson has shown that military servitors of all ranks used the ideas that can be found in historical and polemical texts from Ivan's reign as well as in the tales written about the Time of Troubles (a period of civil war and foreign intervention from 1598 to 1613), as the basis of their own political views. How did the servitor class, from boyar to provincial gentryman, learn this basic vocabulary of political ideas?

While most provincial noblemen probably never set foot inside the Golden Hall, members of boyar clans and the upper ranks of the Moscow gentry spent time, in many cases a lot of time, in the throne room and its adjacent vestibule. Lengthy court rituals, like the exchange of gifts with foreign ambassadors and the ceremonial meals that are well documented in foreigners' accounts,[13] would have left ample time to examine, or at least glance at, the rich golden murals that surrounded the visitor on all sides. Even for the disinterested, the murals could have served as the sixteenth-century equivalent of magazines in a doctor's office. Moreover, the medium of a monumental mural program, so unfamiliar to most modern viewers, was an ordinary part of the experience of most of those who populated the Golden Hall on important court occasions. The presentation of ideas in the form of murals arranged on

---

in the Throne Rooms of Muscovy, 1550 to 1650" (paper presented to the Historians' Seminar at the Davis Center for Russian Studies, Harvard University, April 1996). On the diplomatic rituals, see also L. A. Iusefovich, *"Kak v posol'skikh obychaiakh vedetsia"* (Moscow: Mezhdunarodnye otnosheniia, 1988), and the excellent paper by Maria Solomon Arel, "Muscovite Diplomatic Practice as a Prism Through Which to View Tsarish Power: Encounter with the English" (paper presented at the American Association for the Advancement of Slavic Studies, Boca Raton, September 1998).

12. Valerie Kivelson, "'The Devil Stole His Mind': The Tsar and the 1648 Moscow Uprising," *American Historical Review* 98 (1993): 733–56, and idem, *Autocracy in the Provinces*.

13. For example, see Richard Chancellor's description of the lavish state dinner in the Golden Palace ("golden court"), with mountains of golden serving vessels and "one hundred and forty servitors arrayed in cloth of gold that in the dinner time changed thrice their habit and apparel," to which Ivan IV invited him and his men. Chancellor was mightily impressed. Lloyd E. Berry and Robert O. Crummey, eds., *Rude and Barbarous Kingdom: Russia in the Accounts of Sixteenth-Century English Voyagers* (Madison: University of Wisconsin Press, 1968), 25–27. For similar receptions, see, in the same collection, the accounts of Anthony Jenkinson (who describes what is probably the Palace of Facets with its central pillar) and Sir Thomas Randolph.

the walls and vaults of a church structure was a standard experience within at least metropolitan churches since Kievan times. In fact, the arrangement of image-ideas on the interior surfaces of a church was better suited to the organization and presentation of political ideas than were any textual models available in Muscovy. The literary tradition of Rus' offered no models for sustained textual political discussion in which ideas were organized logically, but the traditional arrangement of images within an Orthodox church described in principle by Otto Demus some years ago[14] gave painters a means to organize political ideas in space. Spatial relations rather than Aristotelian logic thus became the glue that held together and organized discreet political ideas.

Further, the murals in the Golden Hall may have been more accessible to the eye than church murals for the simple reason that they were easier to see. In many of churches, important scenes were placed in difficult-to-see spots at a great height. Others were hidden behind the iconostasis. The modest dimensions of the Golden Hall (the throne room was about twelve meters square, the vestibule, about twelve by eight meters) and its open plan would have made the murals fairly easy to see from almost any vantage point. For those who could read fairly simple Church Slavonic, extensive inscriptions explained the meaning of the images. For those who could not, the images were in many cases self-explanatory, as we shall see. Finally, as teaching experience shows, repetition reinforces understanding. Important texts (like the crucial "Wisdom has built a house" from Proverbs 9) and figures (God, Solomon, the Mother of God) appear in many places. More important, many of the themes and scenes in the Palace (like the Old Testament scenes of Israel's military defeat of its enemies under Moses, Joshua, and Gideon) were found over and over again both in other mural cycles elsewhere in the Kremlin and in various texts.[15] The habit of Metropolitan Macarius and his cultural helpers of repeating the same themes has been remarked on by many commentators;[16] this repetition must have helped to drum these themes into even those heads that otherwise might have been hard to penetrate. It seems fair to conclude, therefore, that the murals in the Golden Hall were potentially potent tools for communicating ideas to the lay elite of Moscow directly, and indirectly, to the rest of the servitor class.

14. Otto Demus, *Byzantine Mosaic Decoration: Aspects of Monumental Art in Byzantium* (London: Routledge and Kegan Paul, 1953).

15. These connections are particularly well laid out by Podobedova in *Moskovskaia shkola.*

16. For example, see Robert Crummey, *The Formation of Muscovy, 1304–1613* (London: Longman, 1987), 199–200, and Podobedova, *Moskovskaia shkola.*

What ideas were conveyed to these military-minded lay courtiers? Any means of communication creates some slippage between the intent of the communicator and the person or persons who gets (or fails to get) the message. My question, therefore, is, "what political messages might a typical courtier have taken away from the repeated visits that we know he must have made to the Golden Palace?" This question is obviously different from the more usual, "What do the murals in the Golden Hall mean?" It is by now a truism that the meaning a person receives from a work of art depends on a variety of factors: the education and life experiences of the viewer, the time spent in viewing (a glance or a measured view),[17] the year or even month in which the viewing takes place and thus the immediate context of events that could be associated with the images and texts, the place of the viewer within the room, and the visual accessibility of the images in question. Available evidence does not allow us to define each of these variables accurately, but I think we can make a fairly shrewd guess, given the consistency of visual political messages at Ivan's court, that several points would strike our imagined military servitor with little or no theological education. I have selected seven themes that I believe resonate with other roughly contemporary monuments of culture, literary or artistic; most of these themes seem also to crop up both in various tales about the Time of Troubles and in Kivelson's gentry petitions. These themes are (1) the descent of political power from God, (2) the protection of Rus' (the name commonly used by the medieval East Slavs to describe themselves) by the Mother of God, (3) the importance of the clan of the ruler, (4) God's protection of the Muscovite army and its role in sacred history, (5) the good order of the realm, (6) the piety and moral behavior of the tsar, and (7) advice and the relationship of the ruler with his courtiers. My hypothesis is that the members of the court absorbed these ideas at least in part through the Golden Hall murals. In later generations, when the need to defend the interests of secular courtiers in the context of a set of political beliefs arose, these themes reappeared.

In order to understand the context of these ideas, a quick overview of the murals is essential. These images are not easy to describe in a few words. They covered the wall both of the vestibule and the throne room itself (numbers 1

---

17. Randolph Starn, "Seeing Culture in a Room for a Renaissance Prince," in *The New Cultural History*, ed. Lynn Hunt (Berkeley and Los Angeles: University of California Press, 1989), 205–32; Randolph Starn and Loren Partridge, *Arts of Power: Three Halls of State in Italy, 1300–1600* (Berkeley and Los Angeles: University of California Press, 1992), 118–31. Art historians have recently devoted a lot of attention to the viewing public. Thomas Crow's works are especially relevant in this respect. See his *Painters in Public Life in Eighteenth-Century Paris* (New Haven: Yale University Press, 1985).

FIG. 2   Reconstruction drawing of the Sanctuary mural over the tsar's throne in the throne room of the Golden Palace by K. K. Lopialo, from an appendix in O. I. Podobedova's *Moskovskaia shkola zhivopisi.* Note here the presence of the Mother of God as part of the theme of Divine Wisdom, but giving the impression of her as protectress of the tsar and his kingdom.

and 2 on fig. 1). The vestibule was devoted largely to Old Testament themes. At the center of the ceiling vault was an image of the Trinity, under which were spread seven scenes of godly governance. In the squinches were depicted the kings of ancient Israel, starting with David and Solomon (fig. 3). On the walls and adjoining vaults was shown the military conquest of the Promised Land by Moses, Joshua, and in the throne room, Gideon.[18] In the throne

18. S. P. Bartenev, *Moskovskii kreml' v starinu i teper'* (Moscow, 1916), 183–93, provides a full description of the murals made in 1672. References to this description, which is the clearest evidence we have about the murals, will be made parenthetically in the text.

FIG. 3 Reconstruction drawing of the upper murals of the vestibule of the Golden Palace by K. K. Lopialo, from an appendix in O. I. Podobedova's *Moskovskaia shkola zhivopisi*. In the middle is Fatherhood (*Otechestvo*, which can also be referred to as the Ancient of Days) surrounded by seven moralizing scenes about divinely inspired rulership. In the squinches are Old Testament rulers of Israel, while around the walls are scenes of the conquest of the Promised Land by Moses and Joshua. In general, the vestibule murals show Old Testament rulership, military and political, as a prefiguration of and model for rulership in Rus'.

FIG. 4   Reconstruction drawing of the upper murals of the throne room of the Golden Palace by K. K. Lopialo, from an appendix in O. I. Podobedova's *Moskovskaia shkola zhivopisi*. Beneath the complex iconography centering on Divine Wisdom in the dome are the rulers of Rus', arranged to parallel the Old Testament rulers in the vestibule. On the walls and lower vaults are scenes of Gideon's military victories, the conversion of Rus' to Christianity under Saint Vladimir, and the transfer of charismatic regalia from Byzantium to Rus' in the reign of Vladimir Monomakh, as well as depictions of several parables and historical episodes. The scenes about Saint Vladimir and Vladimir Monomakh show the importance of advisers, while the parables and historical scenes emphasize the moral responsibilities of earthly life in general and rulership in particular.

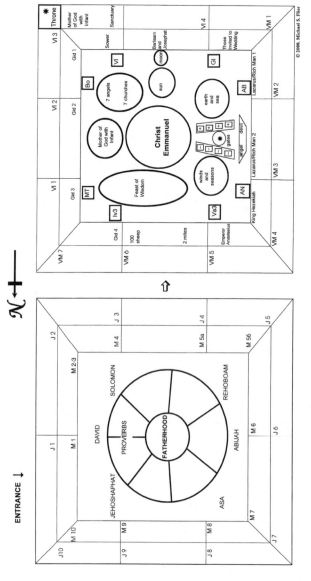

Vestibule

Golden Hall

© 2000. Michael S. Flier

ENTRANCE

FIG. 5 Diagram of the overall scheme of the murals of the Golden Palace. Reconstruction by Michael S. Flier, reproduced with his permission. In the vestibule (on the left) the rulership scenes around Fatherhood (*Otechestvo*) are numbered 1 through 7. Below are the cycles about Moses (M 1–10) and Joshua (J 1–10). In the throne room itself (on the right), we see among the rulers of Rus', Boris (Bo) and Gleb (Gl), on either side of Saint Vladimir (Vl). Following clockwise from Gleb are Andrei Bogoliubskii (AB), Aleksandr Nevskii (AN), and Vasilii III (Va3). Following counter-clockwise from Boris are Michael of Tver (MT) and "Grand Prince Ivan Vasil'evich (probably Ivan III) (Iv3). In the outside part of the diagram, reflecting the lower vaults and walls, are scenes devoted to Gideon (Gid 1–4), Saint Vladimir (Vl 1–4), and Vladimir Monomakh (VN 1–7), as well as parables and historical scenes.

room itself, God as Sabaoth (Lord of Armies) was shown in the center of the dome, surrounded by complex images connected to the themes of Divine Wisdom, the creation of the world, and the choice between the broad path of sin and the narrow path of righteousness. In the squinches were depicted members of the Riurikovich dynasty, starting with Saint Vladimir and ending with "Ivan Vasilevich" (Ivan III?). On the wall were depicted a series of scenes from Rus' history, including the conversion of Rus' to Christianity and the transfer of charismatic regalia from Byzantium to Rus' in the reign of Grand Prince Vladimir Monomakh (Bartenev, 183–90).[19]

Complicating our task further is the fact that the Golden Hall and its murals were pulled down in 1752 to make room for the Kremlin Palace built for the Empress Elizabeth by the architect Rastrelli. We know the murals from a very careful description made in 1672 by the noted icon painter Simon Ushakov and an associate.[20] This description is almost the sole evidence we have for the murals. Most scholars assume that the murals were painted after the great Moscow fire in 1547, but this date has been contested, as we shall see in our conclusion.

The most obvious political idea in the Hall, and also the most important political idea in Muscovite Russia, is the descent of the tsar's power from God. This point is made over and over again. Most potently, each room had a picture of God at the center of its domed ceiling, surrounded with more or less abstract theological or moral subjects. On the walls were depicted historical events from the history of the Old Testament Israel (in the vestibule) and Rus' (in the throne room). Architecture and image worked powerfully together in the Golden Hall to illustrate this most important of themes. Rulers—Old Testament "tsars" in the vestibule and Rus' princes in the throne room—were placed in squinches or pendentives that structurally and visually linked the round dome above with the rectangular wall below. Set in their V-shaped squinches, these rulers stretched like God's fingers from the heavenly into the earthly realm (fig. 4), thus linking spatially and architecturally the world of historical events in sacred states with the power and authority of God.[21] It is hard to imagine how this point would *not* come across to a viewer. At the level of individual scenes, God was shown blessing, guiding,

---

19. See figures 3 and 4 for a reconstruction of the murals of each room by K. K. Lopialo. Figure 5 is a diagram by my colleague Michael Flier of the overall scheme of the murals.

20. Ushakov's description can be found in Bartenev, *Moskovskii kreml'*, 183–93, and I. E. Zabelin, *Materialy dlia istorii, arkheologii, i statistiki goroda Moskvy* (Moscow, 1884), 1:1238–35.

21. See the sketches of the Golden Hall architecture and murals by K. K. Lopialo in Podobedova, *Moskovskaia shkola*, appendix.

and helping rulers in their quotidian life in a straightforward way. In the many Old Testament battle scenes, for example, God as Sabaoth was explicitly shown helping Israelite leaders the way that the Archangel Michael helps the Muscovite troops in the so-called Church Militant icon. As courtiers and foreigners cooled their heels in the vestibule, they would have seen above them, in the seven moralizing scenes surrounding the Ancient of Days (*Otechestvo* or New Testament Trinity) composition in the center of the dome, God or an angel blessing the tsar. In scene 2, inscribed "the heart of the tsar is in the hands of God," a tsar enthroned holding an orb and scepter is shown next to God as Pantocrator, who is holding out his left hand in a gesture of blessing and has placed his right on the orb that the tsar holds (Bartenev, 190). In scenes 4, 5, and 6, angels directly crown the ruler (note that Lopialo erroneously omits the crown in the angel's left hand in scene 4) or hold the scales of justice (scene 6) (Bartenev, 190). In the throne room, the crowning of Vladimir Monomakh is presided over by God as *Otechestvo* (Bartenev, 189). These images were all very direct and did not depend on knowledge of complex theological notions to be understood.

Far more difficult for our typical courtier to understand was the theme of Holy Wisdom (*Sofiia, premudrost' Bozhiia*), a theme that was perhaps *the* dominant idea of the Palace murals from a theological point of view. The complex iconography of Holy Wisdom occupies the northeast half of the throne room dome and was based largely on ideas that had come to Moscow fairly recently from Novgorod. This theme is based on a mystical reading of the ninth chapter of Proverbs, beginning with the sentence, "Wisdom has built a house for herself." Briefly, the House of Wisdom symbolizes the Church and its seven ecumenical councils, the Mother of God as the "house" of the incarnated God, the altar during the Eucharist, and the Muscovite kingdom itself. This deeply layered interpretation must surely have seemed opaque to all but the most sophisticated courtiers, though an ability to read the inscriptions and an acquaintance with the Orthodox liturgy would have helped. My argument that Wisdom was not all that well understood rests on two points. First, secular courtiers would have had little other experience of this abstract concept. Although Holy Wisdom is a prominent idea in Orthodox liturgical texts, its complex development as a political theme would not have been obvious from common liturgical experience. Second, the theme of Wisdom was *not* used extensively in other parts of Moscow's court culture and was not included as a main theme in the decoration of the Palace of Facets done later, during the reign of Ivan the Terrible's son, Fedor Ivanovich (reigned 1584–98). A likely reason for this latter omission is that the theme of

Wisdom had not by then entered the common vocabulary of political ideas. Similarly, Holy Wisdom plays no role in the various tales about the Time of Troubles.

A theme that was a cornerstone of Rus' culture over many centuries and would surely have been familiar to most courtiers is the protection of the Rus' state by the Mother of God. This theme might well have been *read into* the murals even though, in a strict interpretation, it was relatively unimportant there. She appears unambiguously in this role in the final scene of the Vladimir Monomakh cycle (V7 on fig. 5; Bartenev 189), where she blesses the coronation of Vladimir Monomakh with the regalia recently received from Byzantium and imagined by Ivan IV's contemporaries to be the same as that worn by Ivan himself. She also appears prominently in the throne room in a position close to the throne as the New Testament fulfillment of the House of Wisdom prophecy in Proverbs 9. An untutored viewer, however, might well have seen her presiding with Christ Emmanuel over the entire throne room, and thus understand her as a protectress of the Muscovite *tsarstvo*. This impression would have been strengthened by the composition directly over the tsar's throne (see fig. 2; "Sanctuary" in fig. 5) in which the Mother of God is directly over the throne and the tsar, with Solomon, David, and St. Peter in the space between her and the tsar. A learned viewer would be informed by the inscription in Solomon's scroll "Wisdom has built her house" and by the inscription above the whole composition, "The house of the Lord is a holy sanctuary [*sviataia ograda*]," that the Mother of God is again here as part of the Wisdom iconography (as the "house" of the incarnate God). Our uneducated viewer may well have taken the "holy sanctuary" (if he could read the inscription) to refer to the Russian state (as symbolized by the tsar himself on his throne) under the protection of the Mother of God. Indeed, the composition and placement of this "sanctuary" scene makes one suspect that both interpretations may have been intended (Bartenev, 188–89).

It is not necessary to engage in speculative misinterpretation of the murals in order to describe a number of themes that resonated with other parts of Muscovite culture and had close connections with the lives of lay courtiers. The importance of the ruler's clan is such a theme, for it was a major preoccupation of the court and a matter of great concern in their own sphere to the boyars who frequented the Golden Palace. This theme was emphasized in the two throne-room cycles on the baptism of the first Prince Vladimir (ca. 980–1015) and the transfer of regalia from Byzantium later, under Grand Prince Vladimir Monomakh (1113–25). The clan theme was underlined in the placement of various Riurikovich rulers in the squinches in the throne room and the parallel selection of the lineal descendants of "Tsar and Prophet David" for the same position in the vestibule.

Another theme that would have been obvious to an illiterate lay courtier is the military one. Fighting would have been the main occupation of such a person. Numerous battle scenes appeared in the three cycles describing the liberation of the people of Israel from Egypt and the conquest of the Promised Land by Moses, Joshua, and Gideon. These scenes echoed a number of other roughly contemporary cultural artifacts emphasizing the theme of "Blessed is the host of the Heavenly Tsar."[22] The point of these images was to suggest that the army of Muscovy (including the courtiers present in the throne room) played a vital role in salvation history, a role prefigured by the armies of Israel in the Old Testament, and prefiguring the troops of Christ at Armageddon. Again I want to emphasize the physical accessibility of many of these pictures on the walls or vaults close to the level of the lay courtiers who were lucky enough to get into the palace and the utter familiarity of the activity depicted (fighting) in the lives of these military servitors. If the "Church Militant" icon and the murals of the Archangel Michael Cathedral were typical, then these Old Testament warriors were clothed in contemporary Muscovite military dress, thus increasing the accessibility of these images still further.

The duty of the tsar to preserve the good order of the realm, to rule justly, and to protect the poor is a theme that was prominent in the tales about the Time of Troubles and also in many earlier literary texts. The ideal of the good order of the realm was certainly implied on the dome of the throne room, where depictions of the winds and seasons and the creation of the universe (sun, moon, stars, land, sea) shows God through Holy Wisdom ordering the universe as (it is implied) the tsar orders his *tsarstvo*. The inscription around the central figure of Christ Emmanuel, here signifying Holy Wisdom as the inscription makes clear, strengthens this implication (I use Michael Flier's translation), though whether an illiterate courtier would have gotten the point is unclear: "God the Father has through His Wisdom founded the earth and fixed the ages. O paternal Logos beyond eternity, who in God's image is and constitutes creation from non-being into being, who by his authority [*oblastiiu svoeiu*] has set the seasons and the years, bless the crown [or circle?] of time [*venets letu*] with thy beneficence, grant peace to

---

22. Rowland, "Biblical Military Imagery," 163–81, with further references to other works on this important theme. An important new work is N.V. Kvlividze, "Ikona 'Blagoslovenno voinstvo nebesnogo tsaria' i ee literaturnye paralleli," in *Iskusstvo Khristianskogo mira. Sbornik statei*, vol. 2 (Moscow: Pravolslavnyi Sviato-Tikhonovskii Bogoslovskii Institut, 1997).

thy churches, victories to the true tsar, fruitfulness to the land, and great mercy to us" (Bartenev, 183).

The correspondence between God's orderly creation of the world and the ruler's imposition of order in his realm was a commonplace in halls of state in Western and Eastern Europe. This correspondence seems to explain the even greater emphasis given to the Creation in the Hall of Facets murals, although the role of Holy Wisdom there is much diminished.[23] A few other scenes in the Golden Palace murals emphasize good governance in a more practical sense. In the moralizing scenes around the Ancient of Days (*Otechestvo*) in the vestibule (see fig. 3), Solomon gives money to the poor, seemingly as a sign of his fear of the Lord (scene 4), and in the adjoining fifth scene, an angel with scales and a sword clearly symbolizes royal justice, an attribute of the Godly ruler (Bartenev, 190).

I will conclude with two themes in the Golden Palace murals that had much in common with contemporary political discourse, one of which has been often referred to and the other, much less often: the personal piety and moral behavior of the tsar and the question of advice. Almost all commentators have remarked on the striking attempt in the murals to give moral/religious instruction to the tsar (and presumably, to everyone else in the palace). The seven Proverbs-inspired scenes in the vestibule arranged around the Ancient of Days like seven pillars stress the good deeds of a tsar that are a sign of the presence in him of Holy Wisdom. The ruler (sometimes depicted as Solomon) is shown not only being endowed by God or an angel with the symbols of office as we have already discussed, but worshiping (scene 3), giving money to the poor (scene 4), judging justly (scene 5), teaching his subjects (scene 6), and teaching his son with a book (scene 7) (Bartenev, 190). The New Testament counterparts to these scenes are Jesus' parables, shown in the vaults of the throne room itself. These include, starting at the tsar's throne, the parables of the sower, the wedding guests, the rich man and Lazarus, the lost sheep, and the lost coins. In the corner just opposite the tsar are added scenes of two rulers who foresee their own death: Hezekiah who repents and survives for fifteen more years, blessed by the Lord (2 Kings 20:1–6; Isaiah 38:1–6) and the Emperor Anastasios who does not and dies condemned by his sins (Bartenev, 186–87). Many commentators[24] have seen in the selection of these scenes specific references to the life of the young Ivan IV. Whether

23. Aida Nasibova, *The Faceted Chamber in the Moscow Kremlin* (Leningrad: Aurora Art Publishers, 1978).

24. Ivan Zabelin, *Domashnii byt Russkikh tsarei v XVI i XVII st.* (Moscow: Tipografiia A. I. Mamontova, 1895), 166–67; Podobedova, *Moskovskaia shkola,* 61–62.

or not those specific references were intended, this part of the mural program seems to emphasize the desire of God to pardon sinners, but his harsh judgment and punishment of those who refuse to repent. The parables of the wedding feast and the rich man and Lazarus single out greed as especially effective in separating the sinner from God's mercy. Taken together, these scenes imply the free will of a person before the choice between good and evil. This theme of a moral choice is amplified on the dome above, where two gates, one adorned with virtues and the other with vices, symbolize the choice between the "narrow path" of good and the "broad way" of evil. These moralizing scenes not only urge the tsar to choose good; they also by implication underline the conditionality of royal power: if a tsar chooses the broad way of sin, then he separates himself from God. The salvation of the tsar and God's blessing on the *tsarstvo* depend upon the "good soil" of the tsar's soul. (Incidentally, if indeed this part of the mural program does date from the 1550s, these scenes are evidence of a moralizing tendency in Russian Orthodoxy that Paul Bushkovitch has recently dated mostly to the second half of the seventeenth century.)[25]

Our last subject is the theme of advice. By itself, this theme is not the direct subject of any scene and has not been much noticed before. Yet a courtier approaching the palace with an interest in the relationship between the ruler and himself and his colleagues or advisers would have found considerable material to ponder. Ushakov's careful description of 1672 notes the existence of "boyars" or "grandees" (*vel'mozhi*) in a large number of scenes in both the vestibule and the throne room (see figs. 3 and 4). They were shown prominently in the vestibule in the seven scenes around the Ancient of Days figure in the dome. They appeared in the second scene in front of the God-crowned tsar, in the third scene (as "Israelites") assisting Solomon in the performance of his religious duties, in the third scene (as *vel'mozhi*) accompanying Solomon as he distributes alms, in the sixth scene witnessing the tsar teaching the people, and in the seventh scene observing the tsar teach his son. Advisers/courtiers are thus specifically mentioned in five of the seven scenes (Bartenev, 190). Ushakov specifies "boyars" as present in all four scenes in the cycle devoted to the conversion of Rus' under Prince Vladimir. In scene 1, they listen with the tsar as representatives from various faiths describe their beliefs; in scene 2, boyars are mentioned among the Byzantine emperor's retinue in church; in scene 3, boyars stand behind Vladimir holding his crown and

25. Paul Bushkovitch, *Religion and Society in Russia: The Sixteenth and Seventeenth Centuries* (New York: Oxford University Press, 1992).

royal vestments; in scene 4, four boyars are specified as present at the overthrowing of the idols (Bartenev, 188–89). In the Vladimir Monomakh cycle,
boyars are present every time that the Rus' court is depicted. Monomakh
consults his boyars about a military expedition to Constantinople (scene 1),
collects and organizes his troops with the help of boyars (scene 2), receives
the regalia in the presence of clergymen and boyars (scene 6), and is tri-
umphantly crowned, also in the presence of his boyars (scene 7) (Bartenev,
189). The murals clearly depict boyars or grandees as standard parts of the
royal court and show them consulting with and supporting their ruler in a
wide variety of situations. (In military scenes, the same boyars would presumably be depicted as part of the army.) Whereas in the tales about the
Time of Troubles, advisers were important chiefly as the most convenient
means to correct an erring or sinful tsar,[26] in the Golden Palace wise advisers
are shown as part of the normal running of a pious tsar's court. The consistency with which Ushakov mentions them indicates that the authors of the
Golden Palace mural program considered boyar advisers an essential part of
the tsar's court and made a point of including them in the murals' depiction
of Christian governance. Indeed, "advice" may not be the right rubric for our
discussion here; "boyars" or "grandees" are more accurately depicted as *partners* of the tsar in governance. Perhaps the modern viewer is too influenced
here by a Whig view of history, which posited a constant and inevitable
conflict between the ruler and his nobles: the designers of the Golden Hall
murals seem to have regarded a ruler surrounded by powerful boyars as more
powerful than one who rules by himself.

What can we conclude from this excursion into the meaning of some long-lost
murals? The irony from the point of view of Keenan is that there is room for
serious debate on the dating of the murals in the Golden Hall, and thus the
dating question makes it unclear whether or not the murals disprove his two-
culture hypothesis. We know that some murals were painted in the Golden
Hall after the Moscow fire of 1547. Virtually all of our evidence about the
murals comes from a detailed description compiled by Simon Ushakov and
his assistant in 1672, in connection with a proposed repainting of the Golden
Hall. In between, Moscow suffered from the disastrous invasion of the Tatars
in 1571, which severely damaged many buildings in the Kremlin, and from the
depredations of the Time of Troubles. How old were the murals that Ushakov

26. Daniel Rowland, "The Problem of Advice in Muscovite Tales About the Time of Troubles," *Russian History* 6 (1979): 259–83.

described? There is no evidence clear enough to resolve this question to everyone's satisfaction, at least for the moment. If as some scholars think, the murals date from early in the seventeenth century, then they would neither confirm or contradict Keenan's thesis, that the secular world was not enlightened in most matters of religious culture until around 1600. My own judgment is that the mural program, if not the murals themselves, date from the 1540s. The chief evidence is the surviving documentation on the "Viskovatyi affair," a dispute over recent developments in iconography between a prominent courtier, Ivan Viskovatyi, and Metropolitan Macarius, in which the theological content of some of the most innovative sections of the murals was discussed in some detail. A manuscript containing this evidence and apparently dating from the 1560s survives. There is also the habit, well documented in the seventeenth century, of repainting old murals according to the program that was there before. Even if the murals themselves were destroyed in one or more catastrophes, the program would most probably have been preserved. And, of course, it is the program, not the images themselves, which concerns us.[27]

If the mural program does date from the middle of the sixteenth century, the Golden Hall, by virtue of its central role spatially and politically, would have endowed its murals with a high degree of political influence in the age of Ivan the Terrible. Other Kremlin locations, especially churches, were also well furnished with murals. It is precisely in these spaces, where we know courtiers spent a great deal of time, that an effective education in basic political values may well have taken place. We need not assume that a courtier would become so transformed by the throne-room murals that he would be able to translate Cicero, as Prince Kurbskii is alleged to have done. If the key question is one of education, as Professor Keenan has stated, surely the Golden Hall murals, and the many other images that an average courtier encountered, were potential sources of education. Images could move more easily between the two cultures than texts could, simply because they bypassed the linguistic boundaries that Keenan drew to our attention. Each of the seven themes in the murals that we have discussed should have been transparent to this average courtier, whether or not he was literate in Church Slavonic or conversant with sophisticated theology. If so, the Golden Hall murals would surely have conveyed, over a long period of time from the 1550s to the 1670s, a series of important political messages that fit reasonably well with what servitors seemed actually to have believed in the seventeenth century.

27. On the dating of the Golden Hall murals, see my "Biblical Military Imagery," 194 n. 29, with further references on the opinions of earlier art historians. Podobedova believed that the murals were painted in the 1540s; Lopialo, in the seventeenth century. *Moskovskaia shkola*, 59, 194–98.

Reception theory teaches us that a text or a work of art represents only one side of a kind of conversation that takes place between a particular viewer or reader (or a group of viewers or readers) and any given image or text. In order to understand the viewing experience of an audience, the historian needs to try to understand the socially determined values, concerns, and questions that a particular audience brought to an image, since these expectations formed the complement to the picture, the part of the viewing experience that now has to be reconstituted. As Michael Baxendall wrote in describing the experience of a fifteenth-century Italian audience to Bellini's *Transfiguration,* "the painting is a relic of a cooperation between Bellini and his public: the fifteenth-century experience of the *Transfiguration* was an interaction between the painting, the configuration on the wall, and the visualizing activity of the public mind—a public mind with different furniture and dispositions from ours."[28]

How can we recreate the conversations between the images of the Golden Hall and the boyars and other courtiers who frequented it? At the least, we can say that the choice of meanings of any text, performance, film, and so on, is not a binary one. We are not faced with the question of whether boyars understood the murals or not. They must have understood the mural program in some way, even if they saw only a confused jumble of images. Each courtier brought to his encounter with the murals his own experiences and interests, and each took away slightly different messages. As we try to locate each boyar along a continuum of understanding, with an almost infinite variety of choices along this spectrum, it would therefore be extremely unwise to suggest that all boyars occupied only one position in this possible spectrum of understanding, at either end *or* in the middle. A more likely argument is that, given the little that we can guess about the interests and knowledge of lay courtiers, the perceptions of the court as a whole fell within a range of understandings that would have enabled most people, most of the time, to understand the basic messages we have been discussing.

---

28. Michael Baxendall, *Painting and Experience in Fifteenth-Century Italy* (Oxford: Oxford University Press, 1972), 48. Baxendall, investigating a society with far more surviving documentation than sixteenth-century Russia, was nevertheless pessimistic about the force of his own ingenious arguments. At the end of his chapter "The Period Eye," he concluded ruefully, "It is proper to end this chapter on a faltering note." On the complex matter of reception theory, I have found helpful the following works: Terry Eagleton, *Literary Theory: An Introduction* (Minneapolis: University of Minnesota Press, 1983), 54–90; Eric Fernie, ed., *Art History and Its Methods: A Critical Anthology* (London: Phaidon Press, 1995), 357–58; and Ann Jefferson and David Robey, eds., *Modern Literary Criticism: A Comparative Introduction,* 2d ed. (Totowa, N.J.: Barnes and Noble Books, 1986), 138–44. For a wonderful example of reading architecture in the context of its contemporary society and geography, see Upton, *Holy Things and Profane.*

Court life in Russia, as elsewhere, offered many lessons about politics, in many formats. Courtiers went on military campaigns, took part in precedence disputes, did their best to forward the interests of themselves and their clans, attended lengthy ceremonies at court. Each of these activities produced its own lessons, many brutally practical. Among the many ways in which the political culture of the court took shape, the Golden Hall murals, and associated images elsewhere, may well have played an important role, since, by casting political relations in the language and rich context of Orthodox political culture, they provided answers to a *level* of question quite different from the other, more practical, lessons offered by court life. By emphasizing the divine purpose of the state, they strengthened the power of the tsar and made the growing political structure of the realm seem as if it were a part of the natural order of things, as inescapable as the turning of the seasons. The protection of the Mother of God strengthened the idea of divine support for the state while drawing on a long tradition of Marian veneration among a wide variety of inhabitants of Rus'. The celebration of the clan of the ruler echoed the clan concerns that occupied so much attention of the boyars,[29] while the military theme of God's protection of the Russian army gave spiritual comfort to those on campaign and a role in salvation history not only to the tsar but to his nobles. The active participation of the court came out even more clearly in the various scenes involving advice. The scenes dealing with moral choice served not only to edify the court but at the least to imply the conditionality of royal power.

These beliefs, couched entirely within the context of Orthodox culture, were surely of great importance to the political history of Russia. If we assume, as Keenan does, that the Muscovite state until the second half of the seventeenth century was too weak economically, bureaucratically, and militarily to enforce its will on all its subjects all the time, then these murals (and other images) may have been a particularly cost-effective way to hold the country together. This goal was achieved by giving members of the elite good reasons why, under normal circumstances, they should serve the tsar and support the state. Each of the religious ideas we have discussed worked powerfully toward this end. Each also depended on the kind of crossover of religious ideas into the secular culture that form such an important theme in this collection. Instead of relying on brute force, the ruler persuaded his courtiers that they were an important part of God's plan, that their work as warriors

---

29. See here especially Kollmann, *Kinship and Politics,* and her recent book on precedence: *By Honor Bound: State and Society in Early Modern Russia* (Ithaca: Cornell University Press, 1999).

and advisers was crucial to salvation history. At the same time and using the same religious vocabulary, the murals emphasized that the tsar was to govern with the advice of his nobles, and implied that the power of the tsar was conditional on the tsar's personal piety and morality and on his defense of the Orthodox faith. The Orthodox Church thus not only provided a language for the understanding of political relations, it also provided religious reasons for opposing the tsar. During the Time of Troubles, when a succession crisis led to civil war and an abundance of pretenders of doubtful lineage and questionable religious and moral credentials, the importance of these limitations was to become all too apparent.

3

LETTING THE PEOPLE INTO CHURCH

Reflections on
Orthodoxy and Community
in Late Imperial Russia

VERA SHEVZOV

The study of Orthodox Christianity in Russia, like the study of any religious tradition, entails a certain mental mapping. Students and scholars typically organize and correlate information according to certain categories of thought—official and popular, theological and ritual, sacred and profane, public and private—that initially seem to be convenient and useful. The categories we select, however, and the manner in which we define them greatly influence both how we formulate the questions we ask and how we process what the sources (or data) tell us. Our conceptual framework significantly determines the range of interpretive possibilities, and thus also the quality of any final synthesis and conclusions of our research. In this chapter, I consider the issue of conceptualizing "church," a phenomenon that some would say stands in the forefront in the study of Orthodox Christianity. What does it mean to study "church," and how might certain cognitive approaches influence our understanding of it?

If we look at religious histories of early modern and modern Europe over the past thirty years, we can see a particular trend. Having traced the cultural bifurcation in Europe between the curé and the rural parishioners to the Reformation,[1] historians have sought to unearth the buried voices and practices of the common people in order to offer a balanced perspective to the "official" voices of "the church," whether Catholic or Protestant. Accordingly, it became standard practice for European historians to begin their

---

1. See the discussion in Thomas A. Kselman, *Miracles and Prophecies in Nineteenth-Century France* (New Brunswick: Rutgers University Press, 1983), 28.

studies of devotions and piety of the common folk with a proviso that defines
the parameters by which they understand "the popular."[2] While historians
may have encountered difficulties in agreeing on just who or what constituted "the popular," very few have disagreed over its counterpart, "the official." Identified with "the church," the latter generally has referred to the
clergy, prescriptions of canons and councils, and the realm of "pure" theology. The result in most of these studies has been the presentation of what
appear as coexisting but often opposing religious cultures, with the "church"
on one side and whatever constituted "the popular" on the other.[3]

Despite the successes of the study of popular as opposed to official religion
in premodern and modern Europe, one of its byproducts has been a way of
thinking that continues to isolate the common faithful from that body with
which they themselves identified, that is the "church."[4] Historians of Russia
seem to have inherited this way of thinking. Though more recent historians,
along with ethnographers and folklorists, have enabled common folk to
gain a voice of their own, they nevertheless have often *conceptually* left such
folk outside the "church." An example of this has been the shift to the study
of so-called *bytovoe pravoslavie,* that is, quotidian or everyday Orthodoxy.
Defined by one author as "the religious, everyday complex of beliefs and rituals, relations and behavior which were deeply tied to the familial structure,"
the term frequently has been used, at least in Soviet Russia, in ways that
also implied an Orthodoxy that remained in some way lesser or tainted with

2. See as examples Ellen Badone, ed., *Religious Orthodoxy and Popular Faith in European Society* (Princeton: Princeton University Press, 1990), 3–9; Peter Burke, *Popular Culture in Early Modern Europe* (Brookfield, Vt.: Ashgate, 1994), xvi–xxii; Michael P. Carroll, *Madonnas That Maim: Popular Catholicism in Italy Since the Fifteenth Century* (Baltimore: Johns Hopkins University Press, 1992), 6–8; Steven L. Kaplan, *Understanding Popular Culture* (New York: Mouton, 1984), 1–17; Christopher Marsh, *Popular Religion in Sixteenth-Century England* (New York: St. Martin's Press, 1998), 6–9; James Obelkevich, *Religion and the People* (Chapel Hill: University of North Carolina Press, 1979), 3–7; R. W. Scribner, *Popular Culture and Popular Movements in Reformation Germany* (Ronceverte, W.Va.: Hambledon Press, 1987), 17–18; and Marc Vernard, "Popular Religion in the Eighteenth Century," in *Church and Society in Catholic Europe of the Eighteenth Century,* ed. William J. Callahan and David Higgs (New York: Cambridge University Press, 1979), 138–62.

3. For specific examples, see David Blackbourn, *Marpingen: Apparitions of the Virgin Mary in Bismarckian Germany* (New York: Oxford University Press, 1993), 48, 51; Jean Delumeau, *Catholicism Between Luther and Voltaire: A New View of the Counter-Reformation* (Philadelphia: Westminster Press, 1977), 175–231; Timothy Tackett, *Priest and Parish in Eighteenth-Century France* (Princeton: Princeton University Press, 1977), 214; Keith Thomas, *Religion and the Decline of Magic* (reprint, New York: Oxford University Press, 1997); and Eugen Weber, *Peasants into Frenchmen* (Stanford: Stanford University Press, 1976), 357–74.

4. For evidence supporting the notion of a collective Orthodox identity among common believers that very much included notions of church, see my forthcoming book *Russian Orthodoxy on the Eve of Revolution* (New York: Oxford University Press, 2003).

pagan undertones.[5] In the 1920s and 1930s, for instance, Soviet ethnographers used the phrase in order to segregate people's religious practices from a specifically Orthodox context, in part to hasten believers' detachment from their Orthodox identity.[6] Moreover, it is unclear with what the qualifying term *bytovoe,* or "everyday," was being contrasted. To what, we might ask, would a nonquotidian Orthodoxy refer? Presumably to so-called prescribed Orthodoxy, namely to Orthodox theology and perhaps, depending on one's viewpoint, to liturgical practices. It could certainly be argued, however, that much of these were thoroughly everyday and practical as well. Translating the term *bytovoe pravoslavie* in terms of the currently more fashionable category of "lived" religion might be more productive, but it is somewhat misleading in that it hides the latent two-tiered thinking the Russian term has historically carried.[7]

In any case, the term "church" was, and usually still remains, reserved for the events, activities, and voices of members of the ecclesiastical establishment—bishops, monastics, ordained pastors and clerics, and sometimes trained theologians.[8] "The people" remain conspicuously outside its compound. In many instances, then, scholars have no more integrated devout laymen and -women into their histories of Orthodoxy and the Orthodox Church than they had in the older genre of traditional Protestant, Catholic, and Orthodox church histories.

While I am not challenging the validity of the various approaches to the study of popular religion and agree that their results have often proved enlightening, they are nevertheless at times limited in their heuristic and hermeneutical usefulness. They represent only partial views of the religious culture in question. I propose that broadening our usage and conception of the term "church," or *tserkov',* in the study of lived Orthodoxy can lead to the development of other fruitful perspectives. If in the process the boundaries

5. G. A. Nosova, "Opyt etnograficheskogo izucheniia bytovogo pravoslaviia," *Voprosy nauchnogo ateizma* 3 (1967): 151–63; idem, *Iazychestvo v pravoslavii* (Moscow: Nauka, 1975); idem, *Russkie: istoriko-etnograficheskie ocherki* (Moscow: Rossiiskaia akademiia nauk, Institut etnologii i antropologii im. N. N. Miklukoho-Maklaia, 1997). Also see L. V. Ostrovskaia, "Khristianstvo v ponimanii russkikh krest'ian poreformennoi Sibiri," in *Obshchestvennyi byt i kul'tura russkogo naseleniia Sibiri, XVIII–nachalo XX v.,* ed. L. M. Rusakova (Novosibirsk: Nauka, Sibirskoe otdelenie, 1983), 135–50; L. A. Tultseva, "Religioznye verovaniia i obriady russkikh krest'ian na rubezhe XIX i XX vekov," *Sovetskaia etnografiia* 3 (1978): 31–46.

6. N. Matorin, *Zhenskoe bozhestvo v pravoslavnom kul'te* (Moscow: OGIZ, Moskovskii rabochii, 1931).

7. For a discussion of the current use of the term "lived religion," see David D. Hall, ed., *Lived Religion in America: Toward a History of Practice* (Princeton: Princeton University Press, 1997), vii–xiii.

8. For an example of an exception to this, see R. N. Swanson, *Religion and Devotion in Europe, 1214–1515* (New York: Cambridge University Press, 1995), 6–9.

of such notions as "official" and "popular" become blurred, then we have an opportunity to reassess the utility and scope of these notions—as absolute or relative, axiomatic or conditional, categorical or dimensional—and to gain new vistas on Orthodoxy as well as its church history.

The word *tserkov'*—which is derived from the Greek word *kiriakon*, meaning "house of the Lord"—was ambiguous in Russian.[9] It was used to translate both *ekklesia* (gathering, calling forth) and *naos* (temple). This single word, like the English "church," was used to refer broadly to the community of Christians—their collective identity proper—as well as to the church building. More important, on the basis of its own historical roots, *tserkov'*, or "church," like "nation," can be viewed in terms of a community continually in the making, shaped by all persons who see themselves as belonging to it.[10]

In order to explore "church" in a more inclusive or holistic way, a different perspective is needed than the one that has usually been taken by historians of Russia. To address this need, this essay looks at the manner in which native Orthodox believers in late imperial Russia wrote about the collective religious experience in Orthodoxy. Although the voices in this section will be those of educated laymen and clergy, the point is that these are nevertheless the voices of *believers*. If we were to exclude these members of the sacred community, we would only be perpetuating a stereotypically dichotomous way of thinking about Orthodoxy and religious experience. Indeed, as the historian of religion in America, Robert Orsi, has pointed out, religion is shaped and experienced "in the *mutually transforming* exchanges between religious authorities and the communities of practitioners."[11] Consequently, even discourse among priests and intellectuals can be seen as the product not only of their own experiences but also of the experience of other believers inasmuch as these influenced clergymen's thought. Thus, we here consider such discourse on the part of believers as a kind of religious self-expression that was itself a manifestation of lived Orthodoxy. Then the chapter turns to a common feature in the topography of Russian Orthodoxy, namely miracle-working icons, in order to explore how insights gleaned from "nativist" discourse about the

9. For a detailed discussion of the etymological roots of the word *tserkov'*, see Pavel Florenskii, "Ekkleziologicheskie materialy," *Bogoslovskie Trudy* 12 (1974): 175–78.

10. Peter van der Veer and Hartmut Lehmann, eds., *Nation and Religion: Perspectives on Europe and Asia* (Princeton: Princeton University Press, 1999), 3; Alon Confino, *The Nation as a Local Metaphor: Wurttemberg, Imperial Germany, and National Memory, 1871–1918* (Chapel Hill: University of North Carolina Press, 1997), 1–13.

11. Robert Orsi, "Everyday Miracles: The Study of Lived Religion," in Hall, *Lived Religion in America*, 9. For a similar observation for Orthodox experience in Russia, see Vera Shevzov, "Popular Orthodoxy in Late Imperial Rural Russia" (Ph.D. diss, Yale University, 1994), 2–3.

collective Orthodox experience might be useful in investigating particular aspects of Orthodox practices and relating them to the notion of "church."

In 1872, a brief exchange took place between two Orthodox religious writers about the common practice in churches in late imperial Russian Orthodoxy of opening the royal doors to the sanctuary when a pregnant woman was in difficult labor.[12] That year, a church publicist, K. M-ov, published an article in the journal, *Guide for Rural Clergy,* in which he "descended" into the realm of "popular beliefs" and, in the span of a single page, extended the reader's imagination back some nine hundred years to the pre-Christian epoch in Russia. After discussing the meaning of such a practice in this earlier era, he claimed that one would be hard-pressed to see any "church" meaning in this custom. Having thereby "exposed" this superstitious practice, he called on priests to stop performing this ritual act, claiming that it served only to satisfy the needs that arose from "dark legends" of a pagan past.[13]

That same year, a rural priest, Vasilii Maslovskii, from the village Tomkova in the Iaroslavl diocese, responded to this article and offered a different reading of the same practice.[14] Disagreeing with the interpretation that dismissed this ritual as rooted in "dark legends," Maslovskii focused on the ritual's goal and meaning and situated it in the broader context of other known and established Orthodox rituals and prayers. With his different perspective, Maslovskii showed the practice to be entirely expressive of a Christian idea. He even encouraged clergy to honor it. The only reason why the practice had not been formally sanctioned, he maintained, was that it appeared later in history and entered into Orthodox practice through the parish level, without the direct involvement of the bishops.

While these two articles presented radically different evaluations of a common lived practice in Russian Orthodoxy, they are similar in that they both referred to a criterion of "church quality" in their assessment. The author of the first article openly stated that he saw no "church origin or significance" in this custom. Though he never defined what he meant by "church" in this context, it is evident that for him, "common believers" had no other legitimate means of religious participation or expression than those that were

---

12. The "royal doors" are the central doors in the iconostasis that separate the altar or sanctuary from the nave area of the church.

13. K. M-ov, "Ob obychae otvoriat' tsarskiia vrata pri trudnykh rodakh," *Rukovodstvo dlia sel'skikh pastyrei* 2 (1872): 63–68.

14. Sv. Vasilii Maslovskii, "Obychai otvoriat' tsarskiia vrata pri trudnykh rodakh," *Iaroslavskie eparkhial'nye vedomosti,* no. 34 (1872): chast' neofitsial'naia, 269–72.

FIG. 6   Church of the Dormition from the village of Fominskoe. 1721. Currently at the Ipatievskii Monastery, Kostroma. Photograph by Tim Hofer. Simple wooden churches like this dotted the Russian countryside and, together with local chapels, served as centers for community and worship. The various connotations of the term *tserkovnost'* (churchness) resulted in large part from the ambiguous meaning of its root, *tserkov'*, which could refer to the phenomenon of gathering, the temple building, or an institutional apparatus, all of which constituted the Church.

Fig. 7   St. Nicholas Church in the village of Podlesovo, Nizhegorod province. 1890s.
Dmitriev Collection, the State Archive of Nizhegorod Region. Churches were the sites of all
sorts of local activities, gatherings, markets, rituals, and expressions of faith. According to
one priest, *tserkovnost'* referred to "that entire sacred milieu around the sacred temple . . .
feasts and fasts, processions, and pilgrimages to holy places, all of the rites, rituals, and
prayers that accompany believers at all stages of life from cradle to grave." P. Smirnov,
*O Tserkvi: Chtenie v obshchem sobranii S-Peterburgskago Bratstva vo imeni Presviatoi
Bogoroditsy* (St. Petersburg, 1887), 17.

overtly institutionally provided. The second article, however, takes a different perspective. Its author was interested primarily in the *dynamics,* both spiritual and material, by which a ritual incorporated a life situation into the broader narrative of Christian sacred history.

During the late imperial period, educated Orthodox believers began using the notion of *tserkovnost'*—ecclesiality or "churchness"—with increasing frequency in order to articulate their vision of the communal dynamics underlying religious practices and rituals, even seemingly private ones.[15] Not all persons who used the term defined it precisely; the meaning they attributed to it usually can be gleaned only from the context in which it was applied. In general, believers used the term to refer to a collective religious experience and consciousness.[16] While there appear to have been no explicit disputes over the meaning of the term *tserkovnost'*, it nevertheless remained somewhat elusive and found various shades of interpretation. Its various connotations resulted in large part from the ambiguous meaning of its root, *tserkov'*, which, as mentioned above, could refer to the phenomenon of gathering, the temple building, or an institutional apparatus.[17]

Despite its various connotations, we can point to certain common themes in how *tserkovnost'* was used. First, it suggested a way of thinking and being. It signified a particular orientation toward life and "the world" in which the ongoing reference point was the eternal and the sacred.[18] As one priest said, *tserkovnost'* was life in the spirit of the holy and a continual striving for that spirit.[19] In this sense, he juxtaposed to it an outlook on life that, having "forgotten God," was exclusively anthropocentric.[20]

As a way of thinking and feeling, *tserkovnost'* found its primary space for development in liturgy and ritual. Here believers cultivated and expressed their own "belonging to Orthodoxy." In 1887 the priest P. Smirnov referred

15. While the term *tserkovnost'* could be rendered as "ecclesiality," I keep the term in its original Russian in order to convey the diverse ways of understanding "churchness." My review of diocesan newspapers and theological journals shows that the term *tserkovnost'* can be found with increasing frequency beginning in the 1880s. It was not discussed or used as frequently, however, as its counterpart, *sobornost'*, later came to be in the beginning of the twentieth century.

16. Accordingly, one anonymous religious publicist from the Iaroslavl diocese noted in 1886 that the character of that experience differed among the different Christian groups. See "Osobennosti tserkvei," *Iaroslavskie eparkhial'nye vedomosti*, no. 22 (1886): 344–45.

17. Pavel Florenskii, whose magnum opus, *The Pillar and Ground of the Truth*, was to a certain extent a meditation on *tserkovnost'*, went so far as to insist that the term could not be grasped by logical terms. Yet the very indefinability of the term, he maintained, was the "best proof of its vitality." Pavel Florensky, *The Pillar and Ground of the Truth*, trans. Boris Jakim (Princeton: Princeton University Press, 1997), 8.

18. M. Gribanovskii, "V chem sostoit tserkovnost'," *Tserkovnyi vestnik*, no. 51–52 (1886): 827.

19. Prot. V. Nechaev, "Nechto o tserkovnosti," *Dushepoleznoe chtenie* 1 (1882): 72.

20. Ibid., 62.

to *tserkovnost'* as "that entire sacred milieu around the sacred temple [*khram*] ... feasts and fasts, processions, and pilgrimages to holy places, all of these rites, rituals, and prayers that accompany believers at all stages of life from cradle to grave." He spoke of it as the "air" that "seeds of the sacred" need in order to grow.[21] *Tserkovnost'* in this sense might be seen as refocusing the notion of *bytovoe pravoslavie* on the nurturance of religious phenomena in a temple and ecclesial context rather than on their alleged pagan roots.

While pointing to the same vital strands of *tserkovnost'* in such activities as Smirnov did, the one-time populist turned conservative religious thinker Lev Tikhomirov went even further by following the strands of the activities beyond the immediate temple context. In 1905, for instance, he argued against the viability of the parish church as the center of collective Orthodox life. He based his argument on the behavior of common believers, who in his estimation rarely confined their religious lives to their local parish church. Instead, he maintained, they searched for "gifts of the spirit" wherever they appeared and therefore transcended their immediate locality and identified with a broader, more universal understanding of Orthodoxy.[22]

Despite the association of *tserkovnost'* with that which was "characteristic of church"—namely its broad array of liturgical rites and rituals—it was clearly based on an understanding of church that included but also went beyond its institutional order and forms. Identified by one author with Orthodoxy itself,[23] the term pointed to the sacred experiences and sensibilities that lay behind the purely formal organization of collective religious life.[24]

Some authors identified the experiential center of *tserkovnost'* as the individual. Yet, as the liberal Orthodox thinker M. M. Tareev maintained in his article on this subject, the absolutely personal dimension of Orthodoxy in particular and Christianity in general could not be objectively studied, since individual religious experiences are unique and unrepeatable.[25] Nevertheless, he maintained, one could point to a cultural-historical aspect of Orthodoxy

---

21. P. Smirnov, *O Tserkvi: Chtenie v obshchem sobranii S-Peterburgskago Bratstva vo imeni Presviatoi Bogoroditsy* (St. Petersburg, 1887), 17. Similarly, Vladimir Dal' associated *tserkovnost'* with rites, rituals, and liturgical activity. Vladimir Dal', *Tolkovyi slovar' zhivogo velikorusskogo iazyka*, vol. 4 (Moscow, 1882; reprint, Moscow: Russkii iazyk, 1991), 573.

22. Lev Tikhomirov, *Sovremennoe polozhenie prikhodskago voprosa* (Moscow, 1907).

23. Sv. Nikolai Kameneev, "Tserkovnost' kak didakticheskii printsip," *Missionerskoe obozrenie* 11 (1906): 586.

24. For a contemporary definition of religion that captures this same meaning, see Thomas F. O'Dea, *The Sociology of Religion* (Englewood Cliffs, N.J.: Prentice-Hall, 1966), 27.

25. M. M. Tareev, "Tserkovnost' kak printsip nravstvennogo bogosloviia," *Bogoslovskii vestnik* 9 (1909): 67–69. For a study of Tareev as a modern Orthodox thinker, see Paul R. Valliere, "M. M. Tareev. A Study in Russian Ethics and Mysticism" (Ph.D. diss., Columbia University, 1974).

that stood alongside its subjective, experiential side, and that could be discussed in collective terms. *Tserkovnost'* in this usage, then, had to do with a collective consciousness and an awareness of shared personal experiences.[26] In this regard, Lev Tikhomirov highlighted the contrast between this notion and the modern tendency to speak of religion and religious life in purely individualistic terms. He spoke of an "ecclesial collectivity" (*tserkovnaia kollektivnost'*) and defined *tserkovnost'* as the "supreme manifestation of human collective life."[27] Some writers spoke of this collective or communal principle of Orthodoxy not so much as the goal of religious life but as its point of departure.[28]

As it was often associated with religious sensibilities, the notion of *tserkovnost'* emphasized knowledge through experience more than through intellectual mastery. While those who used the term in the context of education and missionary work wrote of the importance of textual learning—the Bible, conciliar teachings, and so on—they also spoke of the importance of the nondiscursive assimilation of these teachings. As Daniel Rowland and Michael Flier have also indicated in their essays, the intellectual or verbal formulation of the teachings mattered less than their appropriation in the realm of sensibilities and feelings. The theologian Pavel Florensky, for instance, maintained that only through "lived religious experience" could a person gain true knowledge of dogmas.[29] In a similar vein, during the 1917–18 All-Russian Church Council, Professor I. M. Gromoglasov from the Moscow Theological Academy advocated that a sense of *tserkovnost'* be placed ahead of a person's theological education as a qualification for election to the Higher Church Council.[30]

Linking such notions as religious sensibility and community, it is evident that these writers understood *tserkovnost'* as something more than simply a product of institutional structures.[31] Indeed, persons who used this term

---

26. Tareev, "Tserkovnost' kak printsip nravstvennogo bogosloviia," 25, 75. Also see Prot. I. Vostorgov, "Tserkovnost'," in the newspaper *Tserkovnost'*, November 13, 1911.

27. L. Tikhomirov, *Lichnost', obshchestvo i tserkov'* (Moscow, 1894), 2.

28. See as an example "Otnoshenie mezhdu Khristianstvom i tserkovnost'iu," *Iaroslavskie eparkhial'nye vedomosti*, no. 23 (1886): 358.

29. Florensky, *Pillar and Ground of the Truth*, xiv.

30. *Deianiia Sviashchennogo Sobora Pravoslavnoi Rossiiskoi Tserkvi, 1917–1918*, vol. 4, Deianie 48 (Petrograd, 1918; reprint, Moscow: Novospasskii monastyr, 1996), 97–98.

31. From a certain perspective, the notion of *tserkovnost'* can be seen as a nineteenth-century Russian Orthodox parallel to the anthropologist Victor Turner's idea of "communitas"—that "shared awareness of being bound together in a community of shared experience." Victor Turner and Edith Turner, *Image and Pilgrimage in Christian Culture* (New York: Columbia University Press, 1978), 250–55. Also see Victor Turner, *The Ritual Process* (Ithaca: Cornell University Press, 1977), and idem, *From Ritual to Theater* (New York: Performing Arts Journal Publications, 1982).

were usually referring to experiences of "church" in which the institutional structure was only one facet of these experiences. This is a noteworthy point given the context in which the term *tserkovnost'* began to be used. In the late nineteenth and early twentieth centuries, when churchmen perceived a complete "ecclesiastical collapse" in their midst, they took upon themselves the task of reconceptualizing the institutional framework of Orthodoxy on the basis of a fresh reading of their corporate past. As part of their efforts, many of them checked their visions against the litmus test of *tserkovnost'*.[32] Divisions among believers even in these institutional debates, however, arose not over the notion of *tserkovnost'* in and of itself but over the actual form that would best allow for the expression of this ideal in communal Orthodox life.[33]

Broadly speaking, then, *tserkovnost'* belonged to a field of meaning involving the following elements: (1) a nondiscursive, experientially based knowledge of a way of relating to the holy; (2) a reverence for and sense of the sacred and its expression in symbolic (liturgical) forms; and (3) a communal orientation or collective spirit that sees the faith itself as a fundamentally shared phenomenon. In metaphorical terms, one might say that *tserkovnost'* related to the church and Orthodoxy as *narodnost'* (referring broadly to the notion of "belonging to a people" and consequently to "Russianness") related to the state and national identity.[34]

Yet such a comparison has its methodological limitations. The professor of church history, Boris Titlinov, juxtaposed the notion of *tserkovnost'* to that of *obshchestvennost'*, a term that suggests a cross-class social solidarity and which might be described as the dynamics of belonging to society as an "all-inclusive secular space."[35] Similarly, M. M. Tareev insisted that the community of

---

32. *Deianiia Sviashchennogo Sobora*, vol. 5, Deianie 58, pp. 229–32.

33. For examples where *tserkovnost'* was used as a litmus test to support specific church reform proposals, see Sv. P. A. Ivanov, *Reforma prikhoda* (Tomsk, 1914), 39. *Deianiia Sviashchennogo Sobora*, vol. 5, Deianie 58, p. 242.

34. Significantly, some publicists applied the notion of *tserkovnost'* to broader political discourse, since they associated the Russian collective religious experience with a sui generis Russian worldview. They believed, for instance, that a "cosmopolitan" and "humanist" educational system transplanted from Germanic soil was not appropriate for Russian peasants, since it did not cultivate those traits characteristic of the Russian national psyche. See Kameneev, "Tserkovnost' kak didakticheskii printsip," 586–92, and Sv. N. Proikov, "Ideia tserkovnosti v eia znachenii dlia nashei narodnoi shkoly," *Rukovodstvo dlia sel'skikh pastyrei* 38 (1911): 30–44. For useful discussions of the notion of *narodnost'*, see for example, Nicholas V. Riazanovsky, "'Nationality' in the State Ideology During the Reign of Nicholas I," *Russian Review* 19 (1960): 38–46; David B. Saunders, "Historians and Concepts of Nationality in Early Nineteenth-Century Russia," *The Slavonic and East European Review* 60 (1982): 44–62; Katya Hokanson, "Literary Imperialism, *Narodnost'* and Pushkin's Invention of the Caucasus," *Russian Review* 53 (1994): 336–52; and Maureen Perrie, "*Narodnost'*: Notions of National Identity," in *Constructing Russian Culture in the Age of Revolution: 1881–1940*, ed. Catriona Kelly and David Shepherd (New York: Oxford University Press, 1998), 28–36.

35. Catriona Kelly and Vadim Volkov, "*Obshchestvennost'*, *Sobornost'*: Collective Identities," in Kelly

church was not simply one type of community among many others, but a spiritual, relational one (and thus unique), with its own all-inclusive sacred space and its own dynamics of belonging.[36] Consequently, the notion of *tserkovnost'* prompts a reconsideration of the subject of "church" as its own category or paradigm, not easily reducible to secular concepts or models.

As noted, such discussions about *tserkovnost'* in the late nineteenth and early twentieth centuries were not simply exercises in abstract theology. Those authors who used this term found their inspiration, not only in their own experiences, but also in the religious lives of common believers. Given this perception of *tserkovnost'* as operative even at the grassroots of Orthodoxy, how might the perspective offered by this notion help us to reconceptualize the idea of "church," as well as to identify certain dynamics of belonging among believers?

I would like to address this question by referring to a common feature in the topography of Russian Orthodoxy, namely, miracle-working icons.[37] Icons were associated with a variety of religious dynamics that were illustrative of the different ways in which believers identified with and experienced the ecclesial community. Beginning at a simple semiotic level, icons in general, perhaps more effectively than written scriptural and liturgical texts, informed individual believers of a sacred story that offered a way of understanding their world and a shared sense of hope for their lives. Miracle-working icons, however, went one step further than other icons in engaging believers. The association of a particular event with an icon meant in the eyes of believers that the same grace that had been active in the life of the saint or in the sacred event visually depicted had now revealed itself in their own midst.[38] As a sign of a sacred presence, the surfacing of a miracle-working icon usually awakened believers' religious sensibilities and often left them feeling personally connected to a perceived reality greater than themselves.[39] The chapter by Isolde Thyrêt also illustrates this point.

---

and Shepherd, *Constructing Russian Culture;* Talal Asad, "Religion, Nation-State, Secularism," in Van der Veer and Lehmann, *Nation and Religion,* 185. For the juxtaposition between *tserkovnost'* and *obshchestvennost',* see B. Titlinov, "Istoki sobornosti," *Russkoe Slovo,* no. 201 (1917).

36. Tareev, "Tserkovnost' kak printsip nravstvennogo bogosloviia," 81.

37. I have discussed the details of this phenomenon elsewhere. See Vera Shevzov, "Miracle-Working Icons, Laity, and Authority in the Russian Orthodox Church, 1861–1917," *Russian Review* 58 (1999): 26–48, and idem, "Icons, Miracles, and the Ecclesial Identity of Laity in Late Imperial Russia," *Church History* 69 (2000): 610–31.

38. Rossiiskii Gosudarstvennyi Istoricheskii Arkhiv (hereafter, RGIA), *f.* 796, *op.* 177, *ot.* 3, *st.* 2, *d.* 2423 (Kaluga 1896).

39. For examples of believers' comments on the effect such icons had on their religious lives, see RGIA, *f.* 796, *op.* 176, *d.* 2084 (Voronezh 1895); *op.* 176, *d.* 2197 (Eniseisk 1895).

While initially a miracle-working icon may have engaged believers individually, the quality and understanding of their experiences prompted almost immediate collective involvement with the icon. A typical response was that from believers in the Siberian diocese of Eniseisk in the 1860s, who decided collectively to acquire an icon of a crucifix from one of their fellow villagers in order to ensure its continued presence among them and their progeny collectively.[40] Writing about this image, the peasant Kuzma Astrakhantsev noted that the image had always had "a beneficial influence on the souls of sinners." "About this there can be no doubt, since its power . . . has been experienced by those of us, not only in our own village but in surrounding villages, who have received some relief and healing."[41] Believers rotated the icon through their homes until several decades later when they could afford to construct a church in which to house it. While rooted in the personal or private life of each believer, then, a shared recognition or experience of the holy simultaneously "called forth" believers and involved them in a shared "community" that routinely transcended their gender differences as well as their social, political, and, in some unique cases, even confessional identities.[42]

Believers also frequently desired to integrate their personal experiences within what Wilfred Cantwell Smith has termed a "cumulative tradition," which, in the case of icons, was tied to well-known sacred narratives and a rich liturgical heritage.[43] Indeed, believers often went to great efforts to place their experiences within this broader sacred context. In some places, such a contexture can be seen in the placement of special icons within a church's or chapel's iconostasis, which itself portrayed scenes and persons from that sacred history that to one degree or another informed their faith.[44] Believers sometimes also combined their visit to venerate such an icon with the rite of repentance and the partaking of the Eucharist.[45] Moreover, believers often incorporated the celebration of their locally revered miracle-working icons into

40. Believers often avoided speaking in terms of "purchasing" an icon, since it seemed unbefitting to exchange money for a sacred item.

41. RGIA, *f.* 796, *op.* 176, *d.* 2197.

42. Witnesses would usually comment on the mixed social profile of those who gathered to honor such icons. Given that certain miracle-working icons engaged persons of other Christian denominations, such as Catholics, Lutherans, Old Believers, and so on, we might consider the effect that experiences with these icons had in leveling confessional boundaries.

43. Wilfred Cantwell Smith, *The Meaning and End of Religion* (New York: Macmillan, 1962), 194.

44. See, as an example, Prot. S. S. Narkevich, *Chudotvornaia ikona presviatyia Bogoroditsy, vsekh skorbiashchikh radosti (s monetami) nakhodiashchaiasia v chasovne Skorbiashchei Bozhiei Materi v S. Peterburge* (St. Petersburg, 1907), 10–11.

45. As examples, see RGIA, *f.* 796, *op.* 168, *d.* 1439 (Kursk 1887); *op.* 183 (Orenburg 1902); *op.* 190, *ot.* 6, *st.* 3, *d.* 310 (Penza 1909).

the annual liturgical calendar by which they marked sacred time.[46] Finally, the epitome of such contextualization could be found in the construction of a chapel or church in an icon's honor.[47]

The dynamics of belonging associated with icons discussed so far did not necessarily (though it often did) involve much interaction with the ecclesiastical institution. Icons, unlike the Eucharist, provided for a form of "communion" within Orthodoxy that did not technically require the "administration" of ordained clergy. What was the relationship between such modes of communal cohesion or identification and that overt structure of church life and formal symbol of its identity, the hierarchy? This relationship was in fact the subject of much correspondence between lay believers and the church's institutional centers in cases concerning the veneration of miracle-working icons. Many believers rallied around such revered icons and behaved as if they regarded them as more representative or expressive of ecclesial life than the clergy. This view was starkly expressed by residents from the town of Mozdok from the Vladikavkaz diocese, who wrote in 1900 regarding their revered icon of the Mother of God, "The bishop is subordinate to the icon, and not the icon to him."[48] A similar position seemed to be shared by some clergy, though they articulated it in different ways. Even though some icons were officially recognized as miracle-working, the bishop of Kostroma, Platon, maintained in 1872, that there was no icon that had been proclaimed miracle-working by means of a formal investigation. He noted that any icon could be miracle-working as long as believers prayed before it in faith and reverence.[49] Once overt fraud had been ruled out, bishops such as Platon simply took note of such icons and, without agreeing to a "miracle-working" title, left the icons to live out their "lives" by either having their commemoration institutionalized (on the parish, diocesan, or national level), or being forgotten with time.

Not all bishops and parish priests, however, shared such a view. In certain cases, diocesan and synodal authorities chose to have such icons removed

---

46. As examples, see Russkii Muzei Etnografii, *f.* 1, *d.* 63, *l.* 6 *ob.* Also see RGIA, *f.* 796, *op.* 174, *d.* 1780 (Kazan 1893).

47. RGIA, *f.* 796, *op.* 169, *d.* 1370 (Orlov 1888); *op.* 176, *d.* 2197 (Eniseisk 1895); *op.* 190, *ot.* 6, *st.* 3, *d.* 291 (Vologda 1909); Narkevich, *Chudotvornaia ikona presviatyia Bogoroditsy.* For an in-depth discussion of these dynamics of sacred contextualization, see Shevzov, "Icons, Miracles, and the Ecclesial Identity of Laity."

48. RGIA, *f.* 796, *op.* 181, *d.* 2580.

49. RGIA, *f.* 796, *op.* 153, *d.* 632. It appears that Platon was not aware of the history of formal investigations concerning icons. Paul Bushkovitch, *Religion and Society in Russia: The Sixteenth and Seventeenth Centuries* (New York: Oxford University Press, 1992), 107. Platon's main point, however, seems to have been that such proclamations and rulings did not in fact make the icon miracle-working. For a similar view that any icon in theory could be miracle-working, see RGIA, *f.* 796, *op.* 195, *d.* 1547, *l.* 8.

from their localities and placed in a monastery or a diocesan cathedral, either in storage or among other icons in church. This was especially the case with icons that surfaced in private homes. Nevertheless, even in these cases, the perspective offered by the notion of *tserkovnost'* can influence the scholarly reading of such clerical reaction. A conventional, institutionally focused reading of such occurrences might portray "the church"—consisting of clergy—combating the veneration of those icons being revered as miracle-working, as if such practices took place not in the "church sphere," but in an ill-defined popular religious one instead.[50] While tensions between clergy and laity may have certainly occurred and are not to be denied, a more culturally holistic understanding of "church," as I will now illustrate, can present such tensions and their significance in a different light.

The veneration of icons, including miracle-working ones, was an ancient and central feature of Orthodox Christianity. As Peter Brown has convincingly shown, this became so despite the protest of Byzantine iconoclastic bishops, who saw the presence of the holy as confined to only a few symbols—the Eucharist, the church building, and the sign of the Cross. These iconoclastic bishops resisted the centrifugal pull of both the holy man and the icon as bearers of the holy outside the hierarchically sanctioned sacramental order.[51] The victory of icons, therefore, in part signaled the institutional legitimation of an icon's charismatic authority, and thus also of the religious sensibilities of iconophilic believers.[52] The theology of the icon that arose in Byzantium, then, essentially developed out of preexisting, widespread, icon-related beliefs and practices. This is a case in which an official theological statement could be seen as Orthodoxy *applied* (to the realm of erudition), as itself a product of pervasive religious dynamics among a broad range of believers, rather than as a prescription from "elite" churchmen.

Given this cumulative tradition behind the use of icons, the widespread veneration and discernment of miracle-working icons in late imperial Russia simply provided another occasion for the *accepted* tensions between hierarchical and charismatic authority in Eastern Orthodoxy to surface. In other words, this was not so much a simple confrontation between insiders (church) and outsiders ("the people") as it was a complex set of tensions between two

50. See, for example, Gregory L. Freeze, "Institutionalizing Piety: The Church and Popular Religion, 1750–1850," in *Imperial Russia: New Histories for the Empire*, ed. Jane Burbank and David L. Ransel (Bloomington: Indiana University Press, 1998), 210–49.

51. Peter Brown, "A Dark-Age Crisis: Aspects of the Iconoclastic Controversy," *English Historical Review* 346 (1973): 1–34.

52. This understanding was preserved in Russia's Orthodox tradition as can be seen in the late-fifteenth-century text, Iosif Volotskii, *Poslanie ikonopistsu* (Moscow: Izobrazitel'noe iskusstvo, 1994).

recognized foci of Orthodox identity *within* the body called "church"—the bishop and the icon. Along with their Byzantine iconoclastic counterparts, some, though not all, Russian Orthodox bishops clearly were uncomfortable with such icons precisely because their legitimation did not necessarily come from or through the clerical hierarchy. Many ecclesiastical officials, consequently, preferred either to minimize their numbers altogether or to align themselves with such icons by having them housed and honored in the diocesan cathedral. Laymen and -women who struggled against such policies were not struggling against the church as much as affirming the church as they experienced it.

Finally, it is significant that believers were known to interpret their experiences with icons with respect not only to events in their personal lives or their immediate community but also to events concerning the Russian nation as a whole. Keeping in mind the notion of *tserkovnost'*, we can see that their sense of "churchness" and of belonging transcended their immediate familial or geographic contexts. For example, in 1891, believers from the Kursk diocese attributed further significance to their locally revered icon when they learned that the mother of one of the engineers of the imperial train had been praying before this icon for the safe passage of the imperial family when that train derailed in October 1888. These believers connected the mother's prayers with the miracle that no one on that train had been injured.[53]

Similarly, on October 19, 1917, just a few days before the Bolshevik storming of the Winter Palace, the Holy Synod received a report from the metropolitan of Moscow and Kolomenskoe, Tikhon, about a peasant woman, Evdokiia Andrianova, who had had a series of dreams alerting her to an icon of the Mother of God in the local parish church.[54] When it was found with the help of the local parish priest, believers began flocking to pray before it. Soon they were requesting that the icon be brought to their homes, churches, factories, and monastic communities for special services and blessings.[55] As in numerous cases in the past, members of the Holy Synod took no action on the case.

Since the finding of this icon occurred on March 2, 1917, the day of Tsar Nicholas II's abdication, believers eventually took the occasion of Evdokiia's revelation to make religious sense of events that were transpiring around

53. RGIA, *f.* 796, *op.* 172, *d.* 1579.

54. Ibid., *op.* 445, *d.* 348.

55. "Skazanie o iavlenii ikony Bozhiei Materi pri Voznesenskoi v sele Kolomenskom tserkvi, Moskovskago uezda," *Dushepoleznyi sobesednik* 9 (1917): 314–15. See the discussion about the icon's popularity in Matorin, *Zhenskoe bozhestvo*, 6–8.

them. Two liturgical services and an *akathistos* hymn in honor of the icon of the Mother of God, which came to be known as "She Who Reigneth" because of the way Mary was portrayed on the icon, were composed several years later, in the 1920s.[56] These texts articulated and applied many of the sensibilities that had accompanied believers' recognition of the icon as special and, therefore, offer yet another example of the contexture of icon-related events within the broader "cumulative tradition" of Orthodoxy. The hymns depicted Mary herself revealing her icon to Evdokiia in a dream so that the icon could engage believers in prayer and glorification of God. They also present the icon as providing a light of hope in the self-imposed "darkness of grievous circumstances" and "visitation of God's wrath" that believers were presently experiencing.[57] The miracles that resulted from prayer before it, the hymns maintained, would guide all those "lost on the sea of this life of suffering" along the path of salvation.[58] Though never once mentioning the actual abdication of the tsar, the services instead turned believers' attention to another leader, "She Who Reigneth," for protection and liberation, since only her "dominion and kingdom" was unassailable.[59]

In 1905, Bishop Evdokim, the rector of the Moscow Theological Academy, spoke of the existence of two churches in Russia. "One is fitted in a brilliant uniform," he wrote, "decorated with ribbons and medals and endowed with privileges and rights. It expresses its faith in official memorial services on tsar's days. The other one is clad in a simple gray tunic, and is persecuted, but is full of sincere faith."[60] While Evdokim's (admittedly simplistic) observation supports the current scholarly tendencies to distinguish between an "official" and a "popular" Orthodox culture in late imperial Russia, his metaphor, like the notion of *tserkovnost'*, suggests the need for caution in defining the terms "official" and "church."

---

56. *Mineia*, vol. 3, part 1 (Moscow: Izdanie Moskovskoi Patriarkhii, 1984), 42. Note that this icon has been included in recent post-Soviet publications listing Russia's "great" miracle-working icons. V. E. Suzdalev, ed., *Velikie chudotvornye ikony* (Nizhnii Novgorod: Tsentr tvorcheskogo sotrudnichestva, 1994). In the icon, Mary is portrayed sitting on a throne, wearing a crown. Clothed in a deep red robe, she holds the emblems of imperial authority, the scepter and the orb. The Christ-child sits in her lap, making the sign of a blessing.

57. "Akafist Presviatoi Vladychitse nashei Bogoroditse iavleniia radi chudnoi ee ikony Derzhavnaia," in *Akafisty Presviatoi Bogoroditse*, Ikos 1; *Kondak* 2 (Moscow: "Skit," 1994), 82; "Prazdnovanie Presviatei Bogoroditse v chest' chudotvornyia Eia ikony, naritsaemyia 'Derzhavnaia,'" *Pesn'* 1; *Pesn'* 6, in *Mineia* (March), 21, 24.

58. "Akafist," *Kondak* 5, 85.

59. "Prazdnovanie Presviatei Bogoroditse," *Pesn'* 4, p. 23; "Akafist," *Ikos* 10, p. 90.

60. Ep. Evdokim, "Na zare novoi tserkovnoi zhizni," *Bogoslovskii vestnik* 5 (1905): 157.

First, while Evdokim clearly points to an officialdom in late imperial Orthodoxy, he does not reserve the designation of "church" for it alone. He refers to both aspects of Orthodoxy as "church." Moreover, since clergy belonged to both groupings, his metaphor avoids the dichotomy between "the church" (limited to the official and the clergy) on the one hand, and "the people" on the other, as does the notion of *tserkovnost'*. Likewise, the notion of *tserkovnost'*, while acknowledging the authoritative positions held by clergy within Orthodoxy, certainly does not limit the dynamics that collectively constitute the ecclesial community exclusively to clerical words, behaviors, and ideas.

Second, and related, by helping us to envision the "church" as a complex and vital sacred community and culture extending beyond its institutional shell, Evdokim's metaphor along with *tserkovnost'* challenges the indiscriminate application of such designations as "virtuoso" and "demotic" to Orthodoxy along "official" and "popular" lines.[61] After all, it would not be difficult to find instances when members of the Orthodox institutional establishment recognized an illiterate common believer as a "virtuoso" spiritual superior; it also would not be difficult to argue that aspects of the church "fitted in a brilliant uniform" were demotic. Such turnabouts in our thinking about "church" lead to the realization, as one scholar of folklife has recently stated, that, from one perspective, "official" religion does not in fact exist. In a sense, every Christian is a native and, therefore, "there is no objective existence of practice which expresses 'official religion.'"[62] At the same time, this viewpoint does not mean that Orthodoxy as a religious culture lacked recognizable boundaries. The study of Orthodoxy and church experience does not and should not entail a leveling of that culture to the "popular" experience. As Robert Orsi has pointed out, it is the defenders of "popular" or "lived" religion who lately seem to be in danger of obscuring the full complexity of religious cultures.[63] The notion of *tserkovnost'* in this sense preserves the pertinent though often complex issues of authority that are integral to the Orthodox context.

Similarly, following this line of thinking, the perspective offered by the term *tserkovnost'* as it was frequently used in the late nineteenth and early twentieth centuries suggests that similar reversals might also be made with

61. Freeze, "Institutionalizing Piety," 211.
62. Leonard Norman Primiano, "Vernacular Religion and the Search for Method in Religious Folklife," *Western Folklore* 54 (1995): 45–46. Also see Wendy James and Douglas H. Johnson, eds., *Vernacular Christianity: Essays in Social Anthropology of Religion Presented to Godfrey Lienhardt* (New York: Lilian Barber Press, 1988), and Orsi, "Everyday Miracles," 19–20.
63. Orsi, "Everyday Miracles," 20.

respect to the designations of "prescribed" and "applied" Orthodoxy. Did not laymen and -women in their personal and local experiences with icons help to *prescribe* liturgical response, and was not that response an application of their own sentiments? Might not such phenomena encourage us to recast our thinking and consider the theological and the experiential as correlative categories in the religious life of a community?

Finally, the notion of *tserkovnost'*, along with Evdokim's observation, leads us to ask: How organized was "organized religion" (that is to say, Orthodoxy) in Russia? It is not unusual for scholars who embark on any in-depth study of Orthodoxy in modern Russia to be struck by a kaleidoscopic array of practices and rituals as well as by a wide range of beliefs and theological readings of various subjects. Yet it is misleading to construe such diversity as separate, reified systems of "orthodoxies."[64] Diversity does not preclude unity. And although, as Gregory Freeze has argued, such local diversity might have challenged efforts at institutional centralization, a collective sense of belonging and universal thinking do not depend upon bureaucratic centralization.[65] By looking at the Orthodox Church in late imperial Russia as a sacred community with a cumulative tradition and a matrix of sensibilities and dynamics of belonging, such diversity can become a means to understanding collective Orthodox identity. As the theologian M. M. Tareev wrote in 1909, "The church does not produce believers but is produced by them."[66]

64. Freeze, "Institutionalizing Piety," 215. For a more detailed discussion of this issue, see Shevzov, "Popular Orthodoxy in Late Imperial Rural Russia," 11–12. For a related discussion on "commonality" versus "uniformity," see Anthony P. Cohen, *The Symbolic Construction of Community* (New York: Tavistock Publications, 1985), 20.

65. Note that at the same time the notion of *tserkovnost'* allows for the existence of boundaries by which believers distinguished themselves from others.

66. Tareev, "Tserkovnost' kak printsip nravstvennogo bogosloviia," 83.

PART II

IMAGINING THE SACRED

4

FROM CORPSE TO CULT IN EARLY MODERN RUSSIA

EVE LEVIN

On July 8, 1647, the blacksmith Ostashko Trofimov inadvertently founded the cult of a saint. He had been hired by the *voevoda* of Arkhangel'sk, Prince Iurii Buisonov-Rostovskii, and he was digging a hole to stabilize his anvil when he unearthed a coffin. Physically shaken by his discovery, he took refuge first in the brewery and then in a storeroom. Later, he returned to the site and chanted the requiem for the dead. At that time his agitation eased, and he credited the intercession of the previously unknown saint whose relics he had uncovered. In the days and weeks that followed, numerous other people experienced the power of the new miracle worker, attributing to him healing and visions. By the time an investigatory commission looked into the new cult in November of the following year, veneration was well established, even though the name and identity of the saint remained obscure.[1]

The nameless miracle worker of Arkhangel'sk represents an anomalous type of saint: one who was completely unknown until the discovery of his relics. Unlike most holy persons, these "unidentified corpse" saints garnered no recognition of piety during their lifetimes. After their deaths, memory of their burial places and even their names had passed into oblivion. These saints did not have prehistories; their claim to sanctity rested entirely upon their ability to work miracles through their relics. Their cults arose out of a single incident, the discovery of an unusual corpse, and the imagination and hopes of Orthodox believers drawing on Christian traditions of sainthood.

Research for this paper was supported by a grant from the International Research and Exchanges Board and the Hilandar Research Library at Ohio State University. I appreciate the assistance of Nicholas Breyfogle, Daniel Collins, Alexandra Korros, and Erik Zitser in the preparation of this article, as well as the participants of the Michigan workshop, especially Valerie Kivelson, Nadieszda Kizenko, Isolde Thyrêt, and Christine Worobec.

1. Rossiiskaia Gosudarstvennaia Biblioteka (henceforth, RGB), f. 212, Sobranie Olonetskoi seminarii, d. 75, "Skazanie o chudesakh ot groba neizvestnogo sviatogo." This is an early nineteenth-century copy of a seventeenth-century original. Only the first part is preserved.

The transformation of an unidentified corpse into the focus of a saint's cult raises numerous questions about the religious perspectives of the saints' devotees. In their conception, what were the essential characteristics of sainthood? What constituted a miracle? Who decided whether miracles or visions—and the saints who provided them—were authentic? Why did some cults survive, and others die out? And what conceptions did premodern Russians have of human bodies, living and dead, that allowed them to attribute the healing of living ones to contact with certain dead ones? Because the cults of saints of this type originated exclusively among non-elite believers, they are especially indicative of the mental universe of ordinary people in communities far from centers of ecclesiastical or secular power.[2] The cults came to the attention of outside authorities—for that reason, documentation of them survives—and the official reactions to them reveal the relationship between state religion and folk belief in the early modern period. In addition to the nameless Arkhangel'sk miracle worker, I have identified a dozen similar cases from the sixteenth through eighteenth centuries, recorded in vitae, miracle tales, petitions, and inquest records.[3]

Throughout Christian Europe in the Middle Ages and early modern periods, a multiplicity of definitions of sainthood coexisted.[4] Saints could

2. "Popular religion" has become a popular topic of study, and an enormous literature has been generated. For an evaluation of this concept and the secondary literature useful in the Russian context, see Eve Levin, "*Dvoeverie* and Popular Religion," in *Seeking God: The Recovery of Religious Identity in Orthodox Russia, Ukraine, and Georgia,* ed. Stephen K. Batalden (DeKalb: Northern Illinois University Press, 1993), 31–52.

3. On the use of saints' lives as sources in the Russian context, see V. O. Kliuchevskii, *Drevnerusskiia zhitiia sviatykh kak istoricheskii istochnik* (Moscow: Tipografiia Gracheva, 1871); Ivan Iakhontov, *Zhitiia sv. sievernorusskikh podvizhnikov Pomorskago kraia kak istoricheskii istochnik* (Kazan: Imperatorskii universitet, 1881); L. A. Dmitriev, *Zhitiinye povesti russkogo severa kak pamiatniki literatury XIII–XVII vv.* (Leningrad: Nauka, 1973); on miracle tales as sources, see Isolde Thyrêt, "Muscovite Miracle Stories as Sources for Gender-Specific Religious Experience," in *Religion and Culture in Early Modern Russia and Ukraine,* ed. Samuel H. Baron and Nancy Shields Kollmann (DeKalb: Northern Illinois University Press, 1997), 115–31. For a thoughtful evaluation of scholars' use of these sources in the medieval Roman Catholic context, see Patrick Geary, *Living with the Dead in the Middle Ages* (Ithaca: Cornell University Press, 1994), chap. 1, pp. 9–29.

4. The literature on saints and sainthood in the Christian tradition is vast. For basic bibliography, see Stephen Wilson, ed., *Saints and Their Cults: Studies in Religious Sociology, Folklore and History* (Cambridge: Cambridge University Press, 1983). These works were most influential in forming my thinking, as expressed in the paragraphs that follow (with all apologies to the authors for any oversimplification or misconstruction of their ideas): Peter Brown, *The Cult of the Saints: Its Rise and Function in Latin Christianity* (Chicago: University of Chicago Press, 1981); idem, "The Rise and Function of the Holy Man in Late Antiquity," in his *Society and the Holy in Late Antiquity* (Berkeley and Los Angeles: University of California Press, 1982); William A. Christian, *Local Religion in Sixteenth-Century Spain* (Princeton: Princeton University Press, 1981); Pierre Delooz, "Towards a Sociological Study of Canonized Sainthood in the Catholic Church," in Wilson, *Saints and Their Cults,* 189–216; Geary, *Living with the Dead;* Ronald C.

demonstrate their spiritual excellence—show themselves to be "friends of God"—in a variety of ways: through leading a pious and ascetic life; building religious communities; administering the church; defending confessional orthodoxy; converting, governing, and defending Christian populations; or dying as martyrs to the faith. It was their virtue during their earthly existence that earned them the power to work miracles from Heaven. Indeed, it was their power to work miracles that proved their sanctity in a way their deeds in life could not. Thus the working of miracles, more than any achievements in life, became the sine qua non of sainthood, and the saint's earthly deeds often paled in comparison. But no matter how sketchy the information about saints' earthly biographies—and to modern historians, quite a few appear to be complete fabrications—their existence in this world was an essential prelude to heavenly intercession.

With all the numerous prophets, apostles, martyrs, bishops, abbots, and pious rulers in Heaven already, it would seem to be unnecessary to create still more saints. But established saints already had their clienteles and their geographical settings, and communities located far from the centers of power needed intercessors to answer specifically to their needs. Local saints had a unique stake in the welfare of the community that universal saints might not. Premodern believers conceived of the process of soliciting miracles from Heaven in terms similar to how they thought their own earthly governments worked: a local "contact"—the saint—who had a position in the ruler's—God's—entourage interceded to obtain a grant of royal favor. A local shrine, built around a relic or icon, established the saint's physical presence in a particular community, as well as in the Heaven accessible to all Christians. A shrine created a sort of "moral economy" between the saint and the community, with mutual obligations to render support.[5]

Thus the appearance of new saints continued unabated, especially in the Russian hinterlands of the sixteenth and seventeenth centuries, where dozens of new cults arose. Unlike in the Roman Catholic Church, the Russian

Finucane, *Miracles and Pilgrims: Popular Beliefs in Medieval England* (New York: St. Martin's Press, 1995); Nadieszda Kizenko, "Ioann of Kronstadt and the Reception of Sanctity, 1850–1988," *Russian Review* 57 (1998): 325–44; idem, *A Prodigal Saint: Father John of Kronstadt and the Russian People* (University Park: Pennsylvania State University Press, 2000); Pierre-André Sigal, *L'Homme et le miracle dans la France médiévale (XIe–XIIe siècle)* (Paris: Editions du Cerf, 1985); André Vauchez, "L'influence des modèles hagiographiques sur les représentations de la sainteté dans les procès de canonisation (XIIIe–XVe siècle)," in *Hagiographie cultures et sociétés IVe–XIIe siècles* (Paris: Etudes Augustiniennes, 1981), 585–90; idem, *Sainthood in the Later Middle Ages*, trans. Jean Birrell (Cambridge: Cambridge University Press, 1997); Benedicta Ward, *Miracles and the Medieval Mind* (London: Scolar Press, 1982).

5. On this point, see William A. Christian, *Person and God in a Spanish Valley* (Princeton: Princeton University Press, 1989), xiv–xv, 44–47.

Orthodox Church had no standardized procedures for canonization before the eighteenth century.[6] Apparently most Muscovite saints gained recognition haphazardly, without any formal inquest into their authenticity. But the reforming impulses in the Russian Orthodox Church that led to the Moscow Church Councils of 1666 and 1667 also generated increasing scrutiny of local religious observances. The cults of saints who had no record of pious Orthodoxy during their lifetime—or any record at all—were particularly suspect.

The phenomenon of the veneration of unidentified dead bodies as saints was disquieting enough that the Moscow Church Council of 1667 addressed the issue. Although the council was concerned primarily with countering the Old Believers, traditionalists who opposed recent ecclesiastical reforms, it also warned against irregular practices more generally, including the following:

> Also; uncorrupted bodies that are found in the present time should not be kept to be revered as saints, except upon reliable testimony and the order of the Council. For many bodies are found whole and uncorrupted, and not from sanctity; but [bodies] may be whole and unputrified because they were excommunicated and under anathema from an archbishop or bishop, or because of the transgression of divine and ecclesiastical rules and laws. If you want to venerate among the saints one of these bodies that are found, it is appropriate to investigate each instance, and gather testimony by reliable witnesses before the great and complete council of archbishops.[7]

Only putative saints whose claim to sanctity was based on uncorrupted relics—that is, ones of the type of the Arkhangel'sk miracle worker—fell under this ruling. The Council refrained from ordering investigations into *all* newly revealed saints, and did not question the legitimacy of saints whose uncorrupted relics had become the focus of veneration in times past.

---

6. The standard work on canonization in the Russian tradition is E. Golubinskii, *Istoriia kanonizatsii sviatykh v russkoi tserkvi*, 2d ed. (Moscow: Universitetskaia tipografiia, 1903; reprint, Westmead, England: Gregg International, 1969). It has been rightly criticized for presuming standardization and order in the absence of evidence for it. Cf. Paulus Peeters, "La Canonisation des Saints dans l'Eglise Russe," *Analecta Bollandiana* 33 (1914): 380–420, and Paul Bushkovitch, *Religion and Society in Russia: The Sixteenth and Seventeenth Centuries* (New York: Oxford University Press, 1992), 74–99. See also Eve Levin, "False Miracles and Unattested Dead Bodies: Investigations into Popular Cults in Early-Modern Russia," *Official Religion and Lived Religion in the Early Modern World*, ed. James Tracy (Cambridge University Press, forthcoming).

7. *Dieianiia Moskovskikh Soborov, 1666 i 1667* (Moscow: Sinodal'naia tipografiia, 1893; reprint, The Hague: Mouton, 1970 [Slavistic Printings and Reprintings, vol. 190]), pt. 3, ff. 8–8v.

In the decades after the Church Council of 1667, prelates of the Russian Orthodox Church became increasingly suspicious of locally venerated saints, especially those of recent provenance. A large part of their hostility to new cults rested in concern for the covert spread of Old Belief, which opposed the authority of church and state both. In addition, the new generation of hierarchs, educated in Western-style academies and attuned to Western philosophical debates about the veracity of miracles and relics, demanded proof of sanctity beyond the questionable testimony of ignorant laypeople. The Spiritual Regulation of 1721 called for the investigation of "holy relics, wherever they may be doubtful," and explicitly warned against veneration of "unattested dead bodies."[8] A 1737 decree of the Holy Synod—the church's ruling council as established by the Spiritual Regulation—required bishops to report to the Synod any "unattested dead bodies . . . revered as the true, holy relics of saints," along with the "false miracles" attributed to them.[9]

As the directive from the Moscow Church Council of 1667 suggests, premodern Russians offered two mutually exclusive explanations for the existence of uncorrupted corpses. The first was that incorruptibility testified to God's grace. Unlike their Byzantine and Western European counterparts, Russians had a decided preference for whole bodies rather than fragments of bone.[10] Russians made a direct connection between saints' bodily abstinence, the wholeness of their remains, and their ability to effect physical cures. As a prayer to St. Ioann Iarengskii states, "You preserved your body against defilement, and you bequeathed your indestructible love to those who revere you, exuding an indescribable aroma and pouring out inexhaustible healing."[11] But as the prelates of the Moscow Church Council suggested, there were other, less laudatory, explanations for incorruptibility. According to folk belief, to which even high-ranking clerics gave credence, the earth would refuse to accept the bodies of individuals who had died as outcasts from the

---

8. See part 2, article 6, and "About Bishops," article 8: P. V. Verkhovskoi, *Uchrezhdenie Dukhovnoi Kollegii i Dukhovnyi Reglament*, vol. 2 (Rostov: Warsaw University, 1916), 40.

9. Rossiiskii Gosudarstvennyi Istoricheskii Arkhiv (henceforth, RGIA), *f.* 834, *op.* 2, *d.* 1701. The text of the decree is included on *ll.* 1–2 *ob.* For a brief discussion of this decree, see Golubinskii, *Istoriia kanonizatsii*, 439–40.

10. Gail Lenhoff, "The Notion of 'Uncorrupted Relics' in Early Russian Culture," in *Christianity and the Eastern Slavs*, vol. 1, *Slavic Cultures in the Middle Ages*, ed. Boris Gasparov and Olga Raevsky-Hughes, California Slavic Studies 16 (Berkeley and Los Angeles: University of California Press, 1993), 252–75.

11. Hilandar Research Library, Ohio State University (henceforth, HRL), Saratov State University collection (henceforth, SGU) 1344, "Tale of John and Longinus Iarengsk (Solovki)," f. 12. The original manuscript dates to the 1640s–1660s; the vita is the third redaction by Sergei Shelonin, who was an eyewitness to the transfer of the relics.

community, especially under peculiar circumstances. These unholy dead, sometimes termed *upiry,* "vampires," could wreak havoc among the living. When they did, as evidenced by unexplained illness or natural disasters, they were driven away by mutilating their uncorrupted bodies.[12]

Russian vampires and saints had three characteristics in common. The first was continuing sentience: the ability to express their will to the living after their death, becoming visible and speaking to them. The second was the incorruptibility of their bodies, in contradistinction to the remains of ordinary persons who were neither saintly nor evil, which decayed after death. The third characteristic was their ability, through the medium of their bodies, to affect the health and circumstances of the living, either to their benefit or to their detriment. While uncorrupted remains were the most efficacious, apparently ordinary corpses were not without power, either. Numerous incantations invoked tombs and dead bodies as mediums for the healing of illnesses or, more rarely, causing harm.[13] Dead bodies were not only invoked in the abstract; certain *zagovory* involved the actual use of corpses. For example, a folk prayer and ritual against the temptation of alcohol called for the exhumation of a corpse, who is addressed directly: "And you, dead person N., so much time you lie there, and you do not drink so much intoxicating [liquor], nor do you eat bread, so may I, servant of God N., not drink intoxicating drink, not eat, not want, not see, nor see [*sic*], nor hear, nor think about, until cover of the grave."[14] This texts suggests how the corpse effected the cure: its lack of physical urges for food and drink could generate a similar condition in the speaker of the *zagovor.* A body that seemed to be undamaged

12. On the connection between vampirism and excommunication, see Jan L. Perkowski, *The Darkling: A Treatise on Slavic Vampirism* (Columbus, Ohio: Slavica, 1989), 19, and Paul Barber, *Vampires, Burial, and Death: Folklore and Reality* (New Haven: Yale University Press, 1988), esp. 74, 108, 111. Concern about the return of evil-working dead is reflected in folk custom; cf. D. K. Zelenin, *Izbrannye trudy: Ocherki russkoi mifologii* (Moscow: Indrik, 1995), 93, and Eve Levin, "Supplicatory Prayers as a Source for Popular Religious Culture in Muscovite Russia," in Baron and Kollmann, *Religion and Culture,* 105–6. For a discussion of the survival of these ideas in nineteenth-century folk culture, see Christine D. Worobec, "Death Ritual Among Russian and Ukrainian Peasants: Linkages Between the Living and the Dead," in *Cultures in Flux: Lower-Class Values, Practices, and Resistance in Late Imperial Russia,* ed. Stephen P. Frank and Mark D. Steinberg (Princeton: Princeton University Press, 1994), 11–33, especially 26–32.

13. For an example of such an incantation from the Muscovite period, see V. I. Sreznevskii, *Opisanie rukopisei i knig sobrannykh dlia Imperatorskoi Akademii nauk v Olonetskom krae* (St. Petersburg: Tipografiia Imperatorskoi Akademii Nauk, 1913), 493, 500. For examples of such incantations recorded in the nineteenth century, see V. L. Kliaus, *Ukazatel' siuzhetov i siuzhetnykh situatsii zagovornykh tekstov vostochnykh i iuzhnykh slavian* (Moscow: Nasledie, 1997), 131–32, 135–36, 180, 217, 230, 232, 245, 282, 284–86, 298, 330, 368.

14. Sreznevskii, *Opisanie rukopisei,* 497–98. See also the discussion of this text in Levin, "Supplicatory Prayers," 104–5.

even long after death could similarly be expected to impart its wholeness to people who invoked its aid. Given this premise, it is no wonder Russians claimed miraculous healing from the uncorrupted relics of saints; it is the belief that such bodies represented evil-working vampires that is anomalous. The wording of the ruling of the Moscow Church Council of 1667 itself suggests that Russians were more prone to see preserved corpses as miracle workers than as vampires.

Certainly the blacksmith Trofimov chose to recognize the unidentified dead body as a saint who healed him rather than as a vampire who had caused his illness in the first place. In the similar case of Artemii Verkol'skii, the local population showed initial suspicion. In 1577, a deacon found the uncorrupted body of a boy who had been struck by lightning and been buried in the woods. He brought it back to the village church in Verkola, claiming it belonged to a saint. The local peasants at first insisted upon leaving the body outside the church on the porch—the place where excommunicants and repenting sinners had to stand during services. The placement marked the body's uncertain status: whether it was a miracle-working saint or an evil-doing vampire was yet to be determined. Later that year during an epidemic of *triasavitsa*, "the shaking disease," Artemii's sanctity was proven. The first recipient of healing was a young boy. His father, despairing of his life, took the birchbark cover from the coffin of the unknown youth and laid it on his son's chest and throat. In this way, the father was not invoking a saint, for Artemii Verkol'skii had not yet been revealed as one, but rather was tapping into the general power of dead bodies to heal illness. The boy's recovery, followed by the ebbing of the epidemic, established the saint's reputation.[15] In the case of St. Iakov Borovitskii, the local populace at first refused to retrieve the unknown body from an ice block in the river, and then, according to the miracle tale, treated it "unmercifully," burying it in unconsecrated ground.[16]

While the cult of the nameless Arkhangel'sk saint emerged within hours, sometimes it took years before miracles were credited to the unusual corpse. The body eventually identified as St. Vasilii Mangazeiskii literally surfaced

15. HRL, SGU 996, "Service and Life of the Venerable Artemius Verkol'skii," ff. 30–32. The original manuscript dates to the 1640s–1660s. For a study of this vita, see Dmitriev, *Zhitiinye povesti,* 249–61, and Iakhontov, *Zhitiia,* 183–87. *Triasavitsa* later became the folk name for malaria, but its use in the pre-Petrine period referred to the symptom of ague, or shaking, regardless of the underlying cause, which no one at the time could discern. The symptom of chest congestion reported in this case points to influenza rather than malaria.

16. Gosudarstvennyi Istoricheskii Muzei (henceforth GIM), Sobranie Uvarova 1180 (395) (101), v chetverku, "Zhitie sv. Iakova Borovitskago," *ll.* 26–28. The manuscript dates to the seventeenth century.

in the north Siberian town of Mangazei in 1649. The coffin containing the remains had been buried in a marshy area between the guardpost and the church. When it floated to the surface, a guard spotted it and informed the local military governor, who had the grave fenced in to protect it against livestock. The first miracles credited to the body in the coffin occurred only three years later.[17]

The transfer of the newly discovered relics from the place where they were found into a church or chapel marked the identification of the corpse as a saint. Before the development of formal procedures for canonization in the eighteenth century, the translation of relics with proper pomp itself constituted official recognition. Secular and ecclesiastical authorities personally oversaw the translation, thus identifying themselves as official sponsors of the cult. Within days after the discovery of the relics of the Arkhangel'sk miracle worker Prince Buisonov arranged their transfer to the Church of the Translation of the Cross and hired a carpenter to build a proper tomb for the new saint.[18] A similar situation ensued in the cases of the saints of Sorochintsy and Liuteniia in the early eighteenth century. When building excavations revealed the uncorrupted bodies, local military commanders arranged for their transfer to new resting places.[19] In the case of the nameless miracle worker discovered in the village of Ilinskoe in 1728, the body was found while clearing an old cemetery for the priest to use as his farmland. The local nobleman Stefan Neledinskii-Meletskii took the lead in creating the new cult, providing a casket, a chapel furnished with icons and books, and a pipeline from a nearby spring as a source of holy water.[20] In the isolated village of Veriuzhskaia, a prosperous local farmer similarly provided accoutrements for St. Varlaam Ustianskii.[21] Local clergy also could play the key role, as the deacon of Verkola did in the case of St. Artemii.[22]

The first miracle from newly discovered relics was seldom the last. In the case of the nameless Arkhangel'sk miracle worker, the next miracles followed

17. E. K. Romodanovskaia, "Legenda o Vasilii Mangazeiskom," in *Novye materialy po istorii Sibiri dosovetskogo perioda*, ed. N. N. Pokrovskii (Novosibirisk: Nauka—Sibirskoe otdelenie, 1986), 191–92; S. V. Bakhrushin, "Legenda o Vasilii Mangazeiskom," in his *Nauchnye trudy*, vol. 3, pt. 1 (Moscow: Akademii Nauk SSSR, 1955), 334–35.

18. RGB, f. 212, d. 75, ll. 4–5 ob.

19. RGIA, f. 796, op. 25, d. 723, "Delo o moshchakh," ll. 236, 419–20. This huge compendium of documents consists of materials relating to the Synod's 1744 investigation of unapproved saints.

20. *Polnoe sobranie vostanovlenii i rasporiazhenii po viedomstvu pravoslavnago ispovedaniia Rossiiskoi Imperii*, 19 volumes in 5 series (St. Petersburg/Petrograd: Sinodal'naia tipografiia, 1869–1915) (henceforth, *PSRV*), here, ser. 1, vol. 8 (1898), 265–66.

21. RGIA, f. 796, op. 25, d. 723, ll. 590–91.

22. HRL, SGU 1344, ff. 38v–40, 45–45v.

within days. As Prince Buisonov's carpenter recalled later in his testimony to the inquest commission, a thought had occurred to him while building the new casket: "To whom is this tomb being built? What sort of saint is this?" and he was struck with a sudden panic attack. When he prayed at the coffin for forgiveness for his doubts, his panic subsided, and he credited the nameless saint with another cure. The motif of the doubter's punishment and repentance, familiar from legends of the saints, clearly framed the carpenter's experience. In addition to the blacksmith and the carpenter, recipients of miraculous cures included the church's priest who had sore feet; a soldier suffering from "illness of the mustache"; a three-year-old boy who had hurt his arm in a tumble; and a blind ten-year-old girl whose weak legs regained their strength. Even miracles that had occurred earlier were attributed to the newfound saint. Mariia Khaidutova, wife of a soldier who had suffered from "disease of the womb" for ten years, attributed her cure, which occurred prior to the discovery of the relics, to the new miracle worker.[23]

Once Vasilii Mangazeiskii began to work miracles, three years after his body surfaced, they accumulated rapidly. The first recipient, in January 1652, was a soldier stationed in Mangazei, who had thirteen wounds on his arm. The following August, Dimitrii Evtropiev reported the healing of a painful lump near his left testicle. He had turned to the saint for relief only after a local horse doctor had refused to treat him. By the time the local authorities reported the new saint to the bishop of Tobol'sk in August 1653, eight additional miracles had been recorded: two visions of the saint, a cure of snow blindness, two healings of back trouble, two averted drownings, and one suicide prevention.[24] While all the recipients of Vasilii's first miracles were men, as might be expected in a fortress and trade outpost in northeast Siberia, all the first miracles of St. Iakov Borovitskii went to women. At the inquest in 1544, six women reported miraculous healings: one of lameness, one of persistent headaches, two of blindness, and two of demonic possession.[25] Although Artemii Verkol'skii's first miracle in 1577 was not followed with others—or, at least, others that were recorded—until 1584, over the next twenty-six years, sixty-two miraculous healings were attributed to him: thirty-three of men, twenty-seven of women, and two of infants brought by their mothers. As the sole local saint, Artemii Verkol'skii had to be a general practitioner. Although the largest number of patients consulted him about eye

23. RGB, *f.* 212, *d.* 75, *ll.* 4 *ob.*–5 *ob.*, 7–11, 12–14 *ob.* Because the manuscript is incomplete, it is impossible to know how many miracles were reported by the time of the investigation.

24. Romodanovskaia, "Legenda," 192–96.

25. GIM, Sobranie Uvarova 1180 (395) (101), *ll.* 44–45 *ob.*

ailments and weakness in limbs, he also cured heart trouble, internal pain, chills, toothaches, swollen faces, spitting blood, insanity, demonic possession, loss of appetite, and infertility.[26] While the devotees of these saints seem to have kept quite extensive records of healings, sponsors of other cults, such as that of Mariia of Sorochintsy, were content with oral accounts. When the church's bureaucracy came to favor written documentation over verbal testimony in the eighteenth century, devotees of these cults had a difficult time establishing the authenticity of their saints.

Because the saints were previously unknown, every aspect of their identities had to be invented, including their physical appearances. In the case of established saints of more ordinary types, recipients of visions authenticated their experiences by referring to the iconographic images with which they were familiar. But in the case of newly discovered miracle workers, there was no iconographic image yet, so the initial descriptions of new saints varied quite a bit.

The inquest records for the cult of the Arkhangel'sk miracle worker show that the followers of the new saint envisioned him in quite different ways. The gunner Dmitrei had a vision of the saint's tomb in which he saw merely a "person" (*chelovek*). Mariia Khaidutova, recalling her vision that had occurred before the discovery of the new saint's relics, described him as "a person attired in light with red hair and a graying beard, tall in height and having a large shirt, like snow, on him." She told the soldier Ivan Postnikov about her vision, and a year and a half later his wife, Marfa, saw "the same person." Another soldier envisioned quite a different man: "a person in monastic habit with a cowl on his head." He testified frankly that he "did not see the face and hair of that person who appeared to him." The blind ten-year-old girl described "a person tall in height in a black robe and a black beard." It was the girl's aunt who connected the figure in the girl's vision with the new Arkhangel'sk saint, of whom she had heard. The girl's uncle had a complementary vision of "a man in light visage with a large beard and shirt . . . tall in height with a black beard and black shirt."[27]

The inhabitants of Mangazei similarly pictured their unknown saint in different ways. Dimitrii Evtropiev of the sore testicle dreamed of the saint, "a priest in appearance," who rescued him from drowning at the hands of the malevolent horse doctor. A year later, the businessman Grigorii Korotaev twice saw the miracle worker as "short in height, young, with a white face, a

26. HRL, SGU 996, ff. 37–62.
27. RGB, f. 212, d. 75, ll. 6–10 ob., 12–13.

round face, and hair blond with red." To Grigorii, he seemed in appearance to be "of foreign birth" (*inozemskogo rodu*). Other recipients of visions agreed on the saint's youth and short stature—readily discerned from the size of the coffin—but not on the color of his hair or the shape of his face.[28] Once the proper visage was established, persons appealing to the saint for help would invoke that image mentally, and persons who wished to authenticate their visions would describe the apparition accordingly. Thus when the soldier Antip Kopylov called upon the Mangazei saint to heal his illness, the figure who came to him in a dream was "a young person, with a shining face, short in height, and without a beard on him." Kopylov's innovation concerned the saint's clothing: a ragged dark shirt.[29] Soon after, when the monastic priest Tikhon wished to invoke the saint's approval for his plan to remove the relics from Mangazei to Turukhan, he described the saint's clothing in exactly the same terms.[30]

The person with the greatest need to be able to visualize the saint was the artist who painted the icon. Although icons were not portraits in the conventional sense, but rather stylized images that conformed to prototypes of the genre, the artist did need to know whether to depict the saint as young or old, as a monastic or a layperson, and determine the color of hair and robe. In deciding how to draw the icon, the painter relied upon the testimony of devotees of the saint about apparitions, on any visions he himself received, and the physical evidence of the body itself. In the case of Prokopii Ustianskii, a merchant who commissioned the icon used his own vision of the saint to instruct the icon painter. The icon painter also opened the tomb in order to see the remains firsthand. Obviously, despite their "uncorrupted" state, the appearance of the relics alone did not suffice as a guide to the artist.[31] In the case of Ioann Iarengskii, two recipients of visions had described the saint as having a "black beard" and handsome; one of the two also remarked that he wore ecclesiastical vestments. The icon painter himself had a vision that agreed on the dark beard, but not on the rest, so he depicted St. Ioann's "face like John the Baptist but the beard like the thief Rakh, threadbare cloak and arm bent." After the icon went on display in the church in Iarenga, it influenced the way devotees remembered their encounters with the saint. Thus an old man remembered an apparition he had had "a few years before the

28. Bakhrushin, "Legenda," 338; Romodanovskaia, "Legenda," 194–95, 197.

29. Romodanovskaia, "Legenda," 204; *Sbornik Edomskago*, ed. Nikolai Barsukov, in *Pamiatniki drevnei pis'mennosti i iskusstva*, no. 79 (1889): 19.

30. *Sbornik Edomskago*, 21.

31. RGIA, *f.* 796, *op.* 25, *d.* 723, *ll.* 592 ob.–593.

painting of Ioann's icon" as "a man . . . in a threadbare shirt, long hair on his head, arm bent, his face he did not show."[32]

Devotees' visions not only clarified the saints' external appearances, but also, in many cases, their names. St. Glikeriia of Novgorod and Mariia of Sorochintsy were the exceptions; individuals present at the discovery of the remains claimed to know who they were. But most "unidentified corpse" saints remained nameless, in some cases for years. The unknown miracle worker in the hamlet of Liuteniia lacked a name for a number of years before the parish priest had a vision of the saint in which he called himself "Avtonom."[33] The Arkhangel'sk miracle worker still did not have a name when the inquest into his sanctity was undertaken, although investigators asked recipients of visions about it. Only Maria Khaidutova, whose vision occurred prior to the discovery of the corpse, claimed that the saint had told her his name, which she had since forgotten.[34]

Controversy surrounded the selection of the name for Mangazei's local saint. When the archbishop of Tobol'sk first sought approval from Moscow, the saint was called simply "the miracle worker of Mangazei."[35] Grigorii Korotaev testified in 1653 that the saint appeared to him in a vision and identified himself as "Moisei." That name didn't take, however. Soon after, the *voevoda's* houseservant claimed that the saint appeared to him and gave his name as "Vasilii Feodorov *syn*" and ordered him to "get up and recount my name without any doubt."[36] Even so, the identity of the saint remained uncertain. When Antip Kopylov received his vision of the saint in 1670, the apparition asked him, "Do you know me?" Antip responded, "I do not know who you are, only I recognize you by your voice; it is like [that of] the former Mangazei servitor Vasilii Sychev." The saint replied, "Antip, I am not Vasilii Sychev; my name is Vasilii only."[37] A report to the tsar in 1671 noted that "the accounts of many people about the name by which the relics of the Mangazei miracle worker are called did not coincide."[38] Eventually a consensus formed

32. Rossiiskaia natsional'naia biblioteka (henceforth, RNB), Solovetskoe sobranie 182/182, *ll.* 121 *ob.*, 122 *ob.*, 123 *ob.*–124, 143 *ob.*

33. RGIA, *f.* 796, *op.* 25, *d.* 723, *ll.* 236–236 *ob.* The choice of name is odd, literally "Autonomy." Although there was an early martyr of that name who is mentioned in the Lithuanian Chronicle—see *Polnoe sobranie russkikh letopisei,* vol. 20 (St. Petersburg: Tipografiia M. A. Aleksandrova, 1910), 27—the name was not even in uncommon use. Perhaps the priest heard the neologism referring to a new sort of virtue, autonomy, and applied it to the unnamed miracle worker in his parish church.

34. RGB, *f.* 212, *d.* 75, *ll.* 7 *ob.*–8, 9, 13.

35. Bakhrushin, "Legenda," 336–37.

36. Romodanovskaia, "Legenda," 197–98.

37. Ibid., 204–5; *Sobranie Edomskago,* 19.

38. Quoted in Bakhrushin, "Legenda," 342.

around the name "Vasilii," and the official account of Korotaev's miracle was rewritten to include it.[39] But clearly the lack of a name presented no innate obstacle to the development of a cult, or even recognition from the church hierarchy.

Premodern Russians seem to have been largely unconcerned with the prior earthly lives of their newfound miracle workers. The surviving documentation concerning the unnamed Arkhangel'sk saint gives no hint at all as to who he might have been.[40] Instead, they contented themselves with the merest sketch of the saints' existence in this world; the proof of sanctity lay not in how the saints had lived, but how they could intercede for their devotees. But even the minimal information provided about the saints is very telling of popular estimations of what sort of life merited sainthood. An account of the Vasilii Mangazeiskii's miracles from 1659 reported the local legend about his life: "Many people in the city said that they heard from old people that this commercial person, a shop clerk, was tortured on the basis of a slander, [and died] an untimely [death], and was laid in the place. But how many years ago and what he was called, they don't know."[41] When the saint's earthly biography became more important in the early eighteenth century, St. Vasilii's was expanded. An account from after 1719 described him as a young servant "who served his master honestly and preserved his spiritual and physical purity." The master went bankrupt and accused his servant of embezzlement. The master beat him to try to extract a confession and then turned him over to civil authorities, where he died under interrogation.[42] The date of his martyrdom was set as March 23, which led to another legend that Vasilii died on Easter in imitation of Christ.[43] The precise time of his life and death also

---

39. Romodanovskaia, "Legenda," 194; Bakhrushin, "Legenda," 337, 348. The deposition also gives the witness's name as "Grigorii Sirotaev;" given the handwritten styles of the time, such a misreading would be quite understandable.

40. It is possible that the unnamed Arkhangel'sk miracle worker was later transmuted into St. Evfimii of Arkhangel'sk. Information about him is slight: in 1683, Archbishop Afanasii of Kholmogory forbade veneration of a St. Evfimii of Arkhangel'sk, whose relics had been discovered in 1647, and whose cult was investigated sometime before 1650 by Metropolitan Nikon of Novgorod (the future patriarch). Afanasii forbade veneration because the body could not be connected with any assurance to Evfimii, an early abbot of the Arkhangel'sk monastery who had died over 120 years before. The corpse also supposedly showed the dreaded two-fingered sign of the cross connected with Old Belief. See V. Veriuzhskii, *Afanasii, arkhiepiskop Kholmogorskii: Ego zhizn' i trudy v sviazi s istoriei Kholmogorskoi eparkhii za pervyia 20 let eia sushchestvovaniia i voobshche russkoi tserkvi v kontse XVII veka* (St. Petersburg: Tipografiia I. V. Leont'eva, 1908), 384–86.

41. Quoted in Bakhrushin, "Legenda," 346.

42. Boris Pivovarov, "Sviatoi pravednyi Vasilii Mangazeiskii," *Zhurnal Moskovskoi patriarkhii,* 1977, no. 11, p. 66, note 2; Bakhrushin, "Legenda," 345–46.

43. Pivovarov, "Sviatoi pravednyi," 65.

became more important, and the year was given variously as 1598, 1600, 1601, 1602, and 1622.[44]

The reconstructions of the earthly lives of St. Glikeriia and Mariia of Sorochintsy similarly did not go beyond the barest minimum. Glikeriia was the daughter of a Novgorodian elder; no additional biography was ever attributed to her.[45] In the case of Mariia, the sexton who identified her body described her as a "maiden" who "unfailingly attended church, and lived solely from charity, and never used intoxicants."[46]

In the case of Artemii Verkol'skii, the cause of death and the saint's probable age could be surmised from the body itself. Everything else had to be invented on the basis of models of sanctity. Thus young Artemii's vita described him as the son of pious Christian parents, a boy who rejected childish pleasures and undertook prayer and fasting. Unlike in most vitae, Artemii's obedience to his parents was not set in tension with his devotion to God; the two were presented as being in perfect accord. Furthermore, Artemii was praised for a peasant virtue, hard work. From the age of five, according to the vita, he worked his own field and fed himself from his labors, for "he who does not work shall not eat." More than his pious efforts, however, it was Artemii's death that earned him sainthood. The author of the vita explains how Artemii stood in proper awe of God and yielded up his soul to God's judgment in thunder and storm. In this manner, Artemii's death by lightning, which would seem to make him a more likely candidate for vampire status than for sainthood, was recast as submission to God's will.[47]

Under most circumstances, death by drowning was similarly stigmatized, so the clerical author of the vita of Vassian and Iona Unskie (Pertominskie) began his narrative with an apologia for the means of their demise, concluding, "may nobody . . . doubt that a righteous person in life may experience an evil sort of death." Vassian and Iona's uncorrupted bodies demonstrated their sanctity beyond doubt, but the author acknowledged that he knew nothing whatever about them: "from which country these venerable ones came, or where their habitation was, or their family, or their parentage." He

---

44. Bakhrushin, "Legenda," 349–50; Pivovarov, "Sviatoi pravednyi," 65. Pivovarov, a modern ecclesiastical writer, still was very concerned with identifying the correct date of St. Vasilii's death, but found that in no calendar year did the dates line up properly.

45. M. V. Tolstoi, "Kniga glagolemaia opisanie o Rossiiskikh sviatykh," *Chteniia v imperatorskom obshchestve istorii i drevnostei Rossiiskikh pri Moskovskom universitete,* 1887, bk. 4, p. 264; Nun Taisiia, *Zhitiia sviatykh: 1000 liet russkoi sviatosti,* 2 vols. (Jordanville, N.Y.: Holy Trinity Monastery, 1983–84), 1:226.

46. RGIA, *f.* 796, *op.* 25, *d.* 723, *ll.* 420–420 *ob.*

47. HRL, SGU 996, ff. 26v–29v.

cites "rumor from yore" (*drevle slyshaniem*) that identified the saints as pupils of Metropolitan Filipp of Moscow from the Solovetskii monastery.[48]

Because the quality of the relics and their ability to work miracles in themselves provided all the evidence needed to prove the saint's sanctity, formal inquests into cults paid little attention to collecting information on the saints' identities in life. The charge to the commission sent upon orders of Patriarch Filaret in 1624 to investigate Ioann and Loggin Iarengskie directed the investigators to inquire about the origins of veneration and the evidence of miracles, but said nothing about tracing the saints' premortem existences.[49] The commission sent by Archbishop Feodosii of Novgorod in 1544 concerning Iakov Borovitskii asked about his earthly life, but readily accepted the answer that nothing was known.[50]

Most of the saints under consideration here underwent investigation at some point in the development of the cult, and sometimes more than once. In the case of the nameless Arkhangel'sk miracle worker, both the initial investigation and the formal inquest the next year were conducted by secular officials led by the *voevoda* Iurii Buisonov, who was among the original sponsors of the cult. The commission established by Archbishop Feodosii of Novgorod in 1544 to investigate St. Iakov Borovitskii consisted of ten persons, including six clergy and four laymen. One of the members of the commission was the priest Ivan from the church of Sts. Boris and Gleb in Borovichi, who had authored the petition for recognition of the saint.[51] In these cases, clearly the intent was not to debunk cults, but rather to demonstrate their veracity.

The investigation of the cult of Sts. Ioann and Loggin Iarengskie was more neutral at the outset. At the behest of Patriarch Filaret, Metropolitan Makarii of Novgorod appointed a commission consisting of an abbot and one of his lay servitors, and gave them this charge:

> And having brought [witnesses] before you, question them vigorously about who was sick with what illness, and for how many years, and how they received healing from the miracle workers Ivan and Loggin, either here at the miracle workers' tomb or in their home or on the road. And whatever they state before you under examination,

---

48. RNB, Solovetskoe sobranie 182/182, *ll.* 181–83. The same biography was applied later to Ioann and Iakov Iarengskie; cf. Tolstoi, "Kniga glagolemaia," 159–60.

49. RNB, Solovetskoe sobranie 182/182, *ll.* 126 *ob.*–128 *ob.*

50. GIM, Sobranie Uvarova 1180 (395) (101), *ll.* 43–46 *ob.*

51. Ibid., *ll.* 43–48; Kliuchevskii, *Drevnerusskiia zhitiia,* 425.

seek out their families and kinsmen [to tell] how long their relatives suffered from illness and how many years ago they were healed of their illnesses, and where they were healed.[52]

The commission carried out these instructions, interviewing dozens of individuals and recording testimony to fifteen miracles. All the recipients of miracles, eight men and seven women, were laypeople of modest social standing. Women testified for themselves on a par with men. For example, when the peasant Tikhon Tarutin came forward first to recount a miracle his wife Matrona had experienced, the investigators ordered that she appear in person. Her miracle, the healing of a heart ailment, had taken place thirty years earlier. Indeed, all of the miracles had taken place at least five years before the inquest, and half of them over fifteen years earlier.[53] Thus much of the testimony came from older people, whose word in general was given greater weight in the Muscovite judicial process.

Investigations into miracle-working relics did not always yield the results local patrons intended. Officials in Mangazei had trouble even getting the attention of highers-up. In 1653, after the saint was credited with rescuing a merchant party from a freak summer snowstorm, the *voevoda* of Mangazei sent a list of the saint's miracles to Archbishop Simeon of Tobol'sk. Simeon forwarded it to Moscow, inquiring whether he should "go himself for testimony about the relics, or whom to send." With typical Muscovite bureaucratic efficiency, Simeon's inquiry was filed away in the archives of the Siberian chancellery before any action was taken on it.[54] After waiting six years, the priest of the Mangazei cathedral sent a second letter to Archbishop Simeon, who decided to go ahead with the inquest on his own authority. The results were ambiguous: "The coffin is completely whole, only a little blackened. And in the coffin are the relics: the head and arms and legs are all of ordinary human type, only bones, and there is no flesh on them; it has corrupted."[55] It is not clear what Archbishop Simeon thought of the commission's report,

52. RNB, Solovetskoe sobranie 182/182, *l.* 128.

53. Ibid., *ll.* 129–41.

54. Romodanovskaia, "Legenda," 196; Pivovarov, "Sviatoi pravednyi," 62, 71; Bakhrushin, "Legenda," 336–37.

55. Pivovarov, "Sviatoi pravednyi," 62; Bakhrushin, "Legenda," 337. Curiously, each of these authors provided only a part of the quotation: Pivovarov, the Orthodox author omits the reference to corruption; Bakhrushin, the Soviet scholar, omits the first part of the quotation, stating that the coffin was whole and referring to the body as "relics"—a term used exclusively for the remains of saints. See also N. N. Ogloblin, "Mangazeiskii chudotvorets Vasilii," *Chteniia v imperatorskom obshchestve istorii i drevnostei Rossiiskikh pri Moskovskom universitete*, 1890, bk. 2, pp. 4–5.

but he made no move stamp out the cult. The local population of Mangazei regarded the inquest itself as substantiation of Vasilii's claims to sanctity.

In the case of Iakov Borovitskii, Archbishop Feodosii's commission recorded the condition of the corpse in detail. The flesh had dried to the bones, and the right hand was missing three fingers. However, the commission pointed to the intact head, face, fingernails, and toenails, and declared the body to be substantially incorrupt. The state of the remains and the lack of any information on the saint's earthly life were outweighed by the testimony of seven living witnesses, all women, to the miraculous healing powers of the saint. However, Feodosii did take the precaution of ordering that the saint's relics be housed in a closed tomb when he and Metropolitan Makarii authorized veneration.[56]

Even when the testimony at the inquest was deemed credible, revelations concerning the quality of the relics could impede recognition. After Moscow approved veneration of the two Iarenga saints, a problem arose at the time of the transfer of the relics to a new church. Abbot Varfolomei of the Solovetskii monastery, who presided at the canonization, found St. Ioann's body to be substantially intact, and thus holy. However, St. Loggin's remains were not; it was "as though they could not move before the general resurrection, for they were mixed with dirt." Varfolomei refused to proceed with the translation, doused the remains with myrrh, sprinkled them with holy water, and ordered the grave refilled. But the local priest of Iarenga and some of the Solovetskii monks were upset at the exclusion of St. Loggin, and they begged Varfolomei to reconsider. Even though the relics of the two saints were found at different times and in different places, supporters of the cult argued that they had to be treated alike. "For the Lord Almighty has joined the seas together like brothers, one from the east and another from the west, so these [two] should not be separated one from the other. Just as the Holy Spirit stands together with the Holy Trinity, so their holy relics should not be separated." Varfolomei relented, and allowed them to take another look at St. Loggin's body. When they unearthed it, it exuded the ineffable aroma of sanctity—no doubt the result of the previous day's treatment!—and Varfolomei agreed to proceed with the transfer.[57]

56. GIM, Sobranie Uvarova 1180 (395) (101), *ll.* 43–51 *ob.*; Kliuchevskii, *Drevnerusskiia zhitiia*, 425.

57. HRL, SGU 1344, ff. 60–63v. The author of the vita, Sergei Shelonin, seems to have been aware, at some level, of how the relics were doctored. He records a "miracle" on the return trip to Solovki, when he received a whiff of the ineffable aroma. Confused, he turned to the abbot for an explanation. Varfolomei assured him that, because he had once sensed that odor of sanctity, it would always be with him. See ff. 63v–65.

Similarly, Archbishop Afanasii of Kholmogory yielded to pressure in recognizing Sts. Vassian and Iona Unskie. In 1694, the monks of the Pertominskii monastery prevailed upon Peter the Great, who had taken refuge from a storm there, to grant recognition to the local miracle workers. Peter was willing, but Archbishop Afanasii, who accompanied the tsar's suite, was skeptical. Ultimately, however, he "could not oppose the will of the tsar and the wishes of all the tsar's entourage." But when the time came to transfer the relics, the state of the remains left a great deal to be desired: "The relics of one of the venerable ones [consisted of] the head and bones with dirt; the relics of the second venerable one were not found, through God's watchfulness. Just how and why they were not found, nobody knows; for who can ask God about it? But all the apparitions and miracle-working of these two together, which is recounted everywhere, could hardly be all falsely written." Fortunately for the Pertominskii monks, Afanasii did not use the state of the relics as an excuse to cancel the canonization. Instead, he announced to the tsar, "I know these bones to be holy, and not like those of an ordinary dead person as we know them."[58]

In the case of the Pertominskii monastery saints, attention from high-ranking officials proved beneficial: the monastery received much-needed alms as well as official recognition of the local saints. However, the intervention of outsiders did not always benefit the local cult of the saint. In 1635, St. Artemii Verkol'skii worked a miracle for Afanasii Pashkov, the *voevoda* of Kevrola traveling to his posting. On the road, Pashkov's young son fell ill with *triasavitsa,* and when the father pledged to stop at the saint's shrine in Verkola on the way, the boy recovered.[59] However, Pashkov's method of showing his gratitude to the saint did not play well in Verkola. He established a monastery at the shrine and excluded the local residents from it. They protested and tried to drive out the monks, asserting, "The miracle worker is ours and the monastery is ours." But ultimately the monks had more clout, and in 1648–49, Moscow confirmed their ownership of the relics.[60]

The relics of St. Vasilii Mangazeiskii also underwent a disputed transfer, in this case engineered by the town of Turukhan. In the late 1660s, Turukhan was taking over a large share of the business of Mangazei, as merchants, fur trappers, and government servitors transferred there.[61] So it is not surprising that St. Vasilii—or at least some persons who claimed to speak for him—

58. RNB, Solovetskoe sobranie 182/182, *ll.* 199–200.
59. HRL, SGU 351, ff. 52–53v.
60. Dmitriev, *Zhitiinye povesti,* 257–58.
61. Bakhrushin, "Legenda," 339–40.

decided to go, too. After some collusion between the Turukhanskii monastery and soldiers in the Mangazei garrison in the winter of 1670, the monastic priest Tikhon arrived from Turukhan to secure the relics. He announced that St. Vasilii had appeared to him to complain about the cramped and decrepit state of his lodgings in Mangazei and ask to be moved. Tikhon built up his own credibility by presiding at a miraculous cure of the soldier Antip Kopylov—the same one who got the saint's surname wrong—on Lazarus Saturday, March 28. The groundwork laid, Tikhon packed the saint's remains into a new casket and moved them out on Easter Sunday, where the processions and ceremonies disguised what was little more than the perpetration of a theft.[62] Tikhon's escapade was totally unauthorized; in his report to Moscow, Metropolitan Kornilii of Tobolsk described Tikhon as going to Mangazei "in his arrogance and not having written to me, the metropolitan."[63] But St. Vasilii's body remained in Turukhan.

Most of the saints discussed here came under the scrutiny of reforming church leaders in the first half of the eighteenth century, and the results of those investigations shed light on the growing rift between the religious sentiments of local laity and minor clergy and those of the Westernized ecclesiastical elite. In every case, the local communities vouched for the legitimacy of their saint based on their direct experiences. Meanwhile, ecclesiastical authorities in the capital claimed the prerogative of overruling them.

The best-established cults experienced the least trouble from the Synod's reforming tendencies. Iakov Borovitskii's claims to sainthood were never challenged, recognized as he was by the eminent Metropolitan Makarii in the sixteenth century. While the sanctity of Ioann and Loggin Iarengskie was questioned during the Synod's 1744–45 investigations, the documentation of prior official approval kept the cult viable.[64]

The 1744–45 investigation left the cult of Prokopii Ustianskii in limbo, although its promoters were able to provide substantial documentation. In 1696, Archbishop Afanasii of Kholmogory, that skeptic of the sanctity of Sts. Vassian and Iona, had yielded to popular enthusiasm for St. Prokopii, but had not officially proclaimed the cult.[65] In 1737, Bishop Savva of Arkhangel'sk

62. Romodanovskaia, "Legenda," 199–206; *Sbornik Edomskago*, 13–21. Thefts of relics in Western Europe in the medieval period were accomplished very similarly. See Patrick Geary, *Furta Sacra: Thefts of Relics in the Central Middle Ages* (Princeton: Princeton University Press, 1978).

63. Quoted in Bakhrushin, "Legenda," 340; see also Ogloblin, "Mangazeiskii chudotvorets," 8.

64. RGIA, *f.* 796, *op.* 25, *d.* 723, *ll.* 578–578 *ob.*, 580–587 *ob.*

65. Ibid., *ll.* 588–589 *ob.*; Veriuzhskii, *Afanasii*, 388.

appointed a commission, drawing heavily upon local clergy predisposed to look favorably upon the claims made for the saint. This commission found Prokopii's body to be only partially preserved, but it emphasized that there had been no change from the condition reported in 1696. The commission also collected recent testimony to miraculous healings at the Veriuzhskaia church where the relics lay, noting honestly where one statement could not be confirmed.[66] But in 1745, Archbishop Varsonofii of Arkhangel'sk pushed neither for official approval of the cult nor for its suppression, and supporters continued to agitate for a stronger endorsement from the Synod.[67]

The cults of Avtonom Liutenskii and Mariia Sorochintskaia lacked written documentation, and so did not fare even as well as that of Prokopii Ustianskii. Avtonom's remains became the subject of an inquest during the reformist Varlaam Vanatovich's tenure as archbishop of Kiev. His commission determined the body to be corrupted, and he ordered it buried. The local population, including the parish priest, continued to seek healing at the site, as they testified in response to inquiries by the Synod in 1744. The compiler of that report, a monastic priest, was sympathetic to the claims made on behalf of St. Avtonom, but did not have sufficient time to gather complete testimony.[68] Apparently his report did not convince the Synod that Vanatovich, one of its prior members, had made a mistake. Similarly, in the case of the Sorochintsy saint, the Synod deemed the oral testimony to be insufficient. Seven old men provided statements about the discovery of the relics and the saint's early miracles, and a woman told of the healing of her mother of demonic possession a number of years earlier.[69] But promoters of these cults could not produce written documents from earlier hierarchs or the tsar authorizing the cult, and that was more important to obtaining official sanction from the Synod than testimony by living persons to miracles, which could dismissed as ignorant delusion.

Attempts to close down cults did not always work. Metropolitan Filofei's successors in the see of Tobol'sk tried to eliminate veneration of St. Vasilii Mangazeiskii, first by transferring the remains from the Turukhanskii monastery's main church to a outlying chapel, and then by forbidding commemoration altogether. The Turukhanskii monks remained devoted, however, and later moved the relics back to the main church, using the chapel's state

66. RGIA, f. 796, op. 25, d. 723, ll. 588–589 ob., 594 ob.–597.
67. I appreciate Christine Worobec's efforts in tracking the later history of this cult.
68. RGIA, f. 796, op. 25, d. 723, ll. 236–236 ob.
69. Ibid., ll. 420 ob.–421 ob.

of disrepair as an excuse. Thus the cult was reestablished, and ecclesiastical authorities made no further move to suppress it.[70]

The newest cult, that of the nameless saint of Ilinskoe, received the harshest treatment from the Synod. Like the "unidentified corpse" saints who appeared in the sixteenth and seventeenth centuries, the cult of the Ilinskoe miracle worker grew up locally, sponsored both by the parish priest Afanasii and his deacon Maksim Petrov, and by the local *pomeshchik,* Stefan Neledinskii. For five years, the chapel built to honor the nameless saint welcomed pilgrims from the region: landowners, peasants, and village clergy, "who all recognized this dead person as a saint."[71] Even the archimandrite of the nearby Arkhangel'sk-Polskii monastery recognized the cult, coming to celebrate St. Ilia's Day at the chapel. Nobody informed the bishop of Suzdal of the new saint until 1733, when Deacon Petrov and the nobleman Neledinskii had a falling-out. Neledinskii expelled Petrov from the village, and when the latter went to secular authorities to complain about the loss of his position, the story of the cult came out. The Synod ordered that the chapel be sealed and a full investigation of the "dead body" be undertaken. Eight and a half months later, the Synod condemned the cult as fraudulent, and in violation of the Spiritual Regulation. The priest Afanasii was identified as the chief perpetrator of the crime, and he was deprived of his clerical rank, flogged, and sent to a monastery for hard labor for life. The other clergy and lay trustees of the parish, including Deacon Petrov, received lesser punishments. The Synod ordered the so-called relics and the chapel that housed them burned, and the site leveled.[72] Because "superstition" was deemed a lower-class offense, the members of the elite who had participated in the cult, including Neledinskii himself, escaped punishment.

The cults examined in this article grew up out of nothing more than unknown corpses, and ordinary laypeople's willingness to see in them something extraordinary. These cults reflect their understanding of sanctity, of how God's power could be transmitted to this world through the medium of his saints and their physical remains. For ordinary Russians, the first evidence of supernatural power lay in the unusual state of preservation of the body, which pointed to its enhanced power to affect the physical state of living people. Believing such bodies to have power, people attributed alterations in their physical sensations to them. They credited the dead bodies, who

70. Pivovarov, "Sviatoi pravednyi," 63, Bakhrushin, "Legenda," 341.
71. *PSRV,* ser. 1, 8:266.
72. Ibid., 8:266–68, 10 (St. Petersburg, 1911): 62–63.

thus became living saints, positioned in Heaven to intercede for petitioners on earth.

The testimony of recipients of miracles was critical to the development of the cults of these saints. In every case, the first persons to announce the advent of a new saint were decidedly ordinary: craftsmen, traders, soldiers, housewives, and little children. Their communities, including local clergy and members of the secular elite, believed them—not because provincial Russians were especially credulous, but because their accounts were credible, within their cultural context. Premodern Christians, like modern ones, defined a miracle as a direct intervention by God in the course of ordinary events. But unlike modern people, who expect to be able to explain most happenings, even extraordinary ones, by reference to immutable laws of nature, premodern Christians were much more inclined to see them as manifestations of supernatural power. If the outcome was both unexpected and desired, it could be proclaimed a miracle. In other words, miracles reflected the fulfillment of ardent hopes more than any contravention of natural law. Christian teachings, as enshrined in saints' lives and didactic tales, taught believers to anticipate manifestations of divine power in the world around them. Consequently, it is not surprising that they interpreted their experiences in the language of miracles.

In order to know whom to invoke for help and whom to thank for receiving it, followers of the new saints invented identities for them: a name to call out in prayer, and a visual image to evoke. It could take a number of years for a consensus to build around a single name and visage, but in the meantime the saint's ability to work miracles was unimpaired. The saint's life on earth was deemed of little account, and few details were sketched in. Insofar as believers developed premortem biographies for their miracle workers, they drew from the models of admirable people in their midst: traveling monks, pious maidens, hard-working children. More often it was the tragic deaths of the saints, by drowning, lightning, or murder, that devotees recalled as a prelude to their heavenly existence.

In the case of each of these saints, the uncorrupted state of the body that had originally spurred the development of the cult of the saint proved to be transitory. By the time the remains were examined as part of an inquest or during translation, they had ceased to be whole. But by that time the saints had established a record of miracle-working such that devotees were unwilling to disbelieve, no matter what the physical state of the remains. The ecclesiastical authorities who were called in to verify sanctity paid close attention to the material characteristics of the remains, which they recorded in detail.

They may have wanted to insist upon physical wholeness, but significantly, they chose to defer to the local communities' convictions, stretching their definition of "incorruptibility." Thus the physical state of the remains which originally sparked the cult ultimately had less significance to the local community than it did to the clerical elite.

In the space of sixty years, from the 1660s to the 1720s, the leadership of the Russian Orthodox Church radically changed its attitude to "unidentified corpse" saints. Before the mid-seventeenth century, church hierarchs shared with local communities the idea that previously unknown saints could reveal themselves through miracles performed by their relics. When honest Christians testified that they had experienced God's grace through a particular set of relics, the hierarchs were inclined to accept their word. For was it not to be expected that God would reveal his blessings upon Orthodox Russia, even to the far corners of the *tsarstvo*? Their primary concern, as manifested in the Moscow Church Council of 1667, was to distinguish between dead bodies that were saints and dead bodies that were vampires.

But by the time of the Spiritual Regulation of 1721, Russian Orthodox hierarchs no longer worried about letting vampires slip into the ranks of saints. Instead, inspired by their Western-style educations and their fears of Old Belief, they worried about the proliferation of unregulated cults. Most of all, they valued evidence of official approval by their eminent predecessors. The cults whose sponsors could produce such documentation ultimately withstood the Synod's scrutiny, while those who had continued to depend exclusively on local support and oral tradition did not. However, the criteria Synod authorities enunciated as determinants of sanctity were not all that different from those used by the local population to identify the new saint in the first place: the testimony of miracles and the incorruptibility of the relics. But worried about the gullibility and venality of laypeople and village clergy, eighteenth-century hierarchs denied the veracity of their testimony, not trusting them to distinguish between genuine relics and ordinary bones, between miracles and ordinary occurrences. They preferred physical evidence of the bodies themselves, even though in reality it, too, was ambiguous at best; "incorruptibility" lay, like miracles, in the desire of the beholder.

5

PROTECTORS OF WOMEN AND THE LOWER ORDERS

Constructing Sainthood
in Modern Russia

NADIESZDA KIZENKO

Saints and their cults offer a useful forum for measuring lived Orthodox Christianity. They also, however, show one of the potential pitfalls in suggesting the existence of a "popular," as opposed to "official," Orthodoxy. After all, saints' cults can be (and indeed often were) initiated by the church hierarchy; and however fervent the devotion of the laity to certain holy figures, it is the church hierarchy that ultimately decides whether to enshrine individuals for permanent veneration.

Nevertheless, for all of the caveats that have been made about attempting to draw too extreme a distinction between "official" and "popular," or more recently—and better—"prescriptive" and "lived," saints' cults remain one of the most fruitful ways of observing the interaction between the devotion of the laity and the lower clergy and its acceptance—or lack thereof—by the hierarchy.[1] What makes laypeople regard one of their number (dead or alive) as holy, and to what extent has the hierarchy shared these standards? What forms does the veneration take? Do laypeople actively seek official recognition from their hierarchs—that is, how important is it for them to have their heroes canonized? Finally, once a holy person is canonized, which aspects of his or her life does the hierarchy emphasize? While these questions are relevant

---

1. For terminology, see the discussion in Ellen Badone, ed., *Religious Orthodoxy and Popular Faith in European Society* (Princeton: Princeton University Press, 1990), ii–x, and Michael Carroll, *Veiled Threats: The Logic of Popular Catholicism in Italy* (Baltimore: Johns Hopkins University Press, 1996), 5–6. For the negotiations surrounding sanctity in earlier periods, see Aviad M. Kleinberg, *Prophets in Their Own Country: Living Saints and the Making of Sainthood in the Later Middle Ages* (Chicago: University of Chicago Press, 1992), 1–8.

to Kievan, Muscovite, and imperial periods alike, they acquire a particular importance in the late imperial period, when the amount of documentation increases and when the new elements of the mass media and publicity enter the process of saint-making. Russian saints of the late imperial period, even as they share many issues with their predecessors, also reflect concerns—such as national resonance, consumerism and promotion, the invention of tradition, and a paradoxical relationship with the present—that seem peculiarly modern.[2] The cults of two saints from St. Petersburg shed new light on the issues of "lived" versus "prescriptive" and whether modernity is a useful category for discussing sanctity.

At first glance, the Blessed Kseniia of St. Petersburg and Father Ioann of Kronstadt are indeed as different as can be. One was a woman and a holy fool, an eighteenth-century contemporary of Peter I and Elizabeth. The other was an ordained clergyman whose life spanned the late nineteenth and early twentieth centuries. One seems to have been virtually unknown during her lifetime, with documentation outside oral tradition appearing only a half-century after her death. The other was the focus of a publicity machine, described during his lifetime as being "the most popular man in Russia." These differences alone would seem to make them two extremes appropriate for analyzing the wide range of sanctity in imperial Russia. However, Blessed Kseniia and Father Ioann share illuminating traits as well. Both were associated with women, the lower classes—and the imperial family. In both cases, while the impetus to canonize was already strong in the last years of the Romanov dynasty,[3] the saint was only canonized in the emigration in the 1960s–70s and in Russia in the millennial wave of 1988. Finally, the initiative for these canonizations came largely from the laity, with lay devotion to the saints persisting even during the most hostile atmosphere of the Soviet period.

In this chapter I will examine the circumstances surrounding the cults of Kseniia of St. Petersburg and Father Ioann of Kronstadt to venture some propositions concerning the veneration of saints in late imperial Russia.

2. I share Yanni Kotsonis's notions of modernity as a paradox and of Russia as part of the European continuum. See David L. Hoffmann and Yanni Kotsonis, eds., *Russian Modernity: Politics, Knowledge, Practices* (New York: St. Martin's Press, 2000), 1–13. My use of modernity, however, has more to do with the concept as specifically applied to religion. See Nadieszda Kizenko, *A Prodigal Saint: Father John of Kronstadt and the Russian People* (University Park: Pennsylvania State University Press, 2000), 3, 281–85.

3. Nicholas II actively promoted several canonizations. See the discussions in Robert L. Nichols, "The Friends of God: Nicholas II and Alexandra at the Canonization of Serafim of Sarov, July 1903," in *Religious and Secular Forces in Late Tsarist Russia: Essays in Honor of Donald W. Treadgold*, ed. Charles E. Timberlake (Seattle: University of Washington Press, 1992), 206–29; Lev Lebedev, "Ot Tsarstva zemnogo—k Tsarstvu Nebesnomu," *Russkii Pastyr'*, no. 17–18 (1993–94): 16–17; and Gregory L. Freeze, "Subversive Piety: Religion and the Political Crisis in Late Imperial Russia," *Journal of Modern History* 68 (1996): 308–50.

Because both saints were from the same geographical area and because their cults spanned the late imperial, Soviet, and post-Soviet periods, they also provide useful comparisons for studying lived Orthodoxy in different circumstances. It is not always possible to compare some forms of religious observance, such as participation in the sacraments, across changes in political regime and, hence, in the varying contexts of official support or dissuasion. Saints' cults are one of the few forms in which it is possible to do so. By studying two such cults from the same geographical area, but from a range of political and ecclesiastical contexts, I consider to what extent saints' cults are suited to adapting and expressing lived Orthodoxy to a wide range of circumstances—and what, if anything, sets apart the "modern" Russian saint from those of earlier times.

In many ways, Blessed Kseniia is more typical of a saint of the Muscovite or Kievan period than the imperial one. She was a fool for Christ, and the *only* holy fool to be canonized as such after the seventeenth century.[4] As with many earlier saints, no contemporary documentation of her life survives, so that neither the date of her birth nor that of her death is certain. The earliest written reference to her, a chatty litterateur's guide to St. Petersburg published in 1845, describes Kseniia as "Aksin'ia," the bereaved widow of a man named Andrei Petrovich. When Andrei died, his wife went insane, believing that she was now her husband. She responded only to his name and wore only his clothing. People flocked to look at this curious sight and as a result the street on which she lived was named "Andrei Petrov Street."[5]

---

4. A "fool for Christ" or a "holy fool" in the Orthodox tradition was someone who pretended to be feeble-minded with the aim of being mocked by others and attaining greater humility. See the discussion of the holy fools Ioann the Hairy (of Rostov) and Andrei of Tot'ma in E. Golubinskii, *Istoriia kanonizatsii sviatykh v russkoi tserkvi,* 2d ed. (Moscow: Universitetskaia tipografiia, 1903), 156, 159. During the Synodal, or imperial, period, canonizations focused on figures of authority who might be construed as supporting the autocracy (Metropolitan Dimitrii of Rostov, canonized 1757; Bishop Innokentii of Irkutsk, 1804; Bishop Mitrofan of Voronezh, 1804; Bishop Tikhon of Voronezh, 1861; Archbishop Feodosii [Uglitskii] of Chernigov, 1896; Serafim of Sarov, 1903; Anna Kashinskaia, 1909; Bishop Ioasaf of Belgorod, 1911; Patriarch Germogen, 1913; Bishop Pitirim of Tambov, 1914; and Metropolitan Ioann [Maksimovich] of Tobol'sk, 1916. Metropolitan Ioasif of Astrakhan and Bishop Sofronii, both canonized in 1918, also belong to this period for all practical purposes). See the discussion in Golubinskii, *Istoriia kanonizatsii,* 169–201, and N. S. Gordienko, *Novye pravoslavnye sviatye* (Kiev: "Ukraina," 1991), 261. For the general paucity of women as holy fools, see Alice-Mary Talbot, ed., *Holy Women of Byzantium: Ten Saints' Lives in English Translation* (Washington, D.C.: Dumbarton Oaks, 1996), x–xv. Although the Moscow patriarchate's 1967 Festal Menaion includes Domna, the holy fool and eldress of Tomsk (d. 1872) in its list, I have not found any record of her being canonized for "all-church" veneration. See the discussion in Aleksandr Trofimov, *Sviatye zheny Rusi* (Moscow: n.p., 1993), 5–9, 229–31.

5. E. Grebenko, "Peterburgskaia storona," in *Fiziologiia Peterburga, sostavlennaia iz trudov russkikh literatorov,* part 1 (St. Petersburg: Izdatel'stvo A. Ivanova, 1845), 219–21.

FIG. 8   Earliest known depiction of Kseniia. 1845. A satirical sketch reflecting the author's skeptical viewpoint. Illustration reproduced from E. Grebenko, "Peterburgskaia storona," in *Fiziologiia Peterburga, sostavlennaia iz trudov russkikh literatorov,* part 1 (St. Petersburg: Izd. A. Ivanova, 1845), 220. Courtesy of N. Kizenko.

    What would become the prototypical motifs of Kseniia's life—a young widow who seems to become unhinged after her husband's death and assumes his identity, becoming a local curiosity—are thus present from the start. Most important, the account appears in a decidedly nonreligious publication, and is recounted in an amused and worldly tone. The illustration of Kseniia that accompanies the brief account is a satirical sketch, showing a robust merchant woman in a cutaway (fig. 8). An account published soon afterward modifies the names and adds many new details, but the essential outline remains discernible:

Forty, or perhaps a bit more, years ago, here in Petersburg died Kseniia Grigor'ievna, known in her day as Andrei Fedorovich, the wife of the court singer Andrei Fedorovich. Having many acquaintances, mostly from the merchant estate, she often came to them for charity and took nothing other than "the tsar on the steed": that is how she referred to the old coins which had a depiction of a rider on a horse. . . . Some called her "insane," others "leprous" or "a holy fool," a third group as a "foreteller," because she predicted good or bad fortune to the house she entered, although she uttered her predictions only rarely and reluctantly. At nights she would go off in the fields to pray to God for several hours on end, bowing on the ground in all four directions. Her nocturnal departures at first prompted misgivings in mistrustful people and the police even began to keep track of her, but soon confirmed that she was indeed going to the fields and praying.[6]

Thus, Kseniia made her first written appearances in publications that were as far as possible from being church organs, and were not linked with either the clerical or social aristocracy. (Indeed, the *Vedomosti St. Peterburgskoi gorodskoi politsii* [St. Petersburg Police Gazette] declared huffily that it catered to the *mass* public, and deliberately distanced itself from the intellectual elite.)[7] It is telling that both book and article included her in a collection of local-color "types," ranging from a couple known as "the two hoots" to a man who thought he was the prince of Cabardinia, and declared frankly that "such legends might serve as material for novelists, fiction-writers, and playwrights."[8] I dwell on the provenance because, in the absence of other sources, it might be too easy to dismiss Kseniia as being the creation of journalists looking for good copy. This is especially so because of her remarkable resemblance in later accounts to perhaps the most famous literary holy fool—Pushkin's Nikolka in *Boris Godunov,* down to being abused by boys and weeping over a dead tsarevich.[9]

Nevertheless, Kseniia did exist.[10] The first explicitly religious, and the first

6. "Chast' Neofitsial'naia. Fel'eton Politseiskoi Gazety," *Vedomosti St.-Peterburgskoi gorodskoi politisii,* December 2, 1847, pp. 1–2.

7. Letter from the editor in *Vedomosti St.-Peterburgskoi gorodskoi politisii,* February 13, 1847, p. 1.

8. *Vedomosti St.-Peterburgskoi gorodskoi politisii,* December 2, 1847, p. 1.

9. A. S. Pushkin, "Boris Godunov," in *Polnoe Sobranie Sochinenii v Desiati Tomakh* (Leningrad: "Nauka," 1978), 5:259–60.

10. Records from her parish church—that of Apostle Matthew in the Peterburgskaia storona district—in Tsentral'nyi Gosudarstvennyi Istoricheskii Arkhiv Sankt-Peterburga (henceforth TsGIA SPb), along

apparently factual, identity for Kseniia came ten days after the *Police Gazette* article appeared in letters to the editor. Someone whose grandparents had known Kseniia and told him about her wrote in with many new details, including examples of Kseniia's prescience and her abuse at the hands of street urchins.[11] Thus, what began as chance urbane references to a local oddity seems to have served as the catalyst for publicizing what had been a local tradition connected to Kseniia. This oral tradition and the relatively late appearance of written sources makes her cult resemble those of earlier saints.[12]

The first straws in the wind were followed by others. By the first decade of the twentieth century, several full-length accounts of Kseniia's life had been published, alongside numerous references to her in historical and statistical guides to St. Petersburg.[13] The key additional details were some contemporary and many posthumous miracles reportedly performed by her, dealing almost exclusively with predictions, help with finding a position, and healing. With the exception of the healing miracles, of which more will be said later, three aspects of Kseniia's wonder-working leap out: the homely nature of her prescience, her material help, and the emphasis placed on her being a saint of the common people, especially of women. With the recent scholarly emphasis on the feminization of piety in the nineteenth and twentieth centuries, the latter may not seem remarkable.[14] In the context of nineteenth- and

---

with most *fondy*, were unavailable for consultation in the summer of 1999. A document confirming the untimely death of one Andrei Petrov on February 23, 1724, in TsGIA SPb, *f.* 19, *op.* 1, *d.* 489, *l.* 2, seems too early, given the other information available on Kseniia. See the discussion on the authenticity of the street name and its connection to the historical Kseniia in A. Bovkalo, "Ul. Andreia Petrova," *Vechernii Leningrad,* March 27, 1989, p. 2.

11. Ivan B-r-l-ieev, "Iz pisem k redaktoru," *Vedomosti St.-Peterburgskoi gorodskoi politisii,* December 12, 1847, p. 1.

12. See the discussion in Golubinskii, *Istoriia kanonizatsii,* 40–169, on saints canonized from the Christianization of Russia until the establishment of the Holy Synod.

13. In chronological order: S. I. Opatovich, "Smolenskoe kladbishche v S.-Peterburge," *Russkaia Starina,* vol. 8 (St. Petersburg: Tipografiia V. S. Balasheva, 1873), 194–96; *Istoriko-statisticheskiia sviedieniia o S.-Peterburgskoi Eparkhii,* 4th ed. (St. Petersburg: Tipografiia Departamenta Udielov, 1875), 139–40; F. Belorus, *Iurodivyi Andrei Fedorovich ili raba bozhiia Kseniia, pogrebennaia na Smolenskom kladbishche v Peterburge* (St. Petersburg, 1893); D. N. Loman, comp., *Dostoprimechatel'nosti S.-Peterburga. Chtenie dlia naroda s 124 kartinkami* (St. Petersburg: Tipografiia E. A. Evdokimova, 1898), 97–101; A. Smirnova, *Raba bozhiia Kseniia* (St. Petersburg, 1901); E. Poselianin, "Blazhennaia Kseniia," in *Russkaia tser'kov russkie podvizhniki 18-go veka* (St. Petersburg: Izdatel'stvo I. L. Tuzova, 1905), 292–97; E. Rakhmanin, *Raba bozhiia Kseniia* (St. Petersburg, 1909).

14. See, most notably, Barbara Corrado Pope, "'Immaculate and Powerful': The Marian Revival in the Nineteenth Century," in *Immaculate and Powerful: The Female Sacred Image and Social Reality,* ed. Clarissa W. Atkinson et al. (Boston: Beacon Press, 1985), 55–79; Ann Douglas, *The Feminization of American Culture* (New York: Knopf, 1977), 6–10; and David Blackbourn, *Marpingen: Apparitions of the Virgin Mary in a Nineteenth-Century German Village* (New York: Vintage Books, 1995), 7–41.

twentieth-century Russian canonizations, however, Kseniia is the only non-martyred, nonroyal woman, the only one who lived during the imperial period, and the only one who is emphasized as being particularly beloved by lower-class women. Her miracles are similarly virtually unique for the late imperial period in targeting lower- and middle-class women. Now, Kseniia was not the only well-known female holy fool of the imperial period (Pelageia, Paraskeva, and Mariia Ivanovna of Diveevo were also celebrated), and Father Ioann of Kronstadt also came to be associated with women and the lower classes (although not necessarily lower-class women).[15] But Kseniia was the only female holy fool to be canonized within Russia in the imperial and post-Soviet periods, and thus is of interest not only for what she reveals about non-elite female conceptions of the holy, but also for being the sole example of the acceptance and validation of this mentality in modern Russian hagiography.

Consider, for example, the examples of prescience that she is credited with during her lifetime. When Evdokiia Denis'evna Gaidukova once apologized for serving Kseniia a meager lunch, Kseniia reminded her tartly of the conspicuously absent roast duck she was saving in her oven for her "horse's head" of a husband. The frequent repetition of this incident and its variations suggests the well-founded suspicion of the poor that they were fobbed off with pieties and rarely given the best. On an another occasion, Kseniia told a lonely acquaintance that she could become a mother if she went to a certain intersection: the friend set off, and ended up adopting the baby born as the result of a pregnant woman's being crushed to death by a cabdriver (the incident occurred just as Kseniia was giving her instructions). In an analogous incident, Kseniia told a seventeen-year-old girl to stop drinking coffee with her parents and to rush to a cemetery where her husband "was burying his wife." (The bewildered girl later married the disconsolate widower.) As is characteristic for miracles involving holy fools, there is nothing supernatural about these incidents; they simply serve either to puncture the pride of the targets or to arrange their "family happiness," which take the form of either husbands or children.[16]

Although assiduous researchers would uncover miracles pertaining to such elite men as the courtiers of Paul I,[17] in publications from the second half of

15. Sviashch. Ioann Kovalevskii, comp., *Iurodstvo o Khriste i Khrista radi iurodivye vostochnoi i russkoi tserkvi*, 3d ed. (Moscow: Izdatel'stvo Stupina, 1902), 148–54, 289–370; A. N. Strizhev, comp., *Diveevskie predaniia* (Moscow, 1996), 48–52, 68–75.

16. G. V. Novoselova, comp., *Raba bozhiia blazhennaia Kseniia* (Shanghai, 1948; reprint, Jordanville, N.Y.: St. Job of Pochaev, 1964; London, Ont., 1986; St. Petersburg: n. p., [1990?]), 9–11.

17. See Dumashev's June 15, 1797, letter to Paul describing Kseniia's prediction of his imperial generosity, quoted in "Iz Peterburgskikh Predanii," *Peterburgskii listok*, September 28 / October 10, 1897, p. 5.

the nineteenth century, Kseniia is mostly the patron of lower-class women, who figure prominently as tellers of miracle stories which emphasize her assistance with finding work and healing. Typical of her miracles is the one titled, "The healing of a peasant woman, Tat'iana Prokopieva Ivanova from Gzhatsk uezd, Smolensk guberniia, from a toothache."[18] By the beginning of the twentieth century, another element entered: educated people adopted Kseniia as an example of explicitly popular faith, in contrast to their own "arid" beliefs. In other words, Kseniia was one of several examples in the late nineteenth century of the pious elite's acknowledging forms of popular devotion as "authentic." Accounts by educated people of Kseniia's healing miracles are full of such phrases as:

> So *this* is the popular remedy which one must never forget and which I always recommend to everyone. This is precisely the only remedy which has strengthened and made the Russian Orthodox people, to the amazement of the whole world, a mighty giant, a fabled warrior. If it were not for this remedy, if it were not for this deep, heartfelt, and at the same time simple faith of the Russian people in the Lord God and his holy intercessors, God knows what they would turn into![19]

This emphasis on *popular* faith is all the more striking given that, by the early twentieth century, many of the actual recipients of Kseniia's intercession seem to be middle-class at the very least. The daughter of a woman of "very good family" is saved from marrying a convict disguised as a colonel. Sons are finally admitted into elite military schools. A husband who abandons his wife without her share of his pension is tracked down and forced to pay up.[20] But these signs of supra-classness are only apparent. In all cases, the key to accessing Kseniia turns out to be some representative of the people who shows the well-born beneficiary the way, and who is initially reluctant to share his or her faith for fear of being laughed at or ridiculed. In a 1906 account, the illiterate nanny of a sick three-year-old, for example, tells the child's wealthy parents:

For details of his being granted three hundred desiatinas, see Rossiiskii Gosudarstvennyi Istoricheskii Arkhiv, *f.* 1374, *op.* 1, *d.* 394, *l.* 58.

18. Novoselova, *Raba bozhiia blazhennaia Kseniia*, 38. More than two-thirds of the book (pp. 20–78) consists of stories of posthumous miracles.

19. Ibid., 35.

20. Ibid., 20–24, 41–44.

I wanted to ask you many times to let me go to Kseniia's grave [to pray], but I kept fearing to do so, *I thought you would laugh at me or scold me.* Then, when the young lady almost died, I couldn't bear it any longer and thought, "Let them laugh, let them scold me, but I'll still go, I'll still ask to go to Kseniushka's grave, and even if they don't let me, I'll sneak off somehow. . . . When I got there, there were a lot of people praying. . . . I kept crying and saying over and over again, "Lord, save, Kseniushka, help"; I couldn't think of anything else to say, because *I am stupid, uneducated, and don't know how to pray.*[21]

The nanny also brought home some ground from Kseniia's grave and some oil from a votive lamp at her chapel to put under her young charge's pillow and rub onto her sick ear, respectively. As her employers report, "We marveled at the *simple, artless* faith of our nanny, but there it was: Olechka had gotten better; faith could indeed move mountains."[22] This is far from being the only such incident: a close reading of Kseniia's miracles shows that in many cases, they seem expressly intended to validate forms of piety that are lower-class, or women's, or both. Lieutenant-Colonel Vladimir Ivanovich Nikol'skii's legs are healed, for example, because he does not hire a cab to take him to the Smolenskoe cemetery, but insists on covering most of the route on foot—a typical faithful, and especially peasant, pilgrimage preference.[23] When a ne'er-do-well draftsman and his female companion dare to laugh at his mother's decorating her picture of Kseniia with flowers she knits in wool of different colors (a uniquely feminine pious practice), they both lose their jobs and cannot find work for five years. The mother, on the other hand, continues to pray to Kseniia to "enlighten" her perishing son. Only when the son realizes the error of his ways and asks his mother whether he may visit Kseniia's grave with her does his luck change: within days, he is hired by a railway that had rejected his earlier applications.[24]

Kseniia's cult did not only favor certain devotional practices. Such material objects as earth from her grave, oil from her votive lamps, prayer-belts, brochures, and pictures blessed at her grave also figure prominently in both healings and job-seekings. In another statement of popular piety supposedly triumphing over the intellect in the long term, an early-twentieth-century commemorative brochure pointed out that plenty of famous people had been

21. Ibid., 33–34.
22. Ibid., 34; emphases original.
23. Ibid., 37. M. M. Gromyko, *Mir russkoi derevni* (Moscow: Molodaia gvardiia, 1991), 86–89.
24. Novoselova, *Raba bozhiia blazhennaia Kseniia*, 26.

buried in the Smolenskoe cemetery since Kseniia's day, "but how many of them remain well known today?"

This last is key. Who is the target audience here? I would suggest that both the actual and hoped-for devotees are neither peasants from the provinces nor the cosmopolitan elite, but the many recent arrivals from the village to the capital district, who were, as Barbara Alpern Engel puts it, between the fields and the city.[25] Because they were the fastest-growing part of the population and still held many traditional beliefs, it was vitally important for the church not only to maintain their piety in the face of urban distractions, but to do so in a way appropriate to their circumstances.[26] As a local holy figure who specialized in finding work and success in private life and deriding the snobbery of the well-to-do, Kseniia was an ideal focus. A clear indication of the mentality of the intended readers in the cemetery brochure is that the obscurity of the once-celebrated is not the most damning indictment; the fact of their graves' being either neglected or even lost—something that still resonated for pious Russians—is.[27]

The aspect of validating lower-class piety appears even more strongly in the late-nineteenth- and early-twentieth-century Kseniia accounts which refer to priests' serving constant memorial services at her chapel and giving their blessing to people's bringing home oil and soil. That is, despite clerical skepticism at "unverifiable" miracles,[28] there was nonetheless active official encouragement of this cult which had originated among the laity. After the initial impetus to publish Kseniia recollections, it emerged that people had been visiting Kseniia's grave since the 1820s, taking dirt from it to use in prayers over the sick. As the mound of earth kept having to be replaced, the cemetery management placed a stone slab on top to stave off the pious "grave-pickers"—but this, too, was broken into pieces and brought home by her devotees; the same happened with the second slab. Finally, the cemetery built a fence around the grave and attached a mug for donations to build a chapel, with a memorial plaque stating that Kseniia had been widowed at twenty-six and had lived another forty-five years afterward (but with no mention of either the date of birth or of death). One priest expressed the

25. Barbara Alpern Engel, *Between the Fields and the City: Women, Work, and Family in Russia, 1861–1914* (Cambridge: Cambridge University Press, 1994).

26. See the discussion in Gregory L. Freeze, "'Going to the Intelligentsia': The Church and Its Urban Mission in Post-Reform Russia," in *Between Tsar and People: Educated Society and the Quest for Public Identity in Late Imperial Russia*, ed. Edith W. Clowes, Samuel D. Kassow, and James L. West (Princeton: Princeton University Press, 1991), 215–32.

27. Novoselova, *Raba bozhiia blazhennaia Kseniia*, 76–77.

28. See Opatovich, "Smolenskoe kladbishche," 194–95.

opinion that no one, except perhaps the soon-to-be canonized Serafim of Sarov, had as many *panikhidas* (memorial masses) served in his memory as did Kseniia—suggesting that this form of veneration was already widespread and institutionalized. By 1902, Kseniia's reputation was so well established that devotees could build a new, expensive chapel with a marble iconostasis over her grave and could pay for priests to serve there regularly. Thus, long before official canonization, Kseniia's cult had already been acknowledged and partly appropriated by the local clergy. Publications deliberately pairing her life with the vita of St. Vasilii the Blessed, the fifteenth-century holy fool, only underscored this process of enshrining her within the "official" structure of the Orthodox Church.[29]

The other distinguishing feature of miracles connected with Kseniia is the emphasis placed on jobs, for women and men, married and unmarried, parents and children alike. This feature appears only from the 1880s onward and continues to the present day. It, too, expresses the mentality of Kseniia's modern devotees: the qualities people valued in the saints from the late imperial period reflect their temporal concerns in life. Lack of control felt over one's destiny, competition for good jobs, the difficulty of finding a suitable companion when prospective spouses' family backgrounds were a mystery—all of these realities explain why job- and school-placement miracles became standard features of modern saints' intercessions.

A similar emphasis on women, the lower classes, and practical help characterized the life of Father Ioann of Kronstadt (1829–1908). Because his life is thoroughly documented, he is much easier to connect to his time than is Kseniia. Just at the point when he was ordained in 1855, both state and church authorities embarked on the "Great Reforms" that sought to address people's concerns and to engage them more directly in society. Father Ioann was part of this tendency outward, becoming involved in giving to the poor, creating shelters, employment programs, and participating in the temperance movement.[30] He displays the same catering to people's needs that we can see in Kseniia's cult, with the obvious difference that during their respective periods of greatest fame, she was dead and he was alive; he could be approached in person and through the charities he founded; by the turn of the twentieth century, contact with Kseniia could be had only through prayer and her grave.

---

29. *Khrista radi iurodivaia raba Bozhiia Kseniia, pogrebennaia na Smolenskom kladbishchie, v S.-Peterburgie i zhitie sv. Khrista radi iurodivago Vasiliia Blazhennago i drugikh svv.* (St. Petersburg: Izdatel'stvo A. A. Kholmushina, 1904), 3–94.

30. Adele Lindenmeyr, *Poverty Is Not a Vice: Charity, Society, and the State in Imperial Russia* (Princeton: Princeton University Press, 1996), 170–74.

People initially sought him out, in fact, with no thoughts of sanctity: he was simply an extraordinarily kind and generous priest whom one could count on for help. And, as with Kseniia, his cult has its origins in people telling their friends of the help they had received from him.[31]

Father Ioann quickly went beyond these practical measures, however. Liturgical life was as central for him as material service to others. He celebrated ecstatically, weeping, shouting, and falling to the floor during the service. He exhorted the faithful to approach the chalice, changing the pattern of infrequency that had characterized Russian communion. He succeeded so well that the authorities even allowed him to introduce mass public confessions.[32]

But Christian virtue alone does not a saint make. The practical help that Father Ioann provided, significant though it was, paled next to the quality that seemed to attest to help from above: the ability to heal.[33] At first, Father Ioann's reputation was local. As with Kseniia, fame came through the help of the press. In 1883, the newspaper *Novoe Vremia* (*New Time*) ran an open letter from grateful recipients testifying to their healing at his hands. This brought him international renown and established Kronstadt as one of the leading pilgrimage sites in Russia. People came by the shipload; those who could not inundated the post office with their pleas. He became the first modern Russian religious celebrity, with his image on souvenir scarves, mugs, placards, and postcards; in effect, all of Russia was his parish. In 1894, when he was asked to minister to the dying emperor Alexander III, his fame became international, attracting correspondents from Europe and the United States. Such publicists as Vasilii Rozanov and Mikhail Menshikov called him a saint; such writers as Nikolai Leskov satirized him. His successful combination of social service, liturgical revival, charismatic prayer, and healing seemed to embody the answer of the Orthodox Church to the challenges of secularism, urbanism, and sectarian movements.[34]

In his person, Father Ioann combined two religious types which had hitherto been distinct: that of priest and that of the prophet or holy man, or institutionalized as opposed to personal charisma. As the thousands of letters

31. Compare to the experiences of the devotees in Robert A. Orsi, *Thank You, St. Jude: Women's Devotion to the Patron Saint of Hopeless Causes* (New Haven: Yale University Press, 1996), 70–141.

32. See Karl Felmy, "Liturgicheskoe bogoslovie sv. Ioanna Kronshtadtskogo," *Stranitsy: Bogoslovie, kul'tura, obrazovanie* (The Journal of St. Andrew's Biblical Theological College) 3, no. 1 (1998): 61–73.

33. See Golubinskii, *Istoriia kanonizatsii*, 11–15, on healing as the key criterion of Russian sanctity.

34. Vasilii Rozanov, "Russkoe sektantstvo, kak 3 kolorita russkoi tserkovnosti," *Novoe Vremia*, August 30 / September 12, 1905, p. 4; M. O. Menshikov, "Pamiati sviatago pastyria," in *Ioann Kronshtadtskii*, comp. V. A. Desiatnikov (Moscow: Izdatel'stvo "Patriot," 1992), 360–61; Nikolai Leskov, "Polunoshchniki: peizazh i zhanr," *Vestnik Evropy*, 1891, no. 11–12:92–137, 537–76.

to him show, the root of his popular appeal was precisely his being able to provide *both* the immediacy of personal charisma *and* the sanction, and hence services, of legitimate authority.[35] With both priestly office and personal charisma, Father Ioann was the first example in Russia of a phenomenon that has become characteristic of the modern period. It has been increasingly the priest as often as the monk or pious layperson who both captures the religious imagination and speaks as one having authority, in Roman Catholicism as well as Orthodox Christianity.[36]

As with Kseniia, representations of Father Ioann written after his death added several new elements, with his eventual canonization in mind.[37] The first is a shift from the earlier stress on Father Ioann's "supra-classness" to his being labeled a man of the common people. Lieutenant-General David A. Ozerov wrote in 1912 of a visit Father Ioann had made to Terioki during the 1904–5 war with Japan, for example:

> I am standing next to the Batiushka, our own Father Ioann, I am looking at the crowd near the porch—and it seems to me that all of our Rus' is here, our holy, exhausted, simple, own Rus': *ignorant* little peasants, worn-out little soldiers, nuns who are *none too swift*, and above all them Father Ioann, whose fervent and unwavering faith consoles and heartens everyone—*simply, artlessly, without discourses and intellectualizing*—in the old, Russian, ancient, biblical way.[38]

The second shifting of representations after Father Ioann's death is a greater emphasis on his women followers, which was—as were similar emphases on the feminine in France and the United States—mostly negative.[39] Aleksei Makushinskii, a boy soprano at St. Andrew's from 1891 to 1904, recalled later that "it was mostly women who completely lost their reason

35. Letters to Father Ioann are in TsGIA SPb, *f.* 2219, *op.* 1, *dd.* 1–72 (Ioann Sergiev [Kronshtadtskii], 1856–1908).

36. For the role of the priest in Roman Catholicism, see Philippe Boutry and Michel Cinquin, *Deux Pèlerinages au XIXe Siècle, Ars et Paray-le-Monial*, Bibliotheque Beauchesne 8 (Paris: Editions Beauchesne, 1980), and Gustavo Gutiérrez, *A Theology of Liberation: History, Politics, and Salvation* (Maryknoll, N.Y.: Orbis, 1973).

37. S. L. Firsov, ed., *Sviatoi Ioann Kronshtadtskii v vospominaniiakh sovremennikov* (Moscow: Pravoslavnyi Sviato-Tikhonovskii Bogoslovskii Institut, Bratstvo vo Imia Vsemilostivogo Spasa, 1994), consists of some of these memoirs.

38. Ibid., 61. Emphases are the author's. *Muzhichki* and *soldatiki* in the original.

39. See Pope, "Immaculate and Powerful," 174–76, and Douglas, *Feminization of American Culture*, 6–13.

[when they learned that Father Ioann's carriage would pass], flinging themselves under the hooves of his horse with the words, 'Praise the Lord, I have suffered for Christ!'"[40] Similarly, a priest spoke of Father Ioann's "tearing himself out of the grip of his overly excited admirers and—especially—admiresses [*pochitatel'nits*]."[41] Given that these writers wished to record their *favorable* impressions of Father Ioann, it is striking that they emphasize the lower-class background, "ignorance," and femininity of his audience—particularly when, while he was alive, visitors to Kronstadt took pains to record the variety of ages, social backgrounds, and gender mix. Other eulogists turned this emphasis on women expressly to Father Ioann's advantage. The deaths of Dostoyevsky, Tchaikovsky, and Mendeleev only resonated in the cultured part of the population, "not penetrating to the popular depths at all," they wrote; the deaths of such military leaders as Suvorov or Skobelev were felt more broadly, "but their names are almost alien to the feminine half of the population." It was only "holy" Father Ioann who managed to capture the entire popular imagination, "and all the love of the more loving half of the nation—women." By capturing women, Father Ioann had symbolically captured the nation's heart.[42]

Material help with school and work, healing, help with alcoholism, appeal to women: are the cults of Kseniia and Father Ioann, then, only another example of the general nineteenth- and early-twentieth-century European triumph of feminine and practical piety under the code words of "emotional" and "direct"? Certainly, these cults show the triumph of the theme of "giving the people what they want"—whether that might be what people wanted from their saints, or canonization by the hierarchy of those who were already meeting the people's needs. And as Gregory Freeze and others have noted, this "kinder, gentler" Orthodoxy was a trend that was well established by the mid-nineteenth century.[43] But the Russian situation has its specificities, and these are largely political.

40. Aleksei Makushinskii, "Vospominanie byvshago pevchago Kronshtadtskago Andreevskago Sobora," in *Piatidesiatilietie prestavleniia prisnopamiatnago otsa Ioanna Kronshtadtskago, iubeleinyi sbornik* (New York: All-Slavic Publishers, 1958), 42.

41. Memoirs of Priest V. Il'inskii, in Firsov, *Sviatoi Ioann,* 113.

42. Prot. P. Al'bitskii, "O. Ioann Kronshtadtskii, kak pastyr' i obshchestvennyi deiatel'," *Pastyrskii venok dorogomu batiushke o. Ioannu Kronshtadtskomu* (St. Petersburg: Graficheskii Inst. Br. Lukshevits, 1911), 92.

43. B. V. Sapunov, "Nekotorye siuzhety russkoi ikonopisi i ikh traktovka v poreformennoe vremia," in *Kul'tura i iskusstvo Rossii XIX veka: novye materialy i issledovaniia: sbornik statei,* ed. G. A. Printseva (Leningrad: Iskusstvo, 1985); Gregory L. Freeze, "Institutionalizing Piety: The Church and Popular Religion, 1750–1850," in *Imperial Russia: New Histories for the Empire,* ed. Jane Burbank and David L. Ransel (Bloomington: Indiana University Press, 1998), esp. 231–35.

In their vitae, both Kseniia and Father Ioann were linked with the ruling house. In Father Ioann's case, the connection was manifest. He was invited to pray over Alexander III on his deathbed, and he was among the clergy to officiate at Nicholas and Alexandra's wedding, their coronation, and the christenings of their children. In the last years of his life, and particularly during the revolution of 1905, he became one of the main spokesmen for church-state symphony and autocracy for Russia and one of the chief symbols of the Orthodox Church's support for monarchy. It is difficult to find another saintly clerical figure more linked to the old regime.[44]

In Kseniia's case, the connection rests entirely on rumor. Nineteenth-century accounts describe her as going around the streets of St. Petersburg the day before Empress Elizabeth's death, shouting, "*Bliny, bliny,* start making *bliny;* tomorrow all of Russia will be cooking *bliny.*"[45] Soon before the murder of Ivan VI in the Schlüsselberg fortress, Kseniia wept profusely and kept repeating, "Blood, blood!"[46] After Kseniia's death, her reputed connection to the dynasty grew even stronger. When the future Alexander III was still the heir to the throne and fell ill, a chamberlain told his wife Mariia Fedorovna that he had himself been healed by sand from Kseniia's grave and asked to put some under the Heir's pillow. Mariia Fedorovna gave her consent, and that night had a vision of a woman in tatters who not only reassured her that Alexander would recover, but that the child she was bearing would be a girl who must be called Kseniia, and who would become the spiritual guardian of the family. Ever after, the empress paid an annual visit to Kseniia's grave in gratitude—and both she and her daughter Kseniia were among the few Romanovs to survive the Revolution, living to ripe old ages.[47]

No other confirmation for these accounts has been found—something especially noteworthy in the last case, which could in principle be documented readily.[48] The question, then, is why later writers felt compelled to make the

44. See Kizenko, *A Prodigal Saint,* chap. 8.

45. *Bliny* are the yeast whole wheat pancakes traditionally served at funerals and during the week before Great Lent. Because of this association, people interpreted Kseniia's reference to *bliny* as correctly predicting the empress's death.

46. Poselianin, *Russkaia tserkov' i Russkie podvizhniki,* 295.

47. Ibid., 197; Novoselova, *Raba bozhiia blazhennaia Kseniia,* 39–40. Interestingly, unofficial post-Soviet accounts also stress this link to the Imperial House; by contrast, the official 1990 vita, in recounting this incident, only says that it occurred to "one A. A. Romanov." See Iuvenalii, metropolitan of Krutitsa and Kolomenskoe, ed., *Kanonizatsiia Sviatykh. Pomestnyi Sobor Russkoi Pravoslavnoi Tserkvi Posviashchennyi Iubeliiu 1000-letiia Kreshcheniia Rusi, Troitse-Sergieva Lavra, 6–9 iiunia 1998 g.* (Moscow: Izdatel'stvo Moskovskogo Patriarkhata, 1988), 114.

48. Mariia Fedorovna's diaries are silent on this point, and the Grand Duchess Xenia does not refer to the incident in her reminiscences.

connection between a vaguely legendary woman holy fool and the rulers of Russia—and why the stories continued to be repeated, finally to be incorporated in Kseniia's vita. Part of the reason may be "naïve monarchism" or a calculated bid for hierarchical sympathy. Another reason may be the traditional subversive function of the holy fool with respect to the ruler (think of Nikolai of Pskov and Vasilii the Blessed standing up to Ivan IV).[49] This only goes so far, however: Kseniia, like Father Ioann, demonstrated her support for the rulers, not denunciation; her subversiveness took the form of inverting traditional gender roles—her cross-dressing, violence, being "strong like a man," hauling rocks, and general abusiveness.

The matter is more complicated. Through a combination of circumstances, by the second half of the nineteenth century, holy people had become linked to the ruling house in a way that they had rarely been since Peter I. From the point of view of lay devotion, this link was clearly less important than Kseniia's and Father Ioann's utilitarian aspect. Nevertheless, it is largely this association with the monarchy that doomed the cults of both Kseniia and Father Ioann during the Soviet period. Both major shrines associated with them—the convent built over Father Ioann's sarcophagus in St. Petersburg and its adjoining chapel and the chapel erected over Kseniia's tomb—were either sealed, or turned to other purposes, or both. Statues of Lenin were placed inside Kseniia's chapel and in the Kronstadt park created where Father Ioann's parish church had stood. Father Ioann and his remaining followers were regularly vilified in such Soviet publications as *Ateist* (*The Atheist*).[50] But—as both saints' chief debunker, Nikolai Gordienko, was forced to admit—popular veneration of the two continued, taking the form of notes crammed through chinks in the holes of the two chapels, in flowers left at their resting-places, and in memorial services held. That is, even when official encouragement was replaced by active hostility, reverence and belief in the potency of the still-uncanonized figures persisted.[51]

Both appeared in visions as well. Father Ioann appeared most often during the traumas of collectivization and civil war. One 1919 account has him miraculously inspire Silaev, a Bolshevik sailor from the cruiser *Almaz* and *kommissar* in the Cheka, to repent and become a leading counterrevolutionary; Father Ioann also appears with Saints Sergii of Radonezh and Serafim of

49. Kovalevskii, *Iurodstvo*, 211–14; 227–35.

50. A. Iurin, "Ioannity," *Bezbozhnik*, February 12, 1939, p. 2.

51. Kovalevskii, *Iurodstvo*, 287; Ioann (Snychev), metropolitan of St. Petersburg and Ladoga, comp. and ed., *Ocherki istorii Sankt-Peterburgskoi Eparkhii* (St. Petersburg: "Andreev i synov'ia," 1994), 91.

Sarov to serve requiems for all those who died without burial.[52] Similarly, Kseniia ("a strangely dressed woman with a staff in her hand") appeared during the Second World War to save two soldiers in a cellar.[53]

Why did the Moscow patriarchate canonize Kseniia and Father Ioann in the high perestroika and religious revival years of 1988 and 1990? Was it only their continued veneration among the populace of St. Petersburg? After all, there were other local cults in Russia; there were more verifiable holy fools; there were other women; there were other priests. But Kseniia and Father Ioann, besides being the foci of St. Petersburg-based cults, also share the distinction of having been first canonized by the Russian Orthodox Church Outside of Russia—he in 1964, she in 1978 (fig. 9).[54] Their recognition by Moscow may have been prompted by a desire for an eventual rapprochement—or one-upmanship—as well as by the acknowledgment of the genuine devotion both saints continued to inspire in St. Petersburg in particular.

The answer lies in a combination of continued veneration and the uses to which Kseniia and Father Ioann have been put. First is the purely geographical aspect. Both have been dubbed "holy patrons of St. Petersburg," along with St. Alexander Nevskii and the apostle Peter.[55] But it is not only a question of saint as *genius loci.* Paradoxically, both Kseniia and Father Ioann are defined as rejecting secularism and rationalism as personified first by Peter I and St. Petersburg, then by the Soviet period. The most modern thing about Kseniia and Father Ioann is their rejection of . . . modernity. Contemporary post-Soviet writers stress the triumph of a "traditional, typically old Russian" kind of piety appearing in a new, Western-style capital and restoring it to

52. See Arkhimandrit Panteleimon, comp., *Zhizn', podvigi, chudesa i prorochestva sv. prav. otsa nashego Ioanna, Kronshtadtskago Chudotvortsa* (Jordanville, N.Y.: Holy Trinity Monastery, 1976), 183–208. Cheka refers to the first name of the Soviet regime's secret police organization, followed by the NKVD and the KGB.

53. Trofimov, *Sviatye zheny rusi*, 160–61. For an interpretation of NEP-era omens and signs, see Lynne Viola, *Peasant Rebels Under Stalin: Collectivization and the Culture of Peasant Resistance* (New York: Oxford University Press, 1996), 53–55.

54. As a result of Bolshevik persecution, a significant number of Russian hierarchs under the leadership of Metropolitan Antonii (Khrapovitskii) of Kiev, pastors, and faithful left Russia in 1920, preferring exile to subjugation by an atheistic state. In the same year, Patriarch Tikhon, the last free primate of the Russian Orthodox Church, issued a decree (Ukaze 362; November 20, 1920) that mandated that the Highest Church Administration in exile should continue to exist until such time as the Russian Church could freely administer itself. The Russian Orthodox Church Outside of Russia is the current heir to the Highest Church Administration in exile.

55. Arkhimandrit Avgustin (Nikitin), *Pravoslavnyi Peterburg v zapiskakh inostrantsev* (St. Petersburg: too "Neva," 1995), 64; the verses on the praises in *Sviatoi pravednyi Ioann, Kronshtadtskii chudotvorets*, 98; Trofimov, *Sviatye zheny rusi*, 159.

FIG. 9   First official icon of Blessed Kseniia, by Archimandrite Kiprian (Pishew). 1978. Courtesy of Holy Trinity Monastery, Jordanville, New York. Note the absence of a man's coat and the addition of a modest headscarf. The saint has become more aged and more ascetic.

Orthodoxy and to Russianness: Kseniia and Father Ioann overturn the misguided attempts to build a "heaven on earth" on the banks of the Neva.[56]

Other antimodern aspects have appeared as well. Kseniia's wandering is identified with the "*typically Russian* sense of feeling oneself to be a stranger on this earth . . . which leads to *inner freedom* and *independence from external authority.*"[57] Her calling herself Andrei (meaning "manly" in Greek), transvestitism, and adopting a male identity in general, which might have prompted official disquiet, has been turned into an edifying parable of the evils of modernity: contemporary hagiographers claim that her spiritual *muzhestvo* (a word meaning literally "manliness" but in a larger sense courage and fortitude) was meant to presage the present time when "women have to do much of what men *ought to* do, in both the spiritual and material sphere." Thus, while they acknowledge that many women in Russian society work outside the home, are heads of households, and are assuming greater roles within the church, Kseniia's hagiographers do not think this is a good thing.

The rejection of modernity is far more explicit in Father Ioann's case: his antirevolutionary sermons and support for far-right organizations speak for themselves. And in a sense this is precisely the problem. Because of the lack of documentation, Kseniia can be stretched to suit any image; Father Ioann, because of the abundance of documentation, occasionally has to be explained away. While many share his views, the liberal hierarchy does not. In fact, they deliberately minimize his politics and emphasize his help to the needy, his healing of the sick, his attention to alcoholics, and his Russian-ness. In these respects, they try to make his connection to present-day Russia more immediate and more palatable. Similarly, Father Ioann's difficult relation with his wife, with whom he never consummated his marriage, has been similarly sanitized and repackaged as a loving partnership.[58]

What conclusions, then, may we draw from the cults of Blessed Kseniia and Father Ioann of Kronstadt that may help us reach a working definition of modernity in religion? For someone to succeed as a popular modern saint, the amount of verifiable historical information is not key; success in helping people with their daily problems (especially health, love lives, and work) is. Paradoxically, an emphasis on immediate emotional support and hostility to the "rational" and "enlightened," support of such "irrational," material

56. Ioann (Snychev), *Ocherki istorii*, 91–92, 158.

57. Trofimov, *Sviatye zheny rusi*, 157.

58. See his vita: "Zhitie sv. pravednogo Ioanna, Kronshtadtskogo chudotvortsa," *Zhurnal Moskovskoi Patriarkhii*, 1990, no. 10:58–71.

forms of piety as oil, sand, objects left at the person's grave, and "simple faith" characterize modern piety. In modern Orthodox Christianity, as in modern Roman Catholicism, women are particularly enthusiastic supporters of saints' cults. Support and coverage by the media, followed by several waves of emigration, creates large-scale celebrity and allows modern cults to travel outside their environs and become first national, then international in scope.

Several factors are specific to modern Russia. Downplaying or even active hostility by the reigning hierarchy (in this case, the Moscow patriarchate during the Soviet period) does not affect the persistence of veneration. Outside political factors may affect canonization (in this case, the canonizations by the Russian Orthodox Church Outside of Russia). And at least one element shares characteristics with earlier periods: upon canonization, the saint is recast in an image acceptable to the hierarchy's goals, which may change over time.

One does not want to hazard too many propositions on the basis of only two saints, of course. To gain a fuller picture of lived Orthodoxy through saints' cults in modern Russia, much more research needs to be done on widely venerated figures of the late imperial, Soviet, and post-Soviet periods, whether or not they have been canonized. Particular attention needs to be paid to local figures whose veneration does not spread beyond their environs. Nevertheless, as the only nonmonks, nonmartyrs, and nonprinces (the historical categories of Russian sanctity) canonized in Russia in the twentieth century, Kseniia and Father Ioann deserve attention as the two instances where lived and prescribed, popular and official, "met and embraced," and where forms of piety associated with the lower classes and women were enshrined in canon and liturgy by the Orthodox hierarchy.

PART III

ENCOUNTERING THE SACRED

6

TILL THE END OF TIME

The Apocalypse in
Russian Historical Experience
Before 1500

MICHAEL S. FLIER

> By its very metaphysical nature and its calling in the world, the
> Russian people is a people of the End. The Apocalypse has always
> played a large role, both at our popular level and at the highest
> cultural level among Russian writers and thinkers. In our thinking,
> the eschatological problem occupies an incommensurably greater
> place than it does in Western thinking.
> —*Nikolai Berdiaev (1947)*[1]

> Some scholars hold the view that an eschatological feeling was
> prevalent [in Russia in the late fifteenth century]. We lack,
> however, any convincing witness to the broad dissemination of
> such a feeling. The character of Russian 17th–18th-century spiritual
> life . . . is transposed into the past, and attempts are made to
> discern an eschatological panic or "psychosis" in the 15th century.
> —*Dmitrij Čiževskij (1960)*[2]

Like all good apocalyptic prophecies, the Eastern Orthodox prediction that
the world would come to an end in the late fifteenth century was wrong. The
ominous year 1492—7000 in Byzantine reckoning—came and went without cataclysmic incident: life on earth, and in Muscovite Rus', continued
unabated. Remarkably we find no clear indication of mass hysteria or eschatological panic in this bastion of Orthodoxy immediately before, during, or
after the anticipated End, as Čiževskij correctly points out.

---

1. *Russkaia ideia. Osnovnye problemy russkoi mysli XIX veka i nachala XX veka* (Paris: YMCA Press,
1947; reprinted with new pagination, 1971), 195. Unless otherwise indicated, all translations are mine.

2. *History of Russian Literature from the Eleventh Century to the End of the Baroque*, Slavic Printings and
Reprintings, ed. C. H. van Schooneveld, no. 12 (The Hague: Mouton, 1960), 229.

This is not to say that there was no reaction at all, quite the contrary. Certain representatives of high culture, for example, had something to say about the countdown to the fateful day. But we have no unambiguous evidence documenting popular millenarian agitation, uprisings, or the appearance of messiah figures akin to those experienced in the West for five centuries after the year 1000, and in seventeenth-century Muscovy.[3] Why this was so is an interesting and important issue in and of itself, particularly when considered against Berdiaev's claim that the Apocalypse inflected the lives of all Russians, elite and non-elite alike, from time immemorial.

In this chapter I will include the reaction to 1492 as part of a larger review of evidence gathered to clarify the role of the Apocalypse in Russian historical experience, from the official Christianization of Rus' in 988 through the end of the fifteenth century. I will claim *contra* Berdiaev, that apocalypticism is a relatively late phenomenon in Rus', experienced first and foremost among the elite of church and state from the mid-fourteenth century on. For the early period of East Slavic history, we have no basis for assuming that the largely pagan populace understood the Apocalypse and its implications for a calendrical crisis. Nonetheless, I think it highly unlikely that a popular reaction to apocalypticism appeared only in the seventeenth century, as proposed by Čiževskij. There is evidence that popular awareness had begun to coalesce with elite concern by the late fifteenth century, and merged with it in the sixteenth as optimistic expectation about the destiny of Muscovite Rus' and its people, its "Chosen People" at that. A popular eschatological panic or psychosis suggested by Čiževskij in the seventeenth century did not emerge *ex nihilo* following the Time of Troubles. Rather, the fall of the Rurikid dynasty, civil war, and foreign invasion revealed the vulnerability of the ruling elite and created doubt among significant portions of the people. By now fully attuned to the Apocalypse and its implications, they must have wondered whether the spiritual leadership during these End Times should emanate from the reconfigured Muscovite court and the official church.

For the elite, the watershed experience of 1492 had resulted in the manifestation of an attenuated apocalyptic, millennial mode that shaped the symbolization of state ideology in the late fifteenth and sixteenth centuries. It was expressed in a variety of specific contexts provided by the written word,

3. Norman Cohn, *The Pursuit of the Millennium: Revolutionary Millenarians and Mystical Anarchists of the Middle Ages,* rev. and exp. ed. (New York: Oxford University Press, 1970); Robert O. Crummey, *The Old Believers and the World of Antichrist: The Vyg Community and the Russian State, 1694–1855* (Madison: University of Wisconsin Press, 1970); idem, "Religious Radicalism in Seventeenth-Century Russia: Re-examining the Kapiton Movement," *Forschungen zur osteuropäischen Geschichte* 46 (1992): 171–85.

art, architecture, and ritual, contexts that informed the official presentation of the ruler and his court all the way up to the ascension of Peter the Great at the end of the seventeenth century. This mode was optimistic, chauvinistic, and formalistic, more attuned to the millennial rule of the just preceding the End than the cataclysm itself. Muscovy would fulfill its salvific destiny, but only in a manner pleasing to God, a manner keyed to the expectation of an apparently imminent and terrifying but ultimately positive and rewarding end. I will comment on the popular contribution to the extent that it is manifested in written sources and in linguistic innovation.

I begin by addressing a terminological issue revealed in the epigraphs: the frequently unclear relationship between *eschatology* and *apocalypse,* and their respective derivatives. Christianity is in its very essence an eschatological faith. In counterpoint to the beginning of history, when God created heaven and earth, the followers of Christ set their sights firmly on the end. The broader terms "eschatology" and "eschatological" refer generally to belief concerned with the End of the World.[4] Although this End is often seen as a *terminus*—the End of Time—it may also coincide with the achievement of the goal or telos of historical progression and thus also be understood as *teleological*—the End of History.[5]

Chapters 20 and 21 of the Book of Revelation, for example, declare that the End is preceded by a millennium, during which time Satan is bound in a bottomless pit and Christ rules the world in his Second Coming (*Parousia*) together with his martyrs, restored to life in the First Resurrection.[6] The conclusion of this thousand-year period indicates the approach of the End. Revelation teaches that Satan is released for the final battle between good and evil. He and his followers are devoured by fire sent by God and are cast forever into the lake of fire and brimstone. God sits at the Last Judgment, when all the dead not revived in the First Resurrection are raised in the General Resurrection. Those found to be righteous are granted eternal life; those found wanting are cast into the lake of fire and brimstone, the so-called

4. Cf. Gk. *to eschaton* (the utmost, last, greatest extremity).

5. See Malcolm Bull, "On Making Ends Meet," in *Apocalypse Theory and the End of the World,* ed. Malcolm Bull (Oxford: Basil Blackwell, 1995), 2–3.

6. The words *millennium* and *millennial* "thousand years" and *millenary* "containing one thousand" can both be used metonymically to refer to this thousand-year period of peace and tranquillity, or more generally, to any such period, regardless of its length. Greek counterparts *chiliad* and *chiliastic* are synonymous with *millennium, millenary,* respectively, in their reference to a thousand years, cf. Gk. *chīlias* (thousand) and Lat. *mille* (thousand). See Richard Landes, "Lest the Millennium Be Fulfilled: Apocalyptic Expectations and the Pattern of Western Chronography, 100–800 c.e.," in *The Use and Abuse of Eschatology in the Middle Ages,* ed. Werner Verbeke et al., Mediaevalia Lovaniensia, Series 1, Studia 15 (Leuven: Leuven University Press, 1988), 206.

second death. The onset of the timeless Kingdom of God is represented as a transfigured heaven and earth, without seas and heavenly bodies. The holy city, the New Jerusalem, descends from heaven and serves as the final abode for the righteous favored with eternal life, the telos of human history.

The words *apocalypse, apocalyptic, apocalypticism,* in an eschatological context refer to an End that is imminent,[7] typically preceded by prophecies and signs of a cataclysmic and violent confrontation. This tradition is transmitted through prophetic literature and apocalypses (revelations),[8] which often make use of complex, mystical signs and symbols to set the scene for the inevitable End.[9]

It is useful in considering apocalypticism to recognize the variability of imminence, the need to distinguish *predictive imminence,* with its expression of precise dates and times for the End, from nonpredictive or *psychological imminence,* with no time certain but with life nonetheless "lived under the shadow of the end."[10]

For either kind of imminence, predictive or psychological, Byzantine apocalypticism offered two models for comprehending the period preceding the End.[11] According to the first, the year 6000 would usher in the Second Coming of Christ and a millennium of peace and harmony that would end in 7000 with the Last Judgment (cf. Revelation 20 and 21). According to the second, the year 6000 would mark the beginning of the thousand-year reign of the Antichrist, a period of evil and destruction that would give way in the year 7000 to the Second Coming and the Last Judgment. This latter model,

---

7. Landes, "Lest the Millennium Be Fulfilled," 205–6.

8. Cf. Gk. *apokaluptō* (disclose, uncover), *apokalupsis* (revelation).

9. In Jewish and Christian literature, the nature of the End and its aftermath—the terminus and the kingdom that follows—are conveyed in a number of primary sources. These include the prophetic visions of Daniel, noncanonical apocalypses such as those of Enoch and Paul, the synoptic Gospels (the "Little Apocalypse" in Matthew 24–25, Mark 13, Luke 21), the First and Second Epistles of John with their explicit warnings about Antichrist, and most especially the Revelation of Saint John the Divine with its terrifying imagery, elaborate symbolism and numerology, and its hopeful promise of reward.

10. Bernard McGinn, "The End of the World and the Beginning of Christendom," in Bull, *Apocalypse Theory,* 60. Millenary (chiliastic) measurement has played an especially important role in Jewish and Christian predictive imminence, counting ages as thousand-year increments. The seven days of Creation that begin human history provide the dominant metaphor for organizing the progression of that history toward its inevitable conclusion: the cosmic week of seven millennia (Psalms 90:4, 2 Peter 3:8). The sixth (and last) day of God's work and the seventh day, God's Sabbath, are instantiated in the two most fateful cosmic "days," the millennia preceding years 6000 and 7000, respectively. The turn of the eighth millennium yields the age without time and thus without end, the eternal Kingdom of God. Scriptural tradition, however, has favored nonpredictive imminence: we live in the final age, but it is not for us to know the precise time that it will end (cf. Matthew 24:36, Acts 1:7, 1 Thessalonians 5:1–2).

11. Landes, "Lest the Millennium Be Fulfilled," 138ff.

based on the works of Hippolytus, Kiprianus, Pseudo-Methodius of Patara, and Ephraem the Syrian, was the one that took hold in Rus'.[12]

The complex nature of the written apocalyptic tradition has meant that its interpretation has typically been left to a small clerical or scholarly elite. One of the ways in which the apocalyptic End has been made understandable to a larger community of the faithful has been to link it and its imagery to concrete events of human history.[13] On this view, God's control of historical events implies that the greater the evil perceived in the present, the closer the world is to the End that will punish the wicked and reward the good.[14]

The subjective nature of psychological imminence inclines us to view Christian apocalypticism as a subtype of eschatology, one understood as quantifiably heightened and intensified in spiritual and psychological terms. The eschatological, nonapocalyptic perspective may be contrasted profitably with the more narrowly eschatological, apocalyptic viewpoint: "There is still an important difference between a general consciousness of living in the last age of history and a conviction that the last age itself is about to end, between a belief in the reality of the Antichrist and the certainty of his proximity (or at least of the date of his coming), between viewing the events of one's own time in the light of the End of history and seeing them as the last events themselves."[15]

After the official tenth-century baptism of Rus', expressions of eschatological content were readily apparent in monuments written by representatives of elite culture for their elite audience. In the "Sermon on Law and Grace," traditionally ascribed to the mid-eleventh-century metropolitan Ilarion, for example, there are numerous references to different aspects of the expected End, but they are nonapocalyptic statements about a hopeful future without any sense of impending drama: "And then through his Son, he saved all nations; through the Gospel and baptism he brought them to the renewal of regeneration, to life eternal. . . . The holy Church of Mary, the Holy Mother

12. A. Vasiliev, "Medieval Ideas of the End of the World: West and East," *Byzantion* 16, no. 2 (1942–43 [publ. in 1944]): 497–500; McGinn, "End of the World," 60–63; Landes, "Lest the Millennium Be Fulfilled," 144ff.; George P. Fedotov, *The Russian Religious Mind*, vol. 1, *Kievan Christianity: The Tenth to the Thirteenth Centuries* (Cambridge: Harvard University Press, 1946), 158–75, and vol. 2, *The Middle Ages: The Thirteenth to the Fifteenth Centuries* (Cambridge: Harvard University Press, 1966), 83–86; V. Istrin, *Otkrovenie Mefodiia Patarskogo i apokrificheskie videniia Daniila v vizantiiskoi i slaviano-russkoi literaturakh. Issledovaniia i teksty, ChOIDR*, 1897, bk. 4.

13. Bull, "On Making Ends Meet," 3.

14. McGinn, "End of the World," 60.

15. Cf. Bernard McGinn, *Visions of the End: Apocalyptic Traditions in the Middle Ages*, rev. and exp. ed., Records of Civilization: Sources and Studies, no. 96 (New York: Columbia University Press, 1998), 3–4.

of God [Church of the Tithe in Kiev], which you [Volodimer] built on a foundation of true faith, and where indeed your manly body now lies, awaiting the archangels' trumpets."[16]

In the twelfth century, Kirill of Turov warned about the End in his sermon for the Sunday of the Fathers of the First Ecumenical Council, a week before Pentecost: "Holy men . . . cry out . . . about his Second Coming, when he will come to judge the world and will grant to each according to his deeds."[17] These and similar statements stand as general eschatological clichés rather than apocalyptic predictions of imminent destruction.

One senses a similar rhetorical stance in the Laurentian Chronicle account of the Mongol invasion of Rus'.

> That same year [1223] a nation appeared, about whom no one knows precisely, who they are and where they came from and what their language is and what tribe they are from, and what their faith is. And they are called Tatars, but some say Taurmens and others Pechenegs. Some say that they are the ones to whom Bishop Methodius of Patara attests, that they have come from the desert of Yathrib in the northeast. For thus did Methodius say that at the End Times they would appear. (*Laurentian Chronicle*, s.a. 1223 [MS dated 1377])[18]

Any connection between the Mongols and the onset of the End had been broken by the time of this accounting. Their invasion, reconceived as a consequence of moral collapse in Rus' (they appeared "because of our sins"), was used thereafter by the writers of sermons, chronicles, and miscellaneous didactic works to effect change in social and political behavior among the clergy and the laity, especially the elite. In this particular passage, allusion to the people of the End Times is little more than one of several possible points of reference advanced to help identify the invaders. Similar examples of Orthodox eschatology could be cited from hagiography, for example, the Lives of Andrew the Fool, Avraamii of Smolensk, or Stefan of Perm.

The earliest traces of specifically apocalyptic concerns appeared in the late fourteenth century, then grew in number and urgency as 1492 approached.

---

16. Text cited from MS C-591 (15th c.), as reproduced in A. M. Moldovan, *"Slovo o zakone i blagodati" Ilariona* (Kiev: Naukova Dumka, 1984), fol. 168a, b; 191b.

17. *Slovo na sbor sv. otsev* (13th c. MS), as cited in I. P. Eremin, *Literaturnoe nasledie Kirilla Turovskogo*, Monuments of Early Russian Literature, no. 2 (Oakland, Calif.: Berkeley Slavic Specialties, 1989), 88.

18. *Polnoe sobranie russkikh letopisei* (*PSRL*), 41 vols. to date (St. Petersburg-Moscow, 1846–1995), vol. 1, cols. 445–46.

Metropolitan Kiprian (1390–1405), for example, answered a number of practical questions about lapses in monastic life sent to him by Abbot Afanasii, and then lamented the behavior described and despaired about the future: "Now it is the final time, and the ending of the years approaches, and the end of this age, and the Devil is roaring a great deal, wishing to swallow up everyone, through our carelessness and laziness. For virtue has grown rare, love has ceased, simplicity of the spirit has fled; and envy and craftiness and hatred have settled in, and we are filled with trickery and cunning, and because of that we have cut ourselves off from any kind of spiritual happiness."[19]

Dread about the approaching End was even more forcefully expressed in the Easter tables (*paschalia*) dating from this same period, the late fourteenth–early fifteenth centuries. The Russian philologist Anatolii Turilov has called them "prognosticative" because of their inclusion of eschatological excerpts from Pseudo-Methodius of Patara in the entries for specific years, with predictions about wars, mass deaths, cataclysms, and foreign invasions.[20] In the oldest known of these prognosticative tables (late fourteenth–early fifteenth century), from the Savior-Priluki Monastery near Vologda, we find the following commentary for the year 7000, the last entry in the table. "Terror here! Grief here! Since this cycle was the one at Christ's Crucifixion, it has come around this year at the End as well, the year in which we also expect your universal coming."[21]

19. *Akty istoricheskie, sobrannye i izdannye Arkheograficheskoiu kommissieiu*, vol. 1 (St. Petersburg: Tipografiia vtorogo otdeleniia Sobstvennoi E. I. V. kantseliarii, 1841), 481 (16th c. collection). Metropolitan Fotii voices similar concerns in 1415–16 in an epistle against the ordination of Grigorii Tsamblak as metropolitan of Kiev by Lithuanian bishops: "But as you have accepted holy baptism from the Catholic and Apostolic Church of Christ, so also have you accepted to have one prelate, and since you have accepted [that], preserve it until the end of the ages. But the end of the ages is come near to you." *Russkaia istoricheskaia biblioteka*, 39 vols. (St. Petersburg-Leningrad: Tipografiia imperatorskoi Akademii nauk, 1872–1927), vol. 6, pt. 39, col. 318. Since completing this study, I have obtained a monograph by Andrei Iurganov, *Kategorii russkoi srednevekovoi kul'tury* (Moscow: MIROS, 1998), which cites in addition to Kiprian and Fotii, similar apocalyptic sentiments of Feodosii, archbishop of Rostov, in 1455: "Because with [this] the 63rd year of the last century [6963], the seventh millennium is soon achieved," and an anonymous notation in a fifteenth-century horologion [*chasoslov*] cited by S. P. Shevyrev in 1860: "And the years and the seasons and the days are ending, and the Last Judgment is being readied" (p. 321).

20. A. A. Turilov, "O datirovke i meste sozdaniia kalendarno-matematicheskikh tekstov—'Semitysiachnikov,'" in *Estestvennonauchnye predstavleniia Drevnei Rusi. Schislenie let. Simvolika chisel. "Otrechennye" knigi. Astrologiia. Mineralogiia*, ed. R. A. Simonov (Moscow: Nauka, 1988), 33.

21. Cited in "Drevnie russkie paskhalii na os'muiu tysiachu let ot sotvoreniia mira," *Pravoslavnyi sobesednik*, 1860, pt. 3, 331. In "O datirovke," Turilov suggests that such Easter tables came to Rus' from the Balkans, where mid-fourteenth-century apocalyptic fears rose with every victory of the Muslim Turks over the Orthodox Slavs and Greeks. Similar expressions of agitation appear in later copies of the tables and in chronicle accounts about the year 1459 (thirty-three years before the End, the age of Christ at the Crucifixion). A useful summary of textual evidence is provided in N. V. Sinitsyna, *Tretii Rim. Istoki i evoliutsiia srednevekovoi kontseptii* (Moscow: Indrik, 1998), 183–87. Iurganov cites similar passages from other texts (*Kategorii*, 326–27).

The Byzantines dated Creation (*Annus Mundi*) to 5,508 years before Christ; therefore, the year 7000 A.M. would commence September 1, 1492 C.E. That the earliest traces of apocalyptic expression in Rus' should appear in the late fourteenth century is not unexpected. The primary source of Christian apocalyptic imagery, the Book of Revelation, was apparently not widely disseminated in early Rus', in part a reflection of its uncertain beginnings in the Early Christian tradition. The variety of opinion on the canonicity of the Book of Revelation is represented in the Slavonic translations of canon law.[22] An important consequence of early doubts was that Revelation played no direct role in the liturgy.[23] Although the Commentaries of Andreas of Caesarea, which include the text of Revelation, may have existed in Slavonic translation (by Saint Methodius?) as far back as the ninth century, the earliest extant Slavonic translation of Revelation with commentaries is the thirteenth-century Nikol'skii Apocalypse from Novgorod.[24]

By the mid-fourteenth century, the Book of Revelation was available to resonate with the march of history and the promise of eternal life in the ritual of liturgy. The emergence of Muscovy from the early fourteenth century on as a political and spiritual authority in the East was counterbalanced by the fall of the Orthodox Slavs to the Muslim Turks in the Balkans in the late fourteenth century. Moscow's first major victory over the Mongols at Kulikovo Pole occurred in 1380. The subjugation of Yaroslavl, Rostov, Novgorod, and Tver from 1463 to 1485 signaled the inevitability of Moscow's dominance over the other principalities of Rus' before 1492.

On the spiritual front, the metropolitan's see, which had been transferred *de facto* from Kiev to Vladimir in 1299, was effectively relocated to Moscow itself in 1325 with Metropolitan Peter's close attachment to the court of Muscovite prince Ivan I Kalita. The capitulation of the Byzantines to the Latin church at the Council of Ferrara-Florence in 1438–39 and the consequent *de facto* establishment of the autocephalous Russian Church in 1448 in the midst of such political and military success only solidified Moscow's position in the Orthodox world.

---

22. Thomas Oller provides a useful overview of the problem of canonicity and the earliest Slavonic translations of Revelation. See Thomas Hilary Oller, "The Nikol'skij Apocalypse Codex and Its Place in the Textual History of Medieval Slavic Apocalypse Manuscripts" (Ph.D. diss., Brown University, 1993), chap. 5.

23. *The Oxford Dictionary of Byzantium* (Oxford: Oxford University Press, 1991), s.v. "Apocalypse"; N. Thierry, "L'Apocalypse de saint Jean et l'iconographie byzantine," in *L'Apocalypse de saint Jean* (Geneva, 1979), 319, cited in R. Barthélemy-Vogels and Charles Hyart, *L'iconographie russe de l'Apocalypse. La "mise à jour" des livres saints* (Paris: Société d'Edition "Les Belles Lettres," 1985), 18; Oller, "Nikol'skij Apocalypse," 497, 514–17.

24. Cf. Oller, "Nikol'skij Apocalypse."

None of these political and religious events taken individually could be viewed as a turning point of apocalyptic consequence, but over the course of two centuries they could be readily understood as signs, for those inclined to interpret them as such, that Moscow was destined for dominance as the last bastion of Orthodox Christian purity prior to the End Times.[25]

The news that Constantinople, the New Rome, had fallen to the Turks in 1453 was greeted in Muscovy with shock and dismay, but the net result was to elevate the position of Moscow as a spiritual center. For example, at the end of an alleged eyewitness account of the siege, full of concrete details and battle descriptions heavily influenced by the writings of Josephus Flavius, Nestor Iskander, the author of *The Tale of the Taking of the Imperial City by the Turks in 1453* (or a subsequent editor no later than 1515) included excerpts from Pseudo-Methodius of Patara along with direct references to the potential role of Rus' in liberating the New Rome before the End:

> But you should understand, O accursed ones, that if everything foretold by Methodius of Patara and Leo the Wise and the signs concerning this city have been fulfilled, the final things will not pass by, but will be fulfilled as well. For he writes, "And a blond race along with the original creators [of the city] will defeat all the Ishmaelites, and they along with the previous lawful inhabitants will take back the Seven-Hilled [city of Constantinople] and will rule in it, and the Rusians [inhabitants of Rus'] will hold the Seven-Hilled [city], the sixth people and [together with] the fifth, and will plant fruits in it and many will eat of it in avenging the saints."[26]

It was with the conviction of Moscow's greater earthly and ultimately cosmic destiny, that Ivan III elected to engage in reformative symbolism, adopting some of the trappings and ritual of the Byzantine court and physically rebuilding the spiritual and political core of Moscow's Kremlin to represent in ever clearer terms the "way in which the world is built" at the semiotic center of such a complexly organized and increasingly important

25. See, for example, a citation from the III Pskov Chronicle, written in the 1560s: "He [Ivan IV] wanted to build a tsardom in Moscow, and since it is written in Chapter 54 of Revelation—For five kingdoms have passed, and a sixth is [to be], but had not yet come, but that one had already begun, had come, and he was crowned January 16th." A. N. Nasonov, *Pskovskie letopisi,* vol. 2 (Moscow: ANSSR, 1955), s.a. 1547–50, fol. 211r (p. 231). Cf. N. M. Karamzin, *Istoriia gosudarstva Rossiiskogo* (St. Petersburg, 1842), bk. 2, vol. 8, cols. 57–58 and note 162.

26. *Pamiatniki literatury Drevnei Rusi. Vtoraia polovina XV veka* (Moscow: Khudozhestvennaia literatura, 1982), 264.

society.[27] It was during his reign that the current walls of the Kremlin were designed and erected, and its major cathedrals and royal halls expanded or completely rebuilt, predominately by Italian architects.

In the Byzantine east as well, the fall of Constantinople generated new anxiety that the End would come in or around 1492. In fact, a number of works by Gennadius II (Scholarius), the first patriarch of Constantinople under the Turks, were written under the assumption of an imminent end. In his brief *Chronography* of 1472, he makes a new computation and concludes that the end of the seventh millennium will transpire in twenty-one years (namely, 1493).[28]

The Novgorod heresy of the so-called Judaizers that arose in the late 1470s and reached Moscow by the mid-1480s introduced another evident sign for the apocalyptically inclined that the End was in sight. The Judaizers, a largely elite sect of heretics with some standing at the royal court, apparently did not share the unshakable Orthodox belief in resurrection, the Trinity, the Second Coming, or the Last Judgment, and thus rejected the idea of an apocalyptic End that would occur at a predetermined time. Therefore, the fact that official Orthodox Easter tables offered no calculations beyond the year 7000 provided the heretics with a specific authoritative prediction, a definitive date, that they could challenge. An unfulfilled prophecy about the End would provide explicit evidence after the date in question that the people should abandon their commitment to the official church and follow the heretics. The church elite were thus obliged to handle the issue of Apocalypse specifically in the year 7000 (1492) with great care.

In 1489, for example, the archbishop of Novgorod, Gennadii, wrote a letter to Iosaf, the former archbishop of Rostov, noting that Archpriest Aleksei, a heretic leader from Novgorod, stood ready to exploit any faulty apocalyptic prediction: "'Three years will pass, [and] the seventh millennium ends.' And so I [Gennadii] too heard from Aleksei: 'And then it will be our turn [lit. And we in fact will be the ones needed then],' he says. And so the heretics are acting quite sure of themselves!"[29] It is not only in written form that we see direct expressions of apocalypticism in the century or so leading up to 1492, at least in some elite segments of Muscovite society. Specific artistic

27. See Clifford Geertz, "Centers, Kings, and Charisma: Reflections on the Symbolics of Power," in *Local Knowledge: Further Essays in Interpretive Anthropology* (New York: Basic Books, 1983 [orig. publ. 1977]), 124–5.

28. A. Vasiliev, "Medieval Ideas."

29. N. A. Kazakova and Ia. S. Lur'e, *Antifeodal'nye ereticheskie dvizheniia na Rusi XIV–nachala XVI veka* (Moscow-Leningrad: ANSSSR, 1955), 318.

commissions also indicate interest and concern in the very center of Moscow's political and religious life.

An unusual icon, dated from the 1390s to the first third of the fifteenth century and attributed to the workshop of Theophanes the Greek, indicates similar expectations (fig. 10).[30] Titled *The Great Fast* (*Chetyredesiatnitsa,* or "Fast of the Forty Days") by art historians, the icon was discovered in 1919 in the Ivan the Great bell tower in the Moscow Kremlin, occasionally used as a storehouse for the Cathedral of the Dormition.[31] The icon was apparently inspired by themes of several major services immediately before and during the forty-day fast that ends just before Lazarus Saturday and Palm Sunday, the bridge to Passion Week and Easter.

The icon is divided into four panels. The upper left panel depicts Saint John the Forerunner, with two images from his adult life: the beginning (a voice crying in the wilderness) and the end (his head on a platter). He carries a scroll that renders his warning from Matthew 3:2 ("Repent ye: for the kingdom of heaven is at hand") and Matthew 3:10 ("And now also the axe is laid unto the root ... [of the trees: therefore every tree which bringeth not forth good fruit is hewn down, and cast into the fire]"). The upper right panel presents the Mother of God enthroned in heaven with the infant Christ on her lap. Flanked by Archangels Michael and Gabriel, she serves as an indicator of the promise of the Kingdom of God for all humanity. The two bottom panels actually constitute a single scene, representing various ranks of saints standing by the tombs of the righteous as they resurrect from the dead at the General Resurrection immediately before the Last Judgment.[32] The direct iconographic reference to a singular event of the Last Judgment, the General Resurrection, is rare, justifiably understood as apocalyptic, rather than simply eschatological, in light of the time in which it was painted and in its focus on the human dimension of the End, with the Last Judgment imminent but not directly shown.

30. V. I. Antonova and N. E. Mneva, *Gosudarstvennaia Tret'iakovskaia galereia. Katalog drevnerusskoi zhivopisi. Opyt istoriko-khudozhestvennaia klassifikatsii,* vol. 1, *XI–nachala XVI veka* (Moscow: Iskusstvo, 1963), no. 218 (258–60, pl. 168); G. I. Vzdornov, *Feofan Grek. Tvorcheskoe nasledie* (Moscow: Iskusstvo, 1983), 271–73; Ia. V. Bruk and L. I. Iovlevaia, eds., *Gosudarstvennaia Tret'iakovskaia galereia. Katalog sobraniia,* vol. 1, *Drevnerusskoe iskusstvo X–nachala XV veka* (Moscow: Krasnaia ploshchad', 1995), 147–49.

31. L. I. Lifshits, in Bruk and Iovlevoi, *Katalog,* 149.

32. The discovery of the head of Saint John the Forerunner is celebrated on the Tuesday of Meatfare Week, which ends with Meatfare Sunday, the celebration of the Last Judgment. The Mother of God Enthroned in Heaven alludes to that portion of the Akathist hymn sung on the Saturday of the fifth week of the Great Fast. See Vzdornov, *Feofan Grek,* 271. Cf. the extended intepretation by Lev Lifshits (in Bruk and Iovlevoi, *Katalog*), which suggests that this icon is the central member of a triptych of the Hexameron (*Shestodnev*), "Six Days," in commemoration of the weekly Oktoechos liturgical cycle.

FIG. 10 *The Great Fast.* Quadripartite icon. Workshop of Theophanes the Greek? Moscow
Kremlin. c. 1390s–1430s. An example of one of the earliest Rusian representations of the
General Resurrection before the Last Judgment. Upper left: Saint John the Forerunner.
Upper right: Mother of God Enthroned with Infant Christ, flanked by Archangels Michael
(left) and Gabriel. Lower left and right: The General Resurrection. Reprinted with
permission from the archives of Engelina Smirnova, Institute of Art History, Moscow.

A representation of the Last Judgment, typically found on the western internal wall of post-eighth-century Eastern Orthodox churches, served as a general eschatological representation from the very beginnings of Christianity in Rus'.[33] Recall that it was the eschatological image of Christ in Judgment painted on a cloth (*zapona*) that stimulated Volodimer to consider accepting Christianity, a decision he postponed until he had had the opportunity to weigh the merits of competing belief systems.[34]

The actual pictorial treatment of the Apocalypse, as opposed to the Last Judgment, appears quite late in the Byzantine world. The earliest known rendering of the Apocalypse in the entire Byzantine realm is to be found in the now lost frescoes originally painted in 1405 by Theophanes the Greek for the north and south walls of the Cathedral of the Annunciation in the Moscow Kremlin.[35] Contemporary with the apocalyptic icon described above, the fresco cycle bears witness to an extraordinary interest in the Last Times in the very palace church of the Muscovite prince.

These images of the Apocalypse also roughly coincide in time with the appearance of the first high iconostases (icon screens) in all of Orthodox Christendom, those constructed in northeastern Rus' in the first two decades of the fifteenth century in such large churches as the Trinity Cathedral in the Trinity-Sergii Lavra (fig. 11) and the Cathedral of the Dormition in Vladimir.[36] The effect of the multitiered icon screen was to highlight the Deësis tier (*chin*) with its two rows of holy figures, right and left, inclined in supplication toward the central figure of Christ enthroned as final judge.[37] The tiers

33. The more direct representational development of Last Judgment iconography takes place in Byzantine art in the eighth century, undoubtedly in reponse to the struggle against iconoclasm. See N. V. Pokrovskii, "Strashnyi sud v pamiatnikakh vizantiiskogo i russkogo iskusstva," *Trudy VI arkheologicheskogo s"ezda v Odesse (1884),* vol. 3 (Odessa: Tipografiia A. Shul'tse, 1887), 296–97.

34. *PSRL,* vol. 1 (1926/1962), col. 106.

35. I. Ia. Kachalova et al., *Blagoveshchenskii sobor Moskovskogo Kremlia. K 500-letiiu unikal'nogo pamiatnika russkoi kul'tury* (Moscow: Iskusstvo, 1990), 30. No longer extant, these frescoes are mentioned in a letter by Epifanii the Most Wise to Kirill, dated 1415, and preserved in a seventeenth-century manuscript, reproduced in Vzdornov, *Feofan Grek,* 39–49. Epifanii's statement reads, "and in the masonry church of the Holy Annunciation, he also painted the Tree [Root] of Jesse and the Apocalypse," 43, cited from a seventeenth-century manuscript, Rossiiskaia natsional'naia biblioteka, Sol. 15/1474, f. 130v.

36. For a useful summary of recent research on the development of the Russian high iconostasis, see L. A. Shchennikova, "Drevnerusskii vysokii iconostas XIV–nachala XV v.: Itogi i perspektivy izucheniia," in *Ikonostas. Proiskhozhdenie, razvitie, simvolika,* ed. A. M. Lidov (Moscow: Progress-Traditsiia, 2000), 392–410.

37. L. V. Betin, "Ob arkhitekturnoi kompozitsii drevnerusskikh vysokikh ikonostasov," *Drevnerusskoe iskusstvo* (Moscow: Nauka, 1970), 49–51; idem, "Istoricheskie osnovy drevnerusskogo vysokogo ikonostasa," ibid., 58; Michael S. Flier, "Sunday in Medieval Russian Culture: *Nedělja* versus *Voskresenie,*" in *Medieval Russian Culture,* ed. Henrik Birnbaum and Michael S. Flier (Berkeley and Los Angeles: University of California Press, 1984), 144; Konrad Onasch, "Identity Models of Old Russian Sacred Art," ibid., 186–88.

above featured the Old Testament forefathers and prophets and their prediction of a messiah, and the festival tier, with representations of the events from
the lives of Mary and Christ, celebrated during the major holidays of the
year. Contemplation of these upper tiers that led thematically to the Deësis
tier gave the high iconostasis a pronounced eschatological character. It became
a standard feature for large Muscovite cathedrals by the late fifteenth and sixteenth centuries.

The depiction of the Last Judgment itself began to change in Muscovy
from the late fourteenth century on.[38] The new iconography emphasizes the
immediate consequences of ultimate judgment, introducing themes specifically associated, not only with general eschatology (the older Last Judgment),
but with imminent Apocalypse. It is this change in perspective that accounts
for such innovations as the new focus given Adam and Eve (as the precursors
of all mankind seeking entry into Heaven) and the introduction of Heavenly Jerusalem, among others. The more pressing concern about the testing
of a soul's worth is reflected in the presence of tollhouses projected onto the
serpent/river of fire that winds its way through the iconographic space separating the fires of hell below from the feet of Christ the Judge in the compo-
sitional center above (fig. 12). Each soul will be tested at each tollhouse before
being permitted to ascend higher toward the Final Judge.

It is in the last quarter of the fifteenth century, when belief in the impending Apocalypse had intensified, that we see the highest number of cultural expressions of the End. In addition to the greater number of separate
icons of the Last Judgment produced in major centers such as Novgorod and
Moscow, we note the commission of a large icon of the Apocalypse itself
(figs. 13, 14) for Moscow's major church, the Cathedral of the Dormition in
the Kremlin. This icon is the earliest known panel painting with this theme
in the Byzantine world.[39] The inclusion in the icon of the major elements
from Revelation—the Seven Seals, the Whore of Babylon, the scarlet-colored
Seven-headed Beast with Ten Horns, the Pale Rider, the King of Kings leading his army against the forces of the Antichrist, and many more—provides

---

38. See David M. Goldfrank, "Who Put the Snake on the Icon and the Tollbooths on the Snake? A
Problem of Last Judgment Iconography," *Harvard Ukrainian Studies* 19 (1995): 180–99, and V. K. Tsodi-
kovich, *Semantika ikonografii "Strashnogo Suda" v russkom iskusstve 15–16 vekov* (Ul'ianovsk: Ul'ianovskoe
oblastnoe gazetnoe izdatel'stvo, 1995).

39. M. V. Alpatov, *Pamiatnik drevnerusskoi zhivopisi kontsa XV veka. Ikona "Apokalipsis" Uspenskogo
sobora Moskovskogo kremlia* (Moscow: Iskusstvo, 1964); Carolyn W. Anderson, "Image and Text in the
Apocalypse Icon of the Dormition Cathedral of the Moscow Kremlin" (Ph.D. diss., University of Pittsburgh, 1977); Kachalova et al., *Blagoveshchenskii sobor,* 30.

Fig. 11 *Iconostasis of the Trinity Cathedral,* Trinity-Sergii Lavra, Sergiev Posad. 15th–16th century. The multitiered high iconostasis developed in Muscovite Rus' as a more direct expression of concern about the End Times, each tier from top to bottom adding to the narration about the messiah and ultimate redemption, from the forefathers and prophets, through images celebrating major events in the lives of Christ and the Mother of God, to the Deesis (supplication), with its focus on Christ as Final Judge. Reprinted with permission from the archives of Engelina Smirnova, Institute of Art History, Moscow.

FIG. 12   *The Last Judgment.* Icon. Novgorod. Mid-15th century. A hierarchically arranged representation of the Last Judgment before the End of History, an event expected by many Eastern Orthodox faithful in the year 7000 (1492). Reprinted with permission from the archives of Engelina Smirnova, Institute of Art History, Moscow.

FIG. 13   *The Apocalypse.* Icon. Moscow. Cathedral of the Dormition. End 15th century.
One of the earliest extant images of the Apocalypse of John as presented in the Book of
Revelation, with representations of the Seven Seals, the horsemen of the Apolcalypse, the
Whore of Babylon, and the New Jerusalem. Reprinted with permission from the archives of
Engelina Smirnova, Institute of Art History, Moscow.

FIG. 14   *The Apocalypse.* Detail. The Pale Rider and the Whore of Babylon (seated upon the Scarlet-Colored Seven-Headed Beast with Ten Horns) are only two of the terrifying figures associated with evil at the End Times.

tangible proof that in the elite circles of Orthodox Moscow, eschatological certainty had begun to yield to apocalyptic imminence.

All the products of apocalypticism discussed so far—texts, Easter tables, icons, frescoes, iconostases—were effected in a privileged context; they were produced by elites for elites and do not presuppose popular involvement. It was the church that concerned itself with the calendar, the progression of human history, and the consequences of an apocalyptic end that would move humanity into a new dimension. Such limitation raises severe questions about Berdiaev's claim, quoted at the beginning of this chapter, that "the Apocalypse has always played a large role" in Russian cultural history, low as well as high. Representatives of the popular culture of early Rus' would scarcely have understood such fundamental notions as the counting of millennia, the advance of history, and an apocalyptic end.

It is after all, primarily literate cultures that are concerned with chronologies.[40] Most members of Muscovite society were illiterate, and the majority of non-elite members of that society were rural, living their lives according to the rhythms of nature rather than a succession of years.[41] Any abstract notions of eschatology introduced into the elite culture of Rus' with the tenth-century baptism of Volodimer in Kiev would have been lost on the masses, especially concepts pertaining to millennial endings. The directional thrust of time's arrow would not have made much headway in a society that lived in cyclic time,[42] the sort of model proposed by Mircea Eliade when discussing primitive societies with continual cycles of endings and beginnings, the myth of the eternal return.[43] This was the patterning of primitive East Slavic culture to the extent that existing evidence will allow us to reconstruct it.

Vladimir Propp was able to reconstruct an East Slavic cyclical calendar system, one anchored in the natural world, by analyzing critically the materials collected by nineteenth- and twentieth-century cultural historians.[44] The calendar, shaped by the coordination of astronomical phenomena and the life-sustaining agricultural cycle, was strongly influenced by the cult of ancestors, understood to be a potent force in the other world, and still able to affect the well-being of this one. Ritualized interaction of the living with the ancestral dead through cult meals, offerings, and graveside visits was largely confined to the period between the winter solstice (*Sviatki*) and the summer solstice (*Kupalo*), the time of regeneration and growth that determines the outcome of the harvest for the rest of the year.[45]

The pagan East Slavs celebrated the end of the old year (or season) and the beginning of the new, a cyclical regeneration from chaos to cosmos, from disorder to order. But there was no eschatology on a par with that of the Jews or the Christians, with one final, cataclysmic End, the return or appearance

40. Landes, "Lest the Millennium Be Fulfilled," 137.

41. Population estimates for the latter part of the seventeenth century register that Russia's urban population represented only about 3 percent of the total population of 10.5 million, and Moscow alone accounted for at least a third of that, cf. Ia. E. Vodarskii, *Naselenie Rossii za 400 let (XVI–nachalo XX vv.)* (Moscow: Prosveshchenie, 1973), 22–27, 34–36; idem, *Naselenie Rossii v kontse XVII–nachale XVIII veka* (Moscow: Nauka, 1977), passim; G. Rozman, *Urban Networks in Russia, 1750–1800, and Premodern Periodization* (Princeton: Princeton University Press, 1976), 58–60; and H. L. Eaton, "Decline and Recovery of the Russian Cities from 1500 to 1700," *Canadian-American Slavic Studies* 11 (1977): 225–27.

42. Stephen Jay Gould, *Time's Arrow, Time's Cycle: Myth and Metaphor in the Discovery of Geological Time* (Cambridge: Harvard University Press, 1987).

43. Mircea Eliade, *The Myth of the Eternal Return, or Cosmos and History*, trans. Willard Trask, rev. ed., Bollingen series, no. 46 (Princeton: Princeton University Press, 1965), 51–92.

44. V. Ia. Propp, *Russkie agrarnye prazdniki* (1963; reprint, St. Petersburg: Azbuka, 1995), 3–12.

45. Ibid., 23–34.

of a messiah figure, and the salvation of the righteous once and for all.[46] Accordingly, it is important to distinguish periodic or cyclical regeneration from nonperiodic, noncyclical, directional eschatology that implies an End. The calendar system of the pagan East Slavs might be defined as regenerational, but not eschatological, and therefore certainly not apocalyptic.[47]

This suggests that the Christian Apocalypse, arriving as late as it did in its most expansive form, would not have found an immediate parallel for syncretism in the framework of the double faith (*dvoeverie*), a system of belief with partly or completely overlapping functions for elements of East Slavic paganism and Christianity. But the General Resurrection, a nonchronological concept specifically mentioned in Revelation, might well have found fertile soil in a society devoted to its ancestors. The prospect of being reunited with those kindred spirits who played such a vital and functional role in the everyday lives of simple people must have figured in the attraction of the non-elite population to the General Resurrection and eventually, by association, with the Apocalypse.

A popular connection with so lofty a Christian concept is important because it helps to explain why the emergence and spread of a particular linguistic-calendrical innovation in Muscovite Rus' toward the end of the fifteenth century might appeal to low as well as high culture, even though the former was not particularly attuned to the countdown to 1492. The innovation in question involves the extended use of the word *voskresenie*, "resurrection," in the calendrical meaning "Resurrection-Sunday" and finally "Sunday" in its mundane, nonreligious meaning.

Easter, the most important holiday of the church calendar, had two basic names: *Paskha*, derived from the Greek *Páscha*, and *Voskresenie* (short for *Voskresenie Khristovo* "Resurrection of Christ"), the latter a metonymic creation derived from *den' Voskreseniia Khristova*, "the day of Christ's Resurrection." In the late fifteenth century, the word *Voskresenie*, "Easter Sunday" or "Resurrection Sunday," was extended to two of the most important Sundays in the paschal cycle. A Byzantine Greek-Russian phrase book from that period contains a new phrase, *Verbnoe Voskresenie*, "Willow Resurrection Sunday," instead of the usual *Verbnitsa* or *Nedielia Vaii*, "Palm Sunday."[48]

---

46. Cf. Eliade, *Myth*, 51–92, 124–30.

47. In this respect all the Slavs stand in contrast to the pagan Celts and Germans, who have elaborated myths of a catastrophic destruction of the world that spares neither gods nor men. Certainty of the End is made apparent in tales, poetry, oaths, and sayings. See H. R. Ellis Davidson, *Myths and Symbols in Pagan Europe: Early Scandinavian and Celtic Religions* (Manchester: Manchester University Press, 1988), 188–95.

48. Max Vasmer, *Ein russisch-byzantinisches Gesprächbuch. Beiträge zur Erforschung der älteren russischen Lexikographie* (Leipzig, 1922), 14, 138; Flier, "Sunday," 120, 130.

The motivation for the extension of the term "Resurrection" is at least partly liturgical, since Palm Sunday and the Saturday preceding, Lazarus Saturday, are devoted to the General Resurrection (Rev. 19:11–15). The primary festal hymn (*troparion*), which features the General Resurrection, is sung many times over the course of both holidays.

> Giving us before Thy Passion an assurance of the General
> Resurrection,
> Thou hast raised Lazarus from the dead, O Christ our God.
> Therefore, like the children, we also carry tokens of victory,
> and cry to Thee, the conqueror of death:
> Hosanna in the highest; blessed is He that comes in the Name of
> the Lord.[49]

Another paschal holiday came to have resurrectional status as well, *Sobornoe Voskresenie,* "Synod Resurrection-Sunday," officially known as Orthodoxy Sunday (*Nedielia Pravoslaviia*), the first Sunday of Lent. The inaugural celebration of the Triumph of Orthodoxy occurred in Constantinople on the first Sunday of Lent in 842, following the victory over iconoclasm. The holiday was introduced into Rus' by Metropolitan Kiprian in the late fourteenth century to bolster the faith against heresy. Celebrated in the major cathedrals in the presence of the assembled higher clergy or synod, Orthodoxy Sunday came to be known metonymically as Synod Sunday (*Sobornaia Nedielia*), the basis for the innovation Synod Resurrection-Sunday.

As first and last Sundays of the Great Fast (Lent), Orthodoxy Sunday and Palm Sunday were associated with renewal and reaffirmation, a common connection verified in the emergence of the terms Willow Resurrection-Sunday and then Synod Resurrection-Sunday by the turn of the sixteenth century. Invocation of the willow, the pagan Slavic harbinger of spring rebirth, signals that resources of popular culture underlay the new name for Palm Sunday, an overt mark of high-low (elite-popular) cultural interaction.[50]

49. Translation from the Greek by Mother Mary and Archimandrite Kallistos Ware, *The Lenten Triodion* (London: Faber and Faber, 1978), 476.

50. Flier, "Sunday," 132–34. This neological pairing was supported by the Rusian folk calendar as well. The March New Year apparently competed successfully with the September New Year of the church until at least 1492; see L. V. Cherepnin, *Russkaia khronologiia* (Moscow, 1944), 27. Unfortunately, Cherepnin does not document this claim, simply stating that before 1492 investigators (unnamed) assume coexistence. Be that as it may, the two celestial indicators of the March New Year—the pre-Paschal full moon before the vernal equinox and the Paschal full moon after the vernal equinox—appeared around these two Sundays, respectively, in the Lenten period, the former after a year with twelve lunations, the latter after

The realization of this late-fifteenth-century paschal cycle of Resurrection-Sundays, all using the word *Voskresenie,* may be considered apocalyptic because of its thematic link to the optimistic telos of the Last Judgment, the General Resurrection of the just.[51] Freed from its calendrical meaning "Easter," the word *Voskresenie* "Resurrection-Sunday" over the course of the sixteenth century came to be used alone in the meaning "Sunday" as a religious holiday, and by the turn of the seventeenth, it had replaced *nedielia* as the secular word for the name of the day.

No mandate from above would have produced such innovation in the core vernacular vocabulary of Russian in so short a period of time.[52] It is rather the expression of popular Muscovite belief in the General Resurrection and not ecclesiastical usage alone that drove this development, yielding such innovations as *Verbnoe Voskresenie, Sobornoe Voskresenie,* and ultimately *voskresenie,* "Sunday." The Church Slavonic name for Sunday remains *nedielia* to this day.[53]

Up to this point, we have seen overt evidence, variously expressed, of a general interest in Muscovy about the possibility of an imminent End and the General Resurrection, evidence that takes the form of epistolary statements, literary allusions, artistic images, and calendrical innovation. The nagging problem in this attention accorded the Apocalypse, however, was the concrete prediction of the year 7000. The church was faced with the reality of Easter tables that ended with that fateful year, and the heretics (Judaizers) clearly exploited that fact. One response from the official church was to downplay the idea of a precise timetable.

In a number of letters sent to various prelates between 1487 and 1492, Gennadii, the archbishop of Novgorod, challenged the prediction by questioning the different counting schemes available and accused the heretics of

---

one with thirteen; see N. V. Stepanov, "Edinitsy scheta vremeni (do XIII veka) po Lavrentievskoi i I-i Novgorodskoi letopisiam," *ChOIDR,* 1909, bk. 4, sec. 3: 48–52; idem, "K voprosu o kalendare Lavrentievskoi letopisi," *ChOIDR,* 1910, bk. 4, sec. 3: 4, 36.

51. This was confirmed by the end of the sixteenth century when two more holidays were added to the Resurrection Cycle. *Proshchenoe* (*Prashchal'noe*) *Voskresenie,* "Forgiveness (Farewell) Resurrection," and *Radunichnoe Voskresenie,* "Radunitsa Resurrection," are innovative names referring to the Sunday immediately before the Great Fast, and the first Sunday after Easter, respectively. See Flier, "Sunday," 137–39. The etymology for "Radunitsa" is unclear. See Max Vasmer, *Russisches Etymologisches Wörterbuch* (Heidelberg: Carl Winter Universitätsverlag, 1955). Both Sundays are devoted to the cult of ancestors.

52. Russian is the only Slavic language that changed the word for Sunday; cf. Ukr. *nedilja,* Br. *njadzelja,* Cz. *nedîle,* Pol. *niedziela,* Cr. *nedjelja,* Sb. *nedelja,* Bg. *nedelja.* The conservative nature of such words is evident in the clearly pagan origins of our own names for the days of the week and in the inability of the revolutionary government of France to change the names of the months by fiat.

53. Flier, "Sunday," 106, 113–14.

exploiting them for their own gain.[54] He had carefully studied the translated fourteenth-century Jewish astronomical text *The Six Wings* (*Shestokryl*), and had received commentary from his emissary Dmitrii Trakhaniotes on calculations made in the Latin West.[55] In one such response Gennadii wrote after September 1, 1492, to an unidentified addressee:

> And as for the years, the heretics stir up the simple people [by saying] that the years of our seventh millennium have already run out, and the years from other faiths have not run out—and they are simply lying. The years of all faiths have accrued equally and the infidels and their ilk are just adding more on. . . . After all, astronomy is the same the whole world over. And so the years have been set at 7000: they couldn't make them more or less than that, because of the fact that in the beginning the number seven was set by God himself; for God created the world in six days, and on the seventh he rested from all his works.

From his general, commonsense assessment, Gennadii focuses on the heretical enemy closer to home.

> And as for Archpriest Aleksii, . . . he said: "Just as soon as the years run out, then it will be our turn"—but he didn't live to see it! Seeing his unrepentant soul, God turned him over to Satan! And what was that villain going to do? Was he planning to establish the motion of the heavens all over again? The solar and lunar cycles of heavenly motion and the procession of the stars and the indictions are set in a particular way, that there's no changing that. And for that reason the Easter tables and the lunar tables are designed

54. Kazakova and Lur'e, *Antifeodal'nye ereticheskie dvizheniia*, 309–12, 315–20, 388–91.

55. See A. I. Pliguzov and I. A. Tikhoniuk, "Poslanie Dmitriia Trakhaniota novgorodskomu arkhiepiskopu Gennadiiu Gonzovu o sedmerichnosti schisleniia let," in Simonov, *Estestvennonauchnye predstavleniia Drevnei Rusi,* 53. Dmitrii's work found its way into the views voiced by Archbishop Gennadii in his 1492 pastoral letter and into those of Iosif of Volokolamsk in the Eighth Discourse of *The Enlightener,* written around 1493. See Pliguzov and Tikhoniuk, "Poslanie," 56–75. In his letter to Gennadii, Dmitri claims that there is no authority for the notion that the world will end in 7000, but rather in the seventh age. This is, in fact, incorrect. All three Slavonic redactions of the *Revelation of Methodius of Patara* have specific references to the year 7000. See Istrin, *Otkrovenie Mefodiia Patarskogo,* First Slavonic redaction, 93, line 2; Second Slavonic redaction, 108, line 29; and Interpolated Slavonic redaction, 121, pt. 5, line 1. In 1492–93, Iosif of Volokolamsk referred to the precise prediction of the year 7000 by Nikephoros Ksanphopulos (Kallistos) in the Eighth Discourse of *The Enlightener.* Iosif Volotskii, *Prosvetitel', ili oblichenie eresi zhidovstvuiushchikh,* 4th ed. (Kazan: Imperial University of Kazan, 1903), 333–56.

cyclically, for as many thousand years as God has allowed [the world] to continue.[56]

It is difficult to say how successful the heretics were in stirring up the simple people about the year 7000 in particular. Their other actions—desecration of churches, blasphemous alteration of icons, reciting prayers in Hebrew, cursing at Christ, performing uncanonical rituals—were sufficient in number for the church to convene a synod in 1490 to hear evidence against them. Gennadii's comments on the gullibility of the simple people are instructive.

> A man can [try to] protect himself from a heretic, but how does one guard against these heretics? For they call themselves Christians, but to a thinking person they won't even show themselves, but a stupid one—they'll eat him alive! For that reason, their punishment should be double the usual and damnation on top of that. And as far as faith is concerned, one is not allowed to add or subtract. . . . And our people are still simple, they do not know how to defend [lit. speak about] the traditional books: such people [as the heretics] should not be allowed to put any ideas into their heads. For that alone a synod should be convened to execute them—by burning and hanging![57]

In a letter from 1487, Gennadii underscores the intended outreach of the heretics' mission: "They all philosophize, only they entice people with the Jewish Ten Commandments, since they seem pious. And that temptation has spread not only in the towns here, but among the villages as well. And all this is from the priests whom the heretics installed."[58]

These remarks about the heretics' activity and their reception appear to confirm our characterization of the simple people as illiterate, ill-informed, and most important, unable to understand argumentation of the sort necessary to appreciate the potential consequence of the arrival of 1492 for the immediate world.

Aside from condemning an accurate prediction of the End, Gennadii solved the more practical problem of calculating the paschal cycle for the

56. "Letter from Gennadii, archbishop of Novgorod, to an unknown addressee, after September 1, 1492," in Kazakova and Lur'e, *Antifeodal'nye ereticheskie dvizheniia*, 388.

57. Ibid., 381.

58. "Letter from Gennadii, archbishop of Novgorod to Bishop Prokhor of Sara, 1487," ibid., 310.

future by producing a new Easter table. In a letter sent to the prelates of his jurisdiction in December 1492, he included a preface for a new one that extended the calculations of Easter and correlated holidays for another seventy years, the number seventy motivated by King David's projection of the span of a human life (Psalms 90:10):

> And these seasons mark the course of a human life, whereas an age has no end. Likewise the Alpha[59] provides the course of an Easter table without end. And in this regard it is not fitting to begin expecting the End of Time [lit. the Years] yet again, once the seventy years have elapsed, to think that the world will end, as was written before in the seven thousandth Easter table—when the seventh millennium elapsed, the thought arose that the world would end: these things are false. . . . But it is fitting to remember what Christ himself said: "But of that day and that hour, knoweth no man" and because of that it behooves us to be ready at any hour: for we do not know at what hour the End of the World will be.[60]

Ultimately Gennadii relied on the security of natural rhythms to make his strongest case against the heretics. In the same letter he wrote:

> And when the seventh millennium ended and the successive Easter tables with commentary had expired, someone wrote about that yet again: "Terror here! Grief here! Since this cycle was the one at Christ's Crucifixion, it has come around this year at the End as well, the year in which we also expect your Coming"—there was talk [*ml"va*] about this among the people, [and] not only among the simple people, but among the privileged as well; many had doubts about it. And for that reason we have presented this report about the Alpha and the tables and the solar cycles, running their course without end.[61]

59. The Alpha or Great Indiction refers to the Dionysian period of 532 years (28 solar cycles multiplied by 19 lunar cycles) that constitutes a complete Easter cycle.

60. "December 21, 1492. Gramota novgorodskogo arkhiepiskopa Gennadiia sobornomu dukhovenstvu o paskhalii na os'muiu tysiachu let i predislovie k samoi paskhalii," in *Russkaia istoricheskaia biblioteka*, vol. 6, pt. 1, no. 119, cols. 803–4. The very fact that Gennadii writes this letter in December 1492 casts some doubt on the ubiquity of the view that the End would occur sometime between the feast of SS. Peter and Paul on June 29, 1492, and the beginning of the next paschal cycle, the feast of the Publican and the Pharisee, January 27, 1493. See Pliguzov and Tikhoniuk, "Poslanie," 52.

61. Gennadii, "Gramota (1492)," col. 810.

We cannot know what exactly Gennadii had in mind when speaking about the reaction of the simple people and the privileged (presumably in and around Novgorod) to the threat of the Apocalypse. The word *ml"va* (also spelled *m"lva* or *molva*) can range in meaning from "concerned talk," "uproar," and "clamor" to "disturbance" or even "revolt." But it is doubtful that all historical accounts in contemporary chronicles, chronographs, and tales would have remained completely silent about a massive uprising, had there been one. Gennadii's description suggests only that the heretics tried to use the prophecy of an explicit End to advance their own political and social position at the expense of the official elite church. His response was not to be put into the position of defending predictive imminence, but to adhere to the more defensible stance of psychological imminence ("It behooves us to be ready at any hour: for we do not know at what hour the End of the World will be").

There was apparently no widespread psychological panic, as Čiževskij correctly observed, but in the context of the times, the very idea of the End could raise social concern, at least among the population, urban and suburban, most likely to be exposed to competing claims from church officials and heretical leaders. The possibility of such an effect suggests that life could be lived as if "the last age itself [were] about to end" without the frightening prospect that the end itself was necessarily hours or days away. A generally positive, if serious, reaction to the possibility of the General Resurrection remained (witness *Verbnoe Voskresenie*) even after September 1, 1492, came and went. This is at least in part because elements of the General Resurrection harmonized with the indigenous ancestor cult, whereas a linear, calendrical countdown did not.

However the inhabitants of Muscovy might have arrived at the expectation of the End in the late fifteenth century, through complex theology, historical interpretation, amplified folk belief, or communal agitation, the certainty of Muscovy's unique role in the Christian world as it faced the End did not disappear with the passage of 1492. The most remarkable sign of this fundamental conviction at the top comes in the *Presentation of the Easter Tables for the Eighth Millennium,* written by Metropolitan Zosima by order of Grand Prince Ivan III in 1492. The *Presentation,* already mentioned by Gennadii in the pastoral letter preceding his own Easter tables,[62] establishes important themes that indicate the perspective of the highest authorities of church and state on Muscovy's place in history and its role in the future.

---

62. Gennadii, "Gramota, December 21, 1492," col. 802.

PRESENTATION OF THE EASTER TABLES FOR THE EIGHTH MIL-
LENNIUM IN WHICH WE EXPECT THE UNIVERSAL COMING OF
CHRIST, BY THE RIGHT HONORABLE ZOSIMA, METROPOLITAN
OF ALL RUS' ON THE ORDER OF THE SOVEREIGN GRAND PRINCE
IOANN VASIL'EVICH OF ALL RUS'

Through the mercy and aid of the all-holy and life-giving consub-
stantial and indivisible Trinity ... we have reached the brink of
seven thousand years, and the last year of the Easter tables for the
seventh millennium has ended, in the reign of the pious and Christ-
loving grand prince Ivan Vasil'evich, sovereign and autocrat of all
Rus', in the thirty-first year of his tsardom, in the third year of the
pastorate of the right honorable Zosima, metropolitan of all Rus'.

And as it was in the first years, so it is in the last, since our Lord
said in the Gospels: "And the first shall be last, and the last first"
[Matt. 19:30]; and as it was in the first year after the Ascension of
the Lord God and our savior, Jesus Christ to heaven, the Apostles
gathered together and bore witness, affirming the faith.

At one of the most highly charged times in the history of Muscovy, the
Presentation sets forth in no uncertain terms a belief in an imminent End
at the highest levels of authority. One is struck by the use of "brink" (*krai*)
rather than the more neutral "end" (*konets*) to characterize the extreme nature
of the millennial boundary just reached. The last paragraph of the *Presentation* reintroduces the theme of ending as new beginning.

And having taken his counsel and by the order of the sovereign of all
Rus' ... the humble Zosima, metropolitan of all Rus', has labored
diligently to compose the Easter tables for the eighth millennium, in
which we expect the universal Coming of Christ. "But of that day
and hour, knoweth no man," as the divine Evangelist says, "not even
the angels who are in heaven, [but my] Father only" [Matt. 24:36].
And having taken counsel with the archbishops, and the bishops
and the archimandrites, and the entire right honorable synod of the
Rusian metropolitanate, he has transmitted [these Easter tables] to
God's churches for the affirmation of the faith and to all Orthodox
Christians, who know the path of salvation. . . . And from here we
begin the Easter tables for the eighth millennium.[63]

63. "Mitropolita Zosima izveshchenie o paskhalii na os'muiu tysiachu let: 1492," in *Russkaia istoricheskaia biblioteka*, vol. 6, pt. 1 (1880), no. 118, cols. 795–802.

Zosima's focus on time in its final stages is equally noteworthy: "the *last* year of the Easter tables for the seventh millennium," "as it was in the first years, so it is in the *last*." The contrast of first and last as absolutes in a divine temporal pattern sets up the appropriate linkage in the textual middle of the *Presentation,* from the first glorified Orthodox Christian ruler (Constantine the Great), through the second Constantine (Saint Vladimir), to the new Constantine (Ivan III).

> And after the passage of time, it came to pass that God glorified the first Orthodox emperor, Constantine, and showed him the sign of the honorable cross above, mastery and victory over his enemies, as it indeed came to pass; and he received the scepter, the invincible weapon—the Orthodox faith of Christ, and defeating all enemies, he subjugated all his adversaries, and affirmed the Orthodox faith of Christ, according to the traditions of the Apostles, and those practicing heresy against the Orthodox faith he drove out like wolves, and he was called equal of the Apostles. And through God's will he built a city in his name and called it the city of Constantine, that is, the Emperor's City, and it was called the New Rome: and the Orthodox faith of Christ spread considerably over the whole earth.

The emperor Constantine serves as the basis from which to project God's handiwork onto the future in the newly baptized Rus'.

> And after these years, the Lord God chose for himself from among the idolaters, a pure vessel, the pious and Christ-loving grand prince Vladimir of Kiev and all Rus', who tested many faiths, and accepted from Constantinople, like an invincible shield in his heart, the Orthodox faith of Christ, and he was baptized through holy baptism in the name of the Father and the Son and the Holy Spirit, and smashed idols and brought infidels to the faith, and enlightened the entire Rusian land through holy baptism, and having received from God the invincible weapon . . . and he was called the second Constantine.

Finally, the *Presentation* closes the circle that connects the time of Constantine the Great with that of the current ruler, Ivan III.

> And now, in these last years, as in the first, God has glorified his [Vladimir's] kinsman, who has shone forth in Orthodoxy, the pious

and Christ-loving grand prince Ivan Vasil'evich, sovereign and auto-crat of all Rus', the new emperor Constantine for the new city of Constantine, Moscow, the sovereign of the whole Rusian land and of many other lands, so as the Lord said, "I shall glorify those glori-fying me" [cf. John 17:1] and his name and fame were glorified the whole world over, and the Lord God gave over to him the scepter, the invincible weapon.

The three rulers are presented in virtually formulaic terms,[64] but it is not simply their identification as glorified Orthodox Christian rulers that estab-lishes a typological equation. The three-part comparison is motivated by the metonymic connection of Orthodox ruler and boundary crossing, the demarcation of a new state of being. Constantine is the ruler who initiated the transformation of the Byzantine empire from pagan to Christian. Vladi-mir was *chosen* by God—note the verb *chose* (*iz"bra*)—to effect an analogous transformation of Kievan Rus'. His latter-day kinsman, Ivan III, the ruler of Muscovite Rus', the only major Orthodox land not controlled by infidels, must also be identified with such a transformation. The unspoken message is that he has been chosen by God to preside at the dawning of the age with-out end ("now, in these last years") when the righteous, living and newly risen at the General Resurrection, obtain the salvation of eternal life. He is, indeed, the new Constantine, enthroned in Moscow, the new Constantinople, pre-pared for the promise of the End Times. The title of autocrat (*samoderzhets*) in reference to the grand prince is first used by Zosima in *The Presentation*,[65] a new title appropriate for his exalted status at the beginning of the eighth millennium.

The synod that Zosima convened to present the paschal blueprint for the new age is represented in these "last" years as a contemporary counterpart of the gathering in the very first year, when the Apostles assembled after Christ's Ascension. Their encounter with the timeless occurred with the Descent of the Holy Spirit, conceived as an eschatological event, the Pentecost (cf. Acts 2:1–21). In Jerusalem, the Pentecost marked the dawning of a new age, the beginning of the church. In Kiev, the baptism of Vladimir (Volodimer) marked the beginning of the Christian history of Rus.' Likewise, Zosima and his synod expected their encounter with the timeless to occur in Moscow,

---

64. Sinitsyna, *Tretii Rim*, 122–24.

65. Marc Szeftel, "The Title of the Muscovite Monarch up to the End of the Seventeenth Century," *Canadian-American Slavic Studies* 13 (1979): 65.

when Christ would return in the Second Coming, an event perceived as imminent, but unpredictable.

The *Presentation* also establishes a set of cities inviting comparison. Constantinople is called the New Rome, a reference of the transfer of Christian authority from the apostate city of Peter to the Orthodox city of Constantine. Moscow is called the New Constantinople, an allusion to the same transfer of Christian authority to Moscow after the fall of Constantinople. One can surely agree that in practice, the Rusian church still looked to the patriarch of Constantinople as the authoritative head of Eastern Orthodoxy,[66] but in theory propagated the more optimistic perspective that Moscow was the purer vessel. This is the perspective of a society, certainly its elite, that believed itself to be "living in the shadow of the End," expecting in "these last years" the Second Coming of Christ. Of the five extant texts of the *Presentation,* however, only the one traditionally viewed as oldest calls Constantinople the New Rome; the others, dated to the fifteenth-sixteenth century call it the New Jerusalem. In these latter readings with Constantinople as the New Jerusalem, Moscow as the New Constantinople inherits the promise of Revelation as well.[67]

In this regard, it is worth noting that in 1486, Ivan III donated the Great Zion (*Sion* or *Ierusalim*) and the Small Zion (fig. 15) to the Cathedral of the Dormition in the Moscow Kremlin, during the very period (1475–1505) that he transformed Moscow's Kremlin into a sacred center worthy of its exalted Christian status. These imposing liturgical arks of gilded copper were used in major liturgical ceremonies. Meant to represent the Heavenly Jerusalem,

66. Donald Ostrowski suggests that a highly negative view of Constantinople from around 1448 (the date of the selection of Iona as metropolitan of Moscow without patriarchal approval) gave way to a softened position later in that century that remained in effect. He correctly cites as evidence the petition of Ivan IV for the patriarch's approval of his taking the title *tsar'* in 1547 and the need for the patriarch to approve the creation of the Moscow patriarchate in 1589. *Muscovy and the Mongols: Cross-Cultural Influences on the Steppe Frontier, 1304–1589* (Cambridge: Cambridge University Press, 1998), 139–41, 238.

67. I. A. Tikhoniuk has claimed recently that because the traditionally oldest text (Trinity 46) was found to contain Easter tables beginning with 7004 rather than the expected 7001, it must be a secondary, reworked version of the original (probably by Metropolitan Simon of the Trinity Monastery) and that the texts with the reading "New Jerusalem" represent the prototype. Tikhoniuk, "'Izlozhenie paskhalii' moskovskogo mitropolita Zosimy," in *Issledovaniia po istochnikovedeniiu istorii SSSR, XIII–XVIII vv.* (Moscow: Institut istorii ANSSSR, 1986), 47, 55. But this analysis has been challenged by Sinitsyna, who points out that the Easter tables dated to 7004 are written in a different hand, with different ink, and in a less careful flowing style than that found in the text proper. She treats them as later inserts to the original text. Moreover, she points out that the Trinity 46 manuscript is the only one with a heading, and that heading specifically names Zosima as author, working by order of Ivan III. *Tretii Rim,* 122 n. 14. Moshe Taube cautions (personal communication) that among texts in several copies, those with headings are often secondary. If "New Jerusalem" is indeed the original reading, then the case for Moscow identifying itself with this apocalyptic representation is made even stronger.

FIG. 15 *Small Zion.* Gilded copper. Moscow. Cathedral of the Dormition. c. 1486. Copy of the lost original. Zions were liturgical accoutrements believed to be iconic representations of the Heavenly Jerusalem as instantiated in the Holy Sepulcher in Jerusalem. Reprinted with permission from the archives of Engelina Smirnova, Institute of Art History, Moscow.

they were probably influenced in form by the *aedicula* of the Church of the Holy Sepulcher in Jerusalem, the imposing chapel, surmounted by an onion dome, over the site of Christ's interment.[68]

Although a relatively late cultural phenomenon, the Apocalypse stimulated concern, if not widespread psychological panic, in Muscovite Rus' as 1492 approached. After the fateful year, interest did not wane. Rather, we see overt evidence for the emergence of a nonpredictive apocalyptic mode, centered around the Muscovite ruler and his court, and keyed to expression of a positive and optimistic new millennial age, an age in which the ruling elite invested itself in the idea of Moscow as the New Jerusalem, with all the soteriological implications that association could bring.[69] It was a mode that retained its ideological value among the Muscovite elite well into the seventeenth century, when popular voices came to challenge the state and its official church as the true instruments of salvation in the face of inevitable apocalyptic cataclysm.

68. I. A. Sterligova, "Ierusalimy kak liturgicheskie sosudy v Drevnei Rusi," in *Ierusalim v russkoi kul'-ture*, ed. Andrei Batalov and Aleksei Lidov (Moscow: Vostochnaia Literatura, 1994), 46–47; A. M. Lidov, "Ierusalimskii kuvuklii. O proiskhozhdenii lukovichnykh glav," in *Ikonografiia arkhitektury*, ed. A. L. Batalov (Moscow: Vsesoiuznyi Nauchno-Issledovatel'skii Institut Teorii Arkhitektury i Gradostroitel'stva, 1990), 59–60.

69. See Michael S. Flier, "The Iconology of Royal Ritual in Sixteenth-Century Muscovy," in *Byzantine Studies: Essays on the Slavic World and the Eleventh Century*, ed. Speros Vryonis, Jr. (New Rochelle, N.Y.: Aristide D. Caratzas, 1992), 53–76; idem, "Breaking the Code: The Image of the Tsar in the Muscovite Palm Sunday Ritual," in *Medieval Russian Culture*, vol. 2, ed. Michael S. Flier and Daniel Rowland, California Slavic Studies 19 (Berkeley and Los Angeles: University of California Press, 1994), 213–42; idem, "Filling in the Blanks: The Church of the Intercession and the Architectonics of Medieval Muscovite Ritual," *Kamen' kraeog "l'n": Rhetoric of the Medieval Slavic World*, ed. Nancy S. Kollmann et al., *Harvard Ukrainian Studies* 19, nos. 1–4 (1995): 120–137; idem, "Court Ritual and Reform: Patriarch Nikon and the Palm Sunday Ritual," in *Religion and Culture in Early Modern Russia and Ukraine*, ed. Samuel H. Baron and Nancy Shields Kollmann (DeKalb: Northern Illinois University Press, 1997), 73–95.

7

WOMEN AND THE ORTHODOX FAITH IN MUSCOVITE RUSSIA

Spiritual Experience
and Practice

ISOLDE THYRÊT

While scholars of medieval and early modern Europe have made great strides in the last two decades in discovering the religious life of women in the West and identifying gender-specific expressions of spirituality, historians of the Orthodox East, and specifically medieval Russia, have yet to follow the example of their Western counterparts.[1] The reasons for the lack of studies on gender-specific patterns of piety in medieval Russia are manifold. They range from a problematic medieval Russian source-base to the structural differences between Catholic and Orthodox institutions. Still, in view of recent studies of the impact of medieval Russian Orthodox liturgical practices on Muscovite political culture and expressions of popular piety in prayers and saints' cults, the time seems right to raise the question to what extent a gender-specific spirituality existed in medieval Russia.[2] If indeed Muscovite men and

---

1. The application of the term "medieval" to Russia deserves an explanation, since Russia never participated in the developments of the Middle Ages (ca. 500–1500), which are traditionally defined in Western European terms. Since Russia's political and cultural development started centuries after that of Western Europe, scholars have to decide whether to classify the Muscovite period (ca. 1400–1700) as medieval or early modern. While it may make sense for experts in political or economic history to think of Muscovite Russia in early modern terms, the cultural and religious historian of Muscovy finds greater similarities with the medieval period. In this article the terms "medieval" and "Muscovite" are therefore used interchangeably.

2. See, for example, Michael Flier, "Breaking the Code: The Image of the Tsar in the Muscovite Palm Sunday Ritual," in *Medieval Russian Culture,* vol. 2, ed. Michael S. Flier and Daniel Rowland, California Slavic Studies 19 (Berkeley and Los Angeles: University of California Press, 1994), 213–42; Daniel Rowland, "Biblical Military Imagery in the Political Culture of Early Modern Russia: The Blessed Host of the Heavenly Tsar," in *Medieval Russian Culture,* 182–212; Eve Levin, "Supplicatory Prayers as a Source for Popular Religious Culture in Muscovite Russia," in *Religion and Culture in Early Modern Russia and Ukraine,* ed. Samuel H. Baron and Nancy Shields Kollmann (DeKalb: Northern Illinois University Press, 1997), 96–114.

women experienced the Orthodox faith differently, how did women relate to the holy and experience it in a "feminine" way?

To a large extent the question of women's active involvement in the medieval Russian Orthodox faith has been overshadowed by the exclusive focus of historians of medieval Russian religion on areas in which women did not feature prominently. For example, the few scholars who have paid attention to the issue of medieval Russian monasticism have noted the absence of a specifically female monastic spirituality. Instead they emphasize that Russian monasteries served as receptacles for undesirable or recalcitrant women that presented a threat to the accepted social or political order.[3] Undoubtedly it is true that monasteries in medieval Russia did not present the same kind of opportunities that monastic institutions afforded early medieval Western women (one thinks of the charisma of Merovingian monastics such as Radegund). One should not forget, however, that with few exceptions, such as Saints Sergii of Radonezh and Nil Sorskii, it is difficult to identify truly unique male Russian monastic spiritualities as well.[4] As Caroline Bynum's study of the nuns of Helfta in the thirteenth century has shown, Cistercian monasticism provided a fertile setting for the development of a gender-specific religious experience in the medieval West.[5] The Orthodox tradition, however, lacked defined religious orders, which allowed individual nuns to develop a communal identity and to express their religious experiences within the parameters—and safety—of their monastic communities. This may well have worked against the development of female monastic spiritualities in medieval Russia. In view of the different concepts underlying monasticism in the Latin West and the Orthodox East, it may be unwise to look to monasticism as the main source of both male and female religious expression in medieval Russia.

Another factor that impedes our understanding of the religious experience of medieval Russian women is the general focus of Eastern Orthodoxy on a mysticism of experience rather than a mysticism of the word. From the High Middle Ages on, spirituality in the West took the theological concept of the

---

3. On Russian monasticism, see Igor Smolitsch, *Russisches Mönchtum. Entstehung, Entwicklung und Wesen, 988–1917* (Würzburg: Augustiner Verlag, 1953); Marie A. Thomas, "Muscovite Convents in the Seventeenth Century," *Russian History* 10 (1983): 230–42; and Georgii Fedotov, *Sviatye Drevnei Rusi (X–XVII st.)* (1931; reprint, Rostov-on-Don: Feniks, 1999), 278.

4. On Radegund and other female monastic saints of the early Middle Ages, see Jane Tibbetts Schulenburg, *Forgetful of Their Sex: Female Sanctity and Society, ca. 500–1100* (Chicago: University of Chicago Press, 1998).

5. Caroline Walker Bynum, *Jesus as Mother: Studies in the Spirituality of the High Middle Ages* (Berkeley and Los Angeles: University of California Press, 1982), 170–262.

humanity of Christ as its focus. Within this context women mystics identified the female with Christ's suffering and sacrifice for humankind. For this reason experts on Orthodox spirituality, which in essence concentrates on the spiritual and sensual perception of divine action within the cosmic parameters of the Christian salvation drama rather than the individual experience of the divine, cannot expect to find a gender-specific mysticism of the Catholic type.[6] Medieval Russia produced neither a Bernard of Clairvaux (the famous Cistercian abbot who shaped twelfth-century mystic piety with his emotional language of religious experience) nor female mystics such as Hildegard of Bingen (1098–1179) or Julian of Norwich (1342–?).

Although Eastern forms of monasticism and mysticism differed from those of the West, Muscovite women developed and enacted their own distinctive spirituality. As William Wagner points out in his chapter on the Nizhegorod Convent of the Exaltation of the Cross in the imperial period, the fact that the nuns of the nineteenth century displayed no interest in debates about religious reform does not necessarily mean that they had no spiritual ideals. By focusing on their monastery as a site of ritual performance, they consciously affirmed the existing order in the church. The nuns' decision to de-emphasize their engagement in crafts and instead function as guardians of Orthodox liturgical practices and symbols can be interpreted as the choice of a feminine spiritual path. In this instance, the nuns' practical measures regulating their monastic mode of life expressed their spirituality no less than their pious thoughts might have done. In a similar manner, medieval Russian monastic women often expressed their commitment to their institutions through pious donations. The tonsured royal women Evdokiia Bogdanovna Saburova, Anna Alekseevna Koltovskaia, and Marfa Alekseevna all sought to expand the territories and attached rights of their monasteries "for the sake of their souls."[7] The fact that these women (just as their nineteenth-century

---

6. On the shift of attitudes to the divine in the High Middle Ages and the resulting emphasis on the humanity of Christ, see Caroline Walker Bynum, "The Body of Christ in the Later Middle Ages: A Reply to Leo Steinberg," in *Fragmentation and Redemption: Essays on Gender and the Human Body in Medieval Religion,* ed. Caroline Walker Bynum (New York: Zone Books, 1991), 79–118; idem, "'And Woman His Humanity': Female Imagery in the Religious Writing of the Later Middle Ages," in *Fragmentation and Redemption,* 151–79; also see idem, *Jesus as Mother.*

7. See, for example, *Akty istoricheskie sobrannye i izdannye Arkheograficheskoiu kommissieiu,* 5 vols. (St. Petersburg, 1841–42), vol. 1, no. 218, pp. 414–15 (Evdokiia Bogdanovna Saburova); vol. 1, no. 217, pp. 413–14; vol. 3, no. 41, p. 37; vol. 3, no. 67, pp. 61–62; *Russkaia istoricheskaia biblioteka,* 39 vols. (St. Petersburg-Leningrad: Tipografiia imperatorskoi Akademii nauk, 1872–1927), vol. 35, cols. 671–72; D. Ch. Erdman, "Kopiia s dukhovnoi skhimonakhini tsaritsy Dar'i," *Vremennik obshchestva istorii i drevnostei rossiiskikh* 9 (1851): sec. 3, pp. 61–63 (Anna Alekseevna Koltovskaia); Arkhimandrit Leonid, "Blagovernaia tsarevna, velikaia kniazhna Marfa Alekseevna," *Russkii arkhiv* 20 (1882): 27 (Marfa Alekseevna).

counterparts in Nizhegorod) were intent on mitigating the harsh living conditions of their sisters and providing a social service for widows does not make their endeavors any less spiritual than those of the early medieval Benedictines, whose rule forbade harsh ascetic practices and advocated special treatment for young novices and old and sickly monks.

The need to apply to the study of the spirituality of medieval Russian women a flexible and creative approach, evident in the interpretation of women's monastic experience, also comes to the fore in research on medieval Russian women saints. The small number of officially canonized women saints has led scholars, such as E. Golubinskii and G. Fedotov, to believe that Muscovite Russia did not encourage the concept of holy women.[8] In view of the fact that the concept of canonization, its institutional ramifications, and its meaning to the church hierarchy and the Russian Orthodox community at large still needs detailed investigation, any speculation about female sainthood in Muscovite Russia must remain tentative.[9] Medieval Russians worshiped a wide variety of women that were considered holy, although not from the Western, Catholic perspective, which subjected prospective saints to a rigorous canonization procedure from the twelfth century on.[10] In medieval Russia women gained their reputation for sanctity less through the approval of an official hierarchy than through the popular commemoration of their pious acts. In view of the absence of an established canonization procedure, the line between a woman saint and a saintly woman was often not clearly drawn. As a result, medieval Russia's holy women represent a motley group. As Fedotov points out, the few female native saints acknowledged by the Russian church comprised monastics of no extraordinary social rank, princesses who took the veil, laywomen, and martyrs.[11]

Evdokiia Bogdanovna Saburova was the first wife of Tsarevich Ivan Ivanovich, son of Ivan IV the Terrible. She was forced to take the veil by Ivan IV in 1571. Anna Alekseevna Koltovskaia (m. in 1572, d. in 1627) was the fourth of Ivan IV's seven wives. She, too, was forced by Ivan IV to take monastic vows. Marfa Alekseevna (1652–1707), a daughter of Tsar Aleksei Mikhailovich, was tonsured by her half-brother, Peter the Great, in 1698 because she supported her natal sister, Sofiia Alekseevna, in Peter's and Sofiia's struggle for the Russian throne.

8. The index to Golubinskii's pathbreaking work on canonization in Russia names fewer than two dozen holy women; see E. Golubinskii, *Istoriia kanonizatsii sviatykh v russkoi tserkvi* (Moscow: Universitetskaia tipografiia, 1903), 583–94. Fedotov points out that only twelve Muscovite women were ever canonized. See Fedotov, *Sviatye Drevnei Rusi,* 277.

9. For a recent assessment of the religious and social ramifications of the canonization practice in Muscovite Russia, see Paul Bushkovitch, *Religion and Society in Russia: The Sixteenth and Seventeenth Centuries* (New York: Oxford University Press, 1992), 74–127.

10. On the evolution of the canonization process in the West, see E. W. Kemp, *Canonization and Authority in the Western Church* (London: Oxford University Press, 1948).

11. Fedotov, *Sviatye Drevnei Rusi,* 278–86.

Literary and cultural historians of the medieval West have shed light on the spirituality of nontraditional women, such as Beguines (laywomen practicing charity who live together in communities without formal vows), Tertiaries (lay members of associations attached to the formal orders of the mendicants), and anchorites (women who live in seclusion on the periphery of medieval settlements).[12] In contrast, the topoi of the vitae and religious and popular tales of medieval Russian holy women have not yet been systematically explored. My own work on pious royal women of the Muscovite period, however, suggests that like Western medieval women religious, medieval Russian saintly women shared distinct spiritual features that set them apart from their male counterparts.

Whether we look at the officially canonized ninth-century Kievan ruler saint Ol'ga, the popularly venerated grand princesses Evdokiia Donskaia (the fourteenth-century wife of the Muscovite grand prince Dmitrii Donskoi) and Solomoniia Saburova (the first wife of Grand Prince Vasilii III, who forced her to take the veil in 1525), or tsaritsy esteemed for their piety, such as Ivan IV's first wife, Anastasiia Romanovna (d. 1560), and Tsar Aleksei Mikhailovich's first wife, Mariia Il'inichna (d. 1669), all these women distinguish themselves through their commitment to the Orthodox faith and the maintenance of the Muscovite autocracy. Their commitment to the Orthodox faith manifests itself in their efforts to build a Christian community in Russia and defend it against the encroachments of non-Christian or non-Orthodox believers. The sixteenth-century vita of Saint Ol'ga celebrates the Kievan princess for introducing the Christian faith in Russia and erecting churches all over her realm.[13] According to the contemporary religious tale entitled *Skazanie v male,* Grand Princess Evdokiia Donskaia initiated the translation of the icon of the Virgin of Vladimir, which saved Russia from the attack of the infidel Tatars led by Temir-Aksak. She also distinguished herself by commissioning the construction and decoration of many churches and monasteries, among them the Church of the Birth of the Virgin and the Monastery of the Ascension in the Kremlin.[14] Solomoniia Saburova posthumously saved

12. Caroline Walker Bynum, *Holy Feast and Holy Fast: The Religious Significance of Food to Medieval Women* (Berkeley and Los Angeles: University of California Press, 1987); Sharon K. Elkins, *Holy Women of Twelfth-Century England* (Chapel Hill: University of North Carolina Press, 1988); Elizabeth Alvilda Petroff, *Body and Soul: Essays on Medieval Women and Mysticism* (New York: Oxford Unversity Press, 1994); Emilie Zum Brunn and Georgette Epiney-Burgard, eds., *Women Mystics in Medieval Europe* (New York: Paragon House, 1989).

13. *Polnoe sobranie russkikh letopisei* (hereafter, *PSRL*), 41 vols. to date (St. Petersburg-Moscow, 1846–1995), vol. 21, pt. 1, pp. 21–22.

14. Ibid., pt. 2, pp. 408–9.

the Monastery of the Veil in the town of Suzdal and the town itself from the attack of the Poles during the Time of Troubles.[15] Anastasiia Romanovna and Mariia Il'inichna supported their husbands' military efforts against the Tatars of Kazan and the Polish-Lithuanian realm with prayers and pious deeds, such as care for the poor and imprisoned. With these spiritual efforts the royal women were thought to curry divine favor for their spouses' undertakings.[16]

The saintly royal women of Muscovy gained a reputation for serving the tsardom and its subjects with pious endeavors. Many of them distinguished themselves through their generosity to ecclesiastic and monastic institutions.[17] Saint Ol'ga was celebrated as a model ruler in Muscovite Russia who could keep her realm unharmed with her "sensible government."[18] Her vita states that she "enriched herself through charity. She clothed the naked and fed the hungry, gave the thirsty to drink and provided the homeless with all the necessary means. She had extraordinary mercy on the poor, the widows and orphans, and the sick, and satisfied all their needs."[19] In a similar manner the *Skazanie v male* credited Evdokiia Donskaia with spiritual labors that bene-fited her children and the subjects of her realm and praised her generosity and love for the poor.[20] Moreover, she was credited with approximately thirty healing miracles that benefited her subjects.[21] Solomoniia Saburova as well performed a number of healing miracles in the seventeenth century.[22] As a result of their charity and pious acts, Muscovites considered these women intercessors for the Russian tsardom and its subjects before God.

The theme of spiritual intercession, evident in the portrayal of saintly medieval Russian royal women, was also attributed to the wives of the Mus-covite tsars who did not enjoy explicit veneration, but who were still credited with buttressing the autocracy with their pious deeds. The tsaritsy were

---

15. Rossiiskaia natsional'naia biblioteka (hereafter, RNB), F. XVIII.16, *l.* 681; also see Isolde Thyrêt, *Between God and Tsar: Religious Symbolism and the Royal Women of Muscovite Russia* (DeKalb: Northern Illinois University Press, 2001), 37–38.

16. *PSRL,* vol. 29, p. 79; Thyrêt, *Between God and Tsar,* 128–30.

17. For Solomoniia Saburova's and Anastasiia's gifts to the Trinity-Sergii Monastery and the monastery of Saint Nikita of Pereslavl, see Isolde Thyrêt, "Blessed Is the Tsaritsa's Womb: The Myth of Miraculous Birth and Royal Motherhood in Muscovite Russia," *Russian Review* 53 (1994): 484–88, 492, and idem, *Between God and Tsar,* 25–26, 43.

18. *PSRL,* vol. 21, pt. 1, p. 29.

19. Ibid., p. 22.

20. *PSRL,* vol. 21, pt. 2, p. 410; 408–9. On the *Skazanie v male,* see Gail Lenhoff, "Unofficial Ven-eration of the Daniilovichi in Muscovite Rus'," in *Culture and Identity in Muscovy, 1359–1584,* ed. A. M. Kleimola and G. D. Lenhoff (Moscow: ITZ-Garant, 1997), 411–14.

21. *PSRL,* vol. 21, pt. 2, p. 411.

22. RNB, F. XVII. 16, *l.* 681–682 *ob.*

expected to foster the cults of protector saints of the royal family to guarantee the safety and well-being of the tsar and his immediate relatives.[23] By engaging in public pilgrimages to the shrines of these saints, the tsaritsy were acting as symbolic extensions of their royal husbands through their exercise of charity and justice along the pilgrimage path. Anastasiia Romanovna's display of charity and compassion for the poor was not only appreciated by her husband, who expected her to support his military battles with spiritual deeds on the home front, but is also attested to in the emotional outpouring of the masses during her funeral. A century later, Mariia Il'inichna's involvement with her subjects showed itself in her generous alms-giving and her acceptance of petitions during pilgrimages.[24] In the person of the tsaritsa, religious intercession and social service thus became inextricably intertwined.

A comparison of the topoi associated with the saintly royal wives of Muscovy and the early-seventeenth-century lay saint Ul'ianiia Lazarevskaia Osor'ina of Murom suggests that the royal status of the former does not essentially change this picture of medieval Russian feminine spirituality. During her marriage to Georgii Osor'in, Ul'ianiia, daughter of the steward Iustin Nediurev and his wife, Stefanida, engaged in cloth production and embroidery and used the profit from the sale of her products to support the building of churches in her region.[25] Like Saint Ol'ga, she was esteemed for her wisdom and her ability to maintain her household even in times of severe economic crisis.[26] Like the tsaritsy's piety, Ul'ianiia's spiritual disposition was shaped by her domestic role as a wife and caretaker of her family and servants. In essence her spirituality manifested itself in a life of service to the needy. She clothed the orphans and took care of ailing widows. She deprived herself of food to feed the hungry during a time of starvation. Ul'ianiia organized the burial of the dead. When her parents-in-law passed away, she arranged for their commemoration and sent alms to the prisons.[27] Like in the case of the pious royal women, we encounter the themes of mediation, care for one's family, and charity toward the less privileged in society.

---

23. Thyrêt, *Between God and Tsar*, 41–45.

24. *PSRL*, vol. 29, pp. 79, 287 (Anastasiia Romanovna); Thyrêt, *Between God and Tsar*, 127 (Mariia Il'inichna).

25. Kalistrat Osor'in, "Povest' ob Ul'ianii Osor'inoi," in *Pamiatniki literatury Drevnei Rusi. XVII vek. Kniga pervaia*, ed. T. R. Rudi (Moscow: Khudozhestvennaia literatura, 1988), 98–99; also see Serge A. Zenkovsky, *Medieval Russia's Epics, Chronicles, and Tales*, rev. ed. (New York: E. P. Dutton, 1974), 391–93. Both texts represent the short, that is to say, the oldest, redaction of the source.

26. Osor'in, "Povest'," 98–99, 102–3; Zenkovsky, *Medieval Russia's Epics*, 392, 396–98.

27. Osor'in, "Povest'," 99, 100–101; Zenkovsky, *Medieval Russia's Epics*, 392, 394–95.

The identification of saintly medieval Russian women from all walks of life with a piety of action—characterized by a commitment to service and charity—attests to the existence of a gender-specific spirituality in Muscovite Russia. An extension of the Orthodox concern with good works, female piety in Muscovy both reinforced and transformed the existing patriarchal social order. Through service and intercession the saintly Russian women defused conflicts and upheld the social status quo, but also gently corrected injustices and alleviated misfortune associated with the structure of their society. Not surprisingly, this type of female pious behavior endured into the imperial period when—as Gary Marker points out—women like Anna Labzina constructed their spirituality around the theme of service to the needy and Russian empresses acted as mother-intercessors.

Although medieval Russian women saints were mostly associated with the feminine qualities of service and charity, this identification was not maintained as an absolute principle. Whenever the situation required it, a female saint could take on a masculine image as well. The vita of Saint Ol'ga describes the Kievan princess as a figure that excelled in wisdom and reason and was able to take the reins of government like a man.[28] Saint Solomoniia punished the Lithuanian lord who attempted to destroy the town of Suzdal by torturing him. This type of gender-reversal, which Nadieszda Kizenko observes as well in the characterization of Saint Kseniia of Petersburg in the imperial period, was not perceived as subversive, as in the case of holy fools, but testifies to medieval Russia's ability to embrace role reversal for women saints as an option. As the fresco cycles of the stories of pious Russian, Byzantine, and Georgian women in the Golden Palace of the Tsaritsy suggest, Muscovite Russians were comfortable attributing to their religious heroines masculine qualities if the resulting message supported current political or social agendas. The image of the pious Georgian Princess Dinara, who put on armor, rode into battle, cut off the head of her Persian foe, and displayed it victoriously on a spear, demonstrates that the Muscovite crafters of religious messages attributed to religious women the strength, effectiveness, and commitment of men and held them up as models for members of both sexes.[29]

A striking aspect of female medieval Russian sainthood is the universal appeal of women saints to members of all social strata. Although the posthumous cults of Saints Evfrosiniia of Suzdal and Solomoniia Saburova

28. *PSRL,* vol. 21, pt. 1, p. 29.
29. Thyrêt, *Between God and Tsar,* 96–102.

were initially fostered by the nuns and the staff of their respective monastic establishments, who first experienced and testified to miraculous healings at the saints' tombs, the holy women soon were thought to affect the fate of the entire Muscovite realm.[30] Both saints healed members of either sex indiscriminately.

Scholars searching for clues to expressions of medieval Russian spiritual life by members of the female sex may well discover that, in addition to the traditional study of women saints, an investigation of forms of female lay piety—that is to say, the religious norms and behavior of nonmonastic women of all social strata—can render promising results. As Gary Marker points out in his piece on Russian women's spirituality in the eighteenth century, Russian women tended to display their religious potential—and oftentimes charisma—outside dominant institutions. If, as Marker rightly points out, Russian Orthodoxy was not merely a monolithic belief system but represented a means for common people to give meaning to their lives, a study of the religious behavior and practices of laywomen can render insightful results concerning our knowledge of Russian women's spirituality.

Much information about a feminine experience and practice of the Orthodox faith in medieval Russia can be derived from the vast number of Russian miracle tales that are attached to the *lives* of Russian saints, both male and female. A study of the cults of saints that arose in the Russian north, where the Christian faith had not yet taken deep roots, suggests that women were more inclined than men to seek out the help of the miracle workers. For political or economic reasons men were often hostile to the new shrines and sought out pagan sorcerers. Not surprisingly, in this context we encounter the topos of angry saints who retaliate against the male unbelievers. Women, on the other hand, elicited a more compassionate and forgiving response from the holy figures. The association of women with pagan customs, such as roaming in the forests, was treated as a form of possession, which the saints healed. In many instances women developed affective spiritual relationships with the holy men, who conversed with them and comforted them in times of personal grief. Women often displayed a distaste for the saints' competitors, the pagan sorcerers, which disproves the popular conception of S. I. Smirnov and Mary Matossian that medieval Russian females were the major perpetuators of pagan Russian practices.[31]

---

30. For the posthumous miracles of Evfrosiniia of Suzdal, see "Zhitie pr. Evfrosinii Suzdal'skoi po spisku XVII veka," in V. Georgievskii, *Suzdal'skii rizpolozhenskii zhenskii monastyr'. Istoriko-arkheologicheskoe opisanie* (Vladimir: Tipo-Litografiia Gubernskago Pravleniia, 1900), 57–67.

31. Isolde Thyrêt, "Muscovite Miracle Stories as Sources for Gender-Specific Religious Experience,"

A gender-specific experience of the holy can also be seen in the reaction of medieval Russian men and women to the cults of monastic saints. The vitae of male saints who lived a monastic life often mention that these holy men denied women access, and as a result, spiritual care. Their action is usually ascribed to their concern that females violated the code of monastic life, which insisted on the separation of sexes to protect monks from sexual temptation. The monks who controlled the shrine of one of their own saintly brothers similarly discriminated against female pilgrims. They readily engaged in arranging men's visits to the shrines and played an important part in the liturgical ritual surrounding their healing by the saint at his tomb. Female visitors, however, were expected to make special contributions in the form of alms or liturgical gifts and often received the saints' grace during incubation, that is to say, in dreams while sleeping at the shrine. In many instances women experienced a supernatural cure while they were lying alone at the foot of a shrine.[32]

The different treatment of men and women who visited monastic shrines shaped the experience of the patrons of the cults in a gender-specific way. While male pilgrims embraced the authorities and the ritual surrounding the shrines, women tended to distrust the shrine controllers, who performed services at the tomb for them half-heartedly at best. The episode concerning the healing of the crippled woman Dar'ia in the miracle cycle of Saint Ignatii Vologodskii demonstrates this point:

> She had herself carried to the shrine of the holy miracle workers. She implored the *hegumen*, Afonasii, and the priests that they pray to God, the Immaculate Virgin, and the holy miracle workers for her, and she gave a sufficient amount of alms. The *hegumen* quickly ordered the bell rung, and when the brothers gathered at the tomb of the holy miracle workers and the liturgy had been sung, all of them left the cathedral for their cells. The woman kneeled at the tomb of the holy miracle workers and begged for forgiveness for her sins and for a cure of her ailment. And she left and went to her guest cell, grieving about her affliction.[33]

---

in *Religion and Culture in Early Modern Russia and Ukraine*, 121–22 (I wish to thank Northern Illinois University Press for permitting me to republish some of the findings of this article); S. I. Smirnov, "Baby bogomerzkiia," in *Sbornik statei posviashchennykh Vasiliiu Osipovichu Kliuchevskomu ego uchenikami* (Moscow: Pechatnia S. P. Iakovleva, 1909), 217–43; Mary Matossian, "In the Beginning, God Was a Woman," *Journal of Social History* 6 (1973): 325–43.

32. Thyrêt, "Muscovite Miracle Stories," 123–24.

33. Rossiiskaia gosudarstvennaia biblioteka (hereafter, RGB), *f.* 310, *d.* 302, *ll.* 91 *ob.*–92. The woman was eventually healed by Saint Ignatii in a vision.

Women responded to the neglect by the staff around the monastic shrines by engaging in personal prayers and pious acts that could offset the lack of official intercession. For example, when a certain princess named Anna sent her grandson to Saint Ioasaf Kamenskii for healing, she not only gave alms to assure the monks' liturgical support but also prayed herself day and night and performed God-pleasing deeds to assure a positive outcome.[34] Moreover, in view of the reserved attitude of the monastic staff, it is not surprising that the female clients of saints developed a close spiritual relationship with them. Women are frequently credited with having great faith in their supernatural protectors, who in turn were kindly disposed to them. Miracle tales tend to attribute to women, rather than men, the gift of *umilenie,* the ability to pray with tears. Female clients of saints are also associated with literary motifs such as seeing God with their hearts and minds.[35] The physical and emotional dissociation from the shrine personnel also influenced the way women experienced supernatural cures. In the absence of liturgical mediators, women received healing from the saints more directly, namely, in dreams or visions. Since this personal experience of the saints did not depend on the shrine site, female cures often occurred at home or on the way to the holy tomb—a clear sign that women preferred not to depend on their access to the formal setting of the shrine. The supernatural visitations involving female believers emphasized an intimate relationship between healers and patients. The saints generally inquired about their clients' suffering and calmed their fears. The holy figures often touched their patients, held their hands, or stroked their faces.[36]

The religious experience of laywomen who sought out the thaumaturgical quality of the saints in essence did not change if ecclesiastics rather than monks controlled the shrines of holy figures. To the Muscovite church's credit, clerics encouraged women to give testimony to the power of saints, which resulted in women's contribution to the composition of vitae and the official veneration of holy men and women. Female believers found it easier to gain access to ecclesiastically controlled shrines than to tombs placed in a monastic environment. Moreover, Muscovite clerics often worked to close the gap between female believers and the supernatural, by visiting ill women in their homes and treating them with mobile relics, such as dust from the tomb of saints or water from a well a holy man had dug during his lifetime.[37] In

---

34. Sanktpeterburgskii Filial Instituta rossiiskoi istorii Rossiiskoi akademii nauk, *f.* 238, *opis'* 1, *d.* 162, *ll.* 55 *ob.*–56.

35. Thyrêt, "Muscovite Miracle Stories," 126.

36. Ibid., 124–25.

37. Isolde Thyrêt, "Ecclesiastical Perceptions of the Female and the Role of the Holy in the Religious Life of Women in Muscovite Russia" (Ph.D. diss., University of Washington, 1992), 98–101.

many cases priests not only mediated the thaumaturgical power of the saints, but gave spiritual advice and care to their female parishioners. Still, the traditional ecclesiastical concern with the natural order that subordinated the female to the male and women's circumscribed position in liturgical settings (one notes the segregation of the sexes during the liturgy) hampered women's full participation in the cults of ecclesiastical saints. Many miracle stories contain the topos of ecclesiastical shrine controllers neglecting the spiritual care of female parishioners who came to them for help. A particularly striking example is found in Ioasaf's miracle cycle of Saint Nikita of Novgorod. When the blind woman Kseniia begged Pimen, the archbishop of Novgorod, to intercede with the saint to restore her eyesight, Pimen refused her request. The saint subsequently restored her sight in one eye after she prayed at his tomb. When the woman later asked Pimen to pray that her entire vision be restored, the archbishop treated her unkindly: "Old woman, I see that you are old and have lived many years. One eye will suffice you to serve your body to the time of your death."[38] The saint eventually cured her entire affliction, making up for the archbishop's lack of compassion. Women were also hampered by the public aspects of many ecclesiastically controlled cults. The official feast days in honor of the saints attracted crowds that could prevent sick women from approaching the relics and force a postponement of their visits to the shrines. As a result, the miracle stories of saints whose cults were ecclesiastically controlled feature the same topoi with regard to women's religious experience as those of monastic saints. Hampered by ecclesiastical attitudes and protocol, women found healing in visions at home or en route to shrines. Their spiritual relationship with the saints was more affective than that of their male counterparts. Faith motifs and the themes of *umilenie* and intimate piety appear frequently as well.[39]

An examination of the actual interaction of medieval Russian saints and their clientele also suggests that men and women had different expectations with regard to the saints' supernatural intervention. While men's cures tended to restore their position in society at large, women's healings revolved around problems and restrictions specific to their gender. In a number of miracle cycles women's illnesses are identified exclusively with blindness, paralysis, and possession, conditions that can be read as signs of social dysfunction.[40]

38. RGB, *f.* 304.I, *d.* 673, *ll.* 375–376 *ob.*, 376 (quotation); also see Thyrêt, "Muscovite Miracle Stories," 125–26.

39. Thyrêt, "Muscovite Miracle Stories," 126.

40. Ronald C. Finucane, *Miracles and Pilgrims: Popular Beliefs in Medieval England* (New York: St. Martin's Press, 1995), 73, 146–51.

In such cases supernatural intervention restored women's independence, mobility, and interaction with members of their family and community. Female possession often can be interpreted as a form of depression, evident in the miracles of the robe of Christ that occurred in Moscow in 1624. The relic healed the maiden Marina, who was struck with the "black illness" and blindness and spoke little; Irina Spiridonova, who complained of exhaustion and "knew people little"; and a certain Evfimiia, who struggled with fear and terror of the heart.[41] In all these cases the supernatural powers became the focal points for women's psychological reintegration into their society.

The themes governing the interaction of saints and their female petitioners in many instances revolve around women's dependence on their families and their roles and responsibilities in them. The saints often alleviated intense grief in women who had lost a close family member and thus were deprived of protection and exposed to economic hardship. Saint Nikita of Pereslavl saved a woman from despair after her husband abandoned her and her little girl drowned.[42] In a society where women were charged with taking care of the health and well-being of their children, holy men supported mothers in their arduous task by protecting their offspring from harm and illness. For example, Saint Artemii Verkhol'skii was known for healing sick infants, which their mothers brought to his shrine.[43] The wives of the tsars regularly turned to Saints Sergii of Radonezh and Nikita of Pereslavl when their children suffered from childhood diseases.[44] Women also approached the saints when infertility threatened to break up their marriages. In many cases the saints intervened on the behalf of women who suffered from domestic abuse. For example, Saint Aleksandr Svirskii reprimanded the boyar Aprilev, who beat his wife for producing only female offspring. To teach the boyar a lesson, the saint arranged for the birth of yet another girl.[45] In a similar way, Saints Zosima and Savvatii of Solovki punished Prince I. A. Obolenskii, who had beaten his pregnant wife in anger and nearly caused her to miscarry, with the birth of a female child.[46] By granting the prince a baby girl instead of a

41. *Dvortsovye razriady po vysochaishemu poveleniiu izdannye II-em otdeleniem sobstvennoi ego Imperatorskago velichestva kantseliarii*, 4 vols. (St. Petersburg, 1851–55), vol. 2, 789, 805; also see Isolde Thyrêt, "Miracles of Hope: Saints and Social Justice for Women in Medieval Russia," *Sewanee Mediaeval Studies* 8 (1999): 300–301.

42. Biblioteka Akademii nauk (hereafter, BAN), Sobranie Petra Pervogo, A 37, *ll.* 43–44 *ob.*; also see Thyrêt, "Miracles of Hope," 302–3.

43. BAN, Luk'ianov Collection, *d.* 290, *ll.* 35 *ob.*, 37 *ob.*; for details, see Thyrêt, "Miracles of Hope," 306.

44. Thyrêt, *Between God and Tsar*, 41–44.

45. RGB, *f.* 304.I, *d.* 633, *ll.* 282–83; Thyrêt, "Miracles of Hope," 309.

46. Rossisskii gosudarstvennyi arkhiv drevnikh aktov (hereafter, RGADA), *f.* 181, *d.* 507, *ll.* 234–38; for details, see Thyrêt, "Miracles of Hope," 314.

son, Zosima and Savvatii made sure that he would never forget his offense. In another episode the two saints saved a young woman, who had cut her own throat out of fear of further physical mistreatment by her husband. The holy men not only restored her to life but also made sure that her wounds left no marks so that she would not remember the dark event.[47] In a society that did not shield females from domestic violence, the saints functioned as women's advocates for justice and protectors of their safety.

While the religious experience of Muscovite women shows the difficulty of their social position, it would be wrong to infer from this that their spirituality was primarily characterized by a victim mentality. Although the subject of women's role in the medieval Russian canonization process still awaits detailed investigation, their manner of involvement in this process suggests that they took their participation in defining the holy seriously. Muscovite women frequently testified in the procedural hearings that sought to establish a saint's sanctity. In 1524 the nun Evfrosiniia gave an official statement at the inquest of Grand Prince Iurii Vasil'evich that served as the basis of Saint Makarii Koliazinskii's vita.[48] Women also figured prominently in the establishment of the cults of Saints Ioann and Loggin of Iarenga and Ioann of Ustiug and played a significant role in the institution of the veneration of the robe of Christ.[49] In several instances one detects a gender-specific emphasis on certain traits ascribed to the saints. Evfrosiniia's statement, for example, discussed the parents and the nursemaid of Saint Makarii and his refusal as an infant to nurse on Wednesdays and Fridays, while the vita left out these references.[50] The emphasis on nursing and friendship among spouses reflects common female concerns, which are also attested to in the miracle stories of saints curing women. The opportunity to testify to the action of the holy in the Russian Orthodox community also motivated women to exchange their opinions with female friends and neighbors. Working through these informal female networks Muscovite women managed to put their own stamp on specific cults. For example, the story of Saint Basil punishing a young woman with blindness for mocking his nakedness and healing her after her repentance resonated particularly with his female followers in Moscow. Many of the saint's female clients suffered from blindness, which Saint Basil eventually cured.[51] The development of a separate feminine tradition in the worship of a holy

---

47. RGADA, f. 381, d. 199, ll. 330 ob.–332 ob.; also see Thyrêt, "Miracles of Hope," 315.

48. RNB, Pogodin Collection, d. 1571, ll. 28–29 ob.; for details, see Thyrêt, "Ecclesiastical Perceptions," 93–95.

49. Thyrêt, "Ecclesiastical Perceptions," 172–78.

50. Ibid., 95 n. 181.

51. Ibid., 183–84.

relic is especially noticeable in the evolution of the cult of the robe of Christ. The veneration of the robe resulted from the positive reaction of an over-whelmingly female clientele to the patriarch's call for the verification of the relic in 1624. By attesting to the healing power of the relic, the female wit-nesses met the official ecclesiastical expectation of the robe's authenticity. After the official celebration of the relic, however, women's enthusiasm for the continued support of the official cult seems to have cooled. While women con-tinued to visit the Cathedral of the Dormition where the robe was housed, their cures there were effected by more established thaumaturgical powers, such as the icon of the Virgin of Vladimir and the relics of Metropolitans Peter and Iona. Male visitors, on the other hand, continued to be healed by the robe of Christ.[52] The women's preference for the cult of the Virgin stands in stark contrast to the disposition of their Western medieval counterparts, who focused their spirituality on Christ. Part of the reason for Russian women's affinity to the Mother of God may lie in their identification with her intercessory role, as Gary Marker suggests. The cosmic ramifications of the Virgin's position in the Orthodox view also present the Orthodox Mother of God as a more powerful role model than her humbler Western counterpart.[53] In any case, women's conscious choice of the veneration of the Virgin of Vladimir shows that the Orthodox faith clearly offered women opportunities to express their own spiritual preferences.

The independent religious disposition of Muscovite women often pre-sented a challenge to the Russian Orthodox Church. The Stoglav, a Musco-vite church council taking place in 1551, denounced women who refused to work on the days devoted to Saints Paraskeva Piatnitsa and Anastasiia, pagan-Christian figures who were thought to protect female fertility. Instead of performing their household duties, women on these days roamed the coun-tryside, preaching about their visionary experiences.[54] Ul'ianiia Lazarevskaia avoided going to church one winter, preferring to pray alone at home. A vision her priest experienced in which the Virgin requested her presence dur-ing the service eventually changed her mind.[55]

---

52. Ibid., 184–87.

53. On the evolution of the image of the Virgin Mary in the West, see Marina Warner, *Alone of All Her Sex: The Myth and the Cult of the Virgin Mary* (New York: Alfred Knopf, 1976); Sally Cunneen, *In Search of Mary: The Woman and the Symbol* (New York: Ballantine Books, 1996); and Penny Schine Gold, *The Lady and the Virgin: Image, Attitude, and Experience in Twelfth-Century France* (Chicago: University of Chicago Press, 1985), 43–75.

54. N. Subbotin, *Tsarskiia voprosy i sobornyia otvety na mnogo-razlichnykh tserkovnykh chinekh Stoglav* (Moscow: Tipografiia E. Lissnera i Iu. Romanova, 1890), 185–86.

55. Osor'in, "Povest'," 101–2; Zenkovsky, *Medieval Russian Epics,* 396–97.

In spite of the difficulties the Russian Orthodox Church experienced in its approach to women believers, up to the middle of the seventeenth century it pursued an inclusive strategy with regard to women's input in religious issues. Women's participation in the determination of the miraculous power of relics and icons and their testimony in canonization procedures were not only tolerated but actively encouraged from the time of Metropolitan Makarii into the reign of the first two Romanov tsars. While ordinary women attested to the efficacy of the robe of Christ and the icon of the Virgin of Vladimir in the capital, their counterparts in the outlying provinces busily helped "discover" new saintly bodies and create identities for them, as Eve Levin's research shows. Before the rise of a skeptical attitude toward new local cults among members of the church hierarchy, the association of saints with a female clientele was not necessarily considered negative. This stance is possibly related to the absence of a modern concept of class in pre-Petrine Russia, which facilitated the identification of women with the lower socioeconomic strata of society and a lack of education. The unease with the feminization of the cult of saints, observed in the later posthumous veneration of Saint Ioann of Kronstadt, as Nadieszda Kizenko points out, represents a departure from medieval Russian religious traditions.

A preliminary analysis of medieval Russian hagiographic sources suggests that Muscovite women fostered and expressed a spirituality specific to their gender. As in the case of their Western medieval counterparts, medieval Russian women's religious experience reflected specific needs arising out of their social role. At the same time, the Eastern Orthodox definition of the monastic experience and the Orthodox theology of good works shaped the piety of Russian women. The spirituality of Russian women saints in essence centered on the theme of service—service to their family and community and—in the case of royal women saints—service to their country. Charity and care for the sick appear as prevalent topoi. While service and charity were considered primarily feminine qualities, the image of holy women could transcend this gender stereotype and acquire masculine traits to accommodate political and social expediencies. While in these instances the masculine behavior and appearance of female saints were viewed as a positive feature, they ultimately underscore the theme of women's service to their community and the state.

While the religious heroines of Russia could take on both masculine and feminine characteristics, gender stereotypes played an important role in the development of female lay piety in medieval Russia. In their interaction with supernatural powers during pilgrimages and visits to shrines, Muscovite laywomen tended to treat the saints as arbiters and intercessors who could make up for the inequities and injustices women experienced as a result of their lower social position. As a result, the interaction of saints and their female clients was usually portrayed as intimate, evident in the faith motifs in miracle tales chronicling female cures. The saints also provided Muscovite women with opportunities to shape official veneration practices. A preliminary look at the role women played in canonization procedures suggests that female believers were able to express their feminine experience of the holy within the liturgical structures of the Orthodox Church. In many ways the religious experience of medieval Russian women—the focus on feminine rather than masculine traits in the spirituality of female saints and practical piety of lay believers—parallels that of medieval Western women, who, as Caroline Bynum has pointed out, interpreted the divine in the language of their own physical and social experience.

PART IV

LIVING ORTHODOXY

8

QUOTIDIAN ORTHODOXY

Domestic Life in
Early Modern Russia

DANIEL H. KAISER

Largely on the basis of materials drawn from the history of imperial Russia, historians have routinely denied the importance of Russian Orthodoxy to ordinary Russians, whom they characterize as superstitious rather than religious. The great liberal, secularizing project of the nineteenth century doubted that authentic religious experience could have played much part in the Russians' world. In a memorable phrase, the nineteenth-century radical critic Vissarion Belinskii claimed that Russian peasants were fundamentally atheistic and could conceive of no greater use for household icons than to cover their chamber pots.[1] Since then, our understanding of the role of Orthodox belief and practice in modern Russian society has expanded considerably, but the relevance of these findings for early modern Russia remains in doubt. Not long ago, Edward L. Keenan, observing the "remarkable reluctance of Russians to put to paper authentic description or analysis of . . . the inner life of believers," noted that "we still have relatively little evidence about the quotidian beliefs of Russian laymen. Were they, as it has been argued, still becoming Christians in this period? Was their Christian belief system something we would recognize as such? Can we ever know?"[2]

To probe the inner sancta of Muscovite Christians remains a daunting task. In the absence of a body of confessional texts testifying to an internalized religious experience, the hold of Orthodox Christian tenets upon the lay population of Muscovy is difficult to gauge. On the other hand, the

---

1. V. G. Belinskii, *Sobranie sochinenii v deviati tomakh*, 9 vols. (Moscow: Khudozhestvennaia literatura, 1976–82), 8:284.

2. Edward L. Keenan, "Afterword: Orthodoxy and Heterodoxy," in *Religion and Culture in Early Modern Russia and Ukraine*, ed. Samuel H. Baron and Nancy Shields Kollmann (DeKalb: Northern Illinois University Press, 1997), 201.

surviving evidence confirms that in a very substantial, yet quite ordinary way Orthodoxy did play a central role in Muscovite society, helping to establish and provide meaning to daily life in early modern Russia. As visitors frequently remarked, churches defined most Muscovite communities: their cupolas highlighted the landscape and their buildings dominated the public space of even the humblest of communities.[3] In addition, the celebrations of Orthodox Christianity provided the sensory backdrop to daily life in Muscovy, where the smell, sound, and color of the liturgy contrasted with the world outside the church door. Orthodox ritual defined all the major life-cycle experiences of Muscovite Christians, who were born, baptized, married, and buried to the singing of Orthodox priests. Moreover, the church calendar regulated time in early modern Russia: the years were measured from the ostensible date of creation, as declared by the church, and the annual calendar—complete with the great Christian holidays and a raft of lesser festivals named for heroes and heroines of the faith—served as reference points for confessional and secular obligations alike. Consequently, every sphere of activity in early modern Russia—including altogether secular duties—answered to a distinctly Orthodox architecture of time and culture.

From the earliest days of Rus' civilization, subjects of the Kievan princes had to be aware of Christian practice. For example, the chief law code of medieval Rus', the Pravda Russkaia, provided that when the prince's fee collector came to town on one of the weekly fast days or during Lent, he could expect to receive food provisions that corresponded to fasting restrictions.[4] But in early modern Russia, the connection between governmental exaction and the Christian calendar grew tighter. In the fifteenth and sixteenth centuries, for instance, Russian taxpayers were obliged to supply gifts-in-kind (kormy) to local administrators on the three main holidays of the church calendar—Christmas, Easter, and St. Peter's Day (June 29). Each year, then, Muscovite officials and all taxpayers fulfilled their secular duties to the rhythm of the church's celebrations of salvation and discipleship. Even when the sovereign abolished these gifts late in the sixteenth century, the calculation of official, state time continued to depend upon the church calendar. When in 1584 Tsar Fedor Ivanovich restricted the activity of his officials in

3. As the maps of Muscovite land disputes confirm: "Churches and monasteries with their cross-topped domes dominate the maps, as they must have dominated the visual horizon of seventeenth-century Russia." See Valerie A. Kivelson, "'The Souls of the Righteous in a Bright Place': Landscape and Orthodoxy in Seventeenth-Century Russian Maps," *Russian Review* 58 (1999): 9.

4. See *The Laws of Rus'—Tenth to Fifteenth Centuries*, trans. and ed. Daniel H. Kaiser (Salt Lake City: Charles Schlacks, Jr., 1992), 18–19.

Borisogleb district and condemned the exaction of gifts-in-kind, the sovereign's decree prohibited bailiffs from collecting surety bonds "between the Day of the Annunciation [March 25] and the autumn St. Nicholas Day [December 6]."[5] In other words, just as the church calendar had determined the collection of imposts, so too church holidays marked off limitations on the system.

When the Romanov dynasty reorganized local administration in the seventeenth century, restoring gifts-in-kind as compensation, officials continued to depend upon the ecclesiastical calendar. As before, local adminstrators expected to collect reimbursements on Christmas, Easter, and St. Peter's Day, but in addition they could anticipate a fourth payment, this one on the Day of the Assumption (August 15). Extant records from the Russian North confirm that every year the heads of local administration received rams, beef, pork, fish, butter, eggs, bread, and occasionally, money—all on the main holidays of the Orthodox Church. Additional payments arrived at other times of the year, also timed to the Orthodox calendar. A governor (*voevoda*) might collect gifts on his name-day as well as on the day that commemorated the patron saint of the town to which he was assigned. In Ustiug, for instance, locals had to generate a gift for their governor every July 8, St. Procopius Day, which celebrated the patron saint of Ustiug. Residents of other towns answered to different dates, but responded to the same calendar in discharging their tax-paying responsibilities.[6] It is hardly to be wondered at, then, that Muscovite domestic life also responded to the rhythms of the Orthodox church calendar.

Marriage was especially susceptible to Orthodox influence. Canon law prohibited marriage during the four main fasts of the year—St. Filipp's (Christmas) fast, Lent, St. Peter's fast, which separated Trinity and June 29, and the fast that preceded the Day of the Assumption.[7] As far as we can tell, Muscovites seem to have observed these restrictions scrupulously. Although no parish books reporting wedding dates survive from this era, marriage contracts do, and one of the key features of these documents was the establishment of the wedding date. By no means did every marriage agreement define the date, but many did, sometimes also providing an alternate date,

5. *Namestnich'i, gubnye i zemskie ustavnye gramoty Moskovskogo gosudarstva* (Moscow: Istoriko-filologicheskii fakul'tet Imperatorskogo Moskovskogo universiteta, 1909), 40.

6. E. N. Shveikovskaia, *Gosudarstvo i krest'iane Rossii. Pomor'e v XVII veke* (Moscow: "Arkheografich-eskii tsentr," 1997), 248.

7. V. Iu. Leshchenko, *Sem'ia i russkoe pravoslavie (XI–XIX vv.)* (St. Petersburg: Izdatel'stvo Frolovoi T.V., 1999), 85; S. V. Bul'gakov, *Nastol'naia kniga dlia sviashchenno-tserkovno-sluzhitelei*, 2d ed. (Kharkov: Tipografiia Gubernskogo Pravleniia, 1900), 1146–47.

should circumstances conspire against the wedding. Whenever a date was announced, penalties—sometimes very stiff penalties—served to enforce compliance. Consequently, we can take seriously the wedding dates specified in the surviving marriage contracts.

Study of several hundred of these documents indicates that few men and women of sixteenth- and seventeenth-century Russia married during the prohibited seasons. Not one of the wedding contracts scheduled a marriage during St. Filipp's fast, which stretched from mid-November until Epiphany, or during Lent. Just like their Catholic cohorts further west, men and women in sixteenth- and seventeenth-century Muscovy married most often in late January and February, in the interval between Epiphany and the onset of Lent. Another spurt in weddings took place after Lent, and then a lesser number in the fall, peaking in November just before the Christmas fast commenced.[8] Although there may well have been additional vectors dictating this matrimonial pattern, the total absence of weddings during the Lenten and St. Filipp's fasts can hardly be accidental. And even if some Muscovite men and women planned to marry during the St. Peter's and Assumption fasts, these weddings were rare. By and large, the men and women of early modern Russia arranged their weddings on a schedule that did not challenge the calendar prohibitions laid out in canon law.

Of course, it might be argued that for a ceremony so public as a wedding, the church was able to enforce its will on the prospective couple; as churchmen tirelessly repeated, there was no marriage without the wedding sacrament, which only the clergy could administer.[9] And yet the evidence—scattered and scant though it may be—indicates that Muscovite men and women voluntarily arranged their weddings to correspond to church prescriptions. For one thing, neither church law nor Orthodox tradition dictated marriage contracts, so that churchmen seem to have played no role in composing or executing the marriage agreements. Furthermore, the contracts were enforced in both secular and church courts, making clear that, even though wedding dates corresponded to clerical preference, it was the contracting parties who established and honored them.

8. Daniel H. Kaiser, "The Seasonality of Family Life in Early Modern Russia," *Forschungen zur osteuropäischen Geschichte* 46 (1992): 35–38.

9. See, for example, the missive of Metropolitan Fotii to the Novgorodians: "If anyone lives with his wife outside the law, having married without the priest's blessing, then the penance is three years, just like for a fornicator. . . . Teach them, and lead them to Orthodoxy, so that they marry with the blessing [of the priest]." *Akty sobrannye v bibliotekakh i arkhivakh Russkoi Imperatorskoi Arkheograficheskoiu Ekspeditsieiu*, 4 vols. (St. Petersburg: Tipografiia vtorogo otdeleniia Sobstvennoi E. I. V. kantseliarii, 1836–38), vol. 1, no. 369.

Besides, despite the fact that Muscovite brides and grooms married in harmony with the church's prescriptions, the wedding celebrations themselves included many elements of which clergymen did not approve. A 1649 memo from Siberia, for example, reports that "both in the towns and among rural folk disorderly and foul-mouthed louts prevail at weddings, along with minstrels who with their devilish games incline Orthodox Christians to devilish charms and drunkenness."[10] Even the formal outline of the three-day wedding extravaganza described in the appendix to the *Domostroi* makes but a slight bow to Christian sacrament. As a careful student of Russian domestic life observed some time ago, Muscovite weddings betray at their roots a kinship exchange into which a Christian priest, cross, and church wedding were inserted only later.[11] If this be true, we can hardly attribute to Orthodox priests a stranglehold over the dates on which Muscovite men and women regularized their unions.

Nevertheless, in spite of the claims of other cultural forces, Muscovite men and women arranged their wedding dates in strict conformity to the Orthodox clerics' prescriptions. For the most part, Muscovites declined to marry on the fast days that occupied much of the Orthodox calendar. Church law established every Wednesday and Friday as fast days, and therefore prohibited weddings on those days. Analysis of sixteenth- and seventeenth-century marriage contracts demonstrates that compliance with this norm was not universal, but certainly usual. The overwhelming majority of all weddings whose day of the week can be established were celebrated on Sunday; fewer than 10 percent were planned for either a Wednesday or a Friday. The same pattern recurs for alternative dates mentioned in some wedding contracts: about two-thirds of the alternate dates fell on a Sunday, and only a handful on Wednesday or Friday.

Further evidence for the influence of the Christian calendar on wedding dates comes from the terms of reference. Quite often Muscovite marriage contracts established the wedding date by referring not to the month and date, but rather to one of the holidays of the church calendar. Given the seasonal distribution of weddings, and the hiatus during Lent, many contracts employed language like that in a 1673 agreement that set a wedding date for "the first Sunday after Easter ['The Great Day']."[12] But other agreements

10. *Akty istoricheskie, sobrannye i izdannye Arkheograficheskoiu kommissieiu*, 5 vols. (St. Petersburg: Tipografiia vtorogo otdeleniia Sobstvennoi E. I. V. kantseliarii, 1841–42), vol. 4, no. 35.

11. M. G. Rabinovich, "Svad'ba v russkom gorode v XVI v.," in *Russkii narodnyi svadebnyi obriad. Issledovaniia i materialy* (Leningrad: Nauka, 1978), 10–11.

12. "Riadnye zapisi Iriny Andreevny Suslovoi," *Iaroslavskie Gubernskie Vedomosti*, 1913, no. 5, chast' neofitsial'naia, pp. 2–3.

cited a wide range of church holidays, beginning with Epiphany, Trinity, Assumption of the Virgin, and numerous saints' days. Often, a contract would refer to two church holidays in providing for a primary and alternate date of marriage. For example, the seventeenth-century wedding of Stepan Semenov syn Goriainov was scheduled for the week of St. Il'ia's Day or, if that proved inconvenient or impossible, during the week of the Feast of the Protection of the Virgin.[13]

Consequently, despite the frequent laments of Muscovite churchmen about the carousing, the bawdy behavior, and the non-Christian character of much of the ritual that accompanied weddings in the sixteenth and seventeenth centuries, Russian men and women framed their entry into matrimony in rather strict conformity to the calendar devised by Orthodox churchmen. We need not think of this result as reflecting any special piety or as demonstrating special devotion to Orthodoxy. No doubt some men and women celebrated their weddings full of religious sentiment, but even without such a religious commitment Muscovites who selected their date of marriage responded to a clerical calculus deeply embedded in their culture.

Additional proof of Muscovite compliance with Orthodox norms comes from data on age at marriage. Canon law repeatedly inveighed against those who married young and prohibited marriage to the underage. The 1551 church council, for example, refused to recognize marriages in which the groom was not yet fifteen and the bride had not celebrated her twelfth birthday.[14] These regulations and their frequent iteration have led historians to assume that early marriage was usual in Muscovy, and that clerics were responding to a widespread problem. In point of fact, very little data exist that confirm that suspicion. However, using age data drawn from early-eighteenth-century population inventories (the earliest data on age-at-marriage so far available), one can calculate the "singulate mean age at marriage," a statistical stand-in for actual age at marriage.[15]

This technique, when applied to twelve censuses carried out in ten Russian towns before the death of Peter the Great, demonstrates that in the Petrine era, at least, on average men did not marry before age twenty, and women usually wed in their late teens or perhaps not even until their early twenties. Only very rarely did anyone violate Orthodox expectations on this score. For example, among the many thousands of persons covered by these inventories,

13. *Iaroslavskii arkhiv dvorian Vikent'evykh XVII veka. Sbornik dokumentov* (Yaroslavl: Verkhne-Volzhskoe izdatel'stvo, 1989), 37.

14. *Stoglav* (St. Petersburg, 1863), 82.

15. John Hajnal, "Age at Marriage and Proportions Marrying," *Population Studies* 7 (1953): 130.

only one girl can be proved to have married before age twelve, and all told only about one percent of all women married before reaching age fifteen. Even among fifteen-year-olds, for whom marriage was legal in churchmen's eyes, far from all Muscovite maidens rushed into marriage: more than 93 percent of all fifteen-year-old women remained unwed, as did 84 percent of the sixteen-year-olds, and more than three-quarters of the seventeen-year-olds. Similarly, only a handful of boys married before reaching the age standard dictated by church law; in these towns about 2.2 percent of all men wed before their fifteenth birthday. But teenage men, too, were in no hurry to take a spouse: only 9 percent of the fifteen-year-olds, 16.5 percent of the sixteen-year-olds, and 21.7 percent of the seventeen-year-old males were married. Here again Muscovite practice corresponded rather closely to Orthodox prescription.[16]

The church calendar affected men and women of Muscovy in other ways as well. The frequent fasts that marked the church year laid claim to determining what foods one ate, whether one drank, and even whether one had sexual intercourse. Foreigners who visited Muscovy often reported their amazement at the conscientiousness with which Russians observed the dietary restrictions demanded by frequent fasting. Even more surprising, noted one seventeenth-century visitor, was that Muscovite Christians also abstained from intercourse during the fasts.[17] Of course, neither the foreigners nor local priests could confirm absolutely whether the men and women of Muscovy in fact avoided copulation during Lent, but supplementary evidence, although far from conclusive, gives reason to think that foreigners were not far off the mark.

Learning when men and women in early modern Russia conceived their children is quite difficult. Parish priests in this era had not yet become habituated to maintaining registers in which dates of baptism were recorded, and without baptismal dates, estimating dates of conception is impossible. However, an alternative source provides some evidence on birth dates. When Muscovites prepared for death, many endowed special prayers or feasts in their own memory, often naming two or even three dates on which to be remembered. Donors routinely asked that their names be recalled on the anniversaries of their deaths, but some donors also provided for an additional remembrance on another date without specifying what this second date

16. D. Kaizer (Kaiser), "Vozrast pri brake i raznitsa v vozraste suprugov v gorodakh Rossii v nachale XVIII v.," in *Sosloviia i gosudarstvennaia vlast' v Rossii. XV–seredina XIX vv.*, 2 vols. (Moscow: Moskovskii fiziko-tekhnicheskii institut, 1994), 2:225–37.

17. *Opisanie Moskovii pri Reliatsiiakh gr. Karleilia*, in *Istoricheskaia biblioteka*, 1879, no. 5:30.

commemorated. Although there is not space to develop the argument here, it seems clear that this second remembrance represented birth dates.[18]

With this information, it becomes possible to determine the seasonal distribution of births in early modern Russia, and therefore also calculate approximate dates of conception. The results of this experiment indicate that in Muscovy, as in much of Western Europe of the time, a great many babies were born in January and February—and therefore were conceived after Easter, on the heels of the Lenten fast. In early modern Russia, as in the Christian societies further west, a second wave of newborns appeared in November. These children were conceived in the period that separated the Christmas and Lenten prohibitions, the same period when many Muscovite couples celebrated their weddings. At the other end of the spectrum, the low point for Muscovy, as in Catholic Europe, was December, nine months after Lent, when Christians were enjoined from engaging in sexual relations.[19] So there is reason to think that even in bed the men and women of early modern Russia allowed the Orthodox calendar to temper their behavior.

Children conceived from these unions gave physical expression to the extent to which Christian culture influenced Muscovite life—in the main they bore Christian names. To be sure, a minority, especially in the sixteenth and early seventeenth centuries, answered to names that denoted birth order, ethnic identity, or some physical or personality trait. But most Muscovites, whether rich or poor, aristocrat or slave, townsman or peasant, bore names that linked them to Christian saints whose festivals dotted the church calendar. By the beginning of the eighteenth century, hardly a person could be found who did not answer to a baptismal name drawn from the heavenly throng. As a result, every Muscovite served as a living reminder of the church's history; whenever people called Ivan or Vasilii, Evdokiia or Anna, they sounded the name of an apostle or saint who had helped found and nourish Christianity.[20]

The victory of the Christian naming system—which was already visible in the sixteenth century, but which seems to have become complete by the late seventeenth century—gives substantive expression to the extent to which Orthodoxy had come to define Muscovite society and culture. To name something is, in a way, to claim ownership. The prophet Isaiah quoted to the Israelites the word of their creator and God: "I have called you by name, and

18. Kaiser, "Seasonality," 25–27.

19. Ibid., 28.

20. Daniel H. Kaiser, "Naming Cultures in Early Modern Russia," *Harvard Ukrainian Studies* 19 (1995): 271–91.

you are my own" (43.1). From this perspective, the church had a lien against the life of every man and woman in early modern Russia, whether or not they thought themselves members of the Christian universe.

Behavior within marriage also seems to have been susceptible to Orthodox influence. Most marriages left no trace in the historical record; unless conflict or disaster spilled out into the streets where it demanded public attention, the private domestic behavior of the women and men of Muscovy did not find a place in official documentation. It is therefore ironic that within those unions that drew official attention one can also detect the insistent influence of Orthodox values. For example, a 1676 petition claimed that Petr Spiridonov had murdered his wife, an accusation that Spiridonov denied. Referring for confirmation to his own confessor as well as to his deceased wife's confessor, Spiridonov argued that he and his wife had lived together amicably. The priests' deposition confirmed Spiridonov's claim, noting that the couple had lived together not only peacefully but also "according to the law [and] in love." Spiridonov, they went on to say, "lived with his wife according to the law like other Orthodox Christian men did with their wives."[21]

Muscovite husbands and wives, then, were aware of church teaching on marriage, and in reporting their complaints frequently referred to the expectations of canon law. Grigorii Konev, for example, complained that his son's fugitive wife had defaulted on her obligations; Domna, he observed, was not living a proper married life (*nezakonno*).[22] Similarly in 1628 a man accused his son's wife of violating church law: "Sovereign, that daughter-in-law Ustin'ia began to live in contravention of the canons of the holy fathers, and in the absence of her husband, my son, would not live with me nor obey me, her father-in-law."[23] A 1688 case charged a man with forcing his wife to enter a convent; in denying the charge, the man claimed that he "had lived with his wife, Avdot'itsa according to the law and the canons of the holy apostles and fathers," even if he had found it necessary to beat the woman from time to time.[24] Finally, a jilted wife complained to the authorities that her husband, who had lived with his wife "for three years according to the law, just like good people do," then threw her over. He took up with another woman,

21. Sanktpeterburgskii filial instituta rossiiskoi istorii, *koll.* 117, *op.* 1, *no.* 1139.

22. *Russkaia istoricheskaia biblioteka*, 39 vols. (St. Petersburg-Leningrad: Tipografiia imperatorskoi Akademii nauk, 1872–1927), vol. 25, no. 26.

23. Ibid., no. 61.

24. I. P. Mordvinov, "Tikhvinskaia starina: Sbornik materialov k istorii goroda Tikhvina i Nagornogo Obonezh'ia," *Sbornik Novgorodskogo obshchestva liubitelei drevnosti* 4 (1911): 68–69.

"not according to the law, and began to provide drink for her and her children ... and he installed her like a legal wife, and me, poor orphan and his
legal wife, he chased off."[25]

Of course, being aware of clerical expectations did not guarantee that
Muscovite couples lived as churchmen might have wished. As the records
make abundantly clear, many Muscovite spouses ran roughshod over canon
law, in some cases going so far as to murder their partners. There is therefore no reason to think that in early modern Russia married men and women
unanimously and invariably allowed Orthodox teaching to control their behavior toward one another. On the other hand, as the cases themselves demonstrate, Muscovite spouses had a sense—no doubt an imperfect sense—of
the way that they should behave within marriage, and they were aware that
Orthodox law and spiritual exhortation should moderate some of their
meanest impulses.

That much of Orthodoxy's influence in Muscovy was unconscious is easy
to believe. As noted above, men and women continued to marry in ways that
offended clerics, and some of the tsar's subjects bore names that revealed no
connection with heavenly saints. Like men and women elsewhere in Christian Europe, Muscovites managed to integrate into their world confidence in
numerous powers of the natural world whose mysteries they only dimly
understood. Through it all, however, Orthodox Christianity provided the
primary lens through which to make sense of life, no matter how badly Muscovites may have understood what they saw through that lens.

Childbirth in early modern Russia was private, shrouded in taboos that
Orthodoxy itself recognized. As a result, we still know relatively little about
how Muscovite women delivered their children. Unlike parts of Western
Europe where secular government supervised and regulated midwifery, Muscovy provided no organized oversight to childbirth. The records available
to the historian are therefore few and depend for the most part upon prescription rather than description. All the same, it seems that women in early
modern Russia approached childbirth with the same anxieties and the same
arsenal of assistance as did their parallels in France, Germany, and England.
Medical handbooks, for the most part translations of texts that also circulated
in Western Europe, urged the application of both botanical and magical remedies. In bringing these prescriptions to the lyings-in of parturient women,
Muscovites combined a confidence in the power of the natural world with
their faith in the Christian deity.

25. *Russkaia istoricheskaia biblioteka*, vol. 25, no. 232.

For example, a seventeenth-century Muscovite medical book ceded no space to theology in urging pregnant women to wear a stone "on their body, on their breasts, to strengthen both mother and child, and when labor begins, hold the stone in the right hand, and as a result the birth will go more easily." Slightly more in harmony with Christian sentiment was a fifteenth-century miscellany which suggested that "if some woman is in pain in child-birth, write this prayer on paper, have the priest say it three times over the woman, and then tie it around her head." The remedy, like the prayer itself, mixed biblical images with popular wisdom:

> Our Blessed Lord [and] Father. Our Lord Jesus Christ [said] to St. John the Theologian: "Find the woman, [name supplied], who is giving birth, and who is pained in the womb, and is unable to give birth." And our Lord Jesus Christ said to St. John the Theologian, "Go, John, and say into her right ear, from which God was born and from which God was nourished, 'Come out, child, to Christ! Christ calls you. In the name of the Father, and the Son, and the Holy Ghost, both now and forever, age unto age, Amen.' Say also, 'Lord, remember the sons of Edom in the deeds of Jerusalem, saying, 'Destroy [it], destroy [it].'"[26]

A truncated, version of this text found its way into a seventeenth-century leechbook: "Write these words on an animal's hide, and place it on [the woman's] bosom, and then carry it around the room: "Remember, Lord, the sons of Edom in the deeds of Jerusalem, when they said, 'Destroy it, destroy it even unto the foundations of the earth,' and deliver the child."[27] These texts identify individuals and powers intelligible to Christian theology, yet they also demonstrate a confusion of origin and meaning of texts that began with Christian scripture, but which survive in these charms in corrupt, prac-tically nonsensical form. The resulting rituals, therefore, conflate Christian

---

26. A. I. Almazov, *Vracheval'nye molitvy* (Odessa: Ekonomicheskaia tipografiia, 1900), 75–78. See also Eve Levin, "Childbirth in Pre-Petrine Russia: Canon Law and Popular Traditions," in *Russia's Women: Accommodation, Resistance, Transformation,* ed. Barbara Evans Clements, Barbara Alpern Engel, and Christine D. Worobec (Berkeley and Los Angeles: University of California Press, 1991), 55–56. The final phrase borrows language from Psalm 137.7 (136.7 in the Russian Bible); its exact meaning here is uncer-tain, but may refer to the unknown impediments delaying delivery. This sense carries through in another spell from imperial Russia, the saying of which was alleged to aid women enduring difficult and prolonged births. N. N. Vinogradov, "Zagovory, oberegi, spasitel'nye molitvy i proch.," *Zhivaia starina* 17 (1908): 78.

27. *Redkie istochniki po istorii Rossii,* ed. A. A. Novosel'skii and L. N. Pushkarev, 2 vols. (Moscow: Institut istorii SSSR, AN SSSR, 1977), 1:101.

and mythological values, fashioning unique instruments whose authority depended neither upon rational exegesis nor upon Orthodox Christian practice. Rather, they seemed to draw on two powerful, yet separable worlds to bring their respective curative energies to women in childbed. As Eve Levin has pointed out, prayers of this sort addressed forces of the natural world without overlooking the power of the Christian pantheon.[28] And yet, as noted above, hard on the heels of these births, most babies in Muscovy soon found their way to the baptismal font where Orthodox clerics bestowed on them names that marked them off as inhabitants of a Christian community.

A similarly bifurcated sensibility emerges from study of death in early modern Russia. Here, too, Christian theology is much in evidence, but so are other values that seem to have nothing to do with the Incarnate Son of God. Visitors to Muscovy, on observing Muscovite burials, reported what they called "superstitious and prophane ceremonies." The Englishman Giles Fletcher, for example, noted that before closing the casket the living relayed to the hands of the deceased "a letter to Saint Nicolaus: whom they make their chiefe mediatour, and as it were, the porter of heauen gates, as the Papistes doe their Peter."[29] As other reporters make clear, the document in fact served as confirmation of confession, but no church handbook required such a certificate to be buried with the deceased. Here again one observes in everyday life a mixture of clerical symbols with practices seemingly disconnected from Orthodox theology.

The same picture emerges from descriptions of the transfer of the body to burial. According to reports, the cortege included priests with icons and censers, leading the way to the cemetery. But it was the behavior of women mourners that most attracted the attention of foreigners. Margeret noted that "a number of women lament their dead, ask [the deceased] why he has died—if he was not favored by the emperor, if he did not have enough wealth, enough children, an honest wife. If it is a woman, they ask if she did not have a good husband, and similar foolishness."[30] Fletcher was more graphic; he complained that women mourners "stand howling ouer the bodie, after a prophane, and heathenish manner . . . asking him what hee wanted, and whate he meant to die."[31] Women keeners were not unique to burials in

28. Eve Levin, "Supplicatory Prayers as a Source for Popular Religious Culture in Muscovite Russia," in Baron and Kollmann, *Religion and Culture*, 104.

29. Giles Fletcher, *Of the Russe Commonwealth*, intro. Richard Pipes (Cambridge: Harvard University Press, 1966), 106.

30. Jacques Margeret, *The Russian Empire and Grand Duchy of Muscovy: A 17th-Century Account*, trans. and ed. Chester S. L. Dunning (Pittsburgh: University of Pittsburgh Press, 1983), 24.

31. Fletcher, *Of the Russe Commonwealth*, 106–106v.

early modern Russia, of course, but the reports of outsiders emphasize how their behavior contradicted their perceptions of a Christian's understanding of death. The questions repeatedly put to the dead implied that death was not real, that, despite the funeral and the imminent burial of the deceased, mourners nevertheless regarded the deceased as still alive somehow. Additional commemorative practice reinforced the impression that the deceased continued to dwell among the living, at least for a specific period after death. These practices seemed to deny death, the curse at the root of all Christian theology and the ostensible justification for the Incarnate God. Perhaps worse, Western Christians saw in the howling a denial of the Christians' confidence in the resurrection of the body.

But this aspect of Muscovite death rituals stands in contrast to the great bulk of ceremonies by which the men and women of early modern Russia sent the dead to their graves. Whether boilerplate or not, testaments written in this era invariably begin by invoking the triune God and frequently affirm the dying person's understanding that confession was important before leaving this vale of tears. Although a few testators gave expression to distinctly un-Christian sentiments, for the most part the dying affirmed their confidence in God's salvation and their belief in the eternal life of their spirits. Some testators used the occasion to articulate anxiety over the spiritual welfare of spouse or offspring, in that way leaving behind them an injunction intended to encourage a more faithful attendance to Christian doctrine and ritual.[32] In selecting burial sites close to the altars of their favorite churches, or at worst, in the adjoining cemeteries, Muscovite Christians gave final voice to the same sentiment that years earlier had dictated their names: they belonged to the Christian God, and they wished their earthly bodies to lie in close proximity to the place where Christian clerics regularly addressed their immaterial creator and where the very body and blood of Christ dwelt. In the same way, in requesting and paying for clerical prayers after their demise, the dying associated themselves forever with the same church that had authenticated and overseen their births.[33]

---

32. On this theme, see O. E. Kosheleva, "Blagoslovliaiu chada svoi: Zabota o detiakh (po drevnerusskim dukhovnym gramotam)," *Vestnik Universiteta Rossiiskoi Akademii Obrazovaniia*, 1997, no. 2:108–40, esp. 126–35.

33. Daniel H. Kaiser, *Death and Dying in Early Modern Russia*, Occasional Paper of Kennan Institute for Advanced Russian Studies, no. 228 (Washington, D.C., 1988), and reprinted in *Major Problems in Early Modern Russian History*, ed. Nancy Shields Kollmann (Hamden: Garland Publishing, 1992), 217–57. For a full analysis of Muscovite commemorative practice, see Ludwig Steindorff, *Memoria in Altrußland. Untersuchungen zu den Formen christlicher Totensorge*, Quellen und Studien zur Geschichte des östlichen Europa, vol. 38 (Stuttgart: Franz Steiner Verlag, 1994).

In short, Orthodox Christianity in early modern Russia exerted a powerful influence on quotidian life. It helped Muscovites organize and execute even the most secular of their earthly duties, but it also oversaw and defined all the major domestic celebrations. Life was begun within the strictures of the Orthodox calendar, and new lives generated from these couplings inherited the names of Christian saints. In bringing children into the world and in sending the dead to heaven, Muscovites allowed the Orthodox calendar to organize and inform their behavior. The rhythm of Orthodox celebrations, distributed across the annual calendar, penetrated all aspects of social life in Muscovy, which if not exactly pious and sanctimonious, nevertheless bore the deep imprint of Orthodox Christianity.

9

GOD OF OUR MOTHERS

Reflections on Lay Female
Spirituality in Late Eighteenth- and
Early Nineteenth-Century Russia

GARY MARKER

This chapter is concerned with the difficulties that Russian historiography of the imperial period has had in understanding the place of Orthodoxy in the lives of lay people, in this case educated women, and with suggesting some possible remedies. The root cause of this difficulty derives from our long-standing insistence upon viewing almost the entirety of these two centuries through the lens of an inexorable secularization of Russian life and culture. This insistence is unfortunate, since few times or places were as rich in undirected and uninstructed religious wonderment as eighteenth-century Russia. All the ingredients were there. Gregory Freeze has shown in immense detail that the teachings of the official church were incompletely understood and badly disseminated by much of the parish clergy itself. The flock, so far as he and others have been able to determine, typically had only a fanciful understanding of such basic doctrine as the Trinity, Eucharist, and Resurrection. And yet faith in the supernatural, in God, was ubiquitous.[1] More recently, Alexander Lavrov has produced a broad panorama of Russia's unsanctioned practices and beliefs by linking both magic and religion within the broader rubric of popular supernaturalism.[2]

Female religiosity, the specific focus of this chapter, has typically been conveyed as a story of distance or separation in which "holy women" or "spiritual

---

1. Freeze has produced a prodigious body of detailed scholarship, far too much to enumerate here. See, in particular, "The Rechristianization of Russia: The Church and Popular Religion, 1750–1850," *Studia Slavica Finlandensia* 7 (1990): 101–36, and idem, *The Russian Levites: Parish Clergy in the Eighteenth Century* (Cambridge: Harvard University Press, 1977).

2. A. S. Lavrov, *Koldovstvo i religiia v Rossii, 1700–1740 gg.* (Moscow: Drevlekhranilishche, 2000).

women" have almost always been situated outside the normal parameters of everyday life. This analytical approach is not altogether bad, since many of the women who deemed themselves faith-centered truly did place themselves outside the dominant institutions. The Vyg Old Believer Community, for example, consisted overwhelmingly of women, who, as Robert Crummey has demonstrated, lived in strict sexual segregation, bound by vows of chastity and severe asceticism that reinforced the conviction that they lived outside of the norm of household and family, outside the sinful *byt* (daily life) of the fallen faith of the official church.[3] Similarly, the convents and women's religious communities about which Brenda Meehan has written consisted of individuals, mostly peasants, who had chosen to leave their villages and live in considerable isolation in the exclusive company of other women.[4] Finally, the nuns and pilgrims whom William Wagner examines in this collection, such as Abbess Thaisa and Abbess Serafima, proclaimed themselves to be divinely inspired, called by God to serve faith, a calling which required that they leave their parents, families, and homes in search of purity away from the trappings and temptations of the everyday world.

Histories of pre-Reform intellectuals and intellectual life have also tended to disengage women and religion from the mainstream, most egregiously around discussions of reading habits in which female readers are consigned, usually with almost no evidentiary basis, to "traditional literature" such as saints' lives, menologies, and *Domostroi,* the sixteenth-century guidebook to household management, even though hardly anyone appears to have actually read the *Domostroi* before the Slavophiles, Russia's vaunted Romantic nationalists, invented *domostroinaia Rus'* (the idea that the household in Muscovite Russia was governed by the rules set forth in the text) in the mid-nineteenth century.[5] Educated men, by contrast, read social commentary and modern

---

3. Robert O. Crummey, *The Old Believers and the World of Antichrist: The Vyg Community and the Russian State, 1694–1855* (Madison: University of Wisconsin Press, 1970), esp. chap. 6, "A Community Apart."

4. See, e.g., Brenda Meehan, "Popular Piety, Local Initiative, and the Founding of Women's Religious Communities in Russia, 1764–1907," *St. Vladimir's Theological Quarterly* 30 (1986): 117–42.

5. This observation requires some clarification. Carolyn Pouncy has made a study of *Domostroi's* readers, by which she means the people (mostly nobles) who inscribed owners' inscriptions (*vladel'cheskie zapisi*) on the various manuscript copies that survive. But without data from marginalia or other writings, as Pouncy acknowledges, there is no direct evidence to suggest that the owners actually read or consulted the text. As far as I am aware, sources from the late seventeenth and eighteenth centuries make almost no citations to *Domostroi,* an indication that it was little used. Finally, the fact that there were no printed editions of *Domostroi* until 1849, despite the eighteenth-century mania for self-help and household books, indicates a minimal awareness of it by literate society. By contrast, the fourteenth-century book of useful aphorisms, *Izmaragd* (*The Emerald*) was recopied dozens of times in the early modern period, but because it was never embraced by the Slavophiles, it has received far less acclaim than *Domostroi.* Carolyn Johnston Pouncy, "The Origins of the *Domostroi*: An Essay in Manuscript History," *Russian Review* 46 (1987): 357–73.

novels, newspapers, and histories. To my mind, gendered dichotomies of this sort reflect their own strategy of distancing. In this case, though, the distance is cultural rather than physical or spatial. The realm of progress (secular, learned, conscious) becomes fundamentally male, the antithesis of tradition, domesticity, and faith, which through this calculus emerge as synonyms for backwardness, submissiveness, and—within educated life—female gender. If women emerge even part way from this cage, they become "sentimentalists," capable of reading romance novels with strong emotional content, which are but slightly removed from the emotional reassurances of religious writing.

This construction is particularly ironic in that the style of devotional, penitential reading that is ascribed to women as vessels of tradition appears in fact to have been quite new. As Roger Chartier and others have pointed out, "traditional" reading was typically collective, repetitive, and verbal ("intensive"). Individual or silent reading of new texts ("extensive reading") did not become commonplace until well into the seventeenth century.[6] In other words, from the perspective of reading practices, the clichéd ascription, even if true, constituted not tradition but a confirmation of modernity! Still, there is a nominal plausibility to this binarism, since writing and reading remained primarily the province of men. Catriona Kelly's recent *History of Russian Women's Writing*, for example, identifies very few women writers before the 1860s, and only three worth discussing at length.[7] The few women who do get mentioned repeatedly in the literature—Dashkova, Durova, and others—either are singular figures (the proverbial exceptions that prove the rule), or else they form a passive backdrop as sponsors of salons and literary evenings in which literary men are assigned the active work of literary creation. The recent *Dictionary of Russian Women Writers* is a bit more generous, but it too lists only fifteen female authors for the years between 1760 and 1800.[8]

Herein lies a problem, however. By situating faith-centeredness and female spirituality outside the norms of everyday life and modern thinking we are precluded, a priori, from inquiring into the place of faith in the thinking or discourse of educated society. We may acknowledge that prominent eighteenth-century literati and Freemasons such as Nikolai Novikov, Andrei Bolotov, and Ivan Lopukhin were believers, went to church, and had priests

---

6. Roger Chartier, *The Cultural Uses of Print in Early Modern France* (Princeton: Princeton University Press, 1987), chap. 6, "Urban Reading Practices, 1660–1780," 183–239; Rolf Engelsing, "Die Perioden der Lesergeschichte in der Neuzeit," *Archiv fr Geschichte des Buchwesens* 10 (1970).

7. Catriona Kelly, *A History of Russian Women's Writing, 1820–1990* (Oxford: Clarendon Press, 1994).

8. Marina Ledkovsky, Charlotte Rosenthal, and Mary Zirin, eds., *Dictionary of Russian Women Writers* (Westport, Conn.: Greenwood Press, 1994), 765–66.

as friends. Even archbishops liked them.[9] We give passing notice to their use of biblical language and references to Christ. Alternatively, we have come to absorb the "dual models" of the Tartu-Moscow school of Russian semiotics, which reveal the multifarious reproductions of Christian symbols and binarisms within secular culture.[10] What is missing from all of this, however, is any sense that religion or spirituality could have constituted vibrant modes of discourse in and of themselves for ordinary (that is, nonsectarian) lay people, pathways to making sense out of life in productive ways that did not necessarily require taking sides between faith and secularism. In short, modern scholarship, at least until very recently, seems to have defined out of existence any notion of *popular religion* in the eighteenth century, except as it relates to sectarianism and Old Belief.

We sometimes forget that both the Synod, Peter the Great's new governing body for the Orthodox Church, and the communal structures of the Old Belief were themselves products of the eighteenth century, each deeply suspicious of the other and actively creating themselves in response to those fears. The Synod, still in the early stages of establishing diocesan administrations, was acutely aware of the varieties of relatively unsupervised worship and religious sentiment in which it forever suspected the secret workings of schismatics. A simple survey of the Synod chancellery archive reveals hundreds of inquiries into individual preachers, male and female, during the course of the century. S. M. Solov'ev's *Istoriia Rossii s drevneishikh vremen* (*A History of Russia from Ancient Times*), the classic multivolume text of nineteenth-century Russian historiography, takes note of quite a few of these in the volumes on Peter the Great and his successors. Solov'ev, of course, shared the Synod's disdain for sectarians, and not unlike the Synod, he lumped them with Old Believers as vestiges of backwardness and superstition.[11] But in the process he made it clear that figures such as Bosoi the magician and Samuel the fallen monk had lively theological outlooks of their own. Similarly, as

9. Bolotov's memoirs go on at length about his close friendship with the family priest. Novikov and Lopukhin counted several clergy among their associates, at least until the late 1780s, most notable of whom were Archbishop Platon of Moscow and Evgenii Bolkhovitinov of Voronezh. Novikov also relied heavily on church patronage for the circulation of his Pietistic journal *Utrennii svet* (1777–80), which counted dozens of clergy among its subscribers.

10. The classic essay is, of course, Iurii M. Lotman and Boris A. Uspenskii, "Binary Models in the Dynamics of Russian Culture (to the End of the Eighteenth Century)," in *The Semiotics of Russian Cultural History*, ed. Alexander D. Nakhimovsky and Alice Stone Nakhimovsky (Ithaca: Cornell University Press, 1985), 30–66.

11. Solov'ev's scornful commentary on schismatics, sectarians, and blasphemers recurs in numerous places throughout his many works. See, e.g., S. M. Solov'ev, *Istoriia Rossii s drevneishchikh vremen*, vol. 18 (Moscow: Nauka, 1963), 10–18.

Georg Michels as recently shown, the schism remained largely confined to a few monastic centers until the 1680s, and only during the reign of Peter the Great did discrete Old Believer settlements begin to take shape.[12]

Reginald Zelnik's studies of Semen Kanatchikov and other workers of the late nineteenth century offer splendid examples of how one might tease out the elements of faith and religious sensibilities, which, in these instances, helped nascent proletarians make sense of the perplexing temporal changes they confronted in moving from village to city. "[Village Orthodoxy] was a powerful enough cultural world to retain much of its influence over its constituents even when they strayed from the confines of the village to the alien milieu of the metropolis. Such traditional institutions as the *artel* (craft workshop) and *zemliachestvo* (working and living with other people from one's village or local district) helped extend the influence of the village . . . reinforcing such traditional ritual practices as the keeping of Orthodox dietary laws on fast days and, of course, Sunday church observance."[13] But there are few if any comparable studies for the eighteenth and early nineteenth centuries.

Within literate or educated culture the recourse to God and faith is almost completely unexplored. Some of Marc Raeff's recent work has paid more attention to the religious side of eighteenth-century thinking, but without doing much damage to the interpretive framework with which he is associated. "A revival of religious and spiritual concerns was a significant aspect of the Europeanization of the Russian elites. Ever since the late seventeenth century, the Russian elites had been exposed to German Protestant spiritualist and hermetic literature that served to compensate for the inadequate spiritual fare offered by the official Orthodox Church after Peter's reforms . . . in helping fellow *men* [italics added] to improve their material circumstances one also enabled them to lead a proper Christian life in preparation for the hereafter."[14]

12. Georg Michels, *At War with the Church: Religious Dissent in Seventeenth-Century Russia* (Stanford: Stanford University Press, 1999).

13. Reginald Zelnik, ed. and trans., *A Radical Worker in Tsarist Russia: The Autobiography of Semen Ivanovich Kanatchikov* (Stanford: Stanford University Press, 1986), xxii–xxiii. See also idem, "Russian Bebels: An Introduction to the Memoirs of Semen Kanatchikov and Matvei Fisher," *Russian Review* 35 (1976): 249–89, 417–47. Another obvious confirmation of the elasticity of popular religion comes from the popularity of Father Georgii Gapon's movement among some of the most proletarianized workers in St. Petersburg in 1904. Christian faith was, in fact, a condition of membership in Gapon's Assembly of St. Petersburg Workers. See Walter Sablinsky, *The Road to Bloody Sunday: Father Gapon and the St. Petersburg Massacre of 1905* (Princeton: Princeton University Press, 1976), 93ff.

14. Marc Raeff, "At the Origin of a Russian National Consciousness: Eighteenth-Century Roots and Napoleonic Wars," in *Political Ideas and Institutions in Imperial Russia* (Boulder, Colo.: Westview Press, 1994), 67–68.

If this is all there was to Enlightened religiosity in Russia, there really is not much point in continuing with this inquiry. What Raeff is describing here amounts to a kind of deistic mentality that enabled essentially secular thinkers to consume an easily digestible slice of German Protestantism so as to avoid confronting difficult paradoxes regarding the connection between salvation and grace on one hand and this-worldly improvement on the other. A comfortable faith with few questions asked.

Frankly, I am not convinced that this is all there was to it. The transformations of eighteenth-century noble life were arguably no less abrupt—if a good deal less oppressive—than those of nineteenth-century workers, and the frames of reference with which service families made sense of these changes did not require the radical separation of faith and secularity that we insist upon. Elsewhere Raeff himself has shown that the eighteenth-century service nobility endured unresolved doubt and anomie about service, home, hearth, and family—in short about their very identities.[15] One need not subscribe in full to Raeff's alienation thesis to recognize that the service nobility was notorious for representing itself as unanchored and ill-defined by the social categories available to them.[16] Religious faith, oddly enough, was one of the few moorings to the past left to them (along with estate holding, serf-owning, and freedom from direct taxation); and as we know from petitions, *nakazy* (landlords' instructions), and the like, their claims to contemporary privilege were based almost entirely on legitimization via antiquity. Thus one would expect their autobiographical writings to have at least some recourse to faith as a source for stability or reassurance.

If one looks at eighteenth-century education, this expectation grows stronger. By the 1780s Russia's seminaries were educating several times more

---

15. Marc Raeff, *Origins of the Russian Intelligentsia: The Eighteenth-Century Nobility* (New York: Harcourt, Brace and World, 1966), especially chaps. 3 and 4.

16. The controversy over "the alienation thesis" has long since died down, more out of exhaustion than through resolution. Raeff's most searching critic, Arcadius Kahan, pointed out that the experiences that Raeff described ("Westernization") were far too expensive for the overwhelming majority of nobles, for whom boarding school, multiple estates, and a house in the city were unimaginable. From a different vantage point Michel Confino maintained that the memoirs upon which Raeff relied actually spoke quite fondly of childhood and countryside, and they manifested rather little sense of alienation. Arcadius Kahan, "The Costs of Westernization in Russia: The Gentry and the Economy in Eighteenth-Century Russia," *Slavic Review* 25 (1965): 61–85; Michel Confino, "On Intellectuals and Intellectual Traditions in Eighteenth- and Nineteenth-Century Russia," *Daedalus* 101 (1972): 117–49; idem, "Histoire et psychologie: A propos de la noblesse russe au XVIIIe siècle," *Annales: Economies-Societes-Civilisation* 22 (1967): 1163–205; Priscilla Roosevelt, *Life on the Russian Country Estate: A Social and Cultural History* (New Haven: Yale University Press, 1995); Thomas Newlin, "Rural Ruses: Illusion and Anxiety on the Russian Estate, 1775–1815," *Slavic Review* 57 (1998): 295–319. See also Elise Kimerling Wirtschafter, *Social Identity in Imperial Russia* (DeKalb: Northern Illinois University Press, 1997), 36.

students—including hundreds of offspring of laity—than were all the gymnasia, pansions, and service academies combined. Many of their students went on to positions in service rather than to clerical callings. True, most of the instruction focused on an almost unusable Latin, and theology was taught only to a tiny proportion of students who made it through the eight-or-more years of study to the advanced classes. But the lives of seminarians were surrounded by religion, which included daily prayer, catechism, sermons, confession, and hours of incantation. Didacticism aside, they were immersed in a world of belief, religious symbols, and biblical metaphor, even if they didn't always get their patristics straight. It is unimaginable that the years spent in this setting had no bearing on their frames of reference.

One other point: the mental world that Raeff has portrayed appears to be one in which educated men were busily remaking themselves and other men into better men. This celebration of masculinity (*muzhestvo*) was a powerful undercurrent in Russia's Enlightenment, extending to theater, Freemasonry, family albums, salons, and other realms.[17] Women were written into almost all variants of Russian sociability, and they were occasionally noteworthy participants. But the line was drawn, at times explicitly, at manhood, of which Reason was almost always a defining attribute. So long as women were cast, as they almost always were, as the embodiments of femininity, reason lay beyond their grasp. Only by becoming masculine, by taking on the attributes of *muzhestvo* in contradiction to their natural selves (or as one writer put it, "the natural tenderness of their sex") could women be possessed of the same facilities of reason as men. Thus, all of the female rulers and many of the notable women at court took on *muzhestvo* or had it ascribed to them. Because this line-in-the-steppe was drawn not at the gateway to Enlightenment (everyone was open to improvement) but at some point within, it introduced an element of contingency and partiality to participation that undermined the very unity and clarity of Enlightenment precisely at the intersection of gender and reason. Thus, one might expect that women who wrote from within educated society might have a particular and more nuanced reading of Enlightenment and the dynamics of male/female and reason/faith.

An example of what I have in mind comes from the writings of a relatively uncelebrated figure, the memoirist and diarist Anna Labzina (1758–1828). A provincial noblewoman born and raised outside Ekaterinburg, Labzina found herself transported through her two marriages into the elite of Russian

17. See the recent study of Russian Freemasonry by Douglas Smith, *Working the Rough Stone: Freemasonry and Society in Eighteenth-Century Russia* (DeKalb: Northern Illinois University Press, 1999), 91–135.

cosmopolitan society, often to her extreme discomfort. Her autobiographical writings represent her attempts to understand this transformation in circumstances from provincial to cosmopolitan, and her abiding frame of reference was faith.

The life that Labzina described, particularly in her memoir, confronts the reader with so many transgressive blends of sacred and secular that, by the last page (which appropriately stops in mid-sentence and suggests no closure whatever), there is no going back to the clear-cut alternatives with which this chapter began. To give just a few examples: from the age of thirteen she lived within the most exalted circles of educated society, in the care of the writer and educator M. M. Kheraskov and later hobnobbing with the likes of Prince Grigorii Potemkin, Catherine the Great's most prominent favorite and leading adviser at the time, and even the empress herself.[18] She participated in numerous literary evenings, was married for many years to a leading scientist and then to a leading Freemason. She read voraciously, including modern literature, and she engaged in that most modern and individualist of activities—she wrote, and not just idly but with intense feeling about herself and other personalities with whom she came into contact.

"Objectively," then, Labzina lived the quintessential life of *obshchestvo* (educated society), one of a veritable handful of women of her era who lived a life of letters and wrote about it. Moreover, she lived a life that was anything but disconnected from the everyday. Although childless, she was married virtually all her adult life. Rather than cloistering herself or fleeing to a separate space, she surrounded herself with family, friends, and acquaintances (male and female), spent much of her time, whether in the countryside or the city, out of doors, even on the street, and almost always in the company of others. She danced, went to the theater, and spoke her mind quite freely. A modern and social woman, in other words, far removed from *terem* and convent.[19] She even managed to have fun from time to time.

All of this is somewhat reminiscent of Labzina's notorious more-or-less contemporary Nadezhda Durova (the "cavalry maiden" of the Napoleonic wars): these two women wrote in similar tones, shared a love of the outdoors and sport, and were equally strong willed. "Under the clear sky of Little Russia my health became perceptibly better. . . . Here nobody corseted me or wearied me with bobbin lace. With my passionate love for nature and freedom, I

---

18. For a thorough and quite sympathetic recent biography of Potemkin, see Simon Sebag Montefiori, *Prince of Princes: The Life of Potemkin* (London: St. Martin's Press, 2001).

19. The *terem* was the secluded household space to which upper-class women were meant to be confined during the seventeenth century.

spent all my days either running around the forested parcels of my uncle's estate or floating on the Udaj in a large boat."[20] Writing in the late 1870s, the noble memoirist Ekaterina Sabaneeva ascribed similar sentiments to her mother's and grandmother's reminiscences of life in the country in the late eighteenth century.[21]

It has been suggested that this feminine celebration of nature, its connection to personal freedom, derived from the influence of Rousseau, specifically his ideas of "natural upbringing."[22] To the extent that Rousseau and sentimentalism were fashionably "in the air" during the late eighteenth century this affinity makes sense. Among our interlocutors, however, only Dashkova (whose childhood joys, we should note, took place decidedly indoors) mentions Rousseau. It is highly unlikely that Labzina's ascetic and religious mother living in far off Ekaterinburg would have known about or approved of *Nouvelle Heloise*. Moreover, unlike Durova, the categories that Labzina employed to understand her natural surroundings were preeminently spiritual, embedded in a profound and unbreakable faith in the fatherhood of God and the saving power of Christ. She did not celebrate the state of nature per se; indeed, much of what her first husband, the libertine—not to mention incestuous and child-molesting—natural scientist A. M. Karamyshev, deemed "natural" Labzina herself found abhorrent and ungodly, quite unRousseau-ian sentiments. Solace and understanding lay in prayer, hope in God's power of mercy.

When Kheraskov, her friend and benefactor, left her in St. Petersburg, for example, both she and he fretted openly about her renewed vulnerability to her husband's vices and brutality. Kheraskov advised patience, endurance, and silence, even in the face of abominations. "Don't be dazzled by high standing, wealth, or gifts, but be content with what the Lord has provided and will provide. . . . He will grant you strength and fortitude, but you must not depart from Him and must always ask His help."[23] She agreed: "Pray for

20. Nadezhda Durova, *The Cavalry Maiden: Journals of a Russian Officer in the Napoleonic Wars*, trans. Mary Fleming Zirin (Bloomington: Indiana University Press, 1989), 9. By contrast, Ekaterina Dashkova, the only other Russian female memoirist of this era, barely mentions the outdoors (or faith for that matter). Her world was bounded by the city, interior spaces, books, and politics. Ekaterina Dashkova, *The Memoirs of Princess Dashkova*, trans. and ed. Kyril Fitzlyon (Durham: Duke University Press, 1995).

21. E. A. Sabaneeva, "Vospominaniia o bylom, 1770–1828," in *Rossiia v memuarakh: Istoriia zhizni blagorodnoi zhenshchiny*, ed. V. M. Bokova (Moscow: Novoe literaturnoe obozrenie, 1996), 334ff.

22. See, for example, the interesting paper by Olga Glagoleva, "Dream and Reality of *Provintsial'nye Baryshni*," delivered at the annual convention of the American Association for the Advancement of Slavic Studies, Boston, 1996, p. 19.

23. All of the quotations from Labzina's memoir and diary are taken from my own translation in Gary Marker and Rachel May, eds. and trans., *Days of A Russian Noblewoman: The Memories of Anna Labzina* (DeKalb: Northern Illinois University Press, 2001).

me, my father, that God will save me." So too did her mother-in-law: "We shall live together, my friend, and we shall pray for your benefactor. . . . God will help us."

For Labzina, divine intervention was an unfathomable, but salutary, fact of every day life. "Do not be upset, kind mother [-in-law]. . . . Out of love for me you wanted to assure my happiness, but it was useful to God that that not be my lot, so I will submit myself to His decisions and I will bear with it. He has not entirely abandoned me, since He gave me you." Observations such as these infuse all of Labzina's writings. Interestingly, God's reason was open to human conjecture, but ultimately it lay beyond the powers of human reason to comprehend, an acceptance of the doctrine of "mysteries of faith" which continued to have a deep impact upon Orthodox teachings on human understanding.

God was the source of all nature, which to Labzina was bountiful and glorious, a living link between her own physicality and faith. "Very often mother went with me to the bathing area and she would look out with reverence and relate to me the majesty of God. . . . She even taught me to swim in the deep sections of the river. . . . I went boating in lakes . . . and I worked in the garden." [From her nanny]: "Don't you marvel at God's wisdom. . . . Don't you see how He loves humanity, that all creation exists for us, both as sustenance and for pleasure? Man himself was created in [God's] image and likeness." This latter observation suggests a distinctly anthropomorphic outlook on nature ("for us both as sustenance and pleasure"), implying the utility and religiosity of human agency, the synergy of joy-in-life and faith.

Faith in a merciful but unknowable God was, thus, connected simultaneously to patience and to physical activity, both play and work. Work, in turn, meant both tilling one's own garden and an engagement with humanity, particularly the poor, infirm, and imprisoned. As Labzina's mother sermonized, "If you ever are in a position to do good deeds for the poor and unfortunate, you shall be executing God's law, and peace will reign in your heart. God will anoint you with his blessing, your wealth will multiply, and you will be happy . . . visit the sick, console the suffering and discouraged. Always remember that they are as close to you as brothers, and for them you shall be rewarded by the King in Heaven." The theme of tending the helpless and unfortunate is a central theme for Labzina, the synthesis of humility, suffering, human action, and redemption. To a certain extent, this call to serve the poor corresponds to the spirit of Christian charity (*blagotvoritel'nost'*), a familiar theme in saints' lives both of the official church and of the Old

Believers, as in the seventeenth-century *zhitie* (life) of the Old Believer con-
fidant of Avvakum, Feodosiia Morozova (*Povest' o boiaryne Morozovoi*).[24]

In Morozova's vita, a boyar woman endured physical and moral torment on
behalf of her faith (Old Belief) and that of the humble faithful. By enduring
personal torture she spared others who were poorer and weaker from having
to do so. She thus set an example for other aristocratic true believers—male
and female—who are mentioned at length in the text to follow. Labzina also
suffered while remaining true to her faith, and this theme dominates the narrative of her memoir. But her conception of charity took the responsibilities
of the well-to-do woman in a rather different direction than does Morozova's
biographer. Labzina endowed charity with enormous religious and practical
significance, and she unfailingly characterizes them as interventions into relations of authority, specifically as intercession (*zastuplenie*) between the powerful and the powerless in the name of God the Father and Jesus Christ. "I
know that you find this painful and unbearable, but pray to our Intercessor,
Jesus Christ, that he send you his aid. . . . He will not abandon you, but will
reward you with great gifts."

These words, spoken to Labzina by her mother-in-law in regard to staying
with her husband, whose abusive behavior had become intolerable, endow
social action, particularly by women, with importance. Just as Christ interceded
on her behalf, so should she, in Christ's name, intercede on behalf of others
against injustice and suffering. From its divine origins, human intercession,
as she describes it, fell entirely to women (at least in the social sphere), and the
model was her mother. Here we see an enticing hint that spiritual action could
be gender specific, and it may prove useful to investigate further the roots of
this feminized image of intercessor (*zastupnitsa*). In a curious and rarely cited
study, Alexander Konrad once suggested that the female intercessor came
into Russian Orthodoxy by way of Byzantium, through the apocryphal *Journey of the Mother of God Through Hell* (*Khozhdenie Bogoroditsy po mukam*).[25]

24. A. I. Mazunin, "Povest' o boiaryne Morozovoi," in *Pamiatniki literatury Drevnei Rusi. XVII vek*,
bk. 2 (Moscow: Khudozhestvennaia literatura, 1989), 455–84; Rosalind McKenzie, "Women in Seventeenth-
Century Russian Literature," in *Gender and Russian Literature*, ed. Rosalind Marsh (Cambridge: Cam-
bridge University Press, 1996), 46–47. The tale has recently been ably translated into English by Margaret
Ziolkowski. See Margaret Ziolkowski, ed. and trans., *Tale of Boiarynia Morozova, A Seventeenth-Century
Life* (Boulder, Colo.: Lexington Books, 2000).

25. Alexander N. Konrad, *Old Russia and Byzantium: Byzantium and the Oriental Origins of Russian
Culture* (Vienna: Wilhelm Braumüller, 1972), 95–118. The tale itself apparently derives from the early
Christian era and found its way into a Slavonic translation in the twelfth century. A seventeenth-century
manuscript version was published in 1955 in *Khrestomatiia po drevnei russkoi literature*, ed. N. K. Gudzii
(Moscow: Nauka, 1955), 92–98. For an English translation, see Serge A. Zenkovsky, *Medieval Russia's Epics,
Chronicles, and Tales* (New York: E. P. Dutton, 1963), 122–29.

In this tale, the Archangel Michael leads the Mother of God through the many regions of Hell, and exposes her along the way to all manner of sinners and their eternal sufferings. The Holy Virgin is implored to take pity on the sinners and to intervene on their behalf with God. "And a tormented one, seeing her, said, 'How is it, Holy Virgin, that you have visited us? Your blessed Son came upon the earth and did not ask us, nor did Abraham the Patriarch, nor Moses the Prophet, nor John the Baptist, nor Paul the Apostle, the favorite of the Lord. But *you, most Holy Virgin, are an intercessor* [italics added] and protector for the Christian people. You have prayed to God for us.'"[26] At one point the archangel shows her the river of fire in which those who failed to go to church had been submerged up to their necks. Mary is moved by this scene and asks God to allow her to be tortured along with them. After a lengthy interchange in which the Virgin implores the patriarchs and prophets to help her intercede with God on behalf of the damned, Christ responds that the Father has heard her pleas and will give the sinners a respite from Holy Thursday to Pentecost.

Regardless of whether the influence on Slavdom is as direct as Konrad suggests, the parallels between the Intercessor Mother of God and several of the passages in Labzina's memoir are striking. At one point Labzina was living near the border with China, in Nerchinsk, while her husband was on assignment for the Mining College. When his term there ended, the exiles in the town camped out in front of their house begging her to stay because, while doing God's work she tended for them. "You clothed us, and lightened our work load. You tended the sick . . . and managed to procure for us a decent diet. God will not abandon you. What you have given [to us] as a loan will be returned to you tenfold by the Heavenly Father." A similar scene took place in the Siberian town of Irkutsk, where prisoners thanked her for interceding with the warden on their behalf, calling her their mother.

Here we see a specifically feminized social engagement and this-worldly improvement, two hallmarks of Russian Enlightenment, that in this instance derived explicitly from religious, even traditionally Orthodox, sources, with no mention of Rousseau, Voltaire and the *Encyclopedistes,* Pietism, or any other specifically modern, secular authority. In her most recent study of French feminism, Joan Scott has coined the apt term "reading for paradox" to convey this pursuit of "internal contradictions and incompatibilities within concepts . . . that establish the truth or inevitability of certain views of the world."[27]

26. Zenkovsky, *Medieval Russia's Epics,* 123.
27. Joan Wallach Scott, *Only Paradoxes to Offer: French Feminists and the Rights of Man* (Cambridge: Harvard University Press, 1996), 16–17.

While Labzina was in no sense a protofeminist or republican, her writings do lend themselves to precisely this type of subversive reading in that they challenge innumerable interpretive boundaries of Russian Enlightenment, specifically those relating to gender, reason, and social action.

Perhaps, then, we would do well to revisit Russian Marianism more broadly to see whether the Mother of God as intercessor is a recurring theme, offering an inspiration for female action within the patriarchies of faith and society. First results, in fact, are promising. A prayer attributed to Vladimir Monomakh, the eleventh-century prince of Kiev, includes the following supplication: "Immaculate Virgin, who didst not know marriage, delight of God, guide of the faithful, save me as I perish and call upon thy Son. Have mercy upon me, oh Lord, have mercy when thou shalt judge. Judge me not with fire nor accuse me in thine anger! *The Holy Virgin, who bore thee, intercedes with thee, oh Christ* [italics added], in company with the angelic host and the army of martyrs."[28]

Centuries later, *Domostroi* reproduced this formulation almost exactly and in two separate sections. Chapter 13, "How Men and Women Should Pray in Church, Preserve Their Chastity, and Do No Evil," offers the following advice:

> Also say this:
> Lord Jesus Christ, Son of God, have mercy on me, a sinner.
> Say this prayer six hundred times. For the seventh hundred, pray to the Immaculate Virgin:
>
> *My Lady, Most Holy Mother of God, intercede for me,* [italics added] a sinner.
>
> Then go back to the beginning, and repeat this continually. If someone says these prayers, needing Her help, just as breath comes from the nostrils, so at the end of the first year Jesus, Son of God, will rejoice in him. After the second year, the Holy Ghost will enter into him. . . . The Immaculate Mother of God, with all the heavenly hosts and all the saints, will protect those who pray with faith and

28. *The Russian Primary Chronicle: Laurentian Text,* trans. and ed. Samuel Hazzard Cross and Olgerd P. Sherbowitz-Wetzor (Cambridge: Harvard University Press, 1954), Appendix B, "Prayer Attributed to Vladimir Monomakh," 219. Vladimir Monomakh (1053–1125) was the prince of Kiev who, according to the Chronicle accounts, married the daughter of the Emperor Constantine Monomachus of Constantinople, from whom he is said to have inherited the emperor's hat, the famous cap of Monomakh.

live according to God's commandments from all the Devil's wiles in this age and the one to come.[29]

In the concluding "A Father's Epistle Instructing His Son," the son is told that if he follows the instructions, "God's mercy will grace you, and that of the Immaculate Mother of God, our intercessor, and of the great miracle workers."[30]

This gendered notion of intercession also appears elsewhere in Russian explications of relations of authority. For example, Catherine I, the wife of Peter the Great, received literally hundreds of petitions to intercede with Peter on someone's behalf. Typically, these petitions referred to Catherine as "mother-intercessor," an indication that the two roles were somehow connected, and that they implied an accepted female authority to intervene personally between the powerful and the powerless. Other eighteenth-century *tsaritsy* were expected to play similar roles, much as their sixteenth- and seventeenth-century predecessors had done.[31]

Labzina employed a second important term, 'guardian," in a faith-centered, and equally gendered, way, but in this case the gender was male, and the lines of authority patrilineal. "I have a Guardian [i.e., God], to whom I have turned for guidance since birth and who protects me to this day." "God protects me, and he has guarded over me from my mother's womb until this very day." In Labzina's narrative God (and curiously, never the state, ruler, or government) protected her and her mother at various times against thieves, atamans, Tatars, criminals, and other potential sources of danger, not to mention the depravity of her husband. Moreover, just as Labzina and her mother could themselves incarnate the sacred example of *bogoroditsa zastupnitsa,* so too could kindly men incarnate the example of God the Protector. Thus, Labzina herself had several male guardians, including Kheraskov, her husband's superior officer, and the governor of Irkutsk, whose authority over her lay beyond challenge and was, as her mother(s) explained, ordained by God the Father.

The theme of paternal guardianship under God's presence was hardly unique to Labzina. Writing in 1767, for example, Princess Natal'ia Dolgorukaia referred repeatedly to the unfathomable but blessed guardianship of

---

29. *The Domostroi: Rules for Russian Households in the Time of Ivan the Terrible,* ed. and trans. Carolyn Johnston Pouncy (Ithaca: Cornell University Press, 1994), 89.

30. Ibid., 189.

31. The most extensive discussion of this topic remains M. I. Semevskii, *Tsaritsa Katerina Alekseevna: Anna i Villim Mons, 1692–1725* (St. Petersburg: Tipografiia V. S. Balashova, 1884).

God, both directly and through her beloved husband, as her compass through the difficulties she experienced in the 1720s, a time when she had almost no biological family nearby.[32] Similarly, Sergei Timofeevich Aksakov's *Family Chronicle* includes numerous references to men as guardians or formal protectors of women. "As for Praskovia Ivanovna, she need have no fear of acting; she was under the protection of the Governor and her own good friends, and Michail Maximovitsch would never dare to come to Tschurasovo."[33] "During the night they had received secret visits from peasants on the estate, who had told them all that had happened to their mistress; and they had hurried direct to Stepan Michailovitsch, as Praskovia Ivanovna's natural protector."[34]

Still, Labzina did seem to have been original in connecting paternal guardianship through God with the protectiveness of her mother's womb, from which she also derived her very existence. This linkage is revealing in that it comes perilously close to conflating her biological mother with holiness (in Nerchinsk: "Every day God presented me with the opportunity to do good. . . . I fulfilled my mother's instructions here") and perhaps the Mother of God as well. For her, the womb became the visceral vessel of faith, as when she proclaimed, "My honorable progenitress [*roditel'nitsa*], here is your daughter carrying out your testament! . . . I am here with no guide at all, but may your spirit be my protector." God's love, and—remarkably—individuality and resistance derived from the same source, as she makes clear in the many angry interchanges with Karamyshev.[35] "You find it worthwhile to think the way you do, but leave me be with my own rules! You have the authority to deprive me of my property and peace of mind, but you cannot take away my conscience and good name. . . . So long as the hand of God protects me I shall not stray from the path of virtue, and I shall not accept your advice."

Labzina employed "progenitress" only once in her memoir, but its usage leaps out from the page primarily because of its power and uniqueness. Labzina may not have invented the idea—indeed, "progenitress" would seem

32. *Svoeruchnye zapiski Kniagini Natal'i Borisovny Dolgorukoi docheri g. fel'dmarshala grafa Borisa Petrovicha Sheremeteva* (St. Petersburg: Khudozhestvennaia literatura, 1992), esp. 17ff.

33. S. T. Aksakov, *The Family Chronicle*, trans. M. C. Beverley (New York: Dutton, 1961), 59.

34. Ibid., 64.

35. The sacralization of the womb can be found in saints' lives as well. In the life of St. Sergius of Radonezh (1314?–92), the monk who founded Russia's most important monastery, the Trinity Monastery near Moscow, there is an interchange between Sergius (still called by his pre-ordination name of Bartholomew) and his brother Stephen in which Stephen says, "Why do you ask me, and why put me to the test? You were chosen of God while you were yet in your mother's womb, and he gave a sign concerning you before ever you were born, that the child would be a disciple of the Blessed Trinity." See Zenkovsky, *Medieval Russia's Epics*, 212.

to have an obvious derivation from the Holy Virgin, Mother of God, who required no progenitor to produce an offspring. But the formula is highly unusual, at least in eighteenth-century prose. For that very reason it is interesting to see "progenitress" recur in a letter written in 1818 (several years after Labzina had written her memoir) by Iurii Nikitich Bartenev to his brother, in which he recounts his wish to marry Labzina's niece, who had been her ward since the death of her sister years earlier. Bartenev had received encouragement from his intended, and had gotten the approval from everyone except Labzina, whom he had yet to approach. "I am lacking only the main piece, namely the blessing of her progenitress, without whom even the Lord God will not bless or approve our union. The time for consummating our happiness is still unresolved for I am unable to make any firm resolutions without her mother's [Labzina's] assent [*bez voli matushkinoi*]."[36] Bartenev, clearly intimidated by Labzina, was endeavoring to display his own good intentions and sincere religiosity. Still, he could not have artfully borrowed the term from her memoir, since its existence was a secret, and remained so for many decades after Labzina's death. One suspects, then, that the term had currency within the deeply religious and pietistic Masonic discourse of the Dying Sphinx Lodge, of which Labzina's second husband was grand master and in whose midst Bartenev circulated.

If so, Labzina took the word "progenitress" and made it her own, by linking it to individual will, a hallmark of Enlightenment, and blending the two as a single article of faith. Godly authority, through her mother's legacy, enabled her to make decisions on her own. Because it stood on a higher plane than did human law, faith provided her with a basis for refusal in the face of a temporal authority which otherwise compelled her to obey her husband's will and that of other men whose counsel she found unconvincing. Labzina engaged in a sophisticated and nuanced bit of reasoning to explain her resistance. She went to great lengths to confirm her acceptance of patriarchy and the authority of elders as the stated order of things on earth, and thus as God's will. She showed no interest in overturning or even modifying that order, but, when the temporal authority of men obliged her to violate the laws of God as she understood them, she, like Morozova, refused, basing her refusal on freedom of conscience and the power of her faith.[37]

---

36. "Pis'mo Iu. N. Barteneva bratu Vsevolodu Nikitichu, 25 Oktiabria 1818 goda," in *Sbornik starinnykh, bumag khraniashchikhsia v muzee P. I. Shchukina*, vol. 8 (Moscow, 1901), 422–23.

37. For more on Labzina's interweaving of faith and Enlightenment, see Gary Marker, "The Enlightenment of Anna Labzina: Gender, Faith, and Public Life in Catherinian and Alexandrian Russia," *Slavic Review* 59 (2000): 369–90.

There are several more points (such as regard for the dignity of common people) in both the memoir and the diary at which Labzina's religious outlook engaged rather than countermanded Enlightenment, and in each of these the effect is much the same: to situate herself in a world that was not of her making, and often not to her liking, and to make sense of it on her terms. In each case she employed faith, or the discourse of faith, to engage and creatively formulate conventions of secular ideology and thereby make them her own in a decidedly God- and female-centered religious cosmology.

None of these observations is meant to imply that Labzina's outlook was in any sense typical, or that these were the only defining female images in Russian Orthodoxy, although they surely were among the most important. Rather, I would suggest that the texts of Russian Orthodoxy made these examples of female agency commonplace and, through faith, legitimate. Women such as Labzina could access them, discover a voice and language through them, and creatively reshape them to make sense of their own situations in the secular world of the eighteenth century. For them, faith was alive and vital, and it offered them a good deal more than simply a guide to silent suffering and obedience. Thus, if there were one overarching conclusion to this essay, it would be about the limits of dual models. The oppositions of traditional/ modern and sacred/secular, however useful they may be in understanding Russian culture overall, fail to do justice to writers such as Labzina (and I suspect many others) who blend the binarisms in re-creative ways, or simply ignore the boundaries altogether.

10

PARADOXES OF PIETY

The Nizhegorod
Convent of the Exaltation
of the Cross, 1807–1935

WILLIAM G. WAGNER

In a pattern familiar to historians of modern Europe, nineteenth- and early twentieth-century imperial Russia witnessed a substantial monastic revival. Particularly after the mid-nineteenth century, this revival was predominantly female, to the point that by the outbreak of the First World War Russian Orthodox monasticism had become overwhelmingly female. To the expansion of convents and their memberships, moreover, must be added a growing number of informal women's religious communities and formally sanctioned service communities (Table 1). While increasing in numbers and size, Orthodox convents and other women's religious communities also departed from previous patterns by becoming predominantly communal rather than idiorrhythmic in structure and more heavily engaged in various forms of educational and social welfare work.[1] Hence the trends in the development of Russian Orthodox women's religious communities during the nineteenth and early twentieth centuries broadly paralleled those of women's religious orders in Western Europe, where the proliferation of female service orders formed part of an upsurge of religious activism by women.[2] Yet apart from the pioneering work

I wish to acknowledge with gratitude that research for this paper was supported in part by a grant from the International Research and Exchanges Board (IREX), with funds provided by the National Endowment for the Humanities, the U.S. Department of State, and the U.S. Information Agency. None of these organizations is responsible for the views expressed.

1. In idiorrhythmic monastic institutions, members generally provided for their own meals and accommodation, thus allowing for considerable disparities, and piety was more individualized; in communal institutions, meals were taken in common, both cells and duties were assigned by the head of the convent or monastery, and spiritual life was more collective.

2. For example, see Caitriona Clear, *Nuns in Nineteenth-Century Ireland* (Dublin: Gill and Macmillan,

by Brenda Meehan, the growth and reorientation of female monasticism in prerevolutionary imperial Russia and the "feminization" of Orthodox monasticism that resulted from it have been largely ignored by scholars.[3] The causes, characteristics, meaning, and significance of these phenomena therefore remain little understood, as do their connections with similar developments in Europe generally.

This chapter presents a preliminary consideration of these issues based on a still ongoing study of the Convent of the Exaltation of the Cross in the city of Nizhnii Novgorod from the beginning of the nineteenth century through the early Soviet period.[4] The chapter seeks in particular to situate

---

1987); Susan O'Brien, "*Terra Incognita:* The Nun in Nineteenth-Century England," *Past and Present* 121 (1988): 110–40; Ralph Gibson, *A Social History of French Catholicism, 1789–1914* (London: Routledge, 1989); Frances Lannon, *Privilege, Persecution, and Prophecy: The Catholic Church in Spain, 1875–1975* (Oxford: Clarendon Press, 1987); and Mary Peckham Magray, *The Transforming Power of the Nuns: Women, Religion, and Cultural Change in Ireland, 1750–1900* (New York: Oxford University Press, 1998). On parallel developments in the United States, see Carol K. Coburn and Martha Smith, *Spirited Lives: How Nuns Shaped Catholic Culture and American Life, 1836–1920* (Chapel Hill: University of North Carolina Press, 1999).

3. Historians employ the term the "feminization of religion" to describe a variety of developments in nineteenth- and early twentieth-century Europe. Here I mean both the disproportionate growth in female monasticism and the changes in monastic organization and social activity which accompanied this growth. Brenda Meehan, *Holy Women of Russia: The Lives of Five Orthodox Women Offer Spiritual Guidance for Today* (San Francisco: Harper, 1993); Brenda Meehan-Waters, "Popular Piety, Local Initiative and the Founding of Women's Religious Communities in Russia, 1764–1907," in *Seeking God: The Recovery of Religious Identity in Orthodox Russia, Ukraine, and Georgia,* ed. Stephen K. Batalden (DeKalb: Northern Illinois University Press, 1993), 83–105; idem, "From Contemplative Practice to Charitable Activity: Russian Women's Religious Communities and the Development of Charitable Work, 1861–1917," in *Lady Bountiful Revisited: Women, Philanthropy, and Power,* ed. Kathleen D. McCarthy (New Brunswick: Rutgers University Press, 1990), 142–56; idem, "Metropolitan Filaret (Drozdov) and the Reform of Women's Monastic Communities," *Russian Review* 50 (1991): 310–23; idem, "The Authority of Holiness: Women Ascetics and Spiritual Elders in Nineteenth-Century Russia," in *Church, Nation and State in Russia and Ukraine,* ed. Geoffrey A. Hosking (New York: St. Martin's Press, 1991), 38–51; and idem, "To Save Oneself: Russian Peasant Women and the Development of Women's Religious Communities in Prerevolutionary Russia," in *Russian Peasant Women,* ed. Beatrice Farnsworth and Lynne Viola (New York: Oxford University Press, 1992), 21–33. See also I. K. Smolich, *Russkoe monashestvo* (Moscow: Tserkovno-Nauchnyi Tsentr "Pravoslanaia Entsiklopediia," 1997), 291–305; P. N. Zyrianov, *Russkie monastyri i monashestvo v XIX i XX veka* (Moscow: Russkoe Slovo, 1999); and Sophia Senyk, *Women's Monasteries in Ukraine and Belorussia to the Period of Suppression,* in *Orientalia Christiana Analecta* (Rome), vol. 222 (1983).

4. The study of the convent itself is based primarily on its archive preserved at the Gosudarstvennyi Arkhiv Nizhegorodskoi Oblasti (hereafter, GANO) and on several published histories: I. Solov'ev (Sviashchennik), "Nizhegorodskoi Krestovozdvizhenskii pervoklassnyi zhenskii monastyr'," *Nizhegorodskiia eparkhial'nyia vedomosti,* 1887, no. 15, *chast' neofitsial'naia* (hereafter, "ch. neof."), pp. 759–73; no. 16, ch. neof., pp. 839–65; and no. 17, ch. neof., pp. 898–913; M. Dobrovol'skii (Protoierei), *Putevoditel' po sviatyniam i tserkovnym dostoprimechatel'nostiam g. Nizhniago-Novgoroda* (Nizhnii Novgorod, 1912), 155–60; P. Al'bitskii (Protoierei), *Tserkovnyi iubilei. Stoletie sushchestvovaniia v gorode N.-Novgorode Krestovozdvizhenskago pervoklassnago zhenskago monastyria (1813–1913 g.g.)* (Nizhnii Novgorod, 1913); P. Al'bitskii (Protoierei) and N. Mamontov (Sviashchennik), *Krestovozdvizhenskii pervoklassnyi zhenskii monastyr' v*

this convent in the context of urbanization, economic change, and political and social revolution that transformed late imperial and early Soviet Russia during these years. Because the history of the convent over this period in most ways typifies the trends noted above, it would seem to be an appropriate case to examine. The convent was reorganized on a communal basis by its new abbess in 1807. A few years later, chiefly as a result of a disastrous fire, it was relocated from a cramped site adjacent to the city's kremlin to a large plot of land on the outskirts of the city, where its relatively spacious new quarters included a hospital, an apothecary, and an almshouse. For the remainder of the imperial period, the convent grew continuously if unevenly, first in membership and then wealth, with this growth coming to a halt only in the wake of the revolutions of 1917. Over the same period, the two male monasteries in the city of Nizhnii Novgorod largely stagnated and eventually declined in membership, a pattern mirrored by most monasteries in Nizhegorod province (Tables 2 and 3). By the late nineteenth century the convent thus had become by far the largest religious establishment in the city, with its membership exceeding the total number of male black and white clergy in the city combined. It appears also to have been the wealthiest monastic institution in Nizhegorod province.[5] If in most ways typical, however, the Nizhegorod Convent of the Exaltation of the Cross also exhibited important distinguishing characteristics. It often led rather than followed trends, for example in reorganizing itself on a communal basis and engaging in social activity.[6] But perhaps most distinctive was its urban location, in contrast to the other convents in Nizhegorod province, which were located in rural areas or small and

---

gorode Nizhnem-Novgorode. Stoletie ego sushchestvovaniia (1813–1913 g.g.). Istoriko-statisticheskii ocherk (Nizhnii Novgorod, 1913); N. Khramtsovskii, *Kratkii ocherk istorii i opisanie Nizhniago-Novgoroda* (Moscow, 1859), vol. 2, pp. 116–30; Iu. G. Galai and O. Iu. Galai, "Nizhegorodskii Krestovozdvizhenskii zhenskii monastyr'," in *Uchenye zapiski Volgo-Viatskogo otdeleniia Mezhdunarodnoi Slavianskoi Akademii nauk, obrazovaniia, iskusstv i kul'tury. Vypusk 2* (Nizhnii Novgorod: Izdatel'stvo Nizhegorodskogo gosudarstvennogo universiteta im N. I. Lobachevskogo, 1998), 80–92; and A. Lushin, "V zemle Nizhegorodskoi prosiiavshaia . . . ," *Seiatel'*, 1995, no. 1–2:61–65.

5. A. Snezhnitskii, *Adres-Kalendar' Nizhegorodskoi eparkhii, v pamiat' ispolnivshagosia v 1888 godu 900-letiia kreshcheniia Rusi* (Nizhnii Novgorod, 1888), 237–345, provides an extensive inventory of the assets of all the monastic communities in the diocese of Nizhegorod and Arzamas, including their capital endowments. The Nizhegorod Convent of the Exaltation of the Cross possessed by far the largest capital endowment, although several convents possessed much more substantial landholdings. This was still the case in 1917. GANO, *f.* 1016, *op.* 2, *d.* 9, *ll.* 1–2.

6. For example, see Meehan-Waters, "Metropolitan Filarét," on the effort to reorganize convents on a communal basis, and idem, "From Contemplative Practice," on the growth of social welfare activity. On the latter issue, see also Smolich, *Russkoe monashestvo*, 293–96, and Adele Lindenmeyr, *Poverty Is Not a Vice: Charity, Society, and the State in Imperial Russia* (Princeton: Princeton University Press, 1996), 125–26, 140.

relatively stagnant towns and cities.[7] In this respect, the ability of the Nizhe-gorod Convent of the Exaltation of the Cross to adapt itself successfully to the rapidly changing urban conditions of late imperial Russia also stands in sharp contrast to the experience of most urban Russian Orthodox institu-tions at this time.[8] This relative success in coping with the processes of social, economic, and cultural change can be represented as a series of three para-doxes that, taken together, suggest that the convent's apparently considerable adaptive capacity lay in part in a combination of astute leadership, relative institutional autonomy and flexibility, the ability to respond to the religious needs of diverse groups within the local and regional community, and good luck that eventually turned very sour. These three paradoxes, which will be examined in turn, involved (1) the ability of a conservative leadership to adapt to changing times and to adopt modern economic strategies for strengthening and enriching the convent; (2) the ability of the convent to retain the support of wealthy patrons despite a sharp change in the social composition of its membership; and (3) the ways in which the Bolshevik Revolution transformed the convent's strengths into weaknesses and led to its suppression by a political regime committed to a program of modernization, despite the convent's evident ability to adapt successfully to the material and cultural conditions of modernity.

To turn to the first of these paradoxes: the generally conservative leader-ship of the convent proved to be remarkably adept at adapting its economy to the emerging capitalist economy of Russia's central industrial region dur-ing the latter part of the nineteenth and the early twentieth centuries. This

7. For a listing of all convents in Nizhegorod province, see Snezhnitskii, *Adres-Kalendar'*; L. I. Denisov, *Pravoslavnye monastyri Rossiiskoi imperii. Polnyi spisok* (Moscow, 1908); A. A. Pavlovskii, ed., *Vseobshchii illiustrirovannyi putevoditel' po monastyriam i sviatym mestam Rossiiskoi imperii i sv. g. Afonu,* 2d ed. (Nizhnii Novgorod, 1907; reprint, New York: Possev, 1988); and *Pravoslavnyia russkiia obiteli. Pol-noe illiustrirovannoe opisanie vsekh pravoslavnykh russkikh monastyrei v Rossiiskoi imperii i na Afone* (St. Petersburg, 1910; reprint, St. Petersburg: Izdatel'stvo "Voskresenie," 1994).

8. This seems to be the general assessment of Gregory Freeze, who is the most prolific contemporary scholar on the Orthodox Church in prerevolutionary imperial Russia. Among his many works, see in particular *The Parish Clergy in Nineteenth-Century Russia: Crisis, Reform, Counter-Reform* (Princeton: Princeton University Press, 1983), and "'Going to the Intelligentsia': The Church and Its Urban Mission in Post-Reform Russia," in *Between Tsar and People: Educated Society and the Quest for Public Identity in Late Imperial Russia,* ed. Edith W. Clowes, Samuel D. Kassow, and James L. West (Princeton: Princeton University Press, 1991), 215–32. See also Simon Dixon, "The Church's Social Role in St. Petersburg, 1880–1914," in Hosking, *Church, Nation and State,* 167–92, and idem, "The Orthodox Church and the Workers of St. Petersburg, 1880–1914," in *European Religion in the Age of Great Cities, 1830–1930,* ed. Hugh McLeod (London: Routledge, 1995), 119–41. But cf. Jennifer Hedda, "Good Shepherds: The St. Peters-burg Pastorate and the Emergence of Social Activism in the Russian Orthodox Church, 1855–1917" (Ph.D. diss., Harvard University, 1998).

characterization of the convent's leadership as conservative, however, must be qualified in at least one respect. Throughout the period under study the convent's leaders demonstrated a consistent if modest commitment to mitigating the harsh conditions faced by women in Russian society in ways that, in the circumstances and vocabulary of the time, could be described as simultaneously progressive and conservative. Reflecting an awareness of the vulnerability particularly of older women, for example, Abbess Dorofeia, who was responsible for the construction of the hospital and the almshouse at the convent, stressed in a petition to Bishop Mefodii of Nizhegorod and Arzamas in 1826 that "women of any social estate who have no kin, who have been abandoned by everyone, who are poor, ill, and aged, have found here peace, sustenance, and shelter, as well as a salvific refuge for their souls."[9] Her successor, Abbess Vera, established a school for girls at the convent in 1838, at a time when education for women was a controversial issue within the church and the opportunities for formal education for women in general were severely limited.[10] Such charitable and educational endeavors contributed to the transformation in the conception and organization of charity that took place in imperial Russia during the nineteenth century and anticipated both the redefinition of the social role of women and the calls for monastic reform that began to be expressed in Orthodox writing especially after mid-century.[11] But at the same time they fell within, and thereby also

9. GANO, *f.* 582, *op.* 1, *d.* 86, *l.* 6. It is worth noting that Abbess Dorofeia herself was the widow of a military officer who had died in service, although she was well-connected socially and appears not to have been in need when she undertook a religious life. In her petition to Mefodii, she was seeking to have the status of the convent elevated from third to first class, which would have increased the state subvention it received. As part of the reform in 1764 that secularized monastic lands, officially supported monastic institutions were divided into three classes, which determined both the level of state subvention and the number of nuns or monks permitted. The convent was finally elevated to first-class status in 1856.

10. GANO, *f.* 582, *op.* 1, *d.* 250, *ll.* 10, 17; *d.* 335, *ll.* 15 ob.–16; *d.* 286, *ll.* 2–2 ob., 4–5; and Al'bitskii and Mamontov, *Krestovozdvizhenskii pervoklassnyi zhenskii monastyr'*, 48, 53, 69–70. See also Freeze, *Parish Clergy*, 178–79. It is worth noting that Abbess Vera was an orphan who had been raised at the convent.

11. On the development of charity, see Lindenmeyr, *Poverty Is Not a Vice*, and Meehan-Waters, "From Contemplative Practice"; on monastic reform, see Arkhimandrit Evdokim, "Inokini na sluzhbe blizhenim," *Bogoslovskii vestnik*, 1902, no. 11:305–58; and N. D. Kuznetsov, *K voprosu o tserkovnom imushchestve i otnoshenii gosudarstva k tserkovnym nedvizhimym imeniiam v Rossii (Doklad IV otdelu Predsobornogo Prisutstviia)* (Sergiev Posad, 1907). The development of the image and ideal of women in Russian Orthodox writing during the nineteenth and early twentieth centuries will be addressed in a separate essay. But briefly, in ways similar to trends in Western Europe, Orthodox writers used the allegedly natural and divinely ordained qualities of women embodied in a domestic and maternal feminine ideal to define and legitimize an expansion of the role of women in society and the church. On this trend in Western Europe, see H. Mills, "Negotiating the Divide: Women, Philanthropy and the 'Public Sphere' in Nineteenth-Century France," in *Religion, Society and Politics in France Since 1789*, ed. Frank Tallett and Nicholas Atkin (London: The Hambledon Press, 1991), 29–54.

reinforced while modifying, existing conceptions of the nature and role of women. As the curriculum of the school makes clear, moreover, the objective was not to challenge the prevailing order, but to enable particularly vulnerable women to survive within it.[12]

Indeed, the leaders of the convent appear in general to have accepted their place in the existing temporal and ecclesiastical orders. Several abbesses, for example, expressed their identity with and loyalty to the imperial order through their participation in and subsequent reflections on the admittedly highly ritualized visits of emperors and other members of the imperial family to the convent that took place on several occasions.[13] The portraits of recent emperors and members of the imperial family, as well as of several church dignitaries, adorning the walls of the convent's formal reception room made a similar statement.[14] Publicly declared contributions to war relief efforts during the Crimean, Russo-Turkish, and Russo-Japanese Wars and the First World War similarly were intended in part as expressions of patriotism.[15] The string of awards for service to the church received by successive abbesses and treasurers were carefully recorded and no doubt displayed on appropriate occasions.[16] In contrast to a few prominent female monastic leaders, none of the convent's leaders appears to have taken part in any of the intra-church debates over church reform in the early twentieth century, even those relating directly to monasticism or the role of women within the church.[17] The

12. GANO, *f.* 582, *op.* 1, *d.* 235, *ll.* 4 *ob.*–6; *d.* 300, *ll.* 1–2; *d.* 335, *ll.* 15 *ob.*–16; *d.* 352, *ll.* 20–20 *ob.*; and *d.* 550, *ll.* 1–8, 65 *ob.*–67. The curriculum included Russian grammar, reading, writing, Church Slavonic, arithmetic, drawing, singing, divine history, Orthodox catechism, and traditional female handicrafts, such as sewing, knitting, gold embroidery, tailoring, and painting.

13. GANO, *f.* 582, *op.* 1, *d.* 122; *d.* 204; *d.* 335, *ll.* 19 *ob.*–20; *d.* 352, *ll.* 7–8 *ob.*; *d.* 412; *d.* 431; and Al'bitskii and Mamontov, *Krestovozdvizhenskii pervoklassnyi zhenskii monastyr'*, 42–46.

14. GANO, *f.* 582, *op.* 1, *d.* 249, *ll.* 6–10. It would appear that this was the only room in the convent to contain portraits of members of secular society, which both suggests the room's ceremonial and symbolic function and provides insight into the sisters' conceptualization of the relationship between the sacred and the secular worlds.

15. GANO, *f.* 582, *op.* 1, *d.* 335, *l.* 18 *ob.*; *d.* 471; *Nizhegorodskiia eparkhial'nyia vedomosti*, 1904, no. 6, chast' ofitsial'naia, pp. 93–97; and *Ocherk deiatel'nosti dukhovenstva i uchrezhdenii Nizhegorodskoi Eparkhii po okazaniiu pomoshchi v voennoe vremia so dnia otkrytiia Eparkhial'nago Komiteta (20 avgusta 1914 g.) po 1-e ianvaria 1916 goda* (Nizhnii Novgorod, 1916), 31–34, 48–63.

16. See the annual reports on membership of the convent in GANO, *f.* 582, *op.* 1, various *dela*.

17. For example, Abbess Ekaterina of the Holy Mother of God Convent in Lesna and Grand Princess Elizaveta Feodorovna, abbess of the Martha and Mary Cloister in Moscow. See Igumen'ia Ekaterina, "O diakonissakh (Po povodu stat'i sviashch. V. Uspenskago)," *Tserkovnyia vedomosti*, 1908, no. 15/16, pribavlenie, pp. 728–29; *Zhurnaly i protokoly zasedanii Vysochaishe uchrezhdennago Predsobornago Prisutstviia* (St. Petersburg, 1906–7), vol. 4, pp. 83–86; Rossiiskii gosudarstvennyi arkhiv drevnikh aktov, *f.* 1204, *op.* 1, *d.* 17518a, *ll.* 788–79 *ob.*, 269–72; and *Materialy k zhitiiu prepodobnomuchenitsy velikoi kniagini Elizavety. Pis'ma, dnevniki, vospominaniia, dokumenty*, 2d ed. (Moscow: Sestrichestvo vo imia prepodobno muchenitsy Velikoi Kniagini Elizavety, 1996), 50–58.

structure of authority within the convent, moreover, conformed to the ideal of patriarchalism projected and embodied by the ecclesiastical order. Indeed, the introduction of communal organization entailed a substantial expansion of the authority and power of a convent's leaders, who once elected assumed formally unlimited control over the activities and movement of the convent's members and over access to and use of the convent's resources. In this regard it is revealing that although biographic accounts of female monastic life generally emphasize the spiritual and moral, as well as the material, benefits derived from communal organization, they also demonstrate the important role of a strong leader in organizing the community and invariably include an episode or two indicating the disorder and moral laxity that resulted from the absence of such leadership.[18] The records of the Nizhegorod Convent of the Exaltation of the Cross suggest that successive and stable groups of leaders managed the affairs and life of the convent over long periods with a firm hand.[19]

The economic organization of the convent, too, was fairly conventional, at least until the latter part of the nineteenth century. As was the case in all the convents in Nizhegorod province, the sisters produced a significant share of the food and clothing that they consumed, and the remaining needs of the convent were met by income derived from donations, candle sales, and the performance of religious services; the production and sale of craft goods; the rent from a few modest landholdings, fishing rights, and a mill; a state subsidy; and various other sources. Throughout most of the nineteenth century the economic position of the convent appears to have been relatively

18. For examples, see Serafima, "Avtobiografiia igumenii Serafimy," *Orlovskiia eparkhial'nyia vedomosti*, 1891, no. 12, ch. neof., pp. 818–52; and no. 13, ch. neof., pp. 879–86; T. Tolycheva, *Spaso-Borodinskii monastyr' i ego osnovatel'nitsa (Posviashchaetsia vsem pochitaiushchim pamiat' Margarity Mikhailovny Tuchkovoi)* (Moscow, 1875); Appolinariia, "Avtobiografiia igumenii Appolinarii, v skhime Amvrosii," *Tverskie eparkhial'nyia vedomosti*, 1908, no. 1/2, ch. neof., pp. 6–12; no. 3, ch. neof., pp. 59–68; no. 4, ch. neof., pp. 102–9; no. 5, ch. neof., pp. 127–34; no. 6, ch. neof., pp. 159–65; no. 7, ch. neof., pp. 181–89; and no. 8, ch. neof., pp. 223–31; "Mavrikiia, igumen'ia Goritskago zhenskago monastyria, v skhime Marii," in *Zhizneopisaniia otechestvennykh podvizhnikov blagochestiia 18 i 19 vekov (s portretami)*, July (Moscow, 1908), 264–74; and S. A. Kel'tsev, *Iverskaia vyksunskaia zhenskaia obshchina i osnovatel' eia Ieromonakh Varnava* (Moscow, 1884), 45–58. See also Meehan-Waters, "Metropolitan Filaret."

19. Women generally held positions of leadership for extended periods and often advanced from one such position to a higher one. See the annual membership lists of the convent in GANO, *f.* 582, *op.* 1, various *dela*. The extent of power that an abbess could wield is illustrated particularly starkly in the case of Abbess Asenefa, who was compelled to retire in 1903 for allegedly mismanaging the convent's funds. Among other things, she was criticized for refusing to allow other members of the convent's leadership to participate in the management of the convent's finances and demanding that they verify documents and reports without being able to examine or read them. Rossiiskii Gosudarstvennyi Istoricheskii Arkhiv (hereafter, RGIA), *f.* 796, *op.* 184, *d.* 538.

precarious, with fluctuations in income being reflected directly in variations in the sisters' diet.[20] Lamenting the detrimental effects of inflation in a letter to Bishop Filaret in 1870, for example, Abbess Dorofeia (II) added that "the means of the convent are not increasing, so that, even with the strictest economy, they are barely sufficient to cover the maintenance expenses for the nearly two-hundred and fifty sisters of the convent, the twelve orphans from the clerical estate being brought up at the convent's school, and the nearly one hundred sisters from convents in other dioceses who each year stay at the convent while collecting donations, as well as the costs of repairing both a convent that is visited frequently by Imperial Personages and other people and a chapel that becomes flooded each spring. For this reason the amount received in income from various sources is spent each year without any balance remaining."[21]

In this context, the convent's leaders were constantly searching for ways to meet the financial needs of a growing community, and their efforts in this regard again appear to have been fairly traditional, if sometimes ingenious. For example, to tap into the substantial wealth generated each year across the Oka River at the annual Nizhnii Novgorod trade fair, by the mid-nineteenth century the largest and most lucrative in Europe, itinerant collection missions generally were timed to begin with the opening of the fair.[22] So that merchants and traders would not have to leave their goods in order to visit the convent, a permanent chapel eventually was erected on the fairgrounds, thereby substantially increasing the flow of donations to the convent.[23] At least until the advent of the last abbess, however, there is little hint that the leaders of the convent sought consciously to "modernize" its economy. Yet in the process of scrounging the funds needed to meet the convent's needs, that is precisely what they managed to do.

This outcome had more to do with the transformation of the surrounding economy and the development of new financial institutions and forms of property during the nineteenth century than it did with the foresight of the convent's leaders, although the latter clearly deserve credit for recognizing and taking advantage of the opportunity that was presented to them. Put briefly, stimulated at least initially by the transfer of the Makar'ev trade fair

---

20. See the annual reports on the convent's finances contained in GANO, f. 582, op. 1, various dela.

21. GANO, f. 582, op. 1, d. 417, l. 11. Dorofeia was seeking an exemption for the convent from a special levy in support of diocesan schools.

22. By "itinerant collection mission" is meant the practice by which, to raise money for the convent, pairs of sisters would travel through several provinces for as long as two years, seeking donations.

23. GANO, f. 582, op. 1, d. 197; Al'bitskii and Mamontov, Krestovozdvizhenskii pervoklassnyi zhenskii monastyr', 40, 58–67. This is the same chapel that flooded each spring.

to Nizhnii Novgorod in 1817, the economy of the city and surrounding region grew substantially during the nineteenth and early twentieth centuries. An enormous amount of wealth flowed through the city, much of it in the hands of the expanding merchant, industrialist, financier, and entrepreneurial and middling strata of society. Because of the trade fair, moreover, merchants, traders, bankers, and so on from Moscow and other cities in the empire visited Nizhnii Novgorod annually for extended periods, developing strong ties with the city as a result.[24] Increasingly, the wealth of such people took the form of capital deposits, stocks and shares, and other financial instruments, and eventually so too did their donations to the convent. This development emerged in the 1830s, experienced two substantial spurts in the 1840–50s and in the 1870s, and accelerated in the early twentieth century, with the capital endowment of the convent reaching nearly 408,000 rubles by 1914. That year the income from this endowment was roughly 14,500 rubles, nearly a third of the convent's income for the year.[25] Such an income enabled the convent's leaders not merely to improve the diet of the sisters but also to expand the welfare and other operations of the convent and to produce a modest surplus that in turn could be reinvested, generally in certificates of deposit. The account books of the convent suggest that the last abbess, Mariia, regularized this process and did much to integrate the convent's operations into the developing market economy. It is perhaps worth noting in this regard that Mariia, who entered the convent in 1902 and took monastic vows and was appointed abbess the following year, thereby completing in months a process that normally took decades, was the widow of a wealthy industrialist and former mayor of Nizhnii Novgorod who had close ties with the Orthodox hierarchy at the national level.[26]

---

24. The growth of the city in the nineteenth century can be traced through Khramtsovskii, *Kratkii ocherk istorii i opisanie Nizhniago-Novgoroda*, vols. 1 and 2; *Pamiatnaia knizhka Nizhegorodskoi gubernii na 1865 g.* (Nizhnii Novgorod, 1864); A. S. Gatsiskii, *Nizhegorodka. Putevoditel' i ukazatel' po Nizhnemu Novgorodu i po Nizhegorodskoi iarmarke*, 3d ed. (Nizhnii Novgorod, 1877); idem, *Beglyi ocherk Nizhniago-Novgoroda i ego proshlago* (Nizhnii Novgorod, 1896); V. I. Vinogradov, *Illiustrirovannyi putevoditel' po Nizhnemu-Novgorodu i iarmarke*, 2d ed. (Moscow, 1896); I. A. Milotvorskii, *Nizhnii-Novgorod, ego proshloe i nastoiashchee (kratkoe opisanie istoricheskago sobytiia Nizhniago-Novgoroda v sviazi s istoriei vsego Nizhegorodskago kniazhestva i Nizhegorodskoi gubernii)* (Nizhnii Novgorod, 1911); D. N. Smirnov, *Kartinki Nizhegorodskogo byta XIX veka* (Gor'kii, 1948); and *Istoriia goroda Gor'kogo* (Gor'kii, 1971). On the growth of the annual trade fair, see also A. L. Fitzpatrick, *The Great Russian Fair: Nizhnii Novgorod, 1840–1890* (London: Macmillan, 1990), and *Makar'evsko-Nizhegorodskaia iarmarka. Ocherki istorii* (Nizhnii Novgorod, 1997).

25. GANO, *f.* 582, *op.* 1, *d.* 671.

26. GANO, *f.* 582, *op.* 1, *d.* 626, *l.* 11; *d.* 640, *ll.* 1 ob.–2; RGIA, *f.* 796, *op.* 184, *d.* 530, *ll.* 50–51; see also GANO, *f.* 582, *op.* 1, *d.* 570. As a wealthy and prominent widow, Mariia (Anna Aleksandrovna Soboleva) could have played an active role as a philanthropist, and even entrepreneur, without entering the convent.

Although by the end of the nineteenth century most of the convents and monasteries in Nizhegorod province were also seeking to build their endowments, none proved as successful at doing so as the Nizhegorod Convent of the Exaltation of the Cross, an outcome that quite likely reflected the convent's advantageous location. An important result was that the convent became much less dependent on the consumption and sale of its own products, and therefore on landholdings, the labor of new members, and the market for its craft production, than the convents located in rural areas and small towns. The latter, by comparison, continued to rely heavily on their own agricultural output and on the sale of craft goods produced by their members. Even here, however, a distinction must be made between the majority of convents, which remained relatively poor and maintained essentially a subsistence economy, and a few—such as the Seraphim-Diveevo Trinity Convent, the Seraphim-Ponetaevka All-Sorrows Convent, the Kutuzovo-Mother of God Convent, and the St. Nicholas and Aleksei Man of God Convents in Arzamas—that established up-to-date commercial farms or derived substantial incomes from the production and sale of high-quality embroidered goods chiefly for religious use, sometimes for an international market.[27] In their efforts to "make do" in a context of developing capitalism, it would seem, the leaders of at least some convents consciously or unconsciously adopted some of its characteristics, thereby enhancing the ability of the institutions they led to survive in a changing economic environment. In the case of the Nizhegorod Convent of the Exaltation of the Cross, its large endowment provided it with an unprecedented degree of security and flexibility. These

---

Fragmentary evidence indicates that she was a deeply religious woman who was well connected to the ecclesiastical hierarchy. It is likely that her position as abbess of a wealthy and prominent convent enabled her to play a socially more prominent and personally more satisfying role than her wealth alone would have allowed. Her reorganization of the accounting methods of the convent undoubtedly also represented a response to the circumstances that had led to her predecessor's removal (see note 19). This case suggests that the growing complexity of the convent's economy may well have necessitated specialized expertise to manage it.

27. For example, see Snezhnitskii, *Adres-Kalendar'*, 237–345; P. V. Ermeev, *Arzamasskie mastera. Rasskazy o narodnom isskustve* (Nizhnii Novgorod, 1992), 236–40; I. N. Chetyrkin, *Istoriko-statisticheskoe opisanie Arzamasskoi Alekseevskoi zhenskoi obshchiny* (Nizhnii Novgorod, 1887), 65–67; "Ob uchastii odnogo monastyria Nizhegorodskoi eparkhii na vsemirnoi vystavke 1900 goda v Parizhe," *Nizhegorodskiia eparkhial'nyia vedomosti*, 1900, no. 3, ch. of., pp. 44–46; T. V. Kuznetsova, "Khudozhestvennye remesla i promysly zhenskikh monastyrei v sinodal'nyi period," in *Nasledie monastyrskoi kul'tury: remeslo, khudozhestvo, iskusstvo. Stat'i, referaty, publikatsii*, vyp. 1 (St. Petersburg: Rossiiskii Institut Istorii Iskusstv, 1997), 30; O. V. Bukova, "Promysly Nizhegorodskogo kraia: ikh sotsial'no-ekonomicheskaia obuslovlennost'," in *IX nauchnaia konferentsiia molodykh uchenykh i spetsialistov Volgo-Viatskogo regiona. Tezisy dokladov, ch. I* (Gor'kii, 1989), 27; and, in general, V. F. Zybkovets, *Natsionalizatsiia monastyrskikh imushchestv v Sovetskoi Rossii (1917–1921 gg.)* (Moscow: Nauka, 1975), 36–44.

advantages, however, were offset by a greater dependence on the performance and—ultimately—the survival of the capitalist economy.

This restructuring of the convent's economy leads to the second paradox through which the history of the convent during this period can be represented. Although the convent received donations and support from a broad range of the population, the wealthy and middling strata of society in effect were heavily subsidizing a religious community composed overwhelmingly of women from the poorer strata of society. It is impossible, of course, to determine precisely either the number or the social identity of the people who regularly contributed small amounts to the convent. The names and very modest contributions recorded in itinerant collection books indicate considerable support for the convent from unprivileged members of society, particularly in Nizhegorod province.[28] But the larger donations and bequests, ranging from fifty to one hundred rubles to occasionally several thousand rubles, especially those that built the convent's endowment, not surprisingly were made chiefly by merchants or members of their families, hereditary honored citizens and officials, members of the clergy or their families, and especially, people listed merely as "ladies" (*gospozha*) or "gentlemen" (*gospodin*). Particularly after the early nineteenth century, few noble donors were listed, although they may have been included in the category of ladies and gentlemen. A reflection of the right of women to control their own property under imperial Russian law, the number of women and men making significant donations and bequests was roughly equal. A significant number of donations, too, were made by people from Moscow and other cities. Without this support from the privileged strata of society, the convent in fact would have had difficulty maintaining itself, at least until its endowment income had grown sufficiently. In effect, throughout the entire period, the convent was a net recipient of charitable donations, if contributions to the convent can be so characterized.[29]

The membership of the convent, by contrast, shifted increasingly toward the poorer and unprivileged strata of society during the nineteenth and the early twentieth centuries. In the late eighteenth and the early nineteenth centuries the majority of members of the convent were widows, mostly of military officers, then of officials, clergy, and other urban groups, and finally

28. For example, see GANO, *f.* 582, *op.* 1, *dd.* 209, 210, 218, 230–33, 242–44, 259, 265–68, 282, 340, 390, 420, 436, 490, 612, 657.

29. The identity of significant donors was determined by using chiefly two sources, annual announcements published in the *Nizhegorodskiia eparkhial'nyia vedomosti* and various lists and correspondence contained in GANO, *f.* 582, *op.* 1, various *dela*. The significance of donations in the overall budget of the convent was determined by using the annual reports submitted by the abbess to the diocesan consistory and the bishop.

of peasants. No doubt reflecting the effects of the continuous wars of this period, this pattern of social composition persisted through the early 1820s, although the share of widows dropped to about 20 percent of the total membership.[30] For the next several decades, however, the majority of new members came roughly equally from the clerical estate, the urban lower middle strata (*meshchanstvo*), and the peasantry, so that by the 1860s and 1870s these three groups dominated the convent's membership at all levels and ranks. The overwhelming majority of these women, moreover, were relatively young (late teens to early thirties) and unmarried. Although women from these three groups continued to provide the majority of new members until the dissolution of the convent, after the late 1880s young (late teens to mid-twenties [fig. 16]) and unmarried peasant women increasingly predominated among the novitiate and the growing number of women living at the convent without inclusion in the novitiate, so that by the 1910s women from the peasantry composed the largest single group in the convent's membership. Very few members, particularly new members, came from those social groups that provided the principal material benefactors of the convent.[31]

Given the nature of the available sources, one can only speculate about what might have led women—particularly women from the poorer and unprivileged strata of society—to enter the convent at this time. Certainly the reasons must have been complex and varied. To some women the convent may have appeared to offer security in a harsh economic world, especially during a period of intense dislocation. Most of the provinces of origin for peasant women entering the convent, for example, experienced significant levels of outmigration and extended departures for seasonal labor by males after the late 1880s, causing an imbalance of women to men in many villages and a consequent difficulty in forming the family groups on which survival depended. In this regard, the low rate of mortality and the high life expectancy of women living in the convent attest to the material security it provided. Women entering the convent could expect to be cared for, and relieved of the burdens of labor, if they fell ill or when they reached old age.[32] To other

---

30. The decline in the number of widows entering the convent may have been due in part to the reorganization of the convent on a communal basis, as particularly widows with means would have lost their relative autonomy as well as the ability to use their property to make their situation more comfortable.

31. See the annual membership lists of the convent in GANO, *f.* 582, *op.* 1, various *dela*.

32. Ibid. Although the overwhelming majority of women entering the convent came from Nizhegorod province, a significant number also came from a large number of other provinces, chiefly the neighboring provinces of Viatka, Kostroma, and Tambov, as well as the more distant Vologda. In at least one documented case, that of the unmarried peasant woman Ol'ga Vasil'evna Potemkina, the motivation appears to have been a combination of religious feeling and poverty. GANO, *f.* 582, *op.* 1, *d.* 629.

women the convent may have appeared to offer a socially acceptable alternative to married life, an escape from an abusive family situation, an opportunity for female sociability and community, or the possibility of self-development and social advancement. In addition to traditional agricultural and domestic tasks, the women in the convent pursued a wide variety of specialized crafts, filled a number of responsible positions, and were able to develop skills in ways that would otherwise have been difficult.[33]

It is worth recalling, however, that entry into the convent required both submission to its discipline and to the authority of its leadership and acceptance by the abbess. Such acceptance was not likely to be forthcoming without some expression of religious motivation and commitment. As the presence in peasant villages of pious single women who often dressed in a religious fashion (*chernichki*) and lived ascetically by themselves (*keleinitsy*) attests, and the formation by peasant women of informal religious groups in rural areas at this time demonstrates, rural Russia was not devoid of deeply pious Orthodox women willing to commit themselves to some form of religious life. It may be too, then, that the loosening of restrictions on peasant movement after the abolition of serfdom enabled, and the expansion of rural parish schools after the mid-1880s encouraged, such women to enter Orthodox convents in increasing numbers, the Nizhegorod Convent of the Exaltation of the Cross included.[34] Certainly life in the convent would have provided such women with expanded possibilities for spiritual fulfillment, including the opportunity to perform liturgical roles normally reserved for men.

---

33. These are generally listed in the annual membership reports. Six formal positions of authority were listed at various times: abbess, treasurer, superintendent, sacristan, eldress, and *ustavnitsa* (who had responsibility for overseeing church services). Other positions of authority included overseeing the choirs, the various crafts, and domestic tasks. Among the duties performed by members of the convent were agricultural work; baking; preparing meals, brewing kvass (a mildly alcoholic fermented drink made from rye flour or bread with malt), and so on; singing in the choirs, reading the Psalter, and serving in one of the convent's three churches and two chapels; serving as apothecaries or paramedics; managing the almshouse, the hospital, and the hostel for guests and pilgrims; teaching in the school; painting icons and other religious images; working at a variety of crafts, such as gold embroidery, sewing, tailoring, and cobbling; and assisting the abbess and the treasurer.

34. Between 1888 and 1903, the number of church-parish and church grammar schools in Nizhegorod province increased from 290 to 619; the number of girls enrolled in such schools in 1903 was 7,788. Nationally, between 1884 and 1905 the number of church-parish schools increased from 4,064 to 43,893, with their enrollments rising from 105,317 to 1,923,698 pupils of both sexes. See "Vedomost' Nizhegorodskago Eparkhial'nago Uchilishchnago Soveta o tserkovnykh shkolakh za 1903 grazhdanskii god," *Nizhegorodskiia eparkhial'nyia vedomosti*, 1904, supplement to no. 13 (Table 1); [I. Smolich], *Istoriia russkoi tserkvi. Kniga 8-aia, chast' 2-aia. 1700–1917* (Moscow: Izdatel'stvo Spaso-Preobrazhenskogo Valaamskogo Monastyria, 1997), 108–10; and O. V. Bukova, "Dukhovnoe obrazovanie v Rossii i Nizhegorodskoi gubernii" (unpublished paper).

FIG. 16   A group of novices at the St. Nicholas Dal'nee-Davydovo Convent in Nizhegorod province, 1890s. The illustration shows the young age at which most women entered convents during the nineteenth and early twentieth centuries. Following a common pattern, the convent initially was established as a women's religious community in 1857 on land donated by a local noble landowner. Transformed into a convent in 1886, the community maintained a shelter for widows and orphaned girls and a parish school for girls. Dmitriev Collection, the State Archive of Nizhegorod Region.

Whatever motivated women to enter the convent, however, the relatively low incidence of withdrawal suggests an effective process of assimilation once they were there, although a change in the convent's internal composition after the 1880s suggests that the increased number of young peasant women coming to the convent each year may have caused some problems in this regard. The members of the convent were divided into primarily four categories: nuns who had taken full monastic vows (which was permitted by law only after a women had reached forty years of age), *riasofor* novices (novices who had taken a form of monastic vow and wore the habit of a nun), novices, and women or young girls who were living at the convent "to determine their suitability for monastic life."[35] From the elevation of the convent to first-class

35. This paragraph is based primarily on the annual membership lists of the convent. GANO, *f.* 582, *op.* 1, various *dela*.

status in 1856 to the early 1880s, the overwhelming majority of the convent's membership consisted of nuns and novices of both types, with the latter always somewhat outnumbering the former. The number of women living at the convent in the fourth category was comparatively small. But this number began to grow in the 1880s, to the point that after 1908 this group constituted over half of the convent's membership (see Table 3). A small but significant number of these women left the convent each year, particularly after about 1900, suggesting that at least some women found the discipline and restrictions of communal monastic life and their subordinate position within the community difficult to bear.[36] Nonetheless, especially considering the social diversity of the convent's membership, the combination of authority, communal pressures and attractions, mutually dependent labor, practical necessity, personal needs and desires, and daily participation in extensive religious rituals produced an impressive stability within the community.

The ability of the convent to draw either membership or support from such diverse social groups suggests that the convent served the religious needs and an important cultural role for a broad spectrum of Nizhegorod society. Although the various roles and the significance of the convent for different social groups and for society as a whole require further study, an illustration of its capacity to bring together diverse social groups through religious ritual—while simultaneously revealing their divisions—is provided by the ceremony marking the annual arrival of the miracle-working Oran Mother of God icon in Nizhnii Novgorod (fig. 17). Both press accounts and photographs attest to the social diversity of the crowd that greeted the arrival of the icon at the convent. At the same time, however, the assemblage of prominent state and local officials at the ceremony testifies to its political dimension, while the segregation of the privileged and the well-to-do from the common people by a file of troops reveals the tensions present in urban society in late imperial Russia.[37] Abbess Mariia again proved to be particularly effective in promoting the convent as a place of religious symbolism, ritual, and pilgrimage. Exercising the office of abbess during a period of revolutionary unrest, increasing secular attacks on the church, intensifying criticisms of monasticism from clerical as well as lay critics, and growing challenges to Orthodoxy from a variety of religious competitors, she moved the convent still further away from the production of traditional crafts and devoted more resources to the convent's role as a site of ritual performance. The size of the choir

36. For example, see the incident reported in GANO, *f.* 582, *op.* 1, *d.* 629.

37. For descriptions of the ceremony, see *Nizhegorodskii tserkovno-obshchestvennyi vestnik,* 1916, no. 16, col. 326, and GANO, *fond* M. P. Dmitrieva, photographs 699, 708, 718.

was increased considerably, for example, new and innovative music was composed, and a workshop for painting icons, in part for sale to visitors, was established.[38] The increased revenue from collections, candle sales, donations, sales of religious artifacts, and similar sources that accompanied these efforts indicates the continued importance of religion, and of the convent as a focal point of religious belief, ritual, and identity, for a significant if probably indeterminable part of the community.[39] Indeed, it may well be that this importance increased in the atmosphere of intensified conflict over religion, the question of religious tolerance, religious and national identity, and reform within the Orthodox Church itself which characterized Nizhnii Novgorod after 1905.[40]

Hence the Nizhegorod Convent of the Exaltation of the Cross appears to have adapted remarkably successfully to the complex set of social, economic, and cultural changes and conflicts that were taking place in Nizhnii Novgorod and urban Russia generally in the last decades of the old regime. Since this success, moreover, appears to have derived in part from this process of change, with the convent attaining unprecedented levels of size, wealth, and quite likely also influence and cultural significance at precisely this period, it would seem inaccurate to characterize the convent as a vestige of Russia's past or a survival of the premodern era, another manifestation of Russia's allegedly peculiar pattern of "uneven development." This conclusion is reinforced by the fact of the parallel expansion of women's religious orders in Western Europe, although a careful comparison of the phenomenon in both places clearly is necessary.[41] Certainly one could foresee future problems for the convent had the Revolution not intervened. The development of secular and ecclesiastical education in the 1890s diminished the need for the convent's

---

38. For example, see Al'bitskii and Mamontov, *Krestovozdvizhenskii pervoklassnyi zhenskii monastyr'*; F. Milovskii (Sviashchennik), *Tserkovnoe penie v Krestovozdvizhenskom monastyre v istekshem sto letii 1813–1913 g. deiateli v etoi oblasti* (Nizhnii Novgorod, n.d.); and *Nizhegorodskii tserkovno-obshchestvennyi vestnik*, 1906, no. 3, col. 72.

39. GANO, *f.* 582, *op.* 1, *dd.* 652, 671.

40. These conflicts are apparent from a reading of *Nizhegorodskii tserkovno-obshchestvennyi vestnik* for 1906–14. See also Al'bitskii, *Tserkovnyi iubilei*, and B. I. Gudkov, E. V. Kuznetsov, and V. V. Sarychev, "Religioznaia obstanovka v Nizhegorodskoi gubernii v kontse XIX veka," *Voprosy istorii i istorii kul'tury Nizhegorodskogo Povolzh'ia (Mezhvuzovskii sbornik)* (Gor'kii, 1985), 78–99. This pattern of growing alienation from the official church, secularization, religious revival, and conflict over religion and religious identity conforms to that for prewar Europe discussed by Hugh McLeod in *Religion and the People of Western Europe 1789–1989*, 2d ed. (Oxford: Oxford University Press, 1997), and his *European Religion in the Age of Great Cities*, 1–39.

41. See the references cited in note 2. The rapid growth of female monasticism in nineteenth-century Europe appears to have peaked in the 1870s, whereas in Imperial Russia it continued until halted by war and revolution.

FIG. 17   Entry into the city of the annual procession bringing the miracle-working Oran Mother of God icon from the Oran Mother of God Monastery to Nizhnii Novgorod. 1890s. Begun in response to a cholera epidemic in 1831, the procession coincided with the opening of the Nizhnii Novgorod Trade Fair. In the latter part of the nineteenth century, the Mother of God icon produced tens of thousands of rubles in income each year for both the Oran Monastery and the Nizhegorod diocese. Dmitriev Collection, the State Archive of Nizhegorod Region.

school, for example, and the eventual introduction of a system of state welfare would have had a similar impact on its almshouse.[42] To the extent that the flow of peasants to the convent was caused by the particular conditions of the Russian countryside in the late imperial period, this movement probably would have slowed if not disappeared entirely. Nor is it difficult to imagine a scenario under which the flow of capital from merchants and other donors into the convent similarly would have diminished. But if and when all this happened, the convent's leaders would have been able to rely on the cushion provided by a substantial endowment.

42. Since the abbess generally included only the daughters, mostly orphaned, of clerics living at the convent and subsidized by the diocese in her annual reports, it is impossible to determine the total number of students at the school for most years. Between the 1840s and the mid-1890s, however, the diocese normally maintained twelve students at the convent's school each year. By 1899 this number had fallen to three, and thereafter the school was not mentioned in either the abbess's annual reports or the annual membership lists until 1918, when Abbess Mariia noted that there were thirty-five students at the school. The number of women in the convent's almshouse began to grow in the 1870s. GANO, f. 582, *op.* 1, various *dela*.

FIG. 18   Pilgrims at the St. Seraphim-Ponetaevka All-Sorrows Convent, Arzamas district, Nizhegorod province. 1890s. Founded as a women's religious community in 1864 on land donated by a local noble landowner, the commune was transformed into a convent in 1869. Largely because of its association with St. Seraphim of Sarov and its renowned icon and art studios, the convent became a major pilgrimage site as well as one of the largest and wealthiest monastic institutions in Nizhegorod province. Dmitriev Collection, the State Archive of Nizhegorod Region.

This leads to the third paradox: in the end, the Nizhegorod Convent of the Exaltation of the Cross succumbed not to the conditions of modernity, material or cultural, capitalist or socialist, but to the actions of a political regime motivated in part by an ideal of modernity that excluded the existence of such religious institutions. While it is impossible here to discuss Bolshevik ideas and Soviet policies with respect to religion, suffice it to say that the party and the new state were committed to the eventual elimination both of religious organizations and of religious belief generally. Put crudely, for Bolsheviks, religious organizations represented a mechanism of class domination and exploitation, while religious belief constituted a complex of superstitions and illusions that perpetuated ignorance and backwardness and thereby impeded effective action in the world. Hence religious organizations and beliefs not only constituted a potential source of political opposition but also were an impediment to the realization of the new regime's socialist ideal and to "modern" development in general. Considering the Orthodox Church to represent a particular threat to their power and objectives, the party and state consequently sought to neutralize and undermine the church, and monastic institutions provided an especially vulnerable target.[43] In this context, the high visibility and the urban location of the Nizhegorod Convent of the Exaltation of the Cross now represented liabilities rather than advantages. Even so, the convent demonstrated remarkable resilience in response to extraordinarily difficult circumstances until finally suppressed in 1928.

In broad terms, the experience of the Nizhegorod Convent of the Exaltation of the Cross was similar to that of the majority of convents in Nizhegorod province and—it would appear—throughout the new Soviet state.[44] Although the economic difficulties resulting from the war intensified during 1917, the membership of the convent continued to grow, no doubt given added impetus by the harsh and disruptive conditions produced by the war and the February Revolution (see Table 3).[45] Conditions at the convent deteriorated markedly after the October Revolution, however, due both to the chaos and hardships caused by the civil war and the collapse of the economy

---

43. Zybkovets, *Natsionalizatsiia,* provides a general overview of Soviet policies and actions with respect to monastic institutions from the October Revolution to 1922. See also Charles E. Timberlake, *The Fate of Russian Orthodox Monasteries and Convents Since 1917,* Donald W. Treadgold Papers in Russian, East European and Central Asian Studies, no. 103 (Seattle: Henry M. Jackson School of International Studies, University of Washington, 1995), and especially Jennifer J. Wynot, "Perseverance under Persecution: Orthodox Convents under the Soviet Regime" (paper presented at the eleventh Berkshire Conference on the History of Women, University of Rochester, June 4–6, 1999). A useful compendium of relevant Soviet legislation, decrees, instructions, and so on, can be found in P. V. Gidulianov, *Otdelenie tserkvi ot gosudarstva. Polnyi sbornik dekretov RSFSR i SSSR, instruktsii, tsirkuliarov i t.d. s raz"iasneniiami V otdela NKIusta RSFSR,* 2d ed. (Moscow, 1924). The process was overseen by the Eighth (Liquidation) (later, the Fifth) Department of the People's Commissariat of Justice. The archive for this department is substantial, but a general flavor of its orientation and activities can be obtained from Gosudarstvennyi Arkhiv Rossiiskoi Federatsii (hereafter, GA RF), *f.* A-353, *op.* 2, *d.* 689, *ll.* 8–10 *ob.*; and *d.* 690; and *f.* 1235, *op.* 7, *d.* 13, *ll.* 1–15. For recent studies of the relationship between the church and the Soviet party-state during these years, see Dimitry Pospielovsky, *The Russian Church Under the Soviet Regime, 1917–1982,* 2 vols. (Crestwood, N.Y.: St. Vladimir's Seminary Press, 1984); Daniel Peris, *Storming the Heavens: The Soviet League of the Militant Godless* (Ithaca: Cornell University Press, 1998); William B. Husband, *"Godless Communists": Atheism and Society in Soviet Russia, 1917–1932* (DeKalb: Northern Illinois University Press, 2000); Arto Luukkanen, *The Party of Unbelief: The Religious Policy of the Bolshevik Party, 1917–1929* (Helsinki: SHS, 1994); and Glennys Young, *Power and the Sacred in Revolutionary Russia: Religious Activists in the Village* (University Park: Pennsylvania State University Press, 1997).

44. Largely because of the nature of their organization, activities, and composition, male monasteries appear to have had more difficulty adapting to early Soviet conditions, although the experience of a particular monastic institution depended on a number of variables.

45. GANO, *f.* 1016, *op.* 2, *d.* 9, *ll.* 1–2, 42–43.

and to the efforts of the new Soviet state to undermine and suppress especially Orthodox monastic institutions. To be sure, the development and implementation of Soviet policy with respect to monastic institutions and the monastic clergy was complicated by the sometimes differing priorities and attitudes of central, provincial, and local authorities and by the unclear relationship between them. But in general, Soviet authorities sought to disrupt and disperse monastic communities and to limit their influence by depriving them of resources, severely restricting their activities, isolating them administratively and socially, suppressing their leadership, promoting "class conflict" between what authorities perceived as being the "working" and "exploitative" elements within them, and in some cases, "sovietizing" them.[46]

The systematic implementation of Soviet policy with respect to Orthodox monastic institutions and clergy—and religious institutions in general—began in Nizhegorod province in April 1918, when, prodded by the People's Commissariat of Justice, the provincial soviet organization established special provincial and district departments charged with putting into effect the decree of January 23, 1918, on the separation of church and state.[47] Declaring the closure of monastic institutions to be one of his principal objectives, the head of the provincial department, K. S. Karpov, proposed to concentrate first on the monastic institutions in the city of Nizhnii Novgorod, "dispersing the parasitic upper crust [verkhi] and attracting the working monastic element to the general construction of a new life."[48] As the largest monastic institution in the city, the Nizhegorod Convent of the Exaltation of the Cross became a principal target of Karpov's department. An initial attempt by a detachment sent by this department to conduct an inventory of the convent's property provoked a violent confrontation with a crowd that had been summoned by the sisters to defend the convent, suggesting some level both of social support for the convent and of popular opposition to Soviet religious policies.[49] The inventory eventually was completed successfully, however, and shortly thereafter the convent's capital deposits and property holdings were

46. See the references cited in note 43. The attempt by Soviet authorities to provoke "class war" within monastic communities reflects a general tactic, also evident, for example, in the formation of "committees of the poor" in peasant villages.

47. GA RF, f. A-353, op. 2, d. 690, ll. 1–1 ob.; d. 691, ll. 31–32, 38–40, 47–49, 62–69, 75–77 ob., 90–94, 134–49 ob., 193–98, 207, 212–14, 222–25, 237–38; d. 695, ll. 211–13, 245–50 ob.; d. 700, ll. 1–1 ob.; and d. 701, ll. 17–18 ob.; and GANO, f. 1016, op. 2, d. 44, l. 145 ob. See also Iu. G. Galai, "Poslerevoliutsionnaia khronika Blagoveshchenskogo monastyria," in Nizhegorodskii Pravoslavnyi Sbornik, vyp. 1 (Nizhnii Novgorod, 1997), 27–28; and in general, Zybkovets, Natsionalizatsiia, 51–57. The principal legislative acts can be found in the appendix to Gidulianov, Otdelenie.

48. GANO, f. 1026, op. 1, d. 2, ll. 13–14; Galai, "Poslerevoliutsionnaia khronika," 27–28.

49. GANO, f. 56, op. 1, d. 61, l. 109 ob.; GA RF, f. A-353, op. 2, d. 691, l. 237 ob.; and d. 696, ll. 212–13; Revoliutsiia i tserkov', 1919, no. 1:45; Galai and Galai, "Nizhegorodskii Krestovozdvizhenskii zhenskii

confiscated, leaving the convent with severely limited means with which to support its members. An economic structure that had constituted an advantage in a growing capitalist economy now also became a serious liability in comparison with that of convents located in rural areas, whose members for the time being at least still could produce their own food, although the seizure of land by local peasants, returning soldiers, and local Soviet organizations placed even rural convents in a very difficult position.[50] Members of the convent now supported themselves by growing what they could in the convent's gardens and by baking and selling communion bread, selling candles, providing religious services at the convent's cemetery, making and selling crafts, and collecting donations. But with the economy and ecology of the convent disrupted, most of the elderly members had died within a few months. Beginning in 1918, too, various Soviet organizations began to occupy buildings within the convent, in particular the Red Army, which established an archive and then also a divisional staff headquarters within its walls.[51] In 1919, in an effort both to further limit the convent's income and to confine it to narrowly religious functions, the local soviet took control of the convent's cemetery and school. Such actions so reduced the resources of the convent that, as Abbess Mariia reported to Bishop Evdokim in 1919, "there have been difficult days when at the convent there has been neither flour nor bread," and procuring heating fuel, lamp oil, and candles for the churches was difficult.[52] Already deprived of its property, livestock, and the use of most

monastyr'," 88–89; Zybkovets, *Natsionalizatsiia*, 84–85; and William B. Husband, "Soviet Atheism and Russian Orthodox Strategies of Resistance, 1917–1932," *Journal of Modern History* 70 (1998): 81–82. Relying on the account in *Revoliutsiia i tserkov'*, Husband cites this incident as an example of clerical efforts to undermine Soviet power in general. Although the available evidence does not reveal the motives and objectives of the sisters, it is certainly plausible that they were opposed to the new regime in principle and to its policies toward the Orthodox Church in particular. Nonetheless, the incident occurred only as the result of an attempt by armed Soviet officials to intrude into the convent; and according to the leader of the Soviet detachment, the violence resulted chiefly from "the misunderstanding of the police who were stationed near the convent." GANO, *f.* 56, *op.* 1, *d.* 61, *l.* 109 *ob.*

50. The inventories can be found in GANO, *f.* 1026, *op.* 1, *d.* 20. The reports of abbesses of several convents on conditions in 1918 and 1919 can be found in *f.* 1016, *op.* 1, *d.* 10, and *op.* 2, *dd.* 11, 44, 46, 50.

51. GANO, *f.* 582, *op.* 1, *dd.* 676, 678; *f.* 1016, *op.* 1, *d.* 10, *ll.* 28–30, 36–37; and *op.* 2, *d.* 50, *ll.* 5–6. According to local lore, the convent was also used as a camp for political detainees during 1918–19, although archival sources cast doubt on this claim. Abbess Mariia does not mention such detainees in her reports for these years, and none of the prisons or compulsory labor camps maintained in Nizhnii Novgorod by either the Commissariat of Internal Affairs or the Commissariat of Justice was located at the convent. See items in GANO just cited and GA RF, *f.* A-353, *op.* 3, *d.* 610, *l.* 10, and *f.* A-393, *op.* 89, *dd.* 39, 111, 214–15. See also Galai and Galai, "Nizhegorodskii Krestovozdvizhenskii zhenskii monastyr'," 89–91, and M. Smirnova, *Nizhnii Novgorod do i posle* (Nizhnii Novgorod: Begemot, 1996), 102–7.

52. GANO, *f.* 1016, *op.* 2, *d.* 50, *l.* 6, and *ll.* 5–6 in general; see also *d.* 44, *ll.* 60–60 *ob.*, and *op.* 1, *d.* 10, *ll.* 28–30. Despite these conditions, a significant number of women still continued to enter the convent. See Abbess Mariia's letter to Archbishop Evdokim of May 18 (31), 1919, in ibid., *op.* 2, *d.* 77, *ll.* 6–6 *ob.*

of its buildings, the convent saw its churches stripped of their plate, vestments, the precious metals and gems decorating icons, and various other religious objects in March and April 1922 as part of the state's campaign to confiscate "church valuables," ostensibly for famine relief.[53]

The leadership of the convent, often in conjunction with diocesan authorities and the heads of other monastic institutions in the diocese, employed a variety of strategies to cope with this situation. In doing so, from a fairly early point they attempted to work within the provisions of Soviet law. Frequently, of course, there was no alternative. Hence, in order to secure the use of the convent's churches, plate, and vestments and of at least parts of some other buildings, in 1919 Abbess Mariia and the sisters concluded an agreement with local Soviet authorities that recognized state ownership of the convent's former property. Partly for the same reason, and partly to preserve the informal existence of the convent as a religious community, by at least 1921 the convent's members had formally reconstituted themselves into a parish community, which in turn was officially registered as a religious association (*obshchina*) in 1924.[54] As such, they were able to fend off an attempt in 1924 by the leadership of the rival Renovationist Church, abetted by local Soviet authorities, to close the convent's churches.[55]

More inventively, like the majority of convents and a few of the monasteries in the diocese, the leaders and members of the convent took advantage of their skills and social background to form a labor cooperative—the First Nizhegorod Agricultural and Cooperative Handicrafts Association (Artel').[56] Although the available evidence does not specify the organization of the cooperative, most likely it followed the pattern of other such convent cum cooperatives in the diocese, where separate administrative structures existed

53. In fact, as the sisters at the convent claimed at the time would be the case, the proceeds from the confiscated property were used primarily for other purposes. GA RF, *f.* 1235, *op.* 140, *d.* 72, *l.* 42 *ob.*; *f.* 1064, *op.* 2, *dd.* 40, 159, 180; and *op.* 5, *d.* 76. Also Iu. G. Galai, "Prodazha za granitsu sokrovishch nizhegorodskikh pravoslavnykh khramov (1920-e-nachalo 1930-kh godov)," *Nizhegorodskii Pravoslavnyi Sbornik,* vyp. 1 (Nizhnii Novgorod, 1997), 5–11; idem, "Golod 1921 goda v Rossii i sokrovishcha pravoslavnykh khramov," *Nizhegorodskii Pravoslavnyi Sbornik,* 12–19; and Jonathan W. Daly, "'Storming the Last Citadel': The Bolshevik Assault on the Church, 1922," in *The Bolsheviks in Russian Society: The Revolution and the Civil War,* ed. Vladimir N. Brovkin (New Haven: Yale University Press, 1997), 235–68.

54. GANO, *f.* 55, *op.* 2, *d.* 2379, *ll.* 23–24 *ob.*; and *f.* 1104, *op.* 1, *d.* 34, *ll.* 138–41, 145–146 *ob.*, 153–162 *ob.*, 167–170 *ob.*, 230–231 *ob.*

55. Ibid., *f.* 1104, *op.* 1, *d.* 34, *ll.* 149–150 *ob.*, 164–164 *ob.*, 166. Emerging in 1922 and composed of several groups of radical clergy, each having somewhat different objectives, the Renovationist movement attempted to seize control of the church and both reform it from within and reconcile it with the Soviet state. Party and state officials for a while supported the movement as a means of weakening and subverting the church.

56. Ibid., *ll.* 164–164 *ob.*

for the religious and the economic functions of the community. In such cases the abbess, treasurer, superintendent, and other senior sisters constituted the leadership of the religious community, while other sisters from the "exploited classes" formed the administration of the cooperative.[57] Despite this nod to Bolshevik social conceptions and political strategy, however, the individual convents displayed considerable unity in the face of repeated efforts by local and provincial authorities to divide and subvert them. Members of convents generally refused to provide local authorities with lists dividing sisters into "working" and "exploitative" groups, for example, and they tried to circumvent prohibitions against using cooperative or state farm (*sovkhoz*) income to support elderly and infirm sisters.[58] This organizational structure and communal solidarity enabled monastic communities to turn to their advantage one of the main strategies for their subversion employed by local party and state organizations, with the support of the People's Commissariat of Justice, in the first years after the October Revolution. As Karpov's comments above indicate, party and state activists hoped to undermine monastic institutions by converting them into secular cooperatives, in part by promoting "class conflict" within them. But by the spring of 1921 local state organs had

57. GANO, *f.* 1016, *op.* 1, *d.* 10, *ll.* 78–83; *op.* 2, *d.* 44, *ll.* 14–15; *d.* 103, *ll.* 44–45; *d.* 162, *ll.* 11–19a. Party and state activists hoped that this organizational structure would promote conflict between the "working" and "exploiting" members of monastic communities. Ibid., *op.* 2, *d.* 44, *l.* 137. On convents cum workers' cooperatives in Nizhegorod province, see ibid., *op.* 1, *d.* 10, *ll.* 4–4 *ob.*, 67, 78–83; *op.* 2, *d.* 11, *ll.* 42–43 *ob.*; *d.* 44, *ll.* 12–12 *ob.*, 14–15, 17–21, 32–33 *ob.*, 137; *d.* 46, *ll.* 2–7, 13–14 *ob.*, 74–74 *ob.*; *d.* 103, *ll.* 44–45; *d.* 162, *ll.* 11–19a, 45–46; GA RF, *f.* A-353, *op.* 2, *d.* 702, *ll.* 17–41, 86–87; *op.* 3, *d.* 749, *ll.* 19–19 *ob.*, 87, 89, 101–131 *ob.*; *d.* 751, *l.* 3; *d.* 775, *ll.* 17, 45–46 *ob.*; *op.* 4, *d.* 372, *ll.* 118–26; *op.* 7, *d.* 16, *ll.* 87–87 *ob.*; Rossiiskii Gosudarstvennyi Arkhiv Ekonomiki (hereafter, RGAE), *f.* 478, *op.* 3, *d.* 1513, *l.* 42; *op.* 4, *d.* 612, *ll.* 14, 19; *op.* 5, *d.* 1035, *ll.* 38–40, 56–57 *ob.*; *d.* 1036, *ll.* 7, 9–9 *ob.*; and *op.* 6, *d.* 624, *ll.* 50–51 *ob.*; *d.* 1069, *ll.* 2, 80, 82–85; *d.* 1951, *ll.* 76, 108–20; Iu. G. Galai, *Makar'evskii monastyr'* (Nizhnii Novgorod, n.d.), 19–21; S. V. Baruzdina, "Nikolaevo-Georgievskii Ababkovskii zhenskii monastyr' (1818–1928 gody)," in *Pamiatniki istorii, kul'tury i prirody evropeiskoi Rossii. Tezisy dokladov* (Nizhnii Novgorod, 1995), 205–7; Zybkovets, *Natsionalizatsiia*, 107 and 97–109; and Wynot, "Perseverance under Persecution." In addition to the Nizhegorod Convent of the Exaltation of the Cross, other convents forming workers' cooperatives included the Vyksa Iverskii, the Kutuzovo Mother of God, the Makar'ev Zheltovodskii Trinity, the Zelenogorsk Savior, the Malopitsa Mother of God, the Ababkovo St. Nicholas and St. George, the Lukoianov Savior, the Lukoianov St. Tikhon, the Dal'no-Davydovo Mother of God, the Serafim-Diveevo Trinity, the Arzamas St. Nicholas, and the Vvedensko-Iagodkino Convents.

58. GANO, *f.* 1016, *op.* 1, *d.* 10, *ll.* 4 *ob.*, 67; *op.* 2, *d.* 44, *ll.* 17–21, 137, 145 *ob.*; *d.* 46, *ll.* 13–14 *ob.*, 23, 74–74 *ob.* In some instances, local Soviet authorities formed a state farm from a convent's former property and then induced or compelled the sisters to become its employees. With respect to elderly and infirm sisters, central and local Soviet authorities insisted that they should apply to local state welfare organizations for support. The objectives of this policy appear to have been to divide and undermine monastic communities and simultaneously to restrict the activities of religious organizations and to establish a state monopoly over the provision of social welfare. See ibid., *op.* 2, *d.* 44, *ll.* 132–45 *ob.*, pp. 25–29. Given the conditions of the civil war and the low priority given by the state to members of the clergy, however, the policy effectively amounted to a death sentence.

concluded that this strategy had failed. Even when the nuns and former leaders had been expelled from a surviving convent cum cooperative, the continued "religious fanaticism" of the members rendered it politically dangerous and unreliable from the perspective of party and state officials.[59]

As the case of the former Vyksa Iverskii Convent reveals, leaders of convents sometimes also were able to manipulate differences in the priorities and perspectives of different Soviet institutions to the advantage of their communities. In this instance, the convent's leaders successfully enlisted the support of the People's Commissariat of Agriculture—which was concerned with increasing the output of milk and other agricultural products in the region—and of the supply organization of the Red Army—for which the convent cum cooperative was producing uniforms and boots—against the People's Commissariat of Justice, provincial and local Soviet authorities, and local peasants and craftsmen, who for somewhat different reasons each wanted either control over the convent's land, economic inventory, and buildings or closure of the convent altogether. As a result of the intervention particularly of the Commissariat of Agriculture, the cooperative established by the convent survived and was able to gain the use of a greater share of its former property.[60]

By using such devices and strategies, the Nizhegorod Convent of the Exaltation of the Cross and most of the other convents in Nizhegorod province managed to survive the civil war as religious communities and to adapt themselves to the chaotic and dangerous conditions of the early Soviet period, although they had ceased to exist formally as monastic institutions. From the perspective of the Soviet state, two separate institutions existed: a religious association and a workers' cooperative. The memberships of these two institutions overlapped but were not identical. In particular, one effect of becoming first a parish community and then a religious association was the inclusion of laypeople, including men, in both the membership and the leadership of the community; in 1928, in fact, the governing council of the community became predominantly male. The workers' cooperative, by contrast, consisted entirely of women, a large number of whom continued to live in the

59. GA RF, f. A-353, op. 2, d. 696, ll. 211–13; op. 3, d. 730, l. 6; d. 749, ll. 87, 89; d. 774, ll. 11–13; d. 775, ll. 17, 21–21 ob.; and op. 4, d. 372, ll. 118–22 ob.; RGAE, f. 478, op. 5, d. 1035, ll. 38–40, 56–57 ob.; Vestnik Nizhegorodskogo gubernskogo ispolnitel'nogo komiteta, 1919, no. 1 (25 March): 33–35; ibid., 1920, no. 12 (1 December): 7–8; and ibid., 1921, no. 1–2 (January–February): 76, 104. See also Zybkovets, Natsionalizatsiia, 51, who himself reflects this view.

60. GA RF, f. A-353, op. 3, d. 749, ll. 19–19 ob., 87, 89, 101–131 ob.; d. 751, l. 3; d. 775, l. 17; op. 4, d. 372, ll. 118–26; and op. 7, d. 16, ll. 87–87 ob.; RGAE, f. 478, op. 3, d. 1513, l. 42; op. 5, d. 1035, ll. 38–40; d. 1036, ll. 9–9 ob.; and op. 6, d. 624, ll. 50–51 ob.; d. 1069, ll. 2, 80, 82–85; d. 1951, ll. 108–20; and GANO, f. 1016, op. 2, d. 44, ll. 32–33 ob.

buildings of the former convent.[61] These two institutions coexisted uneasily during the NEP years with the other occupants of the convent's former buildings, which included a military archive and divisional staff, a school, and a housing association. The respite of NEP proved short-lived, however, and the return to more radical policies in the late 1920s resulted in the revocation of the license of the workers' cooperative and its eviction from its quarters in the former convent in 1928. In the same year, the religious association was deprived of the right to use the convent's main cathedral and moved to the Kazan Cemetery Church, which had been part of the former convent but was located outside its walls.[62] The remaining sisters managed to preserve a vestige of the former convent until this church, too, was closed during another wave of repression in 1935.[63] The Kazan Cemetery Church eventually was razed, the cemetery was transformed into a playing field, university dormitories were built on part of the convent's former precinct, and the buildings of the former convent were used for a variety of purposes.

Having survived, and even thrived, in a variety of economic, social, and cultural circumstances, the Nizhegorod Convent of the Exaltation of the Cross thus ultimately succumbed to the repressive actions of a political regime committed to the destruction of religious organizations and the eradication of religious belief. The experience of the convent during its brief existence under the Soviet regime, however, places in sharp relief the centrality of religious faith for its members and the resilience this faith imparted to the community. Even when the retention of their identity as a religious community threatened their very existence, both collectively and as individuals, most sisters refused to abandon it and tenaciously sought ways to preserve the convent within the parameters of Soviet decrees and policies. Their tenacity in this regard recalls that of the convent's abbesses in seeking to secure the resources needed to sustain the growing community prior to the Revolution. After the October Revolution, however, the strength of the convent as a religious community also exposed its members to waves of state repression, which eventually proved fatal. Hence, paradoxically, one of the chief strengths of the convent led ultimately to its destruction.[64]

---

61. GANO, *f.* 1104, *op.* 1, *d.* 34, *ll.* 1–3, 35–45, 108–18, 125, 138–41, 145–46 *ob.*, 155, 164–164 *ob.*, 167–85.

62. Ibid., *d.* 34.

63. GANO, *f.* 2209, *op.* 3, *d.* 6829, *ll.* 10–20, 35–39, 97, 98, 102–8, 110–12 *ob.*, 118–21; and *f.* 2626, *op.* 1, *d.* 2641.

64. After the collapse of the Soviet state, the Russian government returned the main cathedral—which at the time was part of a chemical factory—and two of the former buildings of the convent to the Orthodox Church. Although still heavily damaged, the cathedral now serves as a parish church, and there are hopes to reestablish the convent.

TABLE I   Growth of Orthodox Monasticism in Imperial Russia, 1764–1914

| Year | Growth of Monastic Institutions | | Total |
	Monasteries	Convents	
1764	319	68	387
1810	358	94	452[a]
1850	464	123	587
1865	449	138	587
1894	511	263	774
1908	523	408	928
1914	550	475	1025

| | Growth of Monastic Clergy | | | | Total male | Total female | Total |
	Monks	Novices	Nuns	Novices			
1796	4,190		1,671		4,190	1,671	5,861
1840	5,122	3,259	2,287	4,583	8,381	6,870	15,251
1850	4,978	5,019	2,303	6,230	9,997	8,533	18,530
1894	7,582	6,696	8,319	21,957	14,278	30,276	44,554
1908	9,729	8,739	13,712	39,781	18,468	53,593	72,061
1912	10,998	10,203	15,003	55,450	21,201	70,453	91,654
1914	11,845	9,485	17,283	56,016	21,330	73,299	94,629

SOURCE: I. K. Smolich, *Istoriia russkoi tserkvi, 1700–1917* (Moscow: Tserkovno-Nauchnyi Tsentr "Pravoslavnaia Entsiklopediia," 1996), 1:669.

[a]Excluding southern and western Russia.

Note: L. I. Denisov's figures for the year 1907 are higher than one would expect interpolating from Smolich. He reports 540 monasteries with 24,444 monks and novices and 367 convents and 61 unofficial women's religious communities with 65,959 nuns and novices, for a total of 90,403 monastics. He includes in his calculation several types of institutions excluded by Smolich. See Denisov, *Pravoslavnye monastyri rossiiskoi imperii. Polnyi spisok vsekh 1105 nyne sushchestvuiushchikh v 75 guberniiakh i oblastiakh Rossii (i 2 inostrannykh gosudarstvakh) muzhskikh i zhenskikh monastyrei, arkhiereiskikh domov i zhenskikh obshchin* (Moscow: Izdanie A. D. Stupina, 1908), ix–xii.

TABLE 2   Growth of Orthodox Monasticism in Nizhegorod Province, 1843–1917

Year	Monasteries	Monks	Novices	Total	Convents	Nuns	Novices	Total	Women's communities
1843	8	89	120	209	2	48	204	252	4
1853	8	80	161	241	3	61	288	349	—
1866	—	—	—	—	6	151	565	716	—
1883	8	69	32	101	9	360	742	1102	—
1901	8	112	239	351	16	669	4207	4876	4[a]
1907	8			375	17			5541	—
1917	8	143	127	270	17	1178	5445	6623	11[b]

SOURCES: *Izvlechenie iz otcheta Ober-Prokurora Sviateishago Sinoda za 1843 goda* (St. Petersburg, 1843), Tables, pp. 2–4, 6–7; ibid., *za 1853 goda* (St. Petersburg, 1854), Tables, pp. 2–4, 6–7; *Izvlechenie iz vsepoddaneishago otcheta Ober-Prokurora Sviateishago Sinoda Grafa D. Tolstago po vedomstvu Pravoslavnago ispovedaniia za 1866 g.* (St. Petersburg, 1867), Tables, pp. 6–7; *Izvlechenie iz vsepoddaneishago otcheta Ober-Prokurora Sviateishago Sinoda K. Pobedonostseva po vedomstvu Pravoslavnago ispovedaniia za 1883 g.* (St. Petersburg, 1885), Tables, pp. 2–4, 6–7; *Vedomost' muzhskim i zhenskim monastyriam i obshchinam za 1901 god* (St. Petersburg, 1902), 58–63; L. I. Denisov, *Pravoslavnye monastyri rossiiskoi imperii. Polnyi spisok vsekh 1105 nyne sushchestvuiushchikh v 75 guberniiakh i oblastiakh Rossii (i 2 inostrannykh gosudarstvakh) muzhskikh i zhenskikh monastyrei, arkhiereiskikh domov i zhenskikh obshchin* (Moscow, 1908), xi; and V. F. Zybkovets, *Natsionalizatsiia monastyrskikh imushchestv v Sovetskoi Rossii (1917–1921 gg.)* (Moscow, 1975), 149–51.

[a]There were 420 members in three of these communities; the membership of the fourth is not given.

[b]There were 414 members in five of these communities; the membership of the remaining six communities is not given.

Table 3 Growth of the Nizhegorod Convent of the Exaltation of the Cross, 1802–1919

Year	Nuns	Novices assigned to convent	Novices living at convent with permission[a]	Total novices	Total
1802	15[b]		34	34	49
1816	29[c]		51	51	80
1826	32		64	64	96
1836	32	67	43	110	142
1846	32	90	31	121	153
1856	29	103	51	154	183
1866	65[d]	88	15	103	168
1876	84	96	34	130	214
1887	74	104	60	164	238
1896	64	78	109	187	251
1908	76	69	141	210	286
1910	70	65	182	247	317
1917	66	69[e]	230	299	365
1919	93	60	157	217	310

SOURCE: GANO, *f.* 582, *op.* 1, *dd.* 6, 47, 88, 129, 211, 330, 385, 460, 531, 593, 658, 659, 664, 665, 676; and *f.* 1016, *op.* 2, *d.* 9 (*ll.* 42–3) and *d.* 50 (*ll.* 5–6).

[a]Includes students at the convent school between 1838 and 1899.
[b]This is the number allowed by the convent's statute.
[c]The number of nuns allowed at the convent was raised from 15 to 32 in 1807.
[d]The number of nuns allowed at the convent was raised to 100 in 1857.
[e]Thirty-one of these women took full monastic vows in 1918.

II

ORTHODOXY AS ASCRIPTION (AND BEYOND)

Religious Identity on the
Edges of the Orthodox Community,

1740–1917

PAUL W. WERTH

Despite the close historical connection between Russianness and Orthodoxy, Russians were by no means the only Orthodox Christians in the Russian empire. Ukrainians, Belorussians, Georgians, and Moldovans had all accepted Orthodoxy well before their incorporation into Muscovy or the Russian empire, and whole communities of minorities to the east of Russia's Muscovite core were baptized into Orthodoxy as part of the empire's expansion and consolidation. In this essay I wish to offer some insights concerning the meanings of Orthodoxy for such converted communities, drawing principally on the collective experience of the largest such group—the baptized Finnic and Turkic peoples of the region around the confluence of the Volga and Kama rivers.[1]

My goal is threefold. I seek first of all to demonstrate that for communities recently inducted into Orthodoxy and therefore having only tenuous commitments to the religion that they had ostensibly embraced, "lived Orthodoxy" by necessity involved a heavy dose of supervisory discipline designed to forestall the "errors," "deviation," and even "apostasy" that were likely to occur given the nearby presence of communities that remained formally Muslim and "pagan." Indeed, for several generations it was really only the prescriptions of Orthodox religious authorities and the state's willingness

---

1. I have addressed several of the issues raised here at greater length in my monograph, *At the Margins of Orthodoxy: Mission, Governance, and Confessional Politics in Russia's Volga-Kama Region, 1827–1905* (Ithaca: Cornell University Press, 2002), as well as in several articles cited here.

to employ secular power to enforce the irreversibility of baptism that allow us to speak of this population as being Orthodox at all. Second, however, I suggest that while the attachment of some of these converts to Orthodoxy remained almost purely ascriptive and was finally abrogated as a result of the state's religious reforms in 1905, other converts eventually embraced Orthodoxy and used it as a tool in maintaining ethnic and cultural particularity in a time of rapid socioeconomic change and accelerating cultural assimilation, or Russification. Finally, I contend that for all its specificity, in important respects non-Russians' Orthodox experience represented merely a set of variations on the religious experience of Russians themselves. The concern of religious authorities to regulate manifestations of piety; the aspirations of believers for greater autonomy and initiative in religious affairs; and the growth of monasticism—all of these processes were characteristic of Russian and non-Russian Orthodox experience alike. I conclude by suggesting some important insights that we may gain into the changing nature of religion in Russia by investigating Orthodoxy at its margins, where it came into contact with other faiths and confessions.

Located between Moscow and the Ural mountains, the region around the confluence of the Volga and Kama rivers stood at the intersection of three cultural worlds—the Slavic-Orthodox, the Turkic-Islamic, and the Finnic-animist. Following the Russian conquest of the Kazan Khanate in 1552, Russian peasants settled among the Muslim Tatars and animist Maris, Chuvash, and Udmurts; and by the mid-eighteenth century, the region had been largely integrated into the empire's administrative structure. As a result of state-sponsored missionary assaults on the indigenous population (above all in the 1740s and 1750s), most of the region's "idolaters" and about ten percent of the Muslims had been formally baptized by the outset of the nineteenth century.[2] These baptisms served to disrupt a neat correspondence between faith and ethnicity (Russian = Orthodox, Tatar = Muslim, Mari/Chuvash/Udmurt = pagan), although imperial authorities employed the term "the newly baptized" (*novokreshchenye*) in order to situate these new Christians discursively at the edges of the larger Orthodox community. To the extent that these conversions lacked a significant spiritual foundation and were instead based

2. E. A. Malov, *O Novokreshchenskoi kontore* (Kazan: Tipografiia Kazanskogo Imperatorskogo Universiteta, 1878); A. Mozharovskii, *Izlozhenie khoda missionerskogo dela po prosveshcheniiu kazanskikh inorodtsev s 1552 po 1867 goda* (Moscow: Imperatorskoe Obshchestvo istorii i drevnostei pri Moskovskom universitete, 1880); S. L. Ursynovich, "Novokreshchenskaia kontora: K voprosu o roli pravoslavnogo missionerstva v kolonizatsionnoi i natsional'noi politike samoderzhaviia," *Ateist* 54 (1930): 22–50; Michael Khodarkovsky, "'Not by Word Alone': Missionary Policies and Religious Conversion in Early Modern Russia," *Comparative Studies in Society and History* 38 (1996): 267–93.

primarily on a combination of coercion and material incentives, "the newly baptized" themselves usually aspired to uphold their indigenous religious practices or even to receive permission to return to their original religions. Thus at several moments over the course of the nineteenth century baptized Tatars filed petitions with the government seeking formal status as Muslims, while baptized animists continued to conduct indigenous religious rituals in forests and sacred groves. It was primarily in response to such manifestations of converts' weak attachments to Orthodoxy that the church established a set of missions in the region in around 1830 for the "reinforcement" (*utverzhdenie*) of Christianity among these populations that had been formally baptized into that religion several generations earlier.

The fact that non-Russians who continued to practice animism or even sought to "apostatize" back to Islam were still regarded by officials as Orthodox underscores the fundamentally ascriptive dimension of religious identity in imperial Russia. Although in the 1770s Catherine the Great explicitly committed Russia to a policy of "religious toleration,"[3] the state continued to arrogate for itself the right to determine the actual religious status of the empire's subjects, in some cases openly denying them the religious identity that they themselves asserted. A subject was in effect free to practice a non-Orthodox faith openly only if the state had *recognized* him or her as belonging to that faith. To be sure, in many cases the state did in fact accept the claims of its subjects, and the adherents of many non-Orthodox faiths were promised respect for their religions as part of their incorporation into the empire. Nonetheless, certain populations were considered to be fair game for missionary proselytism—particularly the non-Christian populations of the Russian east, but also Uniates (Greek Catholics) in Poland and Ukraine, who were regarded by Russian authorities as having been artificially separated from Orthodoxy as a result of Catholic propaganda and coercion.[4] And the state's official repudiation of coercion in matters of conversion to Orthodoxy could not always prevent officials at different levels of the administration from using their authority over their charges to promote baptism in ways that

3. See Catherine's decree in *Polnoe Sobranie Zakonov Rossiiskoi Imperii*, first series, 19, no. 13996 (June 17, 1773), and Alan W. Fisher, "Enlightened Despotism and Islam under Catherine II," *Slavic Review* 27 (1968): 542–53.

4. The Uniate church had been created as a result of the Union of Brest in 1596, whereby the majority of Orthodox bishops in Ukraine and Belarus recognized the primacy of the pope while retaining the Byzantine-Slavonic rite, Church-Slavonic liturgy, Eastern canon law, married clergy, and a substantial degree of administrative autonomy. On the formation of the Union, see Borys A. Gudziak, *Crisis and Reform: The Kyivan Metropolitanate, the Patriarchate of Constantinople, and the Genesis of the Union of Brest* (Cambridge, Mass.: Harvard Ukrainian Research Institute, 1998).

subtly or egregiously violated both the letter and the spirit of existing laws. In such cases the *fact* of baptism alone usually determined religious status, even when there was substantial evidence that coercion had been used or putative converts themselves clearly expressed their misgivings.[5] In short, the claims of imperial subjects represented only one factor in the determination of official religious identity and could be superseded by the ascriptive determinations of the Russian state.[6]

For "the newly baptized," who by most accounts had only the most rudimentary knowledge of "the Russian faith," Orthodox status as an ascriptive legal identity meant subordination to a series of obligations and prohibitions, many of which seriously disrupted prevailing patterns of veneration and community. To be sure, unscrupulous clergy and local officials were willing to waive certain Orthodox requirements for an appropriate fee. In general, however, certain practices were now prohibited, just as other practices—the baptism of newborns, attendance in church, marriage by Orthodox rite, use of the Bible for oaths, confession and communion at certain intervals, and burial by Orthodox rite (almost all of these involving emoluments for the clergy)—now became obligatory. Violations accordingly resulted in corrective and punitive measures, such as internment in monasteries, various forms of penance, "admonitions" by clergy, and transfer of more serious cases to secular authorities. In cases involving the "instigation" of "apostasy," the accused could even be exiled to Siberia by administrative route. Notably, most of these obligations and punishments were outlined in *civil* and *criminal* law and were upheld by the power of the secular state.

None of this is to imply that ascriptive religious identity for non-Russians was entirely a negative proposition. The adoption of Orthodoxy also involved distinct benefits for the first generation of converts, including a three-year tax break, a lifetime exemption from military service, pardons in cases of minor crimes, and sometimes even outright payment in cash and goods.[7] Moreover, there seems to have been at least some foundation to the arguments of missionaries that a formal ascriptive Orthodoxy identity, no matter how unreflective of a person's actual convictions and allegiances, could serve as

5. For specific cases, see my *At the Margins of Orthodoxy,* 86–94, as well as my article, "Baptism, Authority, and the Problem of *Zakonnost'* in Orenburg Diocese: The Induction of Over 800 'Pagans' into the Christian Faith," *Slavic Review* 56 (1997): 456–80.

6. Compare this state prerogative to ascribe religious confession with the efforts of Soviet authorities in the 1920s and 1930s to ascribe class, as described by Sheila Fitzpatrick in "Ascribing Class: The Construction of Social Identity in Soviet Russia," *Journal of Modern History* 65 (1993): 745–70. In both cases, the state ascribed aspects of social identity that in principle existed independently of state prescription.

7. I address these issues in *At the Margins of Orthodoxy,* 74–86.

the starting point for the conscious and voluntary acceptance of Christian "truths" at a later time.[8] In any event, for those on the edges of the Orthodox community (and most recently inducted into it) there can be no doubt that Orthodoxy as ascription was of tremendous significance.

Nonetheless, the state's ability to ascribe religious identity was not without limits. In several cases imperial subjects refused to accept externally imposed prescriptions, challenged the state's determinations (though usually in highly deferential terms), and thus earned the labels "apostates" (*otstupniki*) or "recalcitrants" (*uporstvuiushchie*). Among the most visible "apostates" were baptized Tatars of the Volga region, many of whom had been superficially converted to Orthodoxy and tirelessly agitated for official recognition as Muslims over the course of the nineteenth century.[9] Other large groups of "recalcitrants" in the empire included former Uniates who refused to acknowledge their official transfer to Orthodox status after the state's abolition of their church in the western provinces (1839) and Poland (1875), and Latvian and Estonian peasants who had converted to Orthodoxy for largely economic reasons in the 1840s but subsequently sought readmission to Lutheranism.[10] The tenacity of these groups was finally rewarded in 1905, when the state, as part of its larger reform of the existing religious order, permitted them to return to the faith of their ancestors—or to Catholicism, in the case of former Uniates.[11] Still, even after 1905, the state set a high standard for the

8. Note that there was a contradiction between the officially established procedure for conversion to Orthodoxy, which presupposed a spiritual transformation *prior* to baptism, and the process of conversion in actual practice, which implied that baptism might in fact precede, and indeed serve as the cause for, such a spiritual transformation.

9. On baptized Tatars, see Agnès Kefeli-Clay, "L'Islam populaire chez les Tatars Chrétiens Orthodoxes au XIXe siècle," *Cahiers du Monde russe* 37 (1996): 409–48; idem, "Constructing an Islamic Identity: The Case of Elyshevo Village in the Nineteenth Century," in *Russia's Orient: Imperial Borderlands and Peoples, 1700–1917*, ed. Daniel R. Brower and Edward J. Lazzerini (Bloomington: Indiana University Press, 1997), 271–91; and Werth, *At the Margins of Orthodoxy*, 45–55, 147–76, 178–83.

10. M. E. Iachevskii, "Zapiska ob otpavshikh iz pravoslaviia v inoverie," Rossiiskii Gosudarstvennyi Istoricheskii Arkhiv (hereafter, RGIA), pechatnye zapiski, folder 2349. On the Uniate problem, see A. Iurashkevich, *Obshchii vzliad na zapadno-russkuiu uniatskuiu tserkov' do i vo vremia vozsoedineniia uniatov s Pravoslavnoiu tserkov'iu v 1839 g.* (Minsk: Tipografiia B. I. Solomina, 1889); *Kniaz' V. A. Cherkasskii i kholmskie greko-uniaty,* 2 vols. (Warsaw: Tipografiia Varshavskogo Uchebnogo Okruga, 1879 and 1882); and Theodore R. Weeks, "Between Rome and Tsargrad: The Uniate Church in Imperial Russia," in *Of Religion and Empire: Missions, Conversion, and Tolerance in Tsarist Russia,* ed. Robert P. Geraci and Michael Khodarkovsky (Ithaca: Cornell University Press, 2001), 70–91. On the Latvian and Estonian converts, see A. V. Gavrilin, *Ocherki istorii Rizhskoi eparkhii XIX veka* (Riga: Filokaliia, 1999), 72–182.

11. See Weeks, "Between Rome and Tsargrad," and Robert Blobaum, "Toleration and Ethno-Religious Strife: The Struggle Between Catholics and Orthodox Christians in the Chelm Region of Russian Poland, 1904–1906," *The Polish Review* 35 (1990): 111–24.

recognition of formally Orthodox subjects as non-Christians. While baptized Tatars encountered little difficulty in receiving official recognition as Muslims, the petitions of baptized Maris seeking recognition as "pagans" or as members of animist sects were most often rejected. In the latter case the state continued to construe itself as the final arbiter of its subjects' religious identity.

Whatever the intricacies of religious reform in 1905, for a good portion of the imperial period the comparatively recent and usually violent or materially induced transfer of non-Russians into the Christian faith ensured that the issues of ascription and discipline would remain central, since indigenous religious allegiances to Orthodoxy often remained weak and Christian "convictions" were in many cases totally absent. Yet as reflected in numerous recent investigations into the tensions between official dictates and popular practice among the Russian peasantry, religious discipline (that is, obligations and prohibitions backed by secular power) in fact pertained to all those people who were formally considered Orthodox—including Russians themselves.[12] Oftentimes practices that might superficially appear strictly "imperial" because they were applied to non-Russian subjects actually pertained to the Russian population as well, if perhaps in slightly different forms. Official efforts to ensure orthopraxy, to establish a monopoly on the sacred, and to delegitimize competing sites and objects of veneration come most readily to mind. Many educated Russian observers were inclined to see in peasant religiosity "paganism," "dual faith" (the coexistence of Orthodox and pre-Christian elements), and other forms of religious deviation. Similarly, the issue of ascription was central in the matter of sectarianism and religious dissent among Russians, since it was, among other things, sectarians' repudiation of official Orthodox affiliation central to prevailing notions of the Russian people as a national community that violated the sensibilities of state and church authorities.[13]

12. Consider recent insightful work on the modern period: Gregory L. Freeze, "The Rechristianization of Russia: The Church and Popular Religion, 1750–1850," *Studia Slavica Finlandensia* 7 (1990): 101–36; idem, "Institutionalizing Piety: The Church and Popular Religion, 1750–1850," in *Imperial Russia: New Histories for the Empire*, ed. Jane Burbank and David L. Ransel (Bloomington: Indiana University Press, 1998), 210–49; Nadieszda Kizenko, *A Prodigal Saint: Father John of Kronstadt and the Russian People* (University Park: Pennsylvania State University Press, 2000); Chris J. Chulos, "Peasant Religion in Post-Emancipation Russia: Voronezh Province, 1880–1917" (Ph.D. diss., University of Chicago, 1994); Glennys Young, "'Into Church Matters': Lay Identity, Rural Parish Life, and Popular Politics in Late Imperial and Early Soviet Russia, 1864–1928," *Russian History* 23 (1996): 367–84; and Vera Shevzov, "Miracle-Working Icons, Laity, and Authority in the Russian Orthodox Church, 1861–1917," *Russian Review* 58 (1999): 26–48.

13. On this point, see Nicholas B. Breyfogle's discussion in "Heretics and Colonizers: Religious Dissent and Russian Colonization of Transcaucasia, 1830–1890" (Ph.D. diss., University of Pennsylvania, 1998), 31–35, and M. A. Reisner, *Gosudarstvo i veruiushchaia lichnost'* (St. Petersburg: Biblioteka "Obshchestvennaia pol'za," 1905).

Moreover, Gregory Freeze's contention that Russian Orthodoxy was itself actually "Russian Heterodoxy," consisting of "an aggregate of local Orthodoxies, each with its own cults, rituals, and customs,"[14] suggests that we need to approach with some care the opposition of a normative Orthodoxy to non-Russian syncretism and even apostasy. We would do well to contemplate how practices that were broadly considered to be Orthodox blended into practices that were not, thereby establishing continuities between Russian center and periphery rather than unambiguous ruptures. In short, issues of ascription and discipline were hardly unique to non-Russian populations, although the specific degree and nature of commonality with Russia proper need to be fleshed out more comprehensively in future research.

Still, for all of the significance of Orthodox ascription for non-Russian converts, it would be misleading to suggest that Orthodoxy remained *merely* an ascribed identity. Indeed, despite the stubborn refusal of nationalist paradigms to acknowledge that non-Russians actually found some Russian cultural configurations to be attractive, Orthodoxy *did* in fact come to appeal to some non-Russians as a system of beliefs, or at least as a set of allegiances and dispositions, especially by the second half of the nineteenth century. Recent studies by Sergei Kan and Andrei Znamenski have demonstrated that certain indigenous communities in Siberia and especially Alaska accepted Russian Orthodoxy and transformed it into native churches.[15] Similar processes are observable among some (though not all) of the much larger convert communities in the Volga-Kama region. Already in the 1840s highland Maris in western Kazan province initiated a "religious movement," characterized by heightened aspirations for literacy and active combat with "pagan" elements in their midst. By 1871 this movement had succeeded in founding the Archangel Michael Mari monastery—to my knowledge the first explicitly *inorodcheskii* (non-Russian) Orthodox monastery in the empire.[16] The movement was also accompanied by the explicit rejection by many highland Maris of their earlier animist beliefs—which led to significant intracommunal conflict

14. Freeze, "Institutionalizing Piety," 215.
15. Andrei Znamenski, *Shamanism and Christianity: Native Encounters with Russian Orthodox Missions in Siberia and Alaska, 1820–1917* (Westport, Conn.: Greenwood Press, 1999); Sergei Kan, *Memory Eternal: Tlingit Culture and Russian Orthodox Christianity Through Two Centuries* (Seattle: University of Washington Press, 1999). Among the most striking aspects of this development in Alaska is that it occurred primarily *after* the sale of that territory to the United States in 1867, when Orthodoxy was deprived of any connection with state power.
16. That is, this was the first monastery that was associated specifically with an ethnic group that had been converted to Orthodoxy in recent historical terms (in contrast to monastic institutions in Ukraine, Georgia, and Bessarabia).

with the so-called paganizers (*iazychestvuiushchie*)—and a profound interest in holy scripture and catechistic questions. Other non-Russian Orthodox monasteries and religious orders followed, including a substantial number of women's orders, which offered non-Russian women more opportunities to express their spirituality and to contribute meaningfully to the religious and moral "development" of their coethnics.[17]

Similarly, while students of "apostasy" frequently highlight that almost 50,000 baptized Tatars returned to Islam after the introduction of new statutes on toleration in 1905, rarely do they note that a much larger number—about 120,000—remained formally Christian.[18] Indeed, Orthodox status served as the foundation for the emergence by the early twentieth century of a conscious, politicized Kräshen (baptized-Tatar) ethnic identity, promoted by an indigenous religious intelligentsia and later acknowledged by Soviet authorities for the better part of the 1920s. Though after 1917 some Kräshen activists (including some who would staff a special Kriashsektsiia of the Tatar Republic's communist party after 1922) attempted to exorcise Orthodoxy from the foundations of their claims to represent a full-fledged nationality, for the majority of Kräshens in the countryside Orthodoxy remained central to their sense of particularity, especially vis-à-vis neighboring Muslim Tatars. Indeed, in the 1920s communist authorities often complained about the "fanatical" and "clerical" character of Kräshen communities.[19]

Central to the development of these non-Russian Orthodox sensibilities in the Volga-Kama region were the interventions of the lay missionary and orientalist N. I. Il'minskii, which featured the use of native languages and native instructors in order to transmit the Christian message to non-Russians. To be sure, these methods were not entirely new when Il'minskii began to

---

17. "Inorodcheskaia zhenskaia obshchina v Permskoi gubernii," *Pravoslavnyi blagovestnik* 9 (1899): 34–39; "Iz zhizni chuvashskoi zhenskoi obshchiny," *Pravoslavnyi blagovestnik* 3, 4 (1899): 130–34, 166–73; "Kuzhenerskii Nikolaevskii cheremisskii zhenskii monastyr' v Urzhumskom uezde, Viatskoi eparkhii," *Viatskiie eparkhial'nye vedomosti*, nos. 30, 31, 33, 35, 37, 44, 47 (1910); N. A. Arkhangel'skii, "Aleksandrinskii zhenskii chuvashskii monastyr' Iadrinskago uezda," *Izvestiia po Kazanskoi eparkhii* 12–13 (1912): 393–407. The notable development of convents also situates non-Russian Orthodox religiosity in a broader Russian context, for in general by the second half of the nineteenth century, monasticism in Russia was being profoundly feminized. See William G. Wagner, "Paradoxes of Piety: The Nizhegorod Convent of the Exaltation of the Cross, 1807–1935," in the present volume.

18. To be sure, some of those who retained formal Christian status nonetheless upheld affinities for Islam, but these so-called *tatarsymaks* apparently accounted for only a portion of those baptized Tatars remaining after 1905. See N. V. Nikol'skii, *Kreshchenye tatary: statisticheskiia svedeniia za 1911 g.* (Kazan: Tsentral'naia tipografiia, 1914), 1.

19. I have treated this emergence of a Kräshen consciousness in "From 'Pagan' Muslims to 'Baptized' Communists: Religious Conversion and Ethnic Particularity in Russia's Eastern Provinces," *Comparative Studies in Society and History* 43 (2000): 497–523.

promote them in an organized fashion in the 1860s. But there *was* something novel in his use of an idiomatic vernacular for translations that were then verified by native non-Russians and in the energy with which he promoted non-Russians into clerical and teaching positions and organized a set of specialized institutions for their training.[20] Deeply convinced that each non-Russian ethnicity had its own worldview that differed significantly from Russian understandings, Il'minskii wrote, "In order to transfer to non-Russians Christian dogmatic and moral teaching, and to transfer it not abstractly, not as a dead letter, but rather in such a way that it might become the foundation for their thinking and life, for that one needs to adapt to their religious conceptions and moral convictions."[21] Non-Russians themselves were obviously in the best position to effect this cultural translation. By 1867, Il'minskii had obtained from the Holy Synod a directive authorizing the training and ordination of non-Russian clergy, exempting them from the normal seminary course.[22] By 1869 the Orthodox liturgy had been translated into Tatar using this new approach, while the Kazan diocesan authorities encouraged the use of native languages in religious discussions and for the most often used prayers and songs. And in 1883 the Synod authorized the conduct of liturgy in non-Russian languages wherever there was "a more or less substantial population" of non-Russians.[23]

In general, as a result of these practices, there emerged a contingent of ethnically conscious non-Russians who were deeply committed to the Orthodox "enlightenment" of their coethnics, especially by the early twentieth century. They regarded Orthodoxy as a way of rejuvenating their respective peoples, who had hitherto remained in a "dark" and "ignorant" state, and recognized that Orthodoxy offered them personally, through appointment to clerical positions in indigenous parishes, the possibility of upward mobility into the ranks of the rural intelligentsia. Enthusiastically promoting a religious mission

---

20. For broad treatments of Il'minskii and his work in English, see Isabelle Teitz Kreindler, "Educational Policies Toward the Eastern Nationalities in Tsarist Russia: A Study of Il'minskii's System" (Ph.D. diss., Columbia University, 1969); Robert Paul Geraci, *Window on the East: National and Imperial Identities in Late Tsarist Russia* (Ithaca: Cornell University Press, 2001); and idem, "The Il'minskii System and the Controversy over Non-Russian Teachers and Priests in the Middle-Volga," in *Kazan, Moscow, St. Petersburg: Multiple Faces of the Russian Empire,* ed. Catherine Evtuhov, Boris Gasparov, Alexander Ospovat, and Mark von Hagen (Moscow: O. G. I., 1997), 325–48.

21. N. I. Il'minskii, ed., *Iz perepiski ob udostoenii inorodtsev sviashchenno-sluzhitel'skikh dolzhnostei* (Kazan, 1885), 9.

22. RGIA, *f.* 797, *op.* 26, *otdel* 2, *razriad* 3, *d.* 251; RGIA, *f.* 796, *op.* 162, *d.* 1417.

23. *Izvestiia po Kazanskoi eparkhii* 11 (1869): 327–31; ibid., 7 (1874): 191–93; "Ob otkrytii v g. Kazani bogosluzheniia na tatarskom iazyke," ibid., 2 (1870): 48–55; N. I. Il'minskii, "O tserkovnom bogosluzhenii na inorodcheskikh iazykakh," *Pravoslavnyi sobesednik* 1 (1883): 258–72.

run by and for *inorodtsy* (non-Russians), these figures made clear that commitments to Orthodoxy and the particularity of *inorodtsy* were entirely compatible. They thus negated the equation of conversion and assimilation, even as they ostensibly articulated support for their own eventual Russification.[24]

Indeed, for at least some of these new activists, Orthodoxy offered a space from which to criticize more heavy-handed policies of assimilation that they believed threatened the existence of their communities as distinct ethnicities. Several of the most prominent figures in the Mari religious movement were deeply dismayed when church authorities installed Russians in key positions in the new Archangel Michael monastery in order to provide oversight and guidance. What bishops regarded as an entirely necessary and appropriate foundation for good monastic governance was interpreted by the Mari religious activists as simply a Russian takeover—that is, an attempt to divest the monastery of its ethnic character and purpose as a specifically *Mari* institution. Some non-Russians began to argue that Russification of their peoples was accompanied by serious moral degradation—the spread of drinking, swearing, sexual promiscuity, and other vices. They even began to suggest that Russians, on the whole, had little to offer non-Russians, in spite of Russians' claims to be the empire's "ruling people." The status of these non-Russian clerics as tireless promoters of Orthodox religious enlightenment empowered them to engage in this critique of the Russian people, while Orthodoxy itself permitted them to assert their ethnic particularity without appearing to be fundamental opponents of the tsarist order.[25]

These episodes do much to pry apart the seemingly close connection between Orthodoxy and Russianness. Just as Old Belief, sectarian dissent, and eventually Evangelical Christianity disrupted this connection from "within" the national community by subtracting ethnic Russians from the ranks of the (officially) Orthodox,[26] so baptized non-Russians disrupted this connection from the "edges" by adding to Orthodoxy "converts" who, in the early stages of Christianization, were scarcely distinguishable from "pagans" and Muslims, and who subsequently, even while accepting the major theological tenets of

24. Geraci, "Il'minskii System," 334–43.

25. I have explored this native Orthodox critique of Russification in "*Inorodtsy* on *Obrusenie:* Religious Conversion, Indigenous Clergy, and the Politics of Assimilation in Late-Imperial Russia," *Ab Imperio* 2 (2000): 105–34.

26. On sectarians, see most recently Breyfogle, "Heretics and Colonizers," and Laura Engelstein, *Castration and the Heavenly Kingdom: A Russian Folktale* (Ithaca: Cornell University Press, 1999). On the rapid growth of Evangelical Christianity among Russians in the early twentieth century, see Heather Coleman, "The Most Dangerous Sect: Baptists in Tsarist Russia and Soviet Russia, 1905–1929" (Ph.D. diss., University of Illinois at Urbana-Champaign, 1998), and S. N. Savinskii, *Istoriia Evangel'skikh Khristian-Baptistov Ukrainy, Rossii i Belorussii, 1867–1917* (St. Petersburg: Bibliia dlia vsekh, 1999).

Orthodoxy, refused to accept the principle of assimilation that many Russians saw as being implicit in conversion. This experience supports Gauri Viswanathan's contention in the Indian case that conversion is not necessarily assimilative, precisely because it involves an effort on the part of the convert to create a new ideal system that does not always accord with what the instigators of conversion have envisioned for him or her.[27] The irony, indeed, is that Russian missionaries, by encouraging conversion and the more conscious acceptance of Orthodoxy among non-Russian subjects, opened the door to alternative outlooks on Orthodoxy's significance for local communities and on their relationship to the broader Russian polity.

All of these processes both reflected and contributed to the elaboration of a more modern, individualistic, conviction-based notion of religion by the second half of the nineteenth century or so. To be sure, Paul Bushkovitch has demonstrated that a more private and personal faith had begun to replace essentially public and collective forms of religious experience as early as the seventeenth century, but he himself emphasizes that this shift was characteristic above all of the court and landholding elite.[28] Otherwise, the collective forms that were focused on practice and community more than on belief and the individual remained prominent well into the nineteenth century. Non-Russians appear to have regarded religion as a communal affair to such an extent that they frequently made any consideration of the decision to convert to Orthodoxy contingent on the agreement of *all* members of a given community to convert as well. Religious authorities, for their part, had historically focused on orthopraxy—the "correct" execution of prescribed religious practices—more than orthodoxy:[29] they had been reasonably satisfied when parishioners fulfilled all prescribed religious obligations, such as church attendance, confession, and communion; and it had taken outright apostasy (the open rejection of Orthodoxy) and flagrant relapses into paganism (such as the ritual slaughter of livestock in animist prayers in the forests) for the newly baptized to earn any real attention from ecclesiastical authorities. The church had also seen few obstacles to the use of material incentives in bringing non-Russians into Orthodoxy, thus at least implicitly acknowledging that religious conviction was not really the standard for confessional affiliation. Without suggesting that religious authorities were indifferent to the religious

27. Gauri Viswanathan, *Outside the Fold: Conversion, Modernity, and Belief* (Princeton: Princeton University Press, 1998), 122.

28. Paul Bushkovitch, *Religion and Society in Russia: The Sixteenth and Seventeenth Centuries* (New York: Oxford University Press, 1992).

29. Clifford Geertz offers this useful distinction in his essay "'Internal Conversion' in Contemporary Bali," in *The Interpretation of Cultures* (New York: Basic Books, 1973), 177.

convictions of non-Russian parishioners, I would contend that the church was nonetheless substantially more concerned with what people *did* than with what they *believed.*

By the mid-nineteenth century, I propose, these older conceptions were eroding to a significant degree. Notably, in 1837 the government dispensed with the provision of cash payments to new converts to Orthodoxy, and by the 1860s the rules regulating the process of conversion to Orthodoxy had been reformed considerably to ensure that the desire of a given person to convert was genuine, spiritual, and carefully considered.[30] Missionaries themselves now wrote more frequently about the need to eschew "forceful" and "external" measures in their work in favor of "purely spiritual ones."[31] Accordingly the last mass baptism of non-Russians—that is, a conversion of several hundred or thousand people at once in suspicious circumstances—occurred in the Volga-Kama region in the late 1850s.[32] At about the same time the idea of the "freedom of conscience" (*svoboda sovesti*) began to appear more frequently in official correspondence, even though the law made reference to this concept beginning only in 1905. Likewise, petitioners seeking official recognition for a change in religious status also began to invoke this phrase or some near-equivalent with increasing frequency. This, surely, was a more individualistic conception of religious freedom than the older idea of "religious toleration" (*veroterpimost'*), which implied protection of collective religious rights for existing confessions or sects. In short, the nature of Orthodoxy (specifically) and religion (more generically), as defined by the state in law and administrative practice, and as experienced by empire's believers, was going through a fundamental shift.

Partly, this shift should be linked to larger changes in Russian society during the Great Reforms in the 1860s, which included the emancipation of the serfs, the transformation of local self-government, and other fundamental alterations. Aspirations in the reform period to create a more inclusive civil order that would draw on the initiative of the empire's population and entrust them with crucial responsibilities of administration and justice required that subjects no longer merely submit passively to the dictates of secular and ecclesiastical authorities, but instead actively engage in the process of reform

---

30. RGIA, *f.* 821, *op.*10, *d.* 253, *ll.* 1–18.

31. These are the words and phrases of one such missionary, E. A. Malov, in "Prikhody starokreshchenykh i novokreshchenykh tatar v Kazanskoi eparkhii," *Pravoslavnoe obozrenie* 17 (1865): 451.

32. In this case roughly one thousand "pagan" Chuvash were converted in the holdings of the Crown Department in Simbirsk province, in apparent response to the Department chief's realization in 1857 that some of the peasants under his jurisdiction were still "pagans." For the details of this case, see Werth, *At the Margins of Orthodoxy,* 89–95.

and improvement of the empire. This active engagement could of course not be created through force. Bases and principles of authority needed to be internalized by the people of Russia, in such a way that they became citizens of a polity rather than merely subjects of an autocracy.[33] Faith was no longer to be just a matter of constituting difference and securing subordination to authority, but was now more explicitly to help shape a virtuous populace for a transformed imperial Russian polity.

But the shift in conceptions of religion had also to do with the resistance of the "apostates" and "recalcitrants," which fostered a deeper appreciation for the significance of religious belief and conviction in the matter of religious identity—that is, a recognition of the existence of a spiritual realm that was resistant, if not impervious, to the ascriptive determinations of state authority. Such a recognition led one bishop to remark in 1858 in response to the persistent problem of baptized-Tatar apostasy, "I consider it a futile matter to attempt ever more forcefully to prove to a Tatar that he is a Christian, when he himself says that he is not a Christian and when he begs the Sovereign not to be considered a Christian."[34] The problem of apostasy, I would thus argue, helped to convince officials that orthopraxy would not necessarily produce Orthodox religious conviction; instead, the converse represented the more likely proposition: it was firm religious conviction that would ensure orthopraxy, as well as other desirable forms of social conformity.

In the end, for the non-Russian convert communities Orthodoxy represented many things. Initially an ascribed identity acquired as a result of a coercive missionary campaign, Orthodoxy for a long time represented a label to be shunned or a set of requirements to be ignored whenever possible. It was the "Russian faith," which implied a rejection of the indigenous ethnic identity on the part of those individuals, households, and communities that embraced it. For some—especially many baptized Tatars—the meaning of Orthodoxy never went much beyond this. But for others, Orthodoxy could be domesticated, indigenized, and ultimately put to uses not envisioned by the agents who had initiated the process of Christianization several generations earlier. For these people, Orthodoxy was lived not only through ascription, but became a foundation for spiritual nourishment, education and literacy, and a greater sense of individual and collective self-worth.

33. For a useful elaboration of these ideas, see Yanni Kotsonis, "Introduction: A Modern Paradox—Subject and Citizen in Nineteenth- and Twentieth-Century Russia," in *Russian Modernity: Politics, Knowledge, Practices*, ed. David Hoffman and Yanni Kotsonis (New York: St. Martin's Press, 2000), 1–6.

34. Bishop of Cheboksary and Vicar of Kazan Nikodim, as quoted in Malov, "Prikhody," no. 18, p. 509.

EPILOGUE

A View

from the West

THOMAS N. TENTLER

Now to get back to my subject, I find, considering all that I have
heard about them, that there is nothing at all savage or barbaric
in that nation [the newly discovered Indians of Brazil], except that
everyone calls barbarous that which is not his own custom. For in
all honesty, we seem to have no other perspective on truth and
reason than the examples, opinions, and customs of the country
where we live. There, always, is the perfect religion, the perfect
political order, the exemplary and perfected way in everything.
—*Michel de Montaigne, "On the Cannibals" (1580)*

For over forty years my research and teaching have been devoted primarily
to the history of Western European Christianity, especially the medieval and
early modern periods (c. 1100 to c. 1750). It is from that perspective that I
have been asked to comment on this collection of essays in the history of
Russian Orthodoxy. In other words, this will be an exercise in comparing
histories—one in which I place what I have known as a scholar against what
I have learned from these enlightening excursions into the Russian Orthodox
past. Given my limited familiarity with Orthodoxy, my comment will be
speculative, but I hope it will be provocative as well, and that in a construc-
tive way.

Comparative history is an approach to our discipline that I want at the
outset to commend and, simultaneously, demystify. For a learned and yet
accessible introduction to comparing histories, I urge readers to consult one
or all of three essays by Raymond Grew,[1] a longtime missionary in the field.

1. Raymond Grew, "The Case for Comparing Histories," *The American Historical Review* 85 (1980):
763–78; idem, "On the Current State of Comparative Studies, in *Marc Bloch aujourd'hui. Histoire com-
parée et sciences sociales,* ed. Hartmut Atsma and André Burguière (Paris: Editions de l'Ecole des hautes

To begin I need only make three simple points about the exercise of historical comparison (a very selective use of Grew) to orient the reader to my remarks.

First, thinking comparatively is natural, perhaps unavoidable, for historians. When we study other people—individuals, societies, ethnicities, religions, eras, nations—we ourselves are situated in time, place, and culture, and we bring to our study a complex knowledge of histories and peoples. The questions we ask, the evidence we think relevant, and the conclusions we draw are inevitably influenced by what we already know (or think we know). In this collection, on a satisfyingly wide range of studies of Russian Orthodoxy, every essay contains references to the history of Western Christianity and to that extent is self-consciously comparative. It would be a happy consequence of this publication if in the near future we could discern a comparable interest in Eastern Christianity among historians of Western Europe.

I suggest, therefore, that readers are bound to react to this material with some form of comparison. The story of a newly discovered frozen body that is made a saint catches our attention because we live in a world in which canonization is familiar but that particular variation on it is not. We respond to women who find religious meaning and economic independence in a thriving convent, or who use religious language and symbols in ways that assert their individuality, because we live at a time when issues of gender touch us deeply, in our scholarship as well as our politics. Birth patterns—and what they imply about the individual sexual behavior of Orthodox believers—become more meaningful when we put them in the context of our knowledge of human fertility and attempts (religious, technological, political) to control it. So it is with every one of the disparate topics in this collection—from an apocalyptic calendar or an iconographic program in a throne room, to lived religion in the households of affluent and ordinary Russians. What we see in and say about saints, icons, religious confrontation, or women with voices implies comparison with what we know as inhabitants of late-modern industrial cultures and what we learn as students of the histories of law, politics, art, social structures, and values in cultures that lie within and outside our special expertise.

Second, what is done "naturally" is better done self-consciously and explicitly. That principle has been worked over for decades in the social sciences and humanities, and I want to make clear my distance from those who have

---

études en sciences sociales, 1990), 323–34; and idem, addendum to "The Case for Comparing Histories," in *Modes of Comparison: Theory and Practice,* ed. Aram Yengoyan (Ann Arbor: University of Michigan Press, forthcoming), a collection of essays honoring Professor Grew.

argued that to accept it requires one to adopt some fully articulated theory of language or social action. There are many ways to pursue comparison—ranging from the highly abstract to the fundamentally empirical. Hypotheses can be generated by a sociological theory predicting testable correlations and outcomes, or comparisons can be generated by hunches about categories widely accepted in historical discourse, such as class, law, morality, sacrament, ecclesiastical authority, sacred texts, sanctity, or any number of institutions.[2] Different data and different problems will require different approaches—and the variety of comparison in these essays confirms that.

My third and final point is my unashamed admission that I favor the empirical over the theoretical. My remarks will eschew all but a few theoretical abstractions, which I shall explain in the simple terms in which I take them. For the most part, however, I take my inspiration from the concrete. I have tried to use my knowledge of the history of Christianity in the West to help me understand another Catholic tradition (and in doing so I shall repeat some comparative observations that the authors themselves have already made). I have read and responded to what I found but did not expect, and what I expected but did not find. The anthropologist Wendy Doniger once subtitled a paper "the dog that didn't bark." She was alluding to the clue that Sherlock Holmes used to solve the murder in "The Hound of the Baskervilles": because the dog had failed to warn the house, Holmes inferred something about the homicidal intruder. My comment is a modest exercise in that kind of inference—an attempt to identify different breeds of dog; or missing, sleeping, or uninterested dogs; or perhaps, puppies who are not as obstreperous as their Western cousins.

I hope that every reader who has followed these remarks on my perspective as a historian of European Christianity and on the method of comparison I have laid out will feel a bit uneasy. I hope the reader will wonder whether such a project in these hands can be free of a garden-variety prejudice. It was in anticipation of that hoped-for response to the obvious danger of my Eurocentric perspective that I have set the well-known words of Michel de Montaigne (1533–92) at the head of this comment. More than three hundred years before a founding father of modern sociology of religion, Emile Durkheim (1858–1917), asserted the interpretive principle that there are no false religions, Montaigne, without the benefit of a single course in anthropology, had a similar insight. I recall it here as a form of assurance that I am

---

2. For suggestions on comparative directions in Reformation history, see Thomas Tentler, "Postscript," in *Penitence in the Age of Reformations*, ed. Katharine Jackson Lualdi and Anne T. Thayer (Burlington, Vt.: Ashgate, 2000), 240–59, esp. 255–59.

aware of the danger this particular kind of comparison poses, and because I suspect that, like me, many readers will find much that is "foreign" in the religious culture we meet in these essays. I choose Montaigne to remind us that rejection of ethnocentrism is not just the province of modern (and post-modern) cultural relativists. That a Renaissance humanist could so incisively expose the injustice of equating the unfamiliar with the irrational, especially in matters of religion, is an instructive surprise and salutary lesson of comparative history. Though rare, that kind of enlightenment was not unknown in the age of European religious wars and imperial expansion—Bartolomé de las Casas (1474–1566), the "Apostle of the Indies," is another example.

I have chosen Montaigne as my antidote to ethnocentrism to make a comparative point—that even early modern religious cultures were capable of producing a tolerant view of alien cultures. But Montaigne is also apt because his hatred of cruelty and fanaticism, amply demonstrated in his essays, reveals the kind of observer whose anthropological objectivity leaves room for strong moral judgments. I think that he would have been fascinated by the religion and customs of tribal Afghanistan, but repelled by terrorism, lawlessness, and the burka. (And I suspect that even the tolerant Montaigne would have been dismayed by the self-castration of the Skoptsy.) Since September 11, 2001, Americans have been made increasingly aware of the perils of ethnocentrism, but also of the necessity of moral judgment.

Turning specifically to the substance of my task, I want to relate the warning against ethnocentrism to the apparent persistence in the historiography of premodern Russian religion of a "two-tiered" approach. Here (as in the history of religion of other areas and eras) specialists in the field have asserted that Orthodox practice and belief exist in two distinct versions. One, grounded in a separate language and sophisticated theology, is the province of a clerical elite. The other is said to be centered on image, ritual, and popular beliefs that resemble folklore—particularly those centered on holy times, places, objects, and persons. In their introductory essay, Valerie Kivelson and Robert Greene have quoted an exaggerated expression of that two-tiered assumption, which, when I view it unsympathetically, seems an unvarnished example of a modernist preference for the abstract and intellectual over the physical and the mundane. Since the principal authors and promoters of that two-tiered view are respected scholars in the field and I am not, I must admit that my own position here is the product of scholarly principle, not of scholarly research in the history of Orthodoxy. Nevertheless I want to set myself on the side of the essayists in this collection, who are looking for an "authentic" Orthodox religious belief and practice even among lowly and unsophisticated practitioners. It is just as important to question the two-tiered approach to religion—with its implication that the modal beliefs and practices of the higher tier are somehow more reasonable than the superstitious practices of the lower tier—as it is to oppose more ordinary forms of ethnocentrism. This work of opposition is all the more important because it is difficult for us, as children of a scientific culture, not to look skeptically on the religious beliefs of illiterate populations, not to call certain practices superstitious. We prefer doctrinal formulations whose manifestations are more spiritual and abstract than instrumental and material. From that perspective, the Trinity is mysterious but respectable; miracle-working icons are, at best, suspect.

In what has become a model for critics of two-tiered cultural history, Peter Brown has analyzed the cult of the saints in the Christianity of late antiquity.[3] Although he deals with an era far removed in time from the subject of these essays, his work is relevant to this discussion in part because he exemplifies the "cast of mind" that Raymond Grew identifies as the most important attribute of good comparison.[4] But the specifics of the ancient case are also applicable to the Orthodox case. For Brown shows that the enthusiasm for the miraculous was not introduced by newly converted, superstitious barbarians but was rather promoted by the intellectual Augustine (354–430) and other esteemed Fathers of the ancient church. For many historians of late antiquity, religious practice centered on miracles and tombs had been incompatible with their vision of the Fathers as heirs of the intellectually superior culture of Rome. They thought of the elites of the Roman world as separate and above the masses. Brown, on the contrary, shows that the bishops actively promoted the cult of the saints, which reflected the political structures and social relationships of late antiquity.

There should have been nothing surprising in that. For if we consider how religions have historically provided the organizing principles of human societies, the whole idea of an elite religion radically divorced from the religion of the people looks implausible on its face.[5] It implies, against sociological common sense, that governing elites have failed to employ prescribed religion

3. Peter Brown, *The Cult of the Saints: Its Rise and Function in Latin Christianity* (Chicago: University of Chicago Press, 1981).

4. Grew, addendum to "The Case for Comparing Histories," 778.

5. Peter Berger, *The Sacred Canopy: Elements of a Sociological Theory of Religion* (Garden City, N.Y.: Doubleday, 1967). See also Guy E. Swanson, *Religion and Regime: A Sociological Account of the Reformation* (Ann Arbor: University of Michigan Press, 1967); idem, *The Birth of the Gods: The Origin of Primitive Beliefs* (Ann Arbor: University of Michigan Press, 1960); and Thomas N. Tentler, "Seventeen Authors in Search of Two Religious Cultures," *Catholic Historical Review* 71 (1985): 248–57.

as an effective source of norms and legitimation binding together a whole society (in which they are genuine participants). There is, to be sure, no lack of evidence of hierarchical distinctions in human societies between governing elites and governed subjects. In early modern Russia royalty, nobility, and Orthodox episcopacy claimed special authority over state and church, and excluded the lower orders from power over this privileged realm. But to discover a hierarchical order—elites with specialized knowledge and claims to superior merit—does not establish the existence of radically separate religions. Every essay in this collection confronts that position. Our authors offer, instead, an alternative body of evidence that respects the diversity of religious experience; they attend seriously to women, peasants, and residents on the peripheries; and they reveal the Orthodox nature of ordinary belief and practice. Like the historians of Western Christianity they cite, they focus not on deviance and heterodoxy, but rather on shared and authentic religious expression. Every author in this collection puts into practice the principle I have just defended. Laura Engelstein and Vera Shevzov mount a frontal attack on the two-tiered assumption. The rest undermine it with concrete examples of its opposite, from Daniel Rowland's throne room to Daniel Kaiser's quotidian mentalities. The feminine dimension of Orthodoxy—as revealed in strikingly different ways by Gary Marker, Isolde Thyrêt, Nadieszda Kizenko, and William Wagner—provides an especially apt example of this challenge to the two-tiered assumption, for if anyone is separated by language and education from the exclusive preserve of the ecclesiastical hierarchy it must be women. Yet these women appear to this observer to be singularly faithful representatives of the faith. Engelstein identifies traditional asceticism as an authentic source even for so aberrant a practice as self-castration. The same sound approach informs the analysis of less extreme cases, as our essayists look for authenticity beneath the variegated surfaces of lived religion.

Transcendence, Immanence, and the Weberian Sociology of Religion

For good or ill, the religious history of early modern Western Europe is still dominated by the ideas of Max Weber (1864–1920), whose *Protestant Ethic and the Spirit of Capitalism* applied the categories of transcendence and immanence to the Reformation and its long aftermath.[6] For Weber the modernity

---

6. Max Weber, *The Protestant Ethic and the Spirit of Capitalism,* trans. Talcott Parsons, introduction by Randall Collins (Los Angeles: Roxbury, 1996). Collins's introduction is excellent.

of Calvinist Protestantism lay in its reaffirmation of transcendence (which he saw as a reclamation of the religion of the Old Testament). Calvinism and, to a lesser extent, Lutheranism were said to have rejected the magical and fairy-tale elements of medieval Catholicism and put in their place a more rational and orderly religion—less open to manipulation by religious ritual, less tolerant of backsliding, and more insistent on theologically correct education for all believers. Calvinism had little or no place for religious art, the observance of holy seasons, and the veneration of holy places and relics. The image of God is, in this characterization, fully transcendent—a "high god" whose providential power rules over us, but is not constantly manifested through the mediation of holy persons, places, and things among us. The most telling aspect of the Calvinistic reformation of religion is its denial that modern miracles are reliable indicators of sanctity or religious truth.

Max Weber's characterization of transcendent Protestantism has elements that are difficult to refute. The sixteenth- and seventeenth-century Roman Catholic response to Protestantism—the Counter or Catholic Reformation—in fact insisted on that whole list of beliefs and practices that we associate with divine immanence, including the veneration of men and women who were really saints, and whose relics transmit the sanctity they had actually possessed when they lived. The list includes pilgrimages to holy places, prayer and devotion aided by religious art, and sacraments that are material causes of an invisible but indisputably real grace that is transmitted to believers and transforms those who are properly prepared. Greek and Russian Orthodoxy were not directly challenged by Protestantism and hence did not need to mount a counterattack. But we have no difficulty in seeing in the religion described in these essays another form of Catholic, immanental Christianity—with its holy places, relics, seasons, pilgrimages, miracles, and saints (with special powers of intercession above and intervention here below).

Weber's interpretation of Protestant theology and its relation to modernity has been a scholarly battleground;[7] and as I have already admitted, there is much to be said for analyzing systems of religious belief in terms of transcendence and immanence. The danger in that use is to oversimplify the evidence and fail to recognize the complex mixture of transcendence and immanence

7. Robert W. Green, ed., *Protestantism and Capitalism: The Weber Thesis and Its Critics* (Boston: D. C. Heath, 1959), and idem, *Protestantism, Capitalism, and Social Science: The Weber Controversy,* 2d ed. (Lexington, Mass.: D. C. Heath, 1973). For examples of Weberian typologies in early modern historiography, see Keith Thomas, *Religion and the Decline of Magic* (New York: Scribner, 1971); Carlos M. N. Eire, *War Against the Idols: The Reformation of Worship from Erasmus to Calvin* (Cambridge: Cambridge University Press, 1986); and Ann W. Ramsey, *Liturgy, Politics, and Salvation: The Catholic League in Paris and the Nature of Catholic Reform, 1540–1630* (Rochester: University of Rochester Press, 1999).

present in every religion. Once that oversimplification is adopted, the next step is virtually inevitable: the transcendent is identified with the modern and rational, and a two-tiered presentation of Western Christianity contrasts a transcendental Calvinism at the top of an upper sphere of religion, against the superstitions of rural (especially southern European) Catholicism toward the bottom of that lower, immanental sphere. It does not take much imagination to guess that in this kind of classification, the Orthodoxy represented in the essays in this collection is likely to nestle with Sicilian peasants in the basement of the sociology of religion.

Whenever this kind of two-tiered model is proposed, we shall do well to follow Peter Brown's example by looking for elements of the "lower" tier among the generators and guardians of the upper tier. Specifically, we should note the immaterial, miraculous, and "credulous" elements in the religion of all early modern religious elites, East and West, Protestant as well as Catholic. Thus we should not forget that the Reformation found a place for prodigies, portents, and signs of divine intervention, and that Luther could attribute the miracles associated with Catholic shrines to the activity of the devil.[8] Luther read the report of the birth of a calf that appeared to have a monk's cowl as a providential sign that God hated monasticism, and the treatise that popularized this divine portent was translated into French and published in Geneva,[9] the capital of Weber's transcendent, de-mystified religion, the very essence of what Western folk religion and Russian Orthodoxy were not. Calvin and Calvinists were also among the vast majority of Christians across Western Europe who believed in witches and demonic possession so literally that they hunted, prosecuted, punished, and executed them in staggering numbers.[10] In this respect Russia, which did not know crazed persecutions

8. Philip Soergel, "Miracles," in *The Oxford Encyclopedia of the Reformation,* 4 vols., ed. Hans J. Hillerbrand (New York: Oxford University Press, 1996), 3:64–66; Robin B. Barnes, "Prodigies and Portents," ibid., 348–50; Brian Levack, "Possession and Exorcism," ibid., 318–20; E. William Monter, "Magic," ibid., 2:482–84; Martin Luther, *To the Christian Nobility of the German Nation,* trans. Charles M. Jacobs, rev. James Atkinson, in *Three Treatises,* 2d rev. ed. (Philadelphia: Fortress Press, 1970), 76–78.

9. Philip Soergel, "Portraying Monstrous Birth in Early Modern Germany," *Arizona Studies in Medieval and Renaissance History* 2 (1998): 129–50; Jean Delumeau, *Sin and Fear: The Emergence of a Western Guilt Culture, 13th–18th Centuries,* trans. Eric Nicholson (New York: St. Martin's Press, 1990), 136. Cf. Robert W. Scribner, *For the Sake of Simple Folk: Popular Propaganda for the German Reformation* (Oxford: Clarendon Press, 1994), 127–32, and for Calvinism in colonial America, David Hall, *Worlds of Wonder, Days of Judgment: Popular Religious Belief in Early New England* (New York: Knopf, 1989).

10. Brian P. Levack, *The Witch-Hunt in Early Modern Europe* (London: Longman, 1987); E. William Monter, "Witchcraft," in *Oxford Encyclopedia of the Reformation,* 1:276–82; H. C. Erik Midelfort, *Witch Hunting in Southwestern Germany, 1562–1684: The Social and Intellectual Foundations* (Stanford: Stanford University Press, 1972); idem, "Witchcraft, Magic, and the Occult," in *Reformation Europe: A Guide to Research,* ed. Steven Ozment (St. Louis: Center for Reformation Research, 1982), 183–209; Christina

and had not mastered the lurid demonology of the witches' sabbath, night flying, and other satanic fantasies, lagged behind the West in a way that, to our modern, rational gaze, is to their advantage.[11] Obviously there is much to learn from comparison between these two Catholic cousins. So too is the counterintuitive lesson of Michael Flier's Russian millennialists, whose eschatological beliefs are not in doubt, but who apparently interpreted them in a more optimistic register than fervent believers in the West, from Luther and his followers to the radicals of the Catholic League.[12]

Since Eastern and Western Christianities are generally depicted in opposition to each other, it is also worth remembering their commonalities, which make their comparison all the more interesting. They both began in the same place and developed in apparent harmony for centuries.[13] Both are religions of roughly the same two-volume Bible, and if there are some disagreements on the contents of the Old Testament, they have little to do with the differences we encounter in the medieval and early modern period. That agreement is even truer of the New Testament, which in East and West is comprised of the twenty-seven books of the Athanasian canon. No doubt some doctrinal differences revolve around contested translations and interpretations of New Testament passages, but it is not likely that any of these textual distinctions could have been significant causes of the cultural differences that appear before us in these essays. Nor is it likely that other disputed theological formulae are causes of divergent paths as much as symptoms that paths have diverged. For example, the *filioque* clause—Rome's insistence that the Holy Spirit proceeds from the Father and the Son (and not from the Father alone, as in the

Larner, *Enemies of God: The Witch-hunt in Scotland* (Baltimore: Johns Hopkins University Press, 1981); Robin Briggs, *Witches and Neighbors: The Social and Cultural Context of European Witchcraft* (New York: Viking, 1996); Alan Macfarlane, *Witchcraft in Tudor and Stuart England: A Regional and Comparative Study* (London: Routledge and Kegan Paul, 1970); Richard Kieckhefer, *European Witch Trials: Their Foundations in Popular and Learned Culture, 1300–1500* (London: Routledge and Kegan Paul, 1976); and Thomas, *Religion and the Decline of Magic.*

11. Valerie Kivelson, "Patrolling the Boundaries: Witchcraft Accusations and Household Strife in Seventeenth-Century Muscovy," *Kamen' kraeog "l'n": Rhetoric of the Medieval Slavic World*, ed. Nancy S. Kollmann et al., *Harvard Ukrainian Studies* 19, nos. 1–4 (1995): 302–23, esp. 302–3, 305, 321–23.

12. Robin B. Barnes, "Apocalypticism" and "Millenarianism" in *The Oxford Encyclopedia of the Reformation*, 1:63–68; 3:61–63; idem, *Prophecy and Gnosis: Apocalypticism in the Wake of the Lutheran Reformation* (Stanford: Stanford University Press, 1988); Barbara B. Diefendorf, "The Catholic League: Social Crisis or Apocalypse Now?" *French Historical Studies* 15 (1987): 332–44; Denis Crouzet, *Les Guerriers de Dieu: La violence au temps des troubles de religion*, 2 vols. (Paris: Champ Vallon, 1990). Contrast, however, Ramsey, *Liturgy, Politics, and Salvation*, 160–65, and esp. Larissa Taylor, "The Good Shepherd: François Le Picart (1504–56) and Preaching Reform from Within," *Sixteenth Century Journal* 28 (1997): 793–810.

13. John Meyendorff, *Byzantine Theology: Historical Trends and Doctrinal Themes* (reprint, New York: Fordham University Press, 1987), 7–11, 78–88, 150–67, 180–90.

Orthodox wording of the Nicene Creed)—was a principal cause of the failure of the reunion of East and West in 1439. Differences in the calendar and disputes over Petrine primacy, purgatory, and original sin are also significant issues in the confessional division.[14] But while ideas and texts can influence historical development—like switchmen, in Weber's phrase—they rarely produce it directly, and that is particularly true of theological abstractions and arguments about grammar and words. Those disputes may and did contribute to political divisions, but they are more likely to have been signs of divergence over authority and practice than fundamental causes of those differences.

Indeed, the early history of ecclesiology—the issue that caused increased separation of the traditions after the formal breach in 1054—might lead one to have predicted harmony rather than division.[15] In the early centuries of Christian history, both East and West developed hierarchical, episcopal ecclesiastical polities and governed through councils that respected canonical legislation wherever it appeared. East and West accepted certain councils as authoritative for the whole church; recognized certain men they called Fathers as the most worthy exponents of the doctrinal component of faith; believed that the visible church was the unique source of salvation; and agreed that certain men and women who lived and died within it were holy in an exemplary way and could be invoked as intercessors. Both traditions were creedal: people stood up in public and recited formulae that began "we" or "I believe." In short, the book of the New Testament, the items of belief, the virtues and vices that define sanctity, the structures of authority, and the ultimate goal of salvation in eternity—all of these might well have produced a common religious culture and practice. Fortunately for us, they did not, and we as historians have a rich comparative field to play in—a field made much richer precisely because, in so many ways, the two traditions start in the same place: Palestine, Judaism, the book, the church, creeds, bishops, saints, fathers, sacraments, and much more. Before I remark on what I did not find, or found but did not expect, I want to stress the utility of the shared elements, which ought to force us to look for explanations that are not superficially textual or prescriptive. As they drifted apart, the courses taken were not clearly determined by some ancient, official shove in a specific direction. And as the mother ships went their separate ways, more and more boats got floated and went in even more, different directions. Hence these essays, and my remarks on what I was surprised to find and not to find.

14. Ibid., 91–101, 109–14, 218–22, and passim.
15. Ibid., 78–88, 150–67, 180–90, and passim.

Universities—Authority and Lived Religion

Among the most interesting differences between the two traditions is the absence in Russia of institutions of higher learning as active centers of authority comparable to the universities of the European Middle Ages. One might perhaps object that attention to intellectuals is out of place in essays that are searching for lived religion, but I would counter that the social or anthropological history of Western Christianity and its heretical and deviant movements would be baffling without reference to universities, which multiplied and grew—in numbers and power—from the late twelfth century onward. It was doctors of theology and canon law who formulated the doctrines and legal norms by which Christian living was measured. They fostered a method of inquiry and pedagogy that lived by precise definition and yet, paradoxically, thrived on debate. When doctrine or legal rights were in doubt, a university was routinely consulted for an authoritative answer—and, in serious cases, more than one university, since the faculties often disagreed. Universities and university-trained professionals produced doctrinal definitions, legal interpretations, theories of civil and ecclesiastical polities, and a huge body of literature—some of it abstract, some of it practical—that patterned and gave meaning to the lived religion of the faithful. A vast body of precedent helped Rome and Western Europe's bishops respond to new practices and either repress the deviant or accommodate and co-opt them.

What to Western eyes is missing in Paul Werth's picture of the treatment of non-Russian converts in the Kama region, for example, is sustained, systematic academic intervention into that cultural exchange. One might call the European university's role in ecclesiastical government "repressive" or "bureaucratic," and their learned professors either agents of a "persecuting society" or architects of an "orderly religion." It is my counterfactual guess, however, that if Rome had encountered Werth's situation, we would have seen university-trained mendicant preachers leading the conversion movement, and we would have been left with a more voluminous record of debates and decisions about what concessions to indigenous belief and practice were permissible, and what forbidden. (The example of the Jesuits, whose worldwide missionary activities included the successful proselytization of Russia's neighbor, Poland, provides a striking alternative model.) Is the late development of universities in Russia related to the absence of an independent, international church that supplied a common ecclesiastical law and supported a network of theological faculties—both of which could stand in opposition to the policies of the state? When Russian universities were finally founded, could they, without centuries of experience, exercise a comparable authority? My Westernized presuppositions lead me to suggest that the answer to the first question is yes, and to the second, no.

Since the authors of this collection teach in universities, and since our readers almost certainly are university-educated as well, we are all likely to hail the early, powerful presence of universities as a sign of cultural superiority. It seems to be an unmitigated good thing. Thus it might be useful to recall two professorial contributions to the religious history of the West that are difficult to regard as beneficent. First, ecclesiastical inquisitors were invariably drawn from or trained by doctors of theology and canon law. Second, these same professionals played an indispensable role in shaping the mythology on which the worst excesses of Western Europe's witchcraft persecutions were built. Global history—a rich mine for historical comparison—has many examples of the mischief created by those trained in an academy of higher learning, and we ought not to assume that an advanced degree will promote "progress" as we generally understand it. In other words, even here comparison is not necessarily to the advantage of the West.

Saints and Sanctity

Identical features of lived religion continued in both traditions into the early modern and modern eras, and among the most notable is the veneration of saintly intercessors whose defining attributes include incorruptibility and miracles. And in spite of some extraordinary cases among Eve Levin's thirteen anonymous bodies that achieved popular and official cult status in early modern Russia, both traditions assumed that saints lead holy lives and, for the same reason, that those who lead holy lives are candidates for canonization. That saint cults celebrated holy men and women seems at first glance to be unremarkable, but that reaction ignores the vehement rejection of the very idea that one might pray to a saint by all branches of the Protestant Reformation. The absence of a Russian Reformation, then, underscores the importance of this shared set of values and assumptions in these two Catholic traditions. Both hold that the true believer and doer of the word becomes intrinsically holy. That may have been easier for the Eastern tradition to accept because of its reluctance to impugn guilt of the Fall to all of Adam's descendants;[16] nevertheless, the agreement that men and women—not just

16. Ibid., 138–49.

God—can and ought to be holy constitutes an important basis for the comparison of the two traditions. So, too, is the contrast with a whole range of Protestant churches who have rejected that proposition. Even the phenomenon of visible saints in the Reformed and Radical Reformations—from Anabaptist Germany and the Netherlands to Calvinist Geneva, England, and New England—does not invalidate the point that the ineradicability of Original Sin is so strong in the churches of the Reformation that they conceive of human holiness as little better than a metaphorical imitation of the real thing. Even John Wesley's Methodism, with its doctrine of perfection, stops short of the Roman and Orthodox Catholic conceptions. Both affirmed, whereas Protestants denied, the efficacy of intercession by saints. And in both traditions, at the apex of holy intercessors, is the most blessed mediatrix herself, the Blessed Virgin Mary—whose various titles by the fifth century guaranteed the unique power and honor of a feminine model of sanctity.[17] Wherever we go in Christian lands, we find churches and museums that house myriad representations of the annunciation, the nativity, the holy family, mother and child, the deposition, the crowning of the Virgin, and other episodes in the second most favored life in traditional Catholic confessions of East and West. The different developments of that devotion (most palpable in artistic representation), and its complex and unpredictable consequences in the cultural developments that ensue, are all the more significant because they begin with this fundamental, un-Protestant, agreement. There is much Orthodox devotional practice—in detail and theological underpinnings—that is reminiscent of Roman Catholicism.

But the histories of making saints in the two traditions also diverge. The West early develops mechanisms for keeping sanctity under hierarchical control, without, it is important to add, eliminating the spontaneous element of popular devotion that is the usual beginning of a successful canonization.[18] Here is another example of the importance of the authority of the university and in particular of the canon lawyers who were trained in universities and

17. Ibid., 146–49, 123–24, 165.
18. André Vauchez, *La sainteté en Occident aux derniers siècles du Moyen Age: d'après les procès de canonisation et les documents hagiographiques,* Bibliothèque des écoles françaises d'Athènes et de Rome, fasc. 241 (Paris: Diffusion de Boccard, 1988), 31–120, translated into English under the title *Sainthood in the Later Midddle Ages* by Jean Birrell (Cambridge: Cambridge University Press, 1997); T. Ortolan, "Canonisation dans l'Église Romaine," in *Dictionnaire de théologie catholique,* ed. A. Vacant, E. Mangenot, and E. Amann, 15 vols. (Paris, 1899–1950), vol. 2, pt. 2 (1932), 1626–34; J. Bois, "Canonisation dans l'Église Russe," ibid., 1659–72; Kenneth L. Woodward, *Making Saints: How the Catholic Church Determines Who Becomes a Saint, Who Doesn't, and Why* (New York: Simon and Schuster, 1990), 4–76; Camilus Beccari, "Beatificaton and Canonization," *Catholic Encyclopedia,* 15 vols. (New York, 1907–12), vol. 2 (accessible at http://www.newadvent.org/cathen).

who rose in that hierarchy. This institutional difference ultimately gave the papacy a monopoly on beatification and canonization in the West. Politics entered in when kings and aristocrats were canonized, in numbers out of proportion to their presence in the population. But movements to canonize royals and other powerful men and women also failed. In the end, only saints canonized according to the rules entered the Roman calendar and achieved widespread devotion.

Russian Orthodoxy's hierarchy also controlled the calendar of saints, but that control developed later and appears to have been less systematic. It seems that in the land of "autarchy" popular spontaneity had a better chance of surviving, that elites had a less firm hand on the sanctification process, that, in short, ecclesiastical bureaucracy was less well organized and less confident than in the West. The systematic investigation of the life of the saint aided Western prelates in exercising that control. With its emphasis on the collective and experiential, Vera Shevzov's *tserkovnost'* supports this counterintuitive Russian, "democratized" answer to the question, "who is the Church?"—especially with its emphasis on the whole body of the faithful. That demotic, yet Orthodox, voice is present in other essays in this collection.

There are expressions of a democratizing ecclesiological impulse in the West that provide suggestive comparisons. Fourteenth-century canonists and theologians, faced with the Great Schism, produced a whole range of conciliarist theories that opposed the centralizing bureaucratization of Rome (and Avignon). Heretical movements in the West before the Reformation (Waldensians, Cathars, Lollards, and Hussites are most prominent) also developed ecclesiologies that rejected papal authority and undermined, to varying degrees, hierarchy. Most obviously, Luther's priesthood of all believers (arguably influenced by conciliarist thought) succeeded in overthrowing the Papacy's version of "autarchy" everywhere that any version of Protestantism was adopted. Nevertheless, the spontaneity and unmanageability of popular religion that is revealed in some of these essays seems distinctive, and for me that means distinctively Russian.

Thus while Eve Levin's saints without lives were exceptional cases in Russia, it is difficult to believe that even these few examples would have escaped the censorious eye of early modern Rome—if for no other reason than the readiness of Protestant polemicists to debunk Catholic legends that had little grounding in the historical record. And that situation evokes another comparison: the balance struck in each of the two religious cultures between acceptance and skeptical critique of the popular origins of saints' legends. As historians whose daily bread is skeptical examination of sources and their reliability, we should be especially mindful here of Durkheim's dictum that for the purposes of sociological study there are no false religions.[19] In addition, to avoid an almost irresistible assumption that "modern" means "rational," we might recall that blind faith in secular schemes of salvation, with their own communions of saints, have been the plague of the twentieth century. With those qualifications in mind, and with some more to come, I shall continue to argue that the West, including the Roman Catholic West, was more willing than the East to suspect and consequently to control the miraculous.

Historical Criticism in the West

A principal source of this occasional restraint on the claims of divine intervention into daily life was the development of historical criticism in the Renaissance. This is not to assert that the Renaissance was really the Enlightenment, or that anywhere in fifteenth- or sixteenth-century Europe it was not routine to see the hand of God in human events, giving them a meaning beyond their human and material causes. Lest we make Russian Orthodoxy seem more alien than it deserves, we should not forget that to this day Roman Catholic orthodoxy endorses, encourages, and even, it can be said, requires belief in the miraculous. Perhaps the most renowned apparition of the Virgin occurred at Lourdes in 1858, and was solemnly approved by Pius IX four years later. Near the end of that century Theresa of Lisieux, a well-educated French nun, remembered her wonder as a child at seeing the room where the Blessed Virgin had received the message of the angel of the Annunciation: she was visiting the holy house of Loreto, the residence of the Virgin, which was believed to have been transported by angels from the Holy Land to Italy in 1295.[20] As we read about the abundance of miracles in early modern Russia, we should remember that there were hundreds of Marian apparitions in Europe and North America in the nineteenth and twentieth centuries and that the few that have gained official recognition include among

19. The corollary "all religions are true" (that is, they all "work" for their faithful) is arguably preferable. I could not object to the proposition that it is antihuman and false to call a suicide bomber whose target is innocent noncombatants "holy." But to the practitioners of some fundamentalist versions of Islam, the idea is true and has become part of a lived, working religion.

20. Theresa of Lisieux, *The Story of a Soul,* trans. Michael Day (Westminster, Md.: Newman Press, 1956), chap. 6, p. 88. According to the legend the house was first transported from Nazareth to Tersato in Ilyria in 1291, and from there to its present location near Ancona: see Herbert Thurston, "Santa casa di Loreto," *Catholic Encyclopedia,* vol. 12.

them cults whose shrines have attracted millions of modern pilgrims.[21] Rome's sanctification process still demands confirmation of miracles before a beatification or canonization can be promoted. That the miraculous is a staple of some forms of Protestant Christianity can be verified by consulting a rich spectrum of evangelical sources—televangelists and web sites. A not unrelated impulse is found in the heart of the Reformation itself, which read history assiduously—ancient pagan, biblical, medieval, and contemporary—to discern the hand of God guiding events. Michael Flier's prophets, reading the events of Russian history through an eschatological lens have their counterpart even in the Protestant West. The most consistent proponent of divine governance of the intimate details of life was Calvin himself—prime source of Max Weber's "rationalization of life" and modernization. Calvin believed that predestination was but a special case of providence, the universal causality of God; and he succeeds in shocking the reader by asserting that the sins and crimes of the reprobate are willed by a God who does not merely view human activity from a watchtower removed from the action, but causes each ineluctable event to happen.[22]

But alongside what will strike many contemporary readers as "credulity," the West (Roman Catholic as well as Protestant) found a larger place for skeptical, historicizing mentalities. Scholarly techniques born in the Renaissance, and nurtured in the Reformation and in the learned historical circles of the seventeenth and eighteenth centuries, were capable of subjecting holy lives, miraculous events, and claims of divine intervention to systematic criticism. The demythologization of St. Jerome that Eugene Rice has so effectively chronicled began with Erasmus's textual and historical insights in the early sixteenth century and continued in the following decades and centuries. In the end the legend and its immensely popular iconography were dismantled. Scholarly critics included not only Protestants with theological motives but also Catholics whose confessional interests were not served by the Jerome

21. David Blackbourn, *Marpingen: Apparitions of the Virgin Mary in Nineteenth-Century Germany* (New York: Knopf, 1994), 3–41.

22. John Calvin, *Institutes of the Christian Religion*, 2 vols., ed. John T. McNeill, trans. Ford Lewis Battles, Library of Christian Classics, nos. 20 and 21 (Philadelphia: Westminster Press, 1960): "as if God sat in a watchtower awaiting chance events" (I.18.1, p. 231); "God's will is . . . the cause of all things" (I.18.2, p. 232); "God wills to take place what he forbids to be done" (I.18.3, p. 234); "God himself both willed that his Son be delivered up and delivered him up to death" (I.18.4, p. 237). Cf. John Calvin, *Antidote to the Council of Trent*, "Antidote to the Canons of the Council of Trent (On Justification)," Canon 6: "His [God's] are the snares, swords, and axes which are directed by his hand; . . . his hiss arouses them to execute what his hand and counsel have decreed." In John Dillenberger, ed., *John Calvin: Selections from His Writings*, American Academy of Religion Aids for the Study of Religion, no. 2 (Missoula, Mont.: Scholars Press, 1975), 1195.

legend's demise.[23] It was an Augustinian mendicant friar who performed a similar service in 1777 for the legend of John Nepomuk (admittedly without undermining the popularity of the cult) by demonstrating that the Bohemian saint's putative martyrdom in the fourteenth century to protect the seal of confession was actually the consequence of a dispute with the emperor over a monastic election.[24] Contemporary with these historical corrections is the whole project of the Bollandists, an association of Jesuit scholars who took up the editorship of the *Acta Sanctorum* in the early seventeenth century.[25] If the Bollandists believed in miracles, they also believed in examining the sources and sorting out apocryphal or suspect evidence in the lives of the saints.

We learn from Eve Levin that, at the end of the seventeenth century, the higher clergy of the Russian church also subjected the claims of anonymous saints to more careful scrutiny, and these efforts were similar to that found in the West. Both were suspicious of enthusiastic piety out of their control. In the West, however, this skepticism came earlier and was supported by a new method. As early as the fifteenth century, historical criticism introduced into Western discourse a set of higher barriers to the establishment of the miraculous.[26] These critics did not, like Calvin or his successors, practically deny the possibility of modern miracles. But they helped make the official church in the West wary of uncritical acceptance of them.

Sin, Repentance, and Discipline

As with canonization, so too with the administration of sacraments, the Roman Catholic hierarchy exercise greater control, and the comparison of penance and confession in East and West is particularly instructive. Yet this history is another example of shared origins and early development. Through the first six or seven centuries of the Christian church, penitential discipline focused on excommunication, repentance, and reconciliation. It was restrictive and demanding, with little patience for recidivism.[27] At the same time

23. Eugene F. Rice, Jr., *Saint Jerome in the Renaissance* (Baltimore: Johns Hopkins University Press, 1985).

24. J. P. Kirsch, "John Nepomucene" (c. 1340–93), in *Catholic Encyclopedia*, 8:467–68; Paul de Vooght, *Hussiana* (Louvain: Publications universitaires de Louvain, [et] Bibliotèque de l'Universite Bureaux de la Revue, 1960), pt. 5, chap. 3, pp. 400–441; Pierre Delooz, "Towards a Sociological Study of Canonized Sainthood in the Catholic Church," in *Saints and Their Cults: Studies in Religious Sociology, Folklore and History*, ed. Stephen Wilson (Cambridge: Cambridge University Press, 1983), 210, 216 n. 32.

25. Charles de Smedt, "Bollandists," in *Catholic Encyclopedia* 2; Woodward, *Making Saints*, 96–106.

26. But Peter Abelard (1079–1142) had publicly doubted the legends surrounding St. Denis.

27. Bernhard Poschmann, *Penance and the Anointing of the Sick,* trans. and rev. Francis Courtney (New York: Herder and Herder, 1964), 19–121.

it reflected the recognition that Christianity, a salvation religion, had to discover some means not only of excluding deviants but also of reconciling
them to the community. As Arthur Darby Nock once put it, the development of systems of discipline and reconciliation was "inevitable from the
moment it was discovered that people sinned after baptism."[28] And in spite
of variations, the Christian churches of the ancient world offered mercy to
sinners in the form of reconciliation. The Council of Nicaea (A.D. 325)
declared that they merely followed ancient custom in not denying forgiveness (probably in the form of Viaticum, the final reception of the Eucharist)
to the faithful at death.[29] All of these generalizations hold for Greek- and
Latin-speaking communities of the Mediterranean world. By the early Middle Ages in the West, denial of forgiveness at death in any form—whether
of the Viaticum, canonical reconciliation, or confession with absolution—
would be taken as an unusual and even cruel exercise of disciplinary rigor. I
suspect that a similar sentiment obtains in the East.

That ordinary Christians—in different eras and distant places—understood these developments should not seem surprising, for once one grasps
the governing regulations, as well as the eternal consequences, a set of logical strategies unfolds. Thus there is a remarkable symmetry between earnest
believers in the fourth century who placed a consecrated wafer—a token of
reconciliation—on the body of the faithful deceased[30] and Daniel Kaiser's
similarly intentioned Russians, who put a certificate of confession in the
Orthodox corpse's hand. The ancient pagan topos of providing the departed
for the journey to the other world becomes Christianized in both customs.
Authorities, ancient Christian and early modern Russian, were "right," in a
sense, to condemn these practices as deviant. On the other hand, if these
symbolic gestures seem too literal for our tastes, are they not logical derivatives of orthodox doctrines? Do they not stem from the institutional rules of
the game, which our quaint deviants understood well? It had been decided
in Christian antiquity that it was safer to have forgiveness certified by priests;
the consequences of that general principle played out in subsequent centuries
in many different ways, but at their core is that ancient sacerdotal value.

28. Arthur Darby Nock, *Early Gentile Christianity and Its Hellenistic Background* (New York: Harper
and Row, 1964), 86.

29. Gregory Grabka, "Christian Viaticum: A Study of Its Cultural Background," *Traditio* 9 (1953):
1–43. Cf. Éric Rebillard, "La Naissance du viatique: se préparer à mourir en Italie et en Gaule au Vᵉ siècle,"
Médiévales 20 (1991): 99–108, and Poschmann, *Penance and Anointing*, 54–58, 65, 74–80, 94–109.

30. Grabka, "Christian Viaticum," 38–39. For a directive by Lanfranc, archbishop of Canterbury
(1070–89), that "a written absolution of sins be placed on the chest of a dead monk in his tomb," see Sarah
Hamilton, *The Practice of Penance 900–1050*, Royal Historical Society Studies in History, New Series
(Woodbridge, N.Y.: Boydell Press, 2001), 180 n. 34.

The differences between confession in the West and East are therefore all the more important given, once again, common origins. By the seventh or eighth century a new form of forgiveness had developed in the West. It was private, secret, and reiterable. As early as 1100 the main outlines of the medieval, early modern, and modern Western practice had been fixed. Confession was theoretically necessary for forgiveness, and absolution was pronounced at the end of confession, before the penitents performed their penances. The law of 1215 made yearly confession obligatory on all who had attained the age of reason. In response, the thirteenth century witnessed the production of a practical literature on how to hear confessions, and a more carefully defined theology explaining how the sacrament worked. At the same time the indicative form of absolution became the norm: priests said "I absolve you" rather than "may God absolve you." The centrality of sacramental confession to the practice of religion in the West had therefore been established in entirely predictable ways. Papal and conciliar legislation, university faculties of canon law and theology, and the exercise of day-to-day (or perhaps, season-to-season) authority by bishops and priests make the practice of penance as routine and uniform as one might hope for in a preindustrial society with limited resources of communication and control.

Development of penance in the Orthodox East reveals important similarities, but the sightings of confession we have in these essays bespeak salient differences between confession under Rome and confession under the other patriarchates. Nowhere in the religious culture of the West is hierarchical and sacerdotal control more firmly established than over the sacraments, and especially over sacramental confession. Nowhere are those other traits peculiar to the Latin church's cultural development more evident than here; where popes and councils legislated the frequency, form, and purposes of confession; where religious authors produced a vast practical literature to achieve a uniformly pious practice; where university professors theorized; where pastors and mendicant preachers taught and exhorted; where bishops and parish priests monitored attendance and punished neglect; and where confession is visible in secular literature and popular imagination. Institutionalized penance also elicited humanist historical criticism, which sharpened issues already raised in scholastic debate and proposed a historicization and demystification of auricular confession. The names of Erasmus, Luther, Calvin, and many other reformers and counter-reformers are associated with that debate.

The history of confession in Europe is the subject of a rich and expanding historical literature providing a detailed narrative of the development of the theory and practice of sacramental penance, its dismantling in Reformation lands, and its restoration and exaltation in early modern and modern

Catholicism. Precisely because of the many features they share, a comparative institutional history of confession in Russia and the West would be illuminating not only for church history but also for the political, intellectual, and cultural histories that help explain how, why, and in what directions these two traditions drifted apart.

From my Western point of view some comparisons are already suggested by these essays, and three topics I have selected reinforce my perception that the West succeeded in establishing a more orderly—or centralized—theory and practice. But before I conclude with reflections on specific differences that might be addressed in a comparative history of confession in Russia and the West, I want to acknowledge the personal and professional bias in my own selectivity. Confession is not only what I know best; it is also a topic that invites invidious comparisons between a more modern, bureaucratized West and a second-world, late-to-the-gate Russia. The very choice of confession leads in that direction, and my own interests make it certain that organization and order will be prominently represented. But within the penitential discourse of East and West there is an equally important pastoral ideal—too subtle and complex to be addressed in a short note, but perhaps even more promising an illuminator of the operative values that divide and unite these two religious cultures. In addition, I want to stress the variety of alternatives for comparison to my choice of confession. Topics in the history of monasticism, private devotion, liturgy, religious education, and art, for example, could inspire a whole range of comparative explorations of the two traditions.[31] And that research into religious practice will also connect, inevitably and unpredictably, with the rest of Russian and European history.

Three topics illustrate the directions that comparative research on confession might take and the benefits that might accrue: (1) the obligation (or necessity) of confession; (2) privacy, guaranteed by the seal of confession; and (3) the theory and practice of priestly absolution.

First, it is perhaps characteristic of differences in ecclesiastical government that the "universal" obligation to confess yearly was legislated in the West as early as the Fourth Lateran Council of 1215. And underlying confession's prominence in the West was the general understanding that, under ordinary circumstances, for a sinner to obtain forgiveness, confession of sins to a priest was a "virtual necessity." The phrase is scholastic—from the thirteenth century—but the assumption was almost universal among religious writers

---

31. Cf. Meyendorff, *Byzantine Theology,* 195–96, for a theological comparison from an Orthodox perspective.

at least since the eleventh century. There is an abundance of evidence to show that the practical consequences of this necessity were gradually understood at all levels of society, not just at the top. The history of the requirement of confession in the West provides many possible subjects for comparison: the rise of more frequent confession; the production of manuals for priest-confessors and a literature, primarily sermons, teaching penitents how to confess; confession in both hagiography and secular literature; confession in Lent, during missions, and before reception of sacraments (including marriage); and above all, confession at death. Concrete comparisons on these subjects would be valuable in themselves, but they would also provide data for more ambitious projects. Among the results might be another perspective on the problem of cultural borrowing, and the timing of parallel developments.

One intriguing bit of evidence cited by Daniel Kaiser—the certificate of confession placed before burial in the hands of the deceased—is a dog with a familiar bark to a historian of confession in the West. Is the existence of that certificate evidence of an imitation of an early modern Western requirement in some jurisdictions that Catholics obtain written verification of the fulfillment of their yearly obligation?[32] If so, to satisfy what regulation? The Muscovite friends of the departed had apparently concluded that this certificate attested to the discharge of an important duty. The obligation to confess yearly had been established by Rome in 1215, with the stipulation that parish priests list and excommunicate those who failed to fulfill it. It was not until 1666–67 that a similar requirement was introduced in Russia, and there is evidence of enforcement in the eighteenth century. A fruitful comparison should not only remark on the delayed appearance of the obligation in Russia, but also examine how it was publicized and how extensively it was enforced.[33] Ultimately the comparative investigation of these features of confession will shed light on other important cultural differences, including sources of guilt and psychological assurance that affect a wide range of social and political relationships.

32. Gertraud K. Eichhorn, *Beichtzettel und Bürgerrecht in Passau: 1570–1630. Die administrativen Praktiken der Passauer Gegenreformation unter den Fürstbischöfen Urban von Trenbach und Leopold I., Erzherzog von Österreich,* Neue Veröffentlichungen des Instituts für ostbairische Heimatforschung der Universität Passau, no. 49 (Passau: Verein für ostbairische Heimatforschung, 1998); Philip Soergel, *Wondrous in His Saints: Counter-Reformation Propaganda in Bavaria* (Berkeley and Los Angeles: University of California Press, 1993), 77; David Myers, *"Poor Sinning Folk": Confession and Conscience in Counter-Reformation Germany* (Ithaca: Cornell University Press, 1996), 120–22; Hermann Rebel, *Peasant Classes: The Bureaucratization of Property and Family Relations under Early Habsburg Absolutism, 1511–1636* (Princeton: Princeton University Press, 1983), 247–48, 316–17; Thomas Deutscher, "The Role of the Episcopal Tribunal of Novara in the Suppression of Heresy and Witchcraft, 1563–1615," *Catholic Historical Review* 77 (1991): 412.

33. Michael Cherniavsky, "The Old Believers and the New Religion," *Slavic Review* 25 (1966): 1–39; Gregory L. Freeze, *The Russian Levites: Parish Clergy in the Seventeenth Century* (Cambridge: Harvard University Press, 1977). My thanks to Robert H. Greene for these citations.

The second comparative possibility concerns the protections of privacy guaranteed in the canon law and moral theology of the seal of confession, an important and neglected feature of Western church history.[34] The academic discussion of threats to that privacy entailed a searching discussion and led to formal regulations that, from the thirteenth century to the twentieth, defined more carefully prohibitions on revealing anything about the penitent or her confession. The earliest and chief adversary of the canonists and theologians was secular authority (at all levels) in pursuit of information about crime. As this discourse evolved, however, ecclesiastical authority itself was seen as a potential threat to the privacy of the penitent and the sanctity of the seal. Throughout this period the professors became more sensitive to the psychological dimensions of the penitent's privacy.

The agenda for a comparative study of the seal begins with simple questions. Was there a comparable learned commentary on this problem in the East? How deeply was Russian hierarchy committed to the privacy of confession? Was it able to protect its clergy from intrusions by secular authority? Most important for lived religion, were Orthodox believers aware of a religiously sanctioned right to the privacy of their confessions? Broader questions about privacy and individual identity in Russian culture inevitably follow. Peter the Great's 1722 injunction that clerics divulge the content of potentially criminal or treasonous confessions is much discussed and decried in the historical literature, but many uncertainties about the actual effect of that injunction and the way it was perceived by contemporaries remain.[35]

A third comparison is suggested by the extraordinary example of Father Ioann, whose popularity as a charismatic pastor of souls led to the dramatic aberration of shouted confessions of sins followed by his public, mass absolution. Even though Father Ioann was not playing by the Orthodox rules, he managed to get away with this extraordinary performance. Contrast him with Jean-Baptiste Vianney (1786–1839), the famous Curé d'Ars, who

---

34. Bertrand Kurtscheid, *A History of the Seal of Confession,* ed. Arthur Preuss, trans. F. A. Marks (St. Louis: B. Herder, 1927); Léon Honoré, *Le Secret de la confession: Étude historico-canonique,* Museum Lessianum, Section théologique 10 (Paris: Charles Beyaert, 1924); Henry C. Lea, *A History of Auricular Confession and Indulgences in the Latin Church,* 3 vols. (Philadelphia: Lea Brothers, 1896; reprint, New York: Greenwood Press, 1968), 1:412–59; R. S. Nolan, "Seal of Confession, The Law of the," in *Catholic Encyclopedia,* 13:649–65; John R. Roos, *The Seal of Confession,* The Catholic University of America, Canon Law Studies 413 (Washington, D.C.: Catholic University of America, 1960); Michael J. Fitzgerald, *The Sacramental Seal of Confession in Relation to Selected Child Abuse Statutes in the Civil Law of the United States,* Dissertatio ad Doctorum in Facultate Iuris Canonici Pontificiae Universitatis Gregorianae (Rome: Pontificia Universitas Gregoriana, 1991).

35. James Cracraft, "Opposition to Peter the Great," in *Peter the Great Transforms Russia,* 3d ed., ed. James Cracraft (Lexington, Mass.: D. C. Heath, 1991), 266–68.

was also admired for hearing confessions by the thousands. But all of the Curé d'Ars's confessions were canonically correct, individual, and private. What was allowed to pass as charismatic spirituality in Russia in the twentieth century would have been branded centuries before in the West as rogue pastoral practice—and it is difficult to imagine any bishop tolerating it. At issue here is *how* the penitent is supposed to confess. The closely related question of *what* the penitent is supposed to confess is perhaps an even richer field for comparison. Sexual sins—their definition by religious authorities and the description expected from penitents—come immediately to mind.[36] But that instinctive response is itself culture-bound, and we would profit also from a comparative analysis of sins relating to anger and greed. Similarly, the confession (or neglect) of sins of disobedience to authority—ranging from church and state to the patriarchal household—might yield an entirely different kind of insight.[37]

With Father Ioann, as with the other two examples, my thoughts turn westward, to a dramatically different religious ideal and exercise of authority. We could select from many different labels to characterize it. Should we choose nice, or neutral, words, like order, discipline, bureaucracy, rationality, rationalization of life; or should we speak of legalism, repression, social control, exploitation, or even persecution?

That provocative question reminds us of where we began this comment— Montaigne's words, cited as a warning against ethnocentric or ideological judgments. I doubt that the question has a simple answer, and I am close to certain that in answering it we cannot *completely* eradicate our culturally determined values and perspectives. I suspect that we really should not want to. I do not doubt, however, the value of the comparative enterprise that underlies the question. Nor do I doubt the value of essays like these on Orthodoxy, to stimulate our comparative searching; expand our knowledge of the historical anthropology of religion in general and Christianity in particular; give multiple answers to complex questions; and challenge two-tiered, binary, or either-or categorizations whenever they obscure, disparage, or otherwise oversimplify the lives and culture of the dead, to whom we historians owe so much.

36. Eve Levin, *Sex and Society in the World of the Orthodox Slavs, 900–1700* (Ithaca: Cornell University Press, 1989).

37. B. N. Floria, "Penitential Formulas in the Relationship of Church and State in Russia in the Sixteenth and Seventeenth Centuries," *Russian Studies in History* 39 (2000–2001): 72–86. My thanks to Robert H. Greene for that citation. Cf. for Western Europe, Miriam Turrini, *La coscienza e le leggi. Morale e diritto nei testi per la confessione della prima Età moderna,* Annali dell'Istituto storico italo-germanico 13 (Bologna: Società editrice il Mulino, 1991).

ANNOTATED BIBLIOGRAPHY

The literature on Russian Orthodoxy is large and growing. This bibliography represents a selective and by no means exhaustive survey of some of the most relevant English-language works to appear over the course of the last several decades. We hope that this historiographic overview will provide some context for understanding the major debates and developments in the field of Russian Orthodoxy and offer useful suggestions for further reading.

ORTHODOX THEOLOGY AND SURVEYS:

The classic studies on Orthodoxy's influence on Russian historical development are George P. Fedotov, *The Russian Religious Mind*, vol. 1, *Kievan Christianity: The Tenth to the Thirteenth Centuries* (Cambridge: Harvard University Press, 1946), and vol. 2, *The Middle Ages: The Thirteenth to the Fifteenth Centuries* (Cambridge: Harvard University Press, 1966); and Georges Florovsky, *Ways of Russian Theology*, 2 vols., ed. Richard S. Haugh, trans. Robert L. Nichols (Belmont, Mass.: Nordland Publishing, 1979). A more recent assessment by the eminent Russian scholar, Dmitrii Likachev, is "Religion: Russian Orthodoxy," in *The Cambridge Companion to Modern Russian Culture*, ed. Nicholas Rzhevsky (Cambridge: Cambridge University Press, 1998), 38–56. See also James H. Billington, *The Icon and the Axe: An Interpretive History of Russian Culture* (New York: Vintage, 1970). Excellent overviews of Eastern Orthodox theology and the development of Eastern Christianity are Timothy Ware, *The Orthodox Church*, 2d ed. (London: Penguin Books, 1997); Jaroslav Pelikan, *The Spirit of Eastern Christendom (600–1700)*, vol. 2 of *The Christian Tradition: A History of the Development of Doctrine* (Chicago: University of Chicago Press, 1974); Vladimir Lossky, *Orthodox Theology: An Introduction* (Crestwood, N.Y.: St. Vladimir's Seminary Press, 1978); and John Meyendorff, *Byzantine Theology: Historical Trends and Doctrinal Themes*, 2d ed. (New York: Fordham University Press, 1983).

ORTHODOXY IN THE KIEVAN AND MUSCOVITE PERIODS:

The legend of Prince Vladimir's conversion to Orthodoxy is recounted in the early Russian chronicles. See *The Russian Primary Chronicle: Laurentian Text*, trans. and ed. Samuel Hazzard Cross and Olgerd P. Sherbowitz-Wetzor (Cambridge, Mass.: Medieval Academy of America, 1953), 96–126. For a wide range of views on the conversion of Rus', see Yves Hamant, ed., *The Christianization of Ancient Russia. A Millenium: 988–1988* (Paris: UNESCO, 1992). A thorough account of the major institutional developments and theological debates during the first centuries of the Russian church is John Fennell, *A History of the Russian Church to 1448* (London: Longman, 1995). For a Soviet interpretation of the church's beginnings in Russia, see Yaroslav N. Shchapov, *State and Church in Early Russia, 10th–13th Centuries* (New Rochelle, N.Y.: A. D. Caratzas, 1993). On the Judaizer heresy of the late fifteenth century, see Andrei Pliguzov, "Archbishop Gennadi and the Heresy of the 'Judaizers,'" *Harvard Ukrainian Studies* 16 (1992): 269–88; David Goldfrank, "Theocratic Imperatives, the Transcendent, the Wordly, and Political Justice in Russia's Early Inquisitions," in *Religious and Secular Forces in Late Tsarist Russia: Essays in Honor of Donald W. Treadgold*, ed. Charles E. Timberlake (Seattle: University of Washington Press, 1992), 30–47; and John Klier, "Judaizing Without Jews? Moscow-Novgorod, 1470–1504," in *Culture and Identity in Muscovy, 1389–1584*, ed. A. M. Kleimola and G. D. Lenhoff (Moscow: ITZ-GARANT, 1997), 336–49.

On Orthodoxy in the Muscovite period, see the outstanding collection of essays in Samuel H. Baron and Nancy Shields Kollmann, eds., *Religion and Culture in Early Modern Russia and Ukraine* (DeKalb: Northern Illinois University Press, 1997). See also Paul Bushkovitch, *Religion and Society in Russia: The Sixteenth and Seventeenth Centuries* (New York: Oxford University Press, 1992). A provocative and influential interpretation of Orthodoxy's role in the course of Russian history is Edward L. Keenan, "Muscovite Political Folkways," *Russian Review* 45 (1986): 115–81. The ways in which Orthodoxy shaped the public and private lives of the early-modern Russian faithful are discussed in Eve Levin, *Sex and Society in the World of the Orthodox Slavs, 900–1700* (Ithaca: Cornell University Press, 1989), and Daniel H. Kaiser, "The Seasonality of Family Life in Early Modern Russia," *Forschungen zur osteuropäischen Geschichte* 46 (1992): 21–50. On the spirituality of elite Muscovite women, see Isolde Thyrêt, *Between God and the Tsar: Religious Symbolism and the Royal Women of Muscovite Russia* (DeKalb: Northern Illinois University Press, 2001).

Advocates of the *dvoeverie* school posit a layered form of Russian religiosity, with Orthodox Christianity providing a veneer or overlay over traditional pagan practices, For this position, see, for example, Florovsky, *Ways of Russian Theology*, vol. 1, p. 3; Iurii M. Lotman and Boris A. Uspenskii, "Binary Models in the Dynamics of Russian Culture (to the End of the Eighteenth Century)," in *The Semiotics of Russian Cultural History*, ed. Alexander D. Nakhimovsky and Alice Stone Nakhimovsky (Ithaca: Cornell University Press, 1985), 30–66; and the essays collected in Marjorie Mandelstam Balzer, ed., *Russian Traditional Culture: Religion, Gender, and Customary Law* (Armonk, N.Y.: M. E. Sharpe, 1992). The assumption that dualistic belief systems persisted in the Russian countryside well until the twentieth century is found in much of the literature. For an influential statement of this argument, see Moshe Lewin, "Popular Religion in Twentieth-Century Russia," in his collection of essays, *The Making of the Soviet System: Essays in the Social History of Interwar Russia* (New York: New Press, 1994), 49–56. A critique of the dual faith model is made in Eve Levin, "Dvoeverie and Popular Religion," in *Seeking God: The Recovery of Religious Identity in Orthodox Russia, Ukraine, and Georgia*, ed. Stephen K. Batalden (DeKalb: Northern Illinois University Press, 1993), 29–52.

On the relationship between Orthodoxy and political authority in Muscovite Russia, see Marc Raeff, "An Early Theorist of Absolutism: Joseph of Volokolamsk," *The American Slavic and East European Review* 8 (1949): 79–89; Michael Cherniavsky, "Khan or Basileus: An Aspect of Russian Mediaeval Political Theory," *Journal of the History of Ideas* 20 (1959): 459–76; David B. Miller, "The Velikie Minei Chetii and the Stepennaja Kniga of Metropolitan Makarii and the Origins of Russian National Consciousness," *Forschungen zur osteuropäischen Geschichte* 26 (1979): 263–382; Daniel Rowland, "Did Muscovite Literary Ideology Place Any Limits on the Power of the Tsar?" *Russian Review* 49 (1990): 125–56; Michael Flier, "Breaking the Code: The Image of the Tsar in the Muscovite Palm Sunday Ritual," in *Medieval Russian Culture,* vol. 2, ed. Michael S. Flier and Daniel Rowland, California Slavic Studies 19 (Berkeley and Los Angeles: University of California Press, 1994), 213–42; Nancy S. Kollmann, "Pilgrimage, Procession, and Symbolic Space in Sixteenth-Century Russian Politics," in *Medieval Russian Culture,* 163–81; and Ludwig Steindorff, "Commemoration and Administrative Techniques in Muscovite Monasteries," *Russian History* 22 (1995): 433–54.

A recent and radically revisionist interpretation of the Old Believers' schism is Georg Bernhard Michels, *At War with the Church: Religious Dissent in Seventeenth-Century Russia* (Stanford: Stanford University Press, 1999). See also Michael Cherniavsky, "The Old Believers and the New Religion," in his *The Structure of Russian History: Interpretive Essays* (New York: Random House, 1970), 140–88; Robert O. Crummey, *The Old Believers and the World of Antichrist: The Vyg Community and the Russian State, 1694–1855* (Madison: University of Wisconsin Press, 1970); idem, "Old Belief as Popular Religion: New Approaches," *Slavic Review* 52 (1993): 700–712; Boris A. Uspenky, "The Schism and Cultural Conflict in the Seventeenth Century," in Batalden, ed., *Seeking God,* 106–44; and Roy Robson, *Old Believers in Modern Russia* (DeKalb: Northern Illinois University Press, 1995). An abridged version of the autobiography of the seventeenth-century Old Believer, Avvakum, is found in Serge A. Zenkovsky, *Medieval Russia's Epics, Chronicles, and Tales,* 2d rev. ed. (New York: Meridian, 1974), 399–448.

ORTHODOXY IN THE IMPERIAL PERIOD:

The now-classic exposition of church-state relations after the Petrine reforms, which set the study of imperial-era religious history on a new course, is Gregory L. Freeze, "Handmaiden of the State? The Church in Imperial Russia Reconsidered," *The Journal of Ecclesiastical History* 36 (1985): 82–102. Historiographic review articles on the current status of the field include Laura Engelstein, "Paradigms, Pathologies, and Other Clues to Russian Spiritual Culture: Some Post-Soviet Thoughts," *Slavic Review* 57 (1998): 864–77; idem, "Holy Russia in Modern Times: An Essay on Orthodoxy and Cultural Change," *Past and Present* 173 (2001): 129–56; and Gregory L. Freeze, "Recent Scholarship on Russian Orthodoxy: A Critique," *Kritika,* n.s., 2 (2001): 269–78. Paul Bushkovitch offers a sharp reminder of the dangers of relying on nineteenth-century Russian writers as reliable sources for earlier eras of Russian Orthodox history in his "Orthodoxy and Old Rus' in the Thought of P. S. Shevyrev," *Forschungen zur osteuropäischen Geschichte* 46 (1992): 203–20.

The establishment of the Holy Synod in 1721 is discussed in James Cracraft, *The Church Reform of Peter the Great* (Stanford: Stanford University Press, 1971). See also Alexander V. Muller, trans. and ed., *The Spiritual Regulation of Peter the Great* (Seattle: University of Washington Press, 1972). On the church's efforts to deepen the laity's understanding of the basic tenets of the Orthodox faith and standardize religious practice across the empire, see Gregory L. Freeze, "Institutionalizing Piety: The Church and Popular Religion, 1750–1850," in *Imperial Russia: New Histories for the Empire,* ed. Jane Burbank and David L. Ransel (Bloomington: Indiana University Press, 1998), 210–49. The emergence of new forms of spirituality and devotion in the eighteenth century is treated in Robert L. Nichols, "The Orthodox Elders (*Startsy*) of Imperial Russia," *Modern Greek Studies Yearbook* 1 (1985): 1–30; Brenda Meehan-Waters, "Metropolitan Filaret (Drozdov) and the Reform of Women's Monastic Communities," *Russian Review* 50 (1991): 310–23; Eugene Clay, "The Theological Origin of the Christ-Faith (Khristovshchina)," *Russian History* 15 (1988): 21–41; and Laura Engelstein, *Castration and the Heavenly Kingdom: A Russian Folktale* (Ithaca: Cornell University Press, 1999).

The definitive treatments of the Orthodox clergy in the eighteenth and nineteenth centuries are Gregory L. Freeze, *The Russian Levites: Parish Clergy in the Eighteenth Century* (Cambridge: Harvard University Press, 1977), and idem, *The Parish Clergy in Nineteenth-Century Russia: Crisis, Reform, Counter-Reform* (Princeton: Princeton University Press, 1983). See also Gregory L. Bruess, *Religion, Identity and Empire: A Greek Archbishop in the Russia of Catherine the Great* (Boulder, Colo.: East European Monographs, 1997); Alexander M. Martin, trans. and ed., *Provincial Russia in the Age of Enlightenment: The Memoir of a Priest's Son* (DeKalb: Northern Illinois University Press, 2002); and Laurie Manchester, "The Secularization of the Search for Salvation: The Self-Fashioning of Orthodox Clergymen's Sons in Late Imperial Russia," *Slavic Review* 57 (1998): 50–76. A firsthand account of clerical life in the mid-nineteenth century is Gregory L. Freeze, trans. and ed., *Description of the Clergy in Rural Russia: The Memoir of a Nineteenth-Century Parish Priest* (Ithaca: Cornell University Press, 1985). On changing conceptions of the clergy's role and function in late imperial society, see Gregory L. Freeze, "A Social Mission for Russian Orthodoxy: The Kazan Requiem of 1861 for the Peasants in Bezdna," in *Imperial Russia, 1700–1917: State, Society, Opposition. Essays in Honor of Marc Raeff,* ed. Ezra Mendelsohn and Marshall S. Katz (DeKalb: Northern Illinois University Press, 1988), 115–35; idem, "The Orthodox Church and Serfdom in Pre-Reform Russia," *Slavic Review* 48 (1989): 361–87; Jennifer Hedda, "Good Shepherds: The St. Petersburg Pastorate and the Emergence of Social Activism in the Russian Orthodox Church, 1855–1917" (Ph.D. diss., Harvard University, 1998); and Argyrios Pisiotis, "Orthodoxy Versus Autocracy: The Orthodox Church and Clerical Political Dissent in Late Imperial Russia, 1905–1914" (Ph.D. diss., Georgetown University, 2000).

For Orthodoxy in its rural setting, see Donald W. Treadgold, "The Peasant and Religion," in *The Peasant in Nineteenth-Century Russia,* ed. Wayne S. Vucinich (Stanford: Stanford University Press, 1968), 72–107; Chris J. Chulos, "Myths of the Pious or Pagan Peasant in Post-Emancipation Central Russia (Voronezh Province)," *Russian History* 22 (1995): 181–216; Vera Shevzov, "Chapels and the Ecclesial World of Pre-Revolutionary Russian Peasants," *Slavic Review* 55 (1996): 585–613; idem, "Miracle-Working Icons, Laity, and Authority in the Russian Orthodox Church, 1861–1917," *Russian Review* 58 (1999):

26–48; Christine D. Worobec, *Possessed: Women, Witches, and Demons in Imperial Russia* (DeKalb: Northern Illinois University Press, 2001); and Jeffrey Burds, *Peasant Dreams and Market Politics: Labor Migration and the Russian Village, 1861–1905* (Pittsburgh: University of Pittsburgh Press, 1998).

In the late nineteenth century, urbanization and industrialization presented new challenges and opportunities for the Orthodox Church. The church's social mission is treated in Simon Dixon, "The Church's Social Role in St. Petersburg, 1880–1914," in *Church, Nation, and State in Russia and Ukraine,* ed. Geoffrey A. Hosking (Basingstoke: Macmillan, 1991), 167–92; idem, "The Orthodox Church and the Workers of St. Petersburg, 1880–1914," in *European Religion in the Age of Great Cities, 1880–1930,* ed. Hugh McLeod (London: Routledge, 1995), 119–41; and W. Arthur McKee, "Sobering Up the Soul of the People: The Politics of Popular Temperance in Late Imperial Russia," *Russian Review* 58 (1999): 212–33. See also Nadieszda Kizenko, *A Prodigal Saint: Father John of Kronstadt and the Russian People* (University Park: Pennsylvania State University Press, 2000). On workers and religion, see Reginald Zelnik, "'To the Unaccustomed Eye': Religion and Irreligion in the Experience of St. Petersburg Workers in the 1870s," in *Christianity and the Eastern Slavs,* vol. 2, *Russian Culture in Modern Times,* ed. Robert P. Hughes and Irina Paperno, California Slavic Studies 17 (Berkeley and Los Angeles: University of California Press, 1994), 49–82; K. Page Herrlinger, "Class, Piety, and Politics: Workers, Orthodoxy, and the Problem of Religious Identity in St. Petersburg, 1881–1914" (Ph.D. diss., University of California at Berkeley, 1996); Mark D. Steinberg, "Workers on the Cross: Religious Imagination in the Writings of Russian Workers, 1910–1924," *Russian Review* 53 (1994): 213–39; and Victoria E. Bonnell, ed., *The Russian Worker: Life and Labor Under the Tsarist Regime* (Berkeley and Los Angeles: University of California Press, 1983). For a firsthand account, see Reginald E. Zelnik, trans. and ed., *A Radical Worker in Tsarist Russia: The Autobiography of Semën Ivanovich Kanatchikov* (Stanford: Stanford University Press, 1986).

In recent years, scholars have begun to focus on Russian Orthodoxy in the context of the multiethnic and multiconfessional empire. Examples of this trend include Yuri Slezkine, "Savage Christians or Unorthodox Russians? The Missionary Dilemma in Siberia," in *Between Heaven and Hell: The Myth of Siberia in Russian Culture,* ed. Galya Diment and Yuri Slezkine (New York: St. Martin's Press, 1993), 15–31; idem, *Arctic Mirrors: Russia and the Small Peoples of the North* (Ithaca: Cornell University Press, 1994), chaps. 1–2; Theodore R. Weeks, "'Defending Our Own': Government and the Russian Minority in the Kingdom of Poland, 1905–1914," *Russian Review* 54 (1995): 539–51; Michael Khodarkovsky, "'Not By Word Alone': Missionary Politics and Religious Conversion in Early Modern Russia," *Comparative Studies in Society and History* 38 (1996): 267–93; idem, "'Ignoble Savages and Unfaithful Subjects': Constructing Non-Christian Identities in Early Modern Russia," in *Russia's Orient: Imperial Borderlands and Peoples, 1700–1917,* ed. Daniel R. Brower and Edward J. Lazzerini (Bloomington: Indiana University Press, 1997), 9–26; John W. Slocum, "Who, and When, Were the *Inorodtsy?* The Evolution of the Category of 'Aliens' in Imperial Russia," *Russian Review* 57 (1998): 173–90; Nicholas B. Breyfogle, "Heretics and Colonizers: Religious Dissent and Russian Colonization of Transcaucasia, 1830–1890" (Ph.D. diss., University of Pennsylvania, 1998); idem, "Caught in the Crossfire? Russian Sectarians in the Caucasian Theater of War,

1853–56 and 1877–78," *Kritika*, n.s., 2 (2001): 713–50; Robert P. Geraci and Michael Khodarkovsky, eds., *Of Religion and Empire: Missions, Conversion, and Tolerance in Tsarist Russia* (Ithaca: Cornell University Press, 2001); and Paul W. Werth, *At the Margins of Orthodoxy: Mission, Governance, and Confessional Politics in Russia's Volga-Kama Region, 1827–1905* (Ithaca: Cornell University Press, 2002).

On Russian Orthodoxy in the last years of the imperial period, see Gregory L. Freeze, "Subversive Piety: Religion and the Political Crisis in Late Imperial Russia," *Journal of Modern History* 68 (1996): 308–50; Paul R. Valliere, "The Idea of a Council in Russian Orthodoxy in 1905," in *Russian Orthodoxy Under the Old Regime,* ed. Robert L. Nichols and Theofanis George Stavrou (Minneapolis: University of Minnesota Press, 1978), 170–82; idem, "The Problem of Liberal Orthodoxy in Russia, 1905," *St. Vladimir's Theological Quarterly* 22 (1976): 115–31; and Catherine Evtuhof, *The Cross and the Sickle: Sergei Bulgakov and the Fate of Russian Religious Philosophy, 1890–1920* (Ithaca: Cornell University Press, 1997).

ORTHODOXY IN THE SOVIET PERIOD:

An important early work on the Orthodox Church under the Soviet regime is John Shelton Curtiss, *The Russian Church and the Soviet State, 1917–1950* (Boston: Little, Brown, 1953). More recent works which make extensive use of recently declassified archival sources include William B. Husband, *"Godless Communists": Atheism and Society in Soviet Russia, 1917–1932* (DeKalb: Northern Illinois University Press, 2000); idem, "Soviet Atheism and Russian Orthodox Strategies of Resistance, 1917–1932," *Journal of Modern History* 70 (1998): 74–107; Glennys Young, *Power and the Sacred in Revolutionary Russia: Religious Activists in the Village* (University Park: Pennsylvania State University Press, 1997); Daniel Peris, *Storming the Heavens: The Soviet League of the Militant Godless* (Ithaca: Cornell University Press, 1998); Edward E. Roslof, "The Heresy of 'Bolshevik' Christianity: Orthodox Rejection of Religious Reform During NEP," *Slavic Review* 55 (1996): 614–35; Gregory L. Freeze, "Counter-reformation in Russian Orthodoxy: Popular Response to Religious Innovation, 1922–1925," *Slavic Review* 54 (1995): 305–39; Lynne Viola, "The Peasant Nightmare: Visions of the Apocalypse in the Soviet Countryside," *Journal of Modern History* 62 (1990): 747–70; Gregory L. Freeze, "The Stalinist Assault on the Parish, 1929–1941," in *Stalinismus vor dem Zweiten Weltkrieg. Neue Wege der Forschung,* ed. Manfred Hildermeier, Schriften des Historischen Kollegs, Kolloquien 43 (Munich: R. Oldenbourg Verlag, 1998), 209–32; Jennifer J. Wynot, "Keeping the Faith: Russian Orthodox Monasticism in the Soviet Union, 1917–1939" (Ph.D. diss., Emory University, 2000); and Daniel Peris, "'God Is Now on Our Side'": The Religious Revival on Unoccupied Soviet Territory During World War II," *Kritika*, n.s., 1 (2000): 97–118.

For primary documents on religion and the state in the Soviet period, see the collections edited and translated by Felix Corley in *Religion in the Soviet Union: An Archival Reader* (New York: New York University Press, 1996), and Boleslaw Szczesniak, *The Russian Revolution and Religion: A Collection of Documents Concerning the Suppression of Religion by the Communists, 1917–1925* (Notre Dame: University of Notre Dame Press, 1959).

LIST OF CONTRIBUTORS

LAURA ENGELSTEIN is the Henry S. McNeil Professor of Russian History at Yale University. She is the author of *Moscow 1905: Working-Class Organization and Political Conflict* (1982), *The Keys to Happiness: Sex and the Search for Modernity in Fin-de-Siècle Russia* (1992), and *Castration and the Heavenly Kingdom: A Russian Folktale* (1999). With Stephanie Sandler, she edited *Self and Story in Russian History* (2000).

MICHAEL S. FLIER is the Oleksandr Potebnja Professor of Ukrainian Philology and chair of the Department of Slavic Languages and Literatures and the Department of Linguistics at Harvard University. He is the author of *Aspects of Nominal Determination in Old Church Slavic* (1974) and many articles on medieval East Slavic culture. He has edited or coedited numerous volumes, including *Medieval Russian Culture,* vol. 2 (with Daniel Rowland) (1994), and *Medieval Russian Culture* (with Henrik Birnbaum) (1984).

ROBERT H. GREENE is a doctoral candidate in Russian history at the University of Michigan. He is currently working on a dissertation on holy relics and devotion to the cult of the saints in late imperial and early Soviet Russia.

DANIEL H. KAISER is a professor of history and the Joseph F. Rosenfield Professor of Social Studies at Grinnell College, as well as past president of the Early Slavic Studies Association. His first book, *The Growth of the Law in Medieval Russia* (1980), received the John Nicholas Brown Prize from the Medieval Academy of America. He has edited three volumes, most recently *Reinterpreting Russian History, 860–1860s* (with Gary Marker) (1994).

VALERIE A. KIVELSON is an associate professor of history at the University of Michigan. She is the author of *Autocracy in the Provinces: Russian Political Culture and the Gentry in the Seventeenth Century* (1997) and of numerous articles, including "The Souls of the Righteous in a Bright Place: Landscape and Orthodoxy in Seventeenth-Century Russian Maps," *Russian Review* 58 (1999).

NADIESZDA KIZENKO is an associate professor of history at the State University of New York, Albany. Her first book, *A Prodigal Saint: Father John of Kronstadt and the Russian People* (2000), received the Heldt Prize from the Association for Women in Slavic Studies.

EVE LEVIN is an associate professor of Russian and East European History at the University of Kansas and editor of *The Russian Review.* She is the author of *Sex and Society in the World of the Orthodox Slavs* (1989) and numerous articles, including "Supplicatory

Prayers as a Source for Popular Religious Culture in Muscovite Russia," in *Religion and Culture in Early Modern Russia and Ukraine,* ed. Samuel H. Baron and Nancy Shields Kollmann (1997).

GARY MARKER is a professor of history at the State University of New York, Stony Brook. His publications include *Publishing, Printing, and the Origins of Intellectual Life in Russia, 1700–1800* (1985); *Reinterpreting Russian History: Readings, 1860–1860s* (1994), compiled and edited with Daniel H. Kaiser; and most recently, *Days of A Russian Noblewoman: The Memories of Anna Labzina* (2001), translated and edited with Rachel May.

DANIEL ROWLAND is the director of the Gaines Center for the Humanities and an associate professor of history at the University of Kentucky, Lexington. He is the author of numerous articles, including "Ivan IV as a Carolingian Renaissance Prince," *Harvard Ukrainian Studies* 19 (1995), and "Moscow—the Third Rome or the New Israel?" *The Russian Review* 55 (1996). With Michael S. Flier, he coedited *Medieval Russian Culture,* vol. 2 (1994).

VERA SHEVZOV is an assistant professor of religion and biblical studies at Smith College. She is the author of *Russian Orthodoxy on the Eve of Revolution* (forthcoming from Oxford University Press) and a number of articles, including "Poeticizing Piety: The Icon of Mary in Russian Akathistoi Hymns,: *St. Vladimir's Theological Quarterly,* nos. 3 and 4 (2000).

THOMAS N. TENTLER is an emeritus professor in the Department of History at the University of Michigan and an adjunct professor of history at the Catholic University of America. He is the author of *Sin and Confession on the Eve of the Reformation* (1977) and numerous articles on religious topics, including "Seventeen Authors in Search of Two Religious Cultures," *Catholic Historical Review* 71 (1985).

ISOLDE THYRÊT is an associate professor of history at Kent State University and the author of *Between God and Tsar: Religious Symbolism and the Royal Women of Muscovite Russia* (2001). She has also written a number of articles, including "'Blessed is the Tsaritsa's Womb': The Myth of Miraculous Birth and Royal Motherhood in Muscovite Russia," *Russian Review* 53 (1994).

WILLIAM G. WAGNER is the Brown Professor of History and department chair at Williams College. He wrote *Marriage, Property, and Law in Late Imperial Russia* (1994); compiled, with R. Bisha, J. Gheith, and C. Holden, *Russian Women, 1698–1917: Experience and Expression. An Anthology of Sources* (2002); and annotated M. Katz's 1989 translation of Nikolai Chernyshevsky, *What Is to Be Done?*

PAUL W. WERTH is an assistant professor of history at the University of Nevada, Las Vegas. He has published articles in *Social History, Tatarstan, Slavic Review, Nationalities Papers, Kritika, Comparative Studies in Society and History,* and *Russian Review,* and is the author of a monograph, *At the Margins of Orthodoxy: Mission, Governance, and Confessional Politics in Russia's Volga-Kama Region, 1827–1905* (2002).

INDEX

Page numbers in *italics* refer to illustrations.